GRAVEYARD QUEST

BY **KC Green**

COVER BY **Allison Shabet**

DESIGNED BY **Hilary Thompson**

EDITED BY **Charlie Chu**

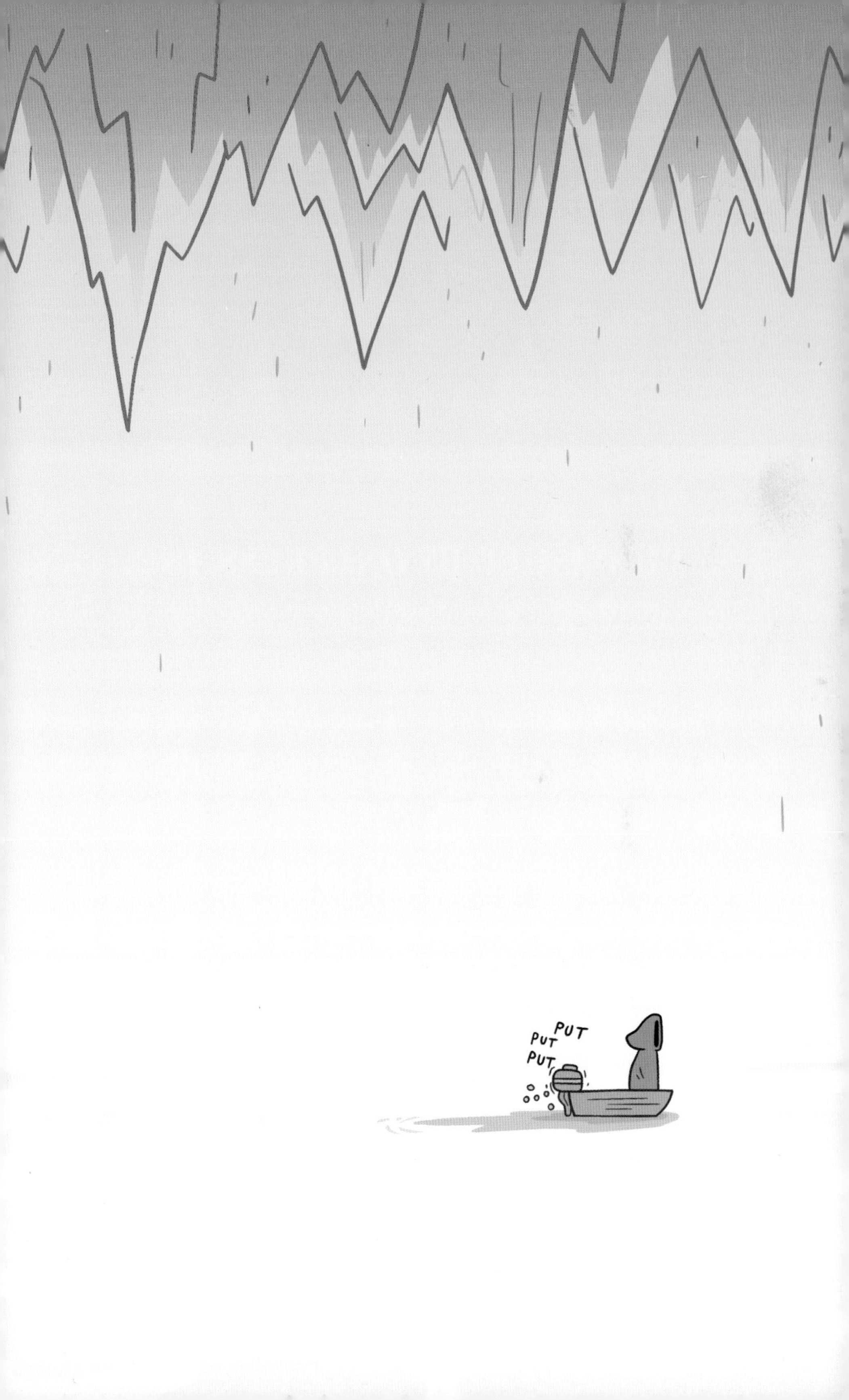
PUT
PUT
PUT

PUBLISHED BY ONI PRESS, INC.

Joe Nozemack, PUBLISHER • **James Lucas Jones**, EDITOR IN CHIEF
Cheyenne Allott, DIRECTOR OF SALES • **Amber O'Neill**, MARKETING COORDINATOR
Rachel Reed, PUBLICITY COORDINATOR • **Troy Look**, DIRECTOR OF DESIGN & PRODUCTION
Hilary Thompson, GRAPHIC DESIGNER • **Jared Jones**, DIGITAL ART TECHNICIAN
Charlie Chu, SENIOR EDITOR • **Robin Herrera**, EDITOR • **Ari Yarwood**, EDITOR
Bess Pallares, EDITORIAL ASSISTANT • **Brad Rooks**, DIRECTOR OF LOGISTICS
Jung Lee, OFFICE ASSISTANT

ONIPRESS.COM • FACEBOOK.COM/ONIPRESS • TWITTER.COM/ONIPRESS
ONIPRESS.TUMBLR.COM • INSTAGRAM.COM/ONIPRESS

KC GREEN CAN BE FOUND ONLINE AT:
KCGREENDOTCOM.COM • @KCGREENN • GUNSHOWCOMIC.COM

ALLISON SHABET CAN BE FOUND ONLINE AT:
DEADWINTER.CC • @REILEY

FIRST EDITION: MARCH 2016

ISBN 978-1-62010-289-3
EISBN 978-1-62010-290-9

PRINTED IN CHINA.

LIBRARY OF CONGRESS CONTROL NUMBER: 2015950764

1 2 3 4 5 6 7 8 9 10

I WORK AT THE GRAVE YARD

IT'S A FAMILY BUSINESS PASSED DOWN TO ME.

I SEEM TO BE LAST IN LINE, HOWEVER.

BUT I DON'T PLAN TO STOP.

I FORGET TO STOP AND JUST KEEP GOING.

WORK TO BE DONE. ALWAYS SOMETHING TO DO.

I'VE BEEN WORKING HERE FOR HUNDREDS OF YEARS.

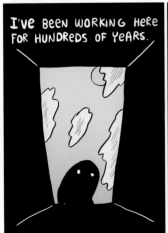

BURYING MORE AND MORE.

IT'S A FAMILY BUSINESS.

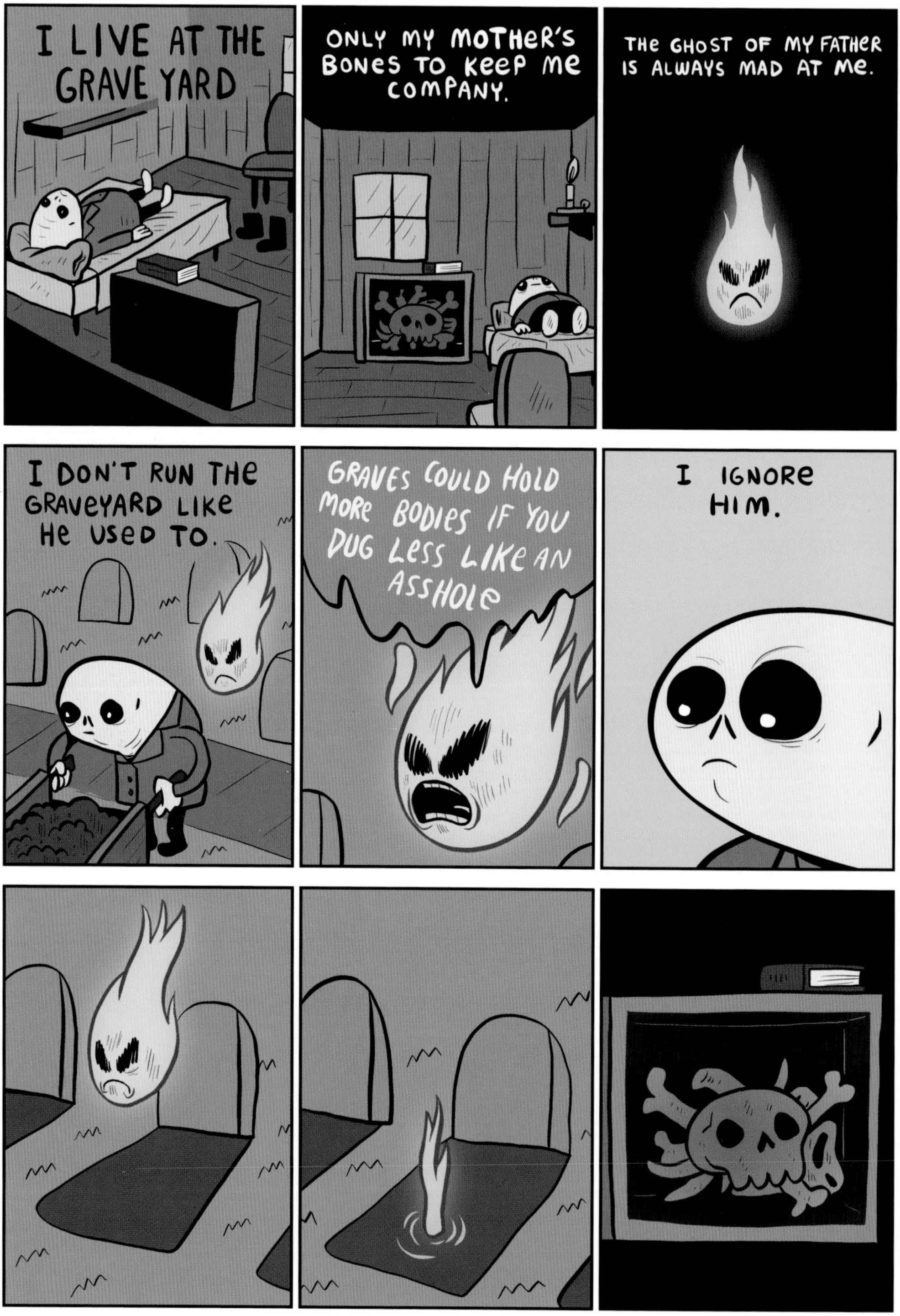
I LIVE AT THE GRAVE YARD
ONLY MY MOTHER'S BONES TO KEEP ME COMPANY.
THE GHOST OF MY FATHER IS ALWAYS MAD AT ME.
I DON'T RUN THE GRAVEYARD LIKE HE USED TO.
GRAVES COULD HOLD MORE BODIES IF YOU DUG LESS LIKE AN ASSHOLE
I IGNORE HIM.

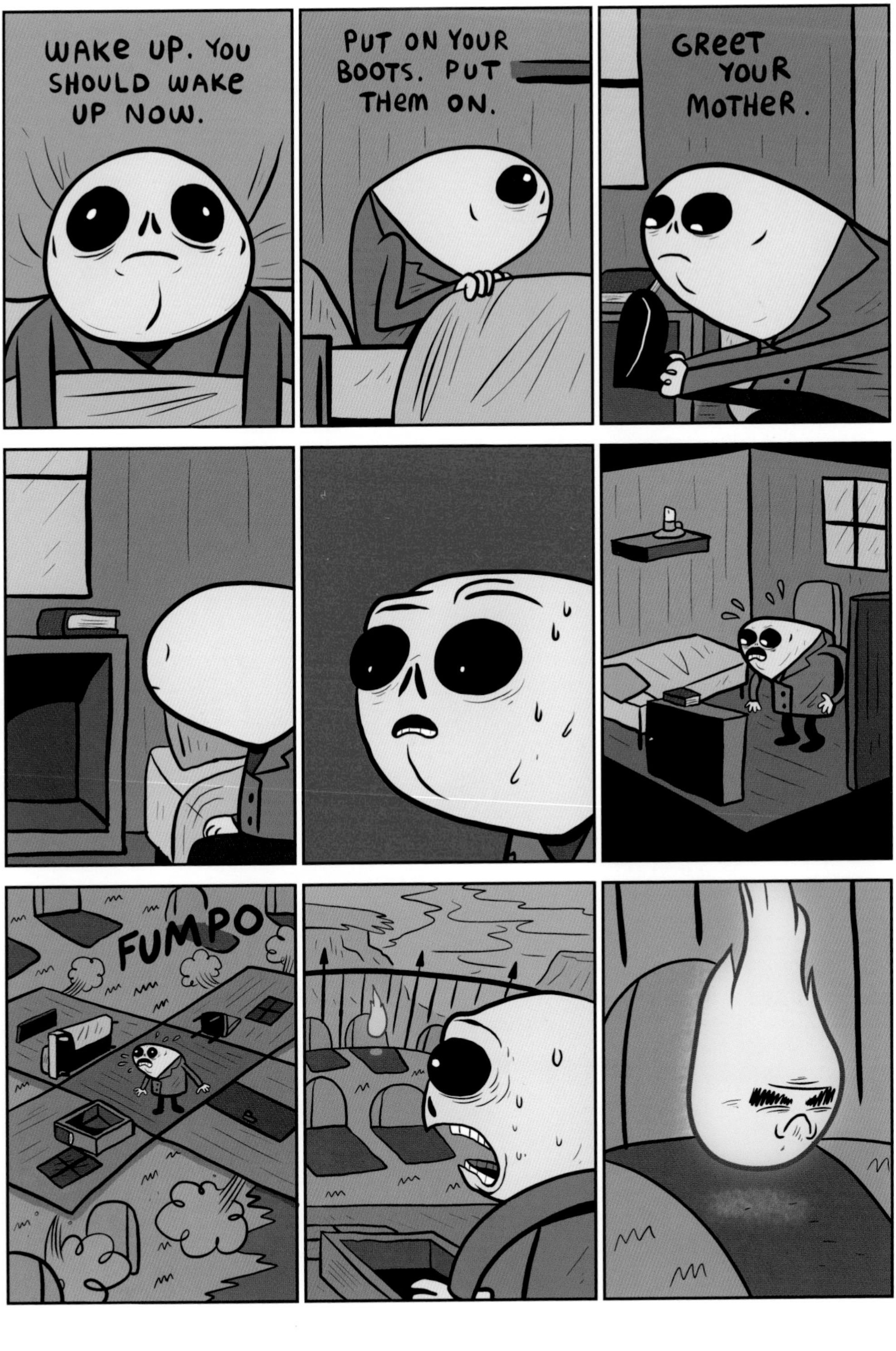
WAKE UP. YOU SHOULD WAKE UP NOW.
PUT ON YOUR BOOTS. PUT THEM ON.
GREET YOUR MOTHER.
FUMPO

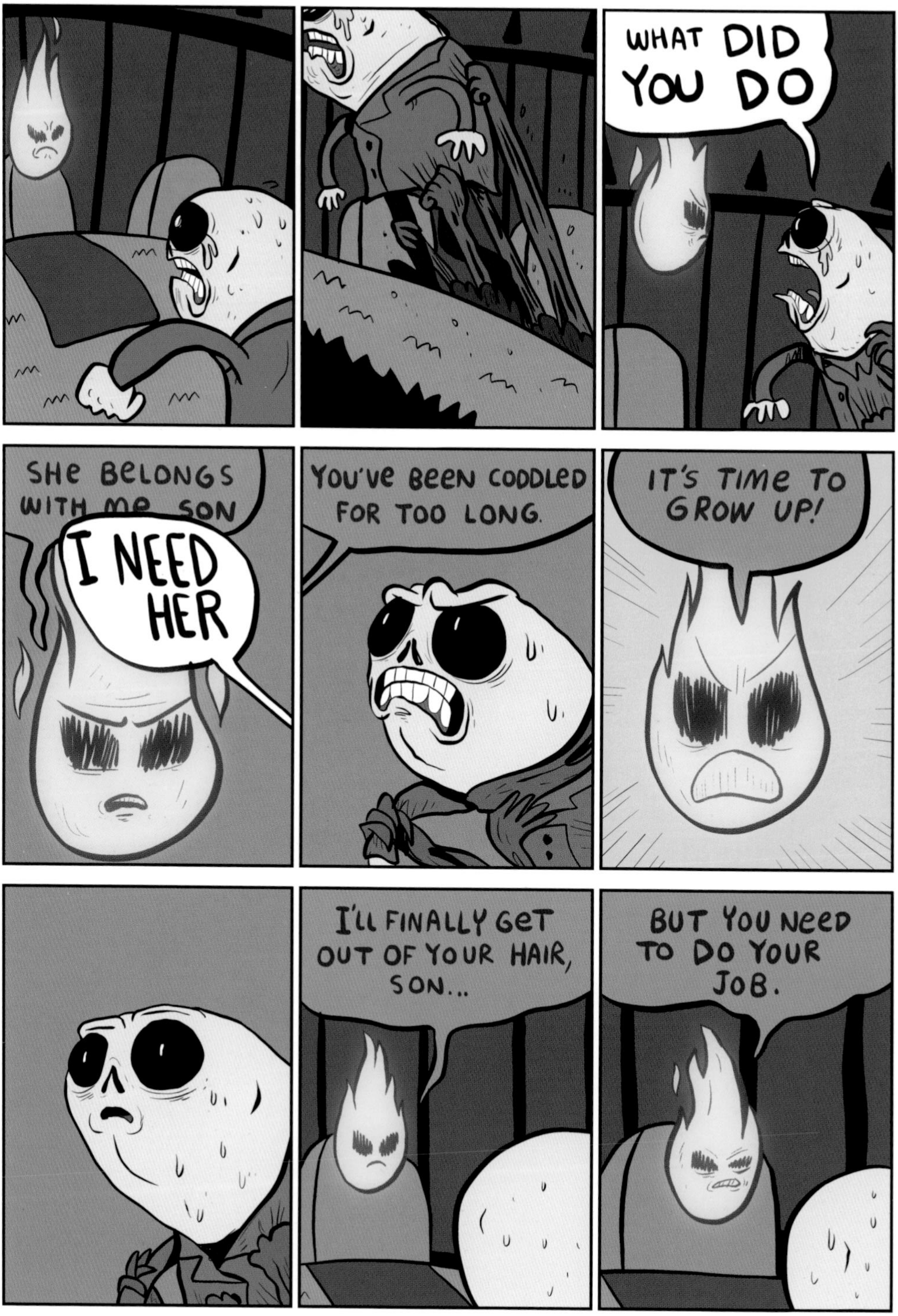
WHAT DID YOU DO
SHE BELONGS WITH ME SON
I NEED HER
YOU'VE BEEN CODDLED FOR TOO LONG.
IT'S TIME TO GROW UP!
I'LL FINALLY GET OUT OF YOUR HAIR, SON...
BUT YOU NEED TO DO YOUR JOB.

DO NOT COME FOR HER OR THERE'LL BE HELL TO PAY

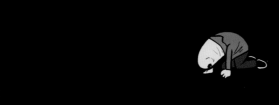

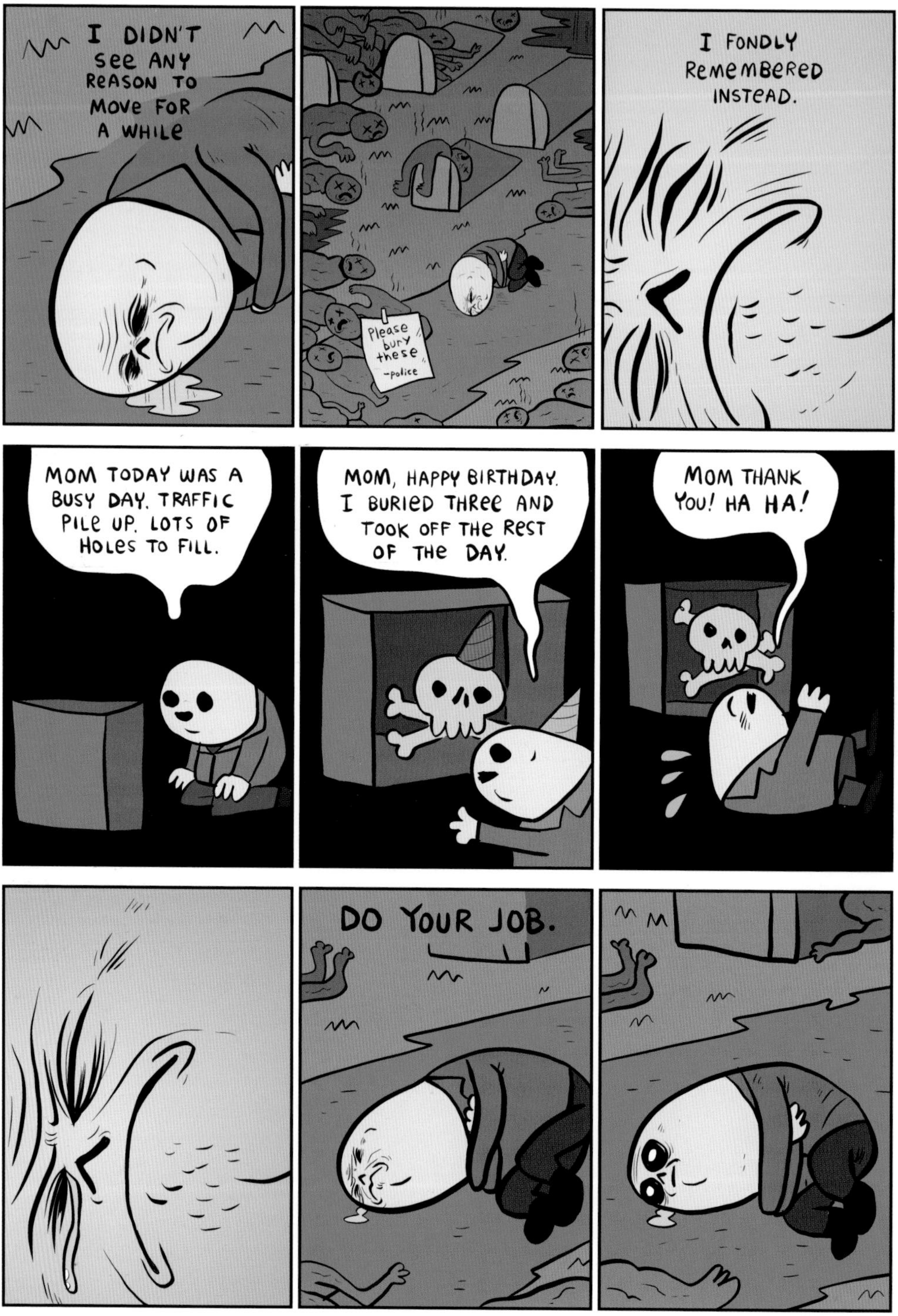
I DIDN'T SEE ANY REASON TO MOVE FOR A WHILE
Please bury these -police
I FONDLY REMEMBERED INSTEAD.
MOM TODAY WAS A BUSY DAY. TRAFFIC PILE UP. LOTS OF HOLES TO FILL.
MOM, HAPPY BIRTHDAY. I BURIED THREE AND TOOK OFF THE REST OF THE DAY.
MOM THANK YOU! HA HA!
DO YOUR JOB.

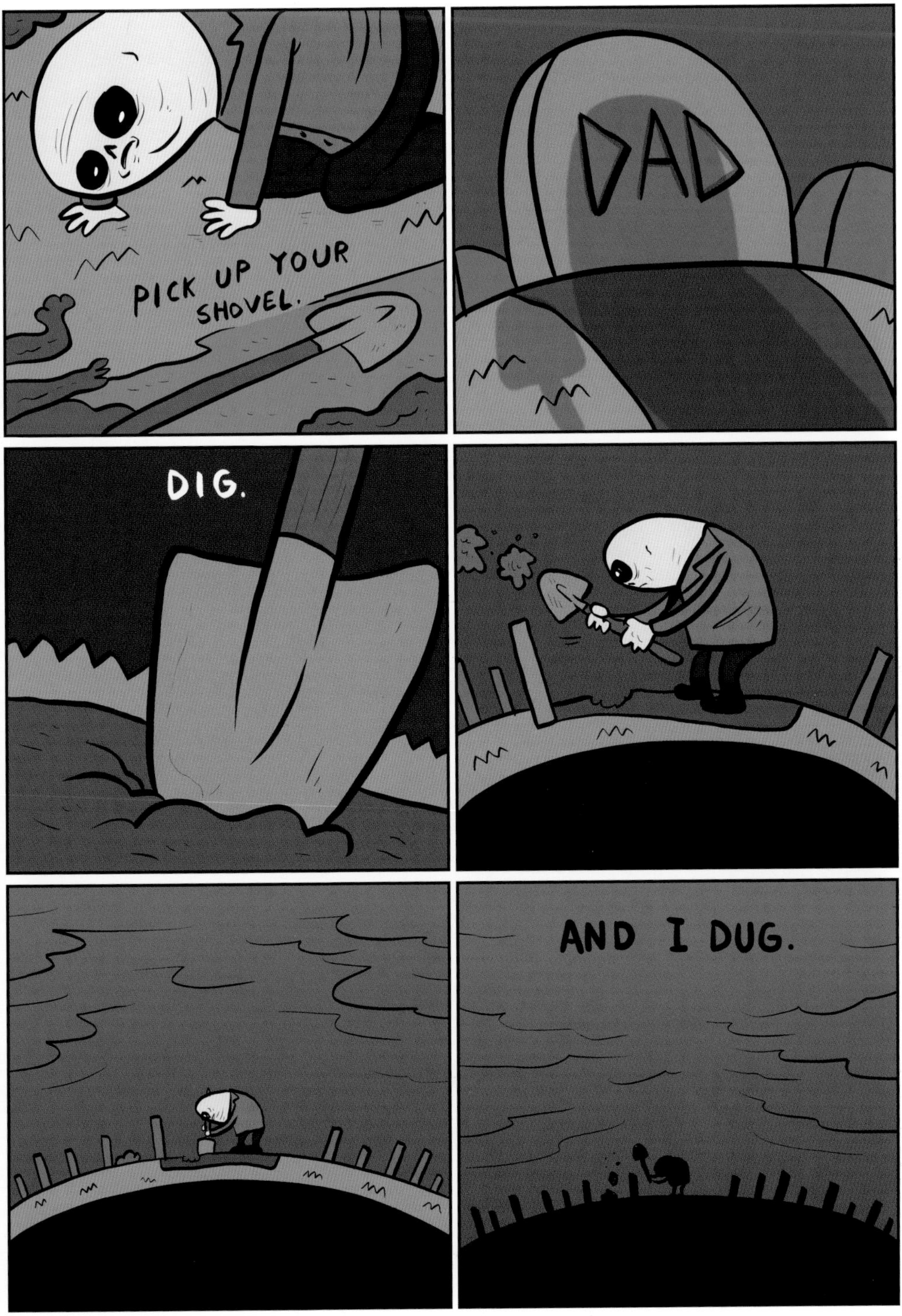
PICK UP YOUR SHOVEL.
DAD
DIG.
AND I DUG.

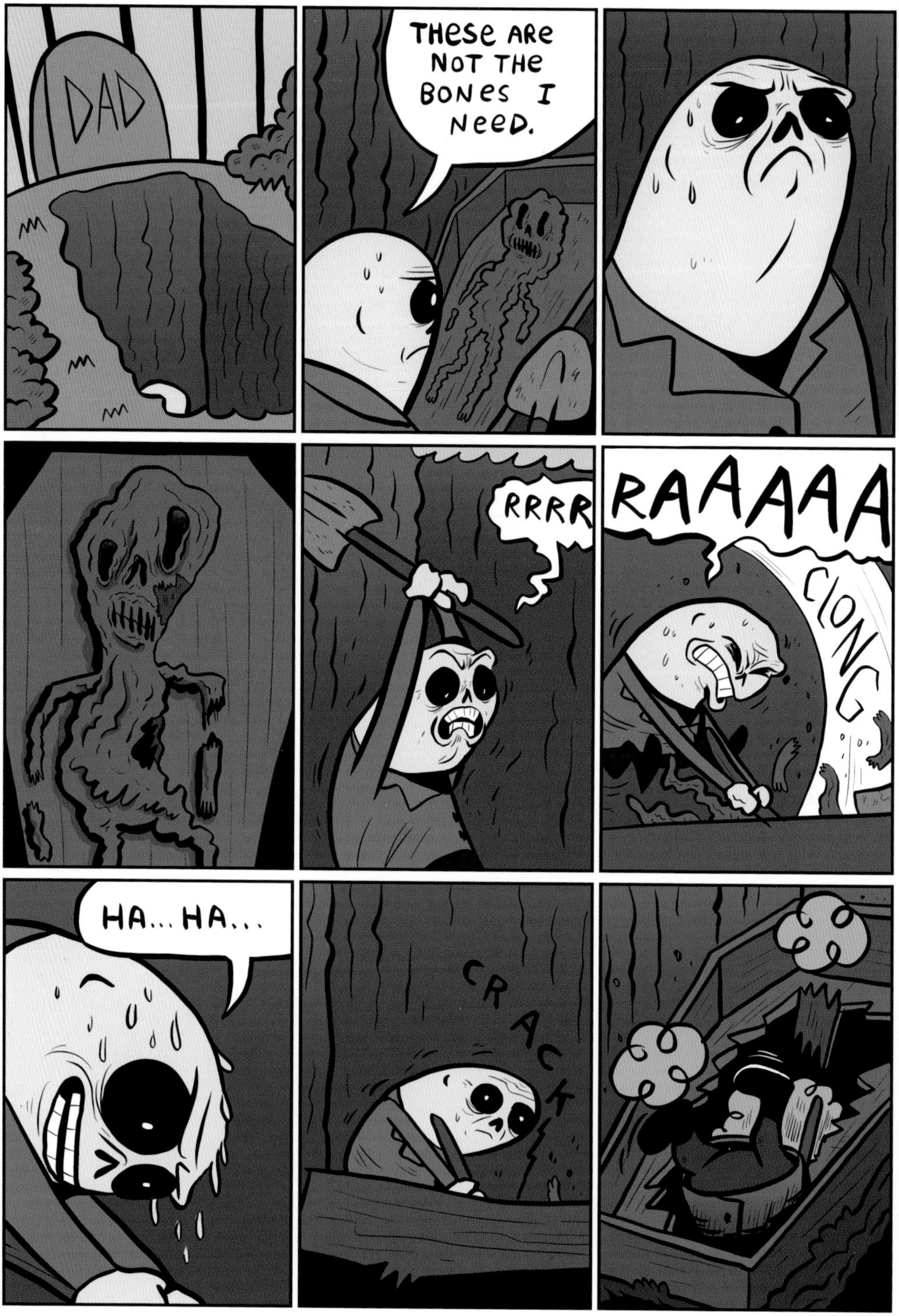
DAD
THESE ARE NOT THE BONES I NEED.
RRRR
RAAAAA
CLONG
HA... HA...
CRACK

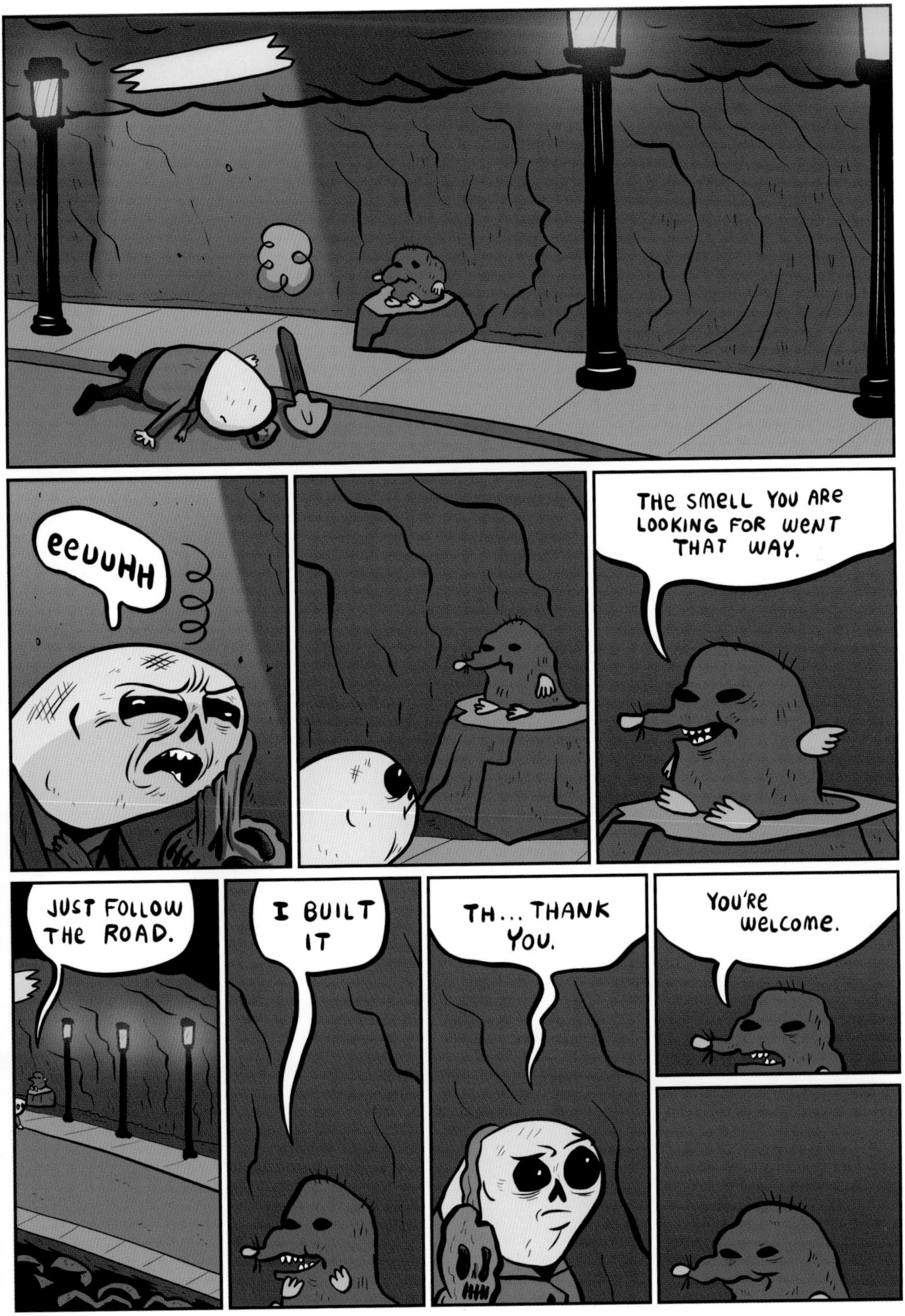
eeuuHH
THe smeLL YOU ARE LOOKING FOR WENT THAT WAY.
JUST FOLLOW THe ROAD.
I BUILT IT
TH... THANK YOU.
YOU'Re weLcome.

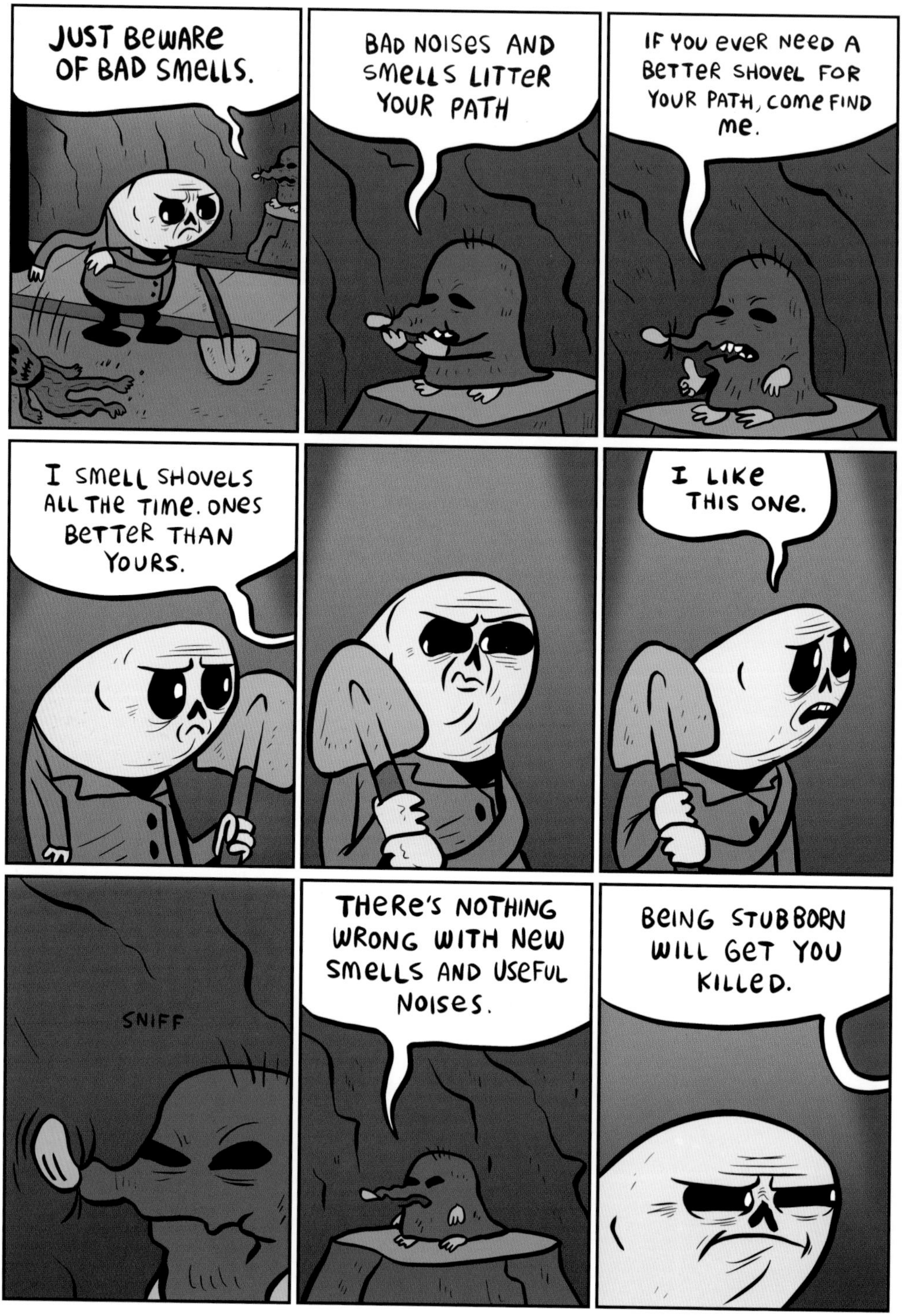
JUST BEWARE OF BAD SMELLS.
BAD NOISES AND SMELLS LITTER YOUR PATH
IF YOU EVER NEED A BETTER SHOVEL FOR YOUR PATH, COME FIND ME.
I SMELL SHOVELS ALL THE TIME. ONES BETTER THAN YOURS.
I LIKE THIS ONE.
SNIFF
THERE'S NOTHING WRONG WITH NEW SMELLS AND USEFUL NOISES.
BEING STUBBORN WILL GET YOU KILLED.

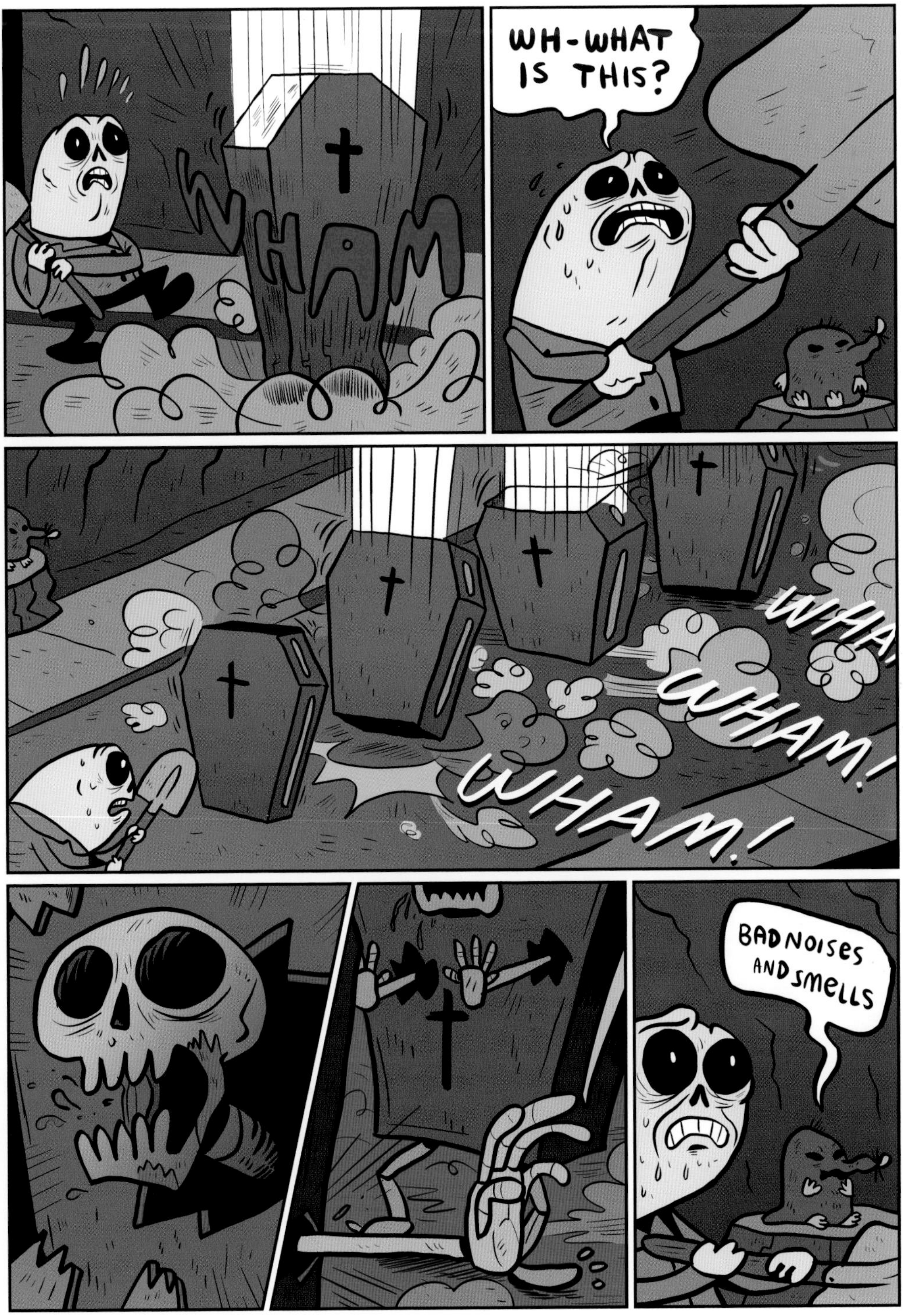
WHAM
WH-WHAT IS THIS?
WHAM!
WHAM!
WHAM!
BAD NOISES AND SMELLS

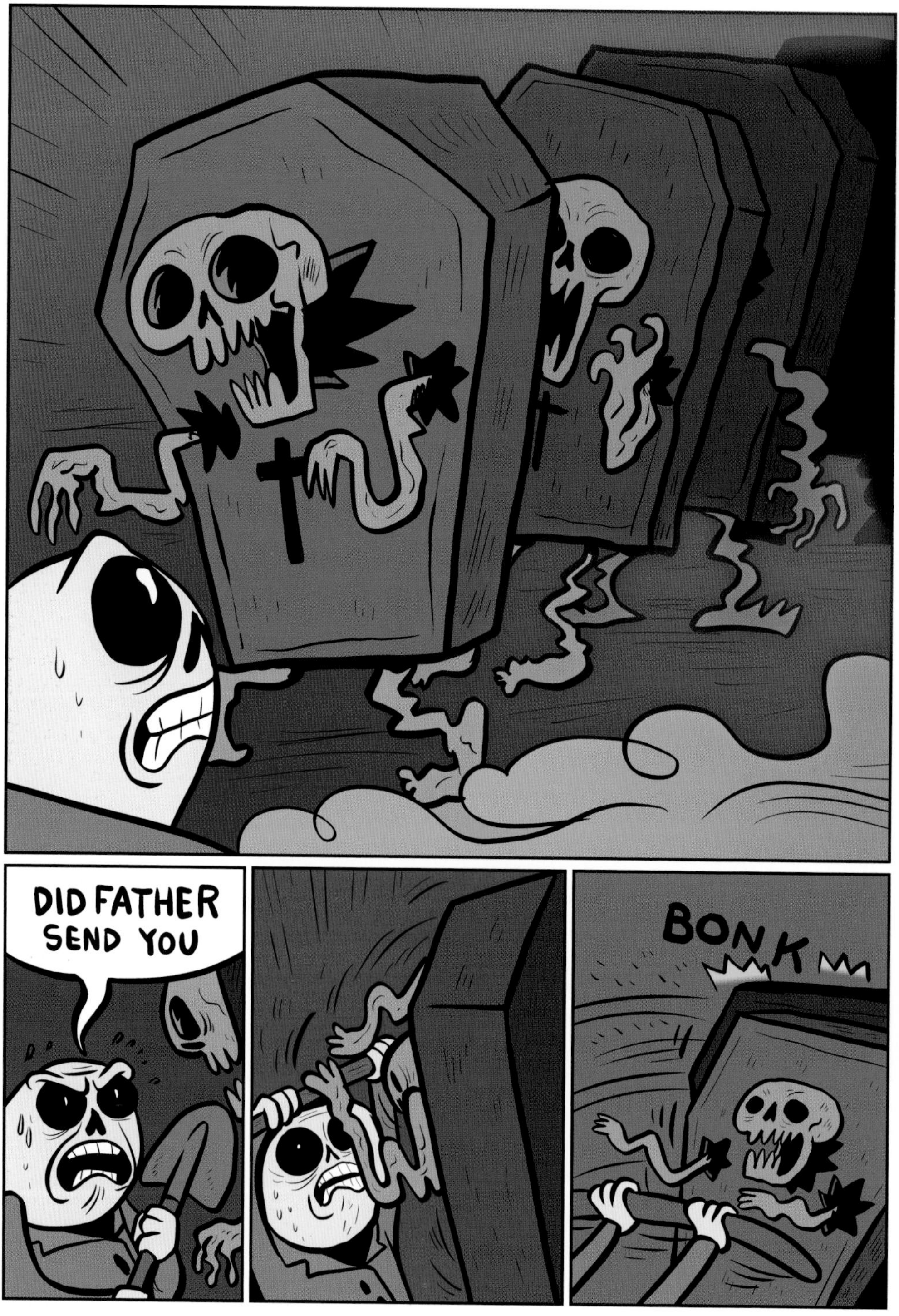
DID FATHER SEND YOU
BONK

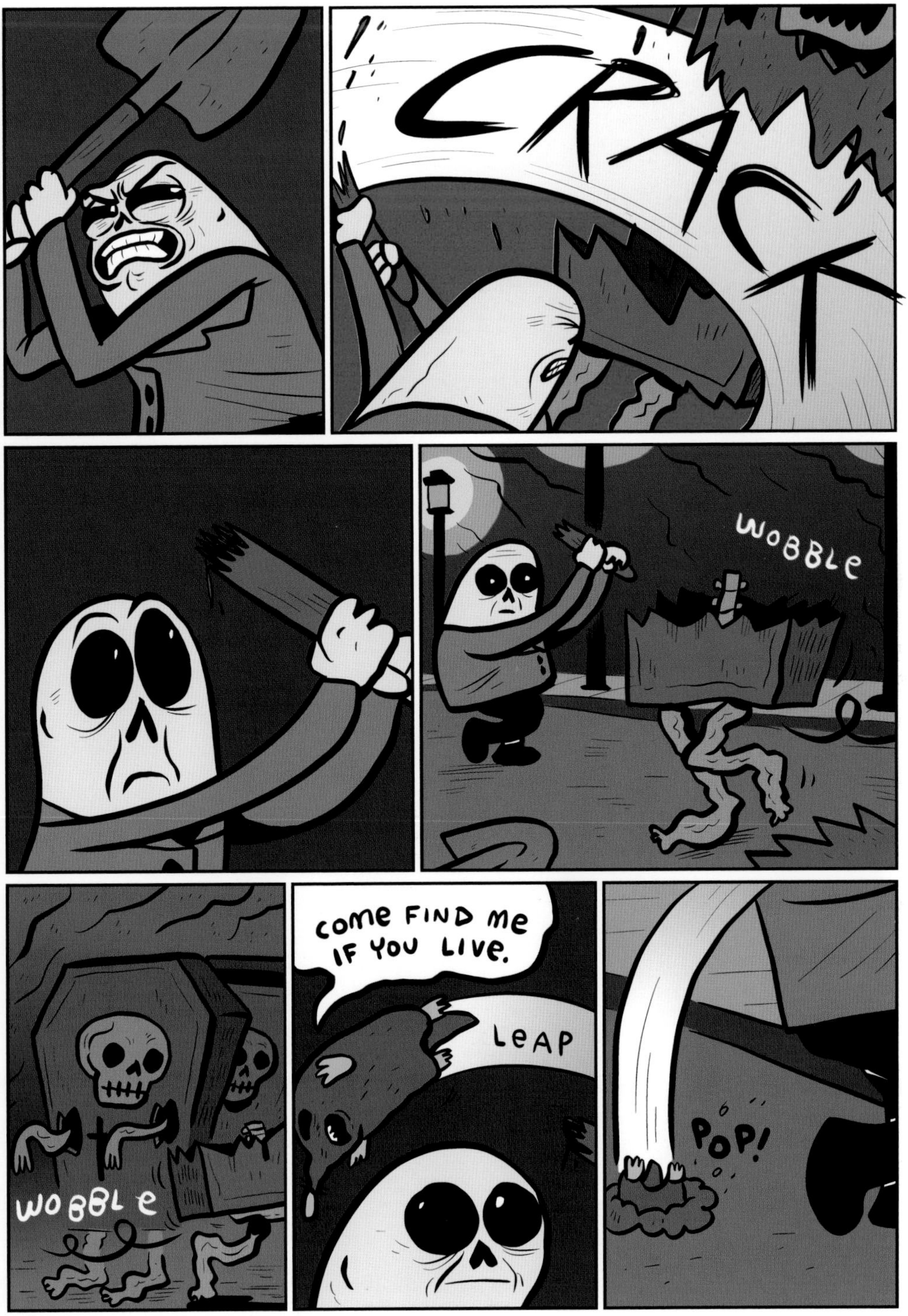
CRACK
WOBBLE
WOBBLE
COME FIND ME IF YOU LIVE.
LEAP
POP!

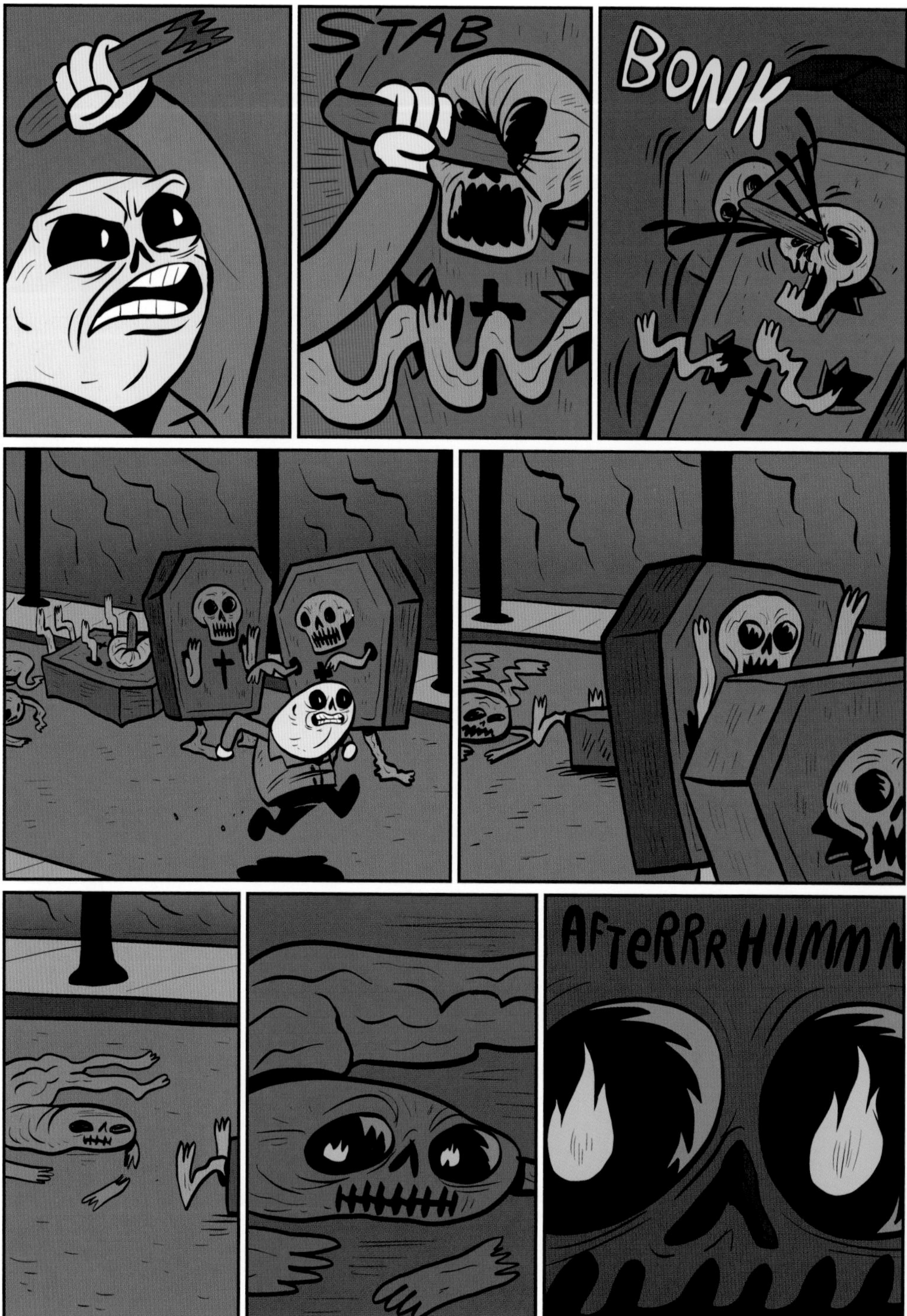
STAB
BONK
AFTERRR HIIMM

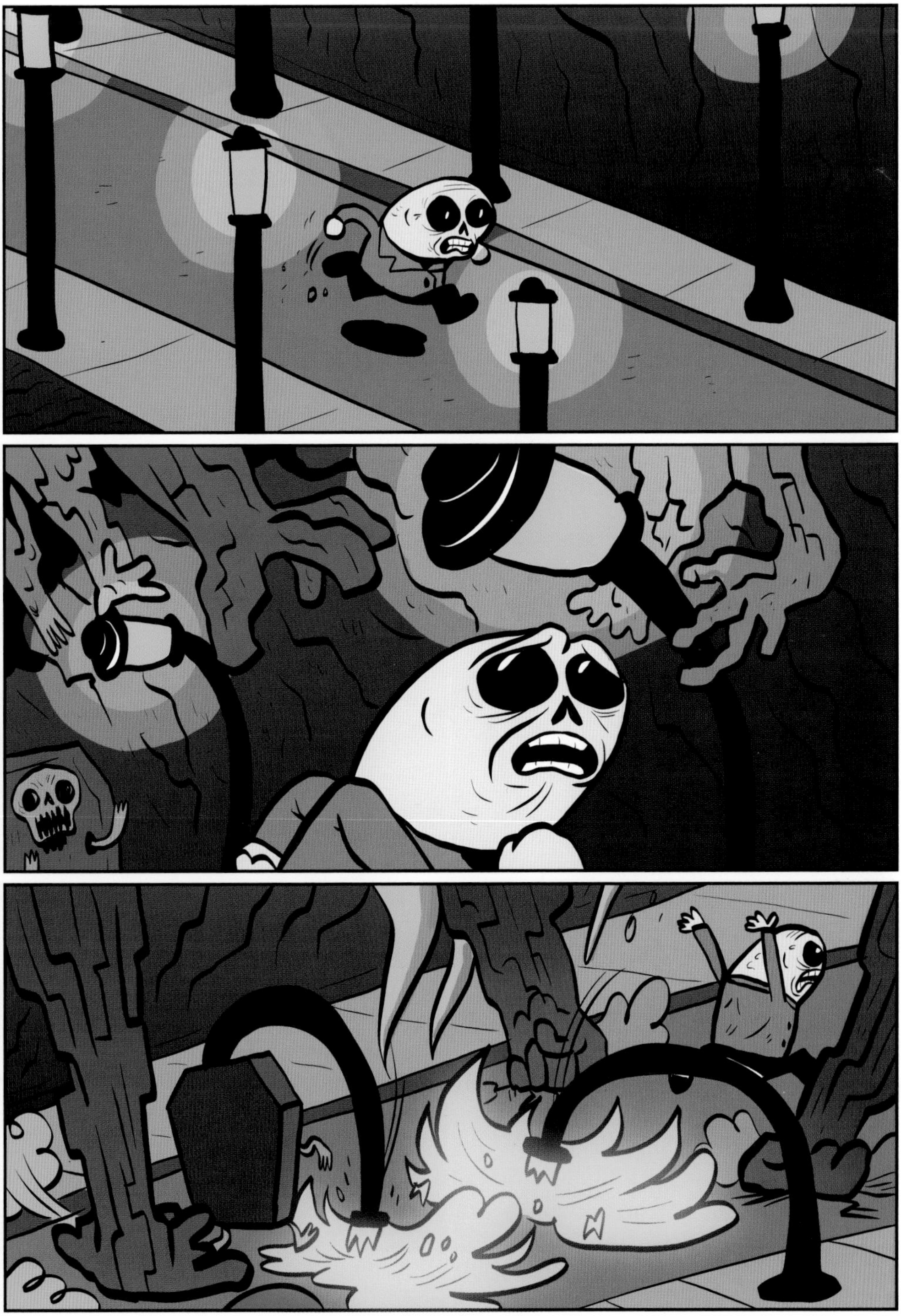

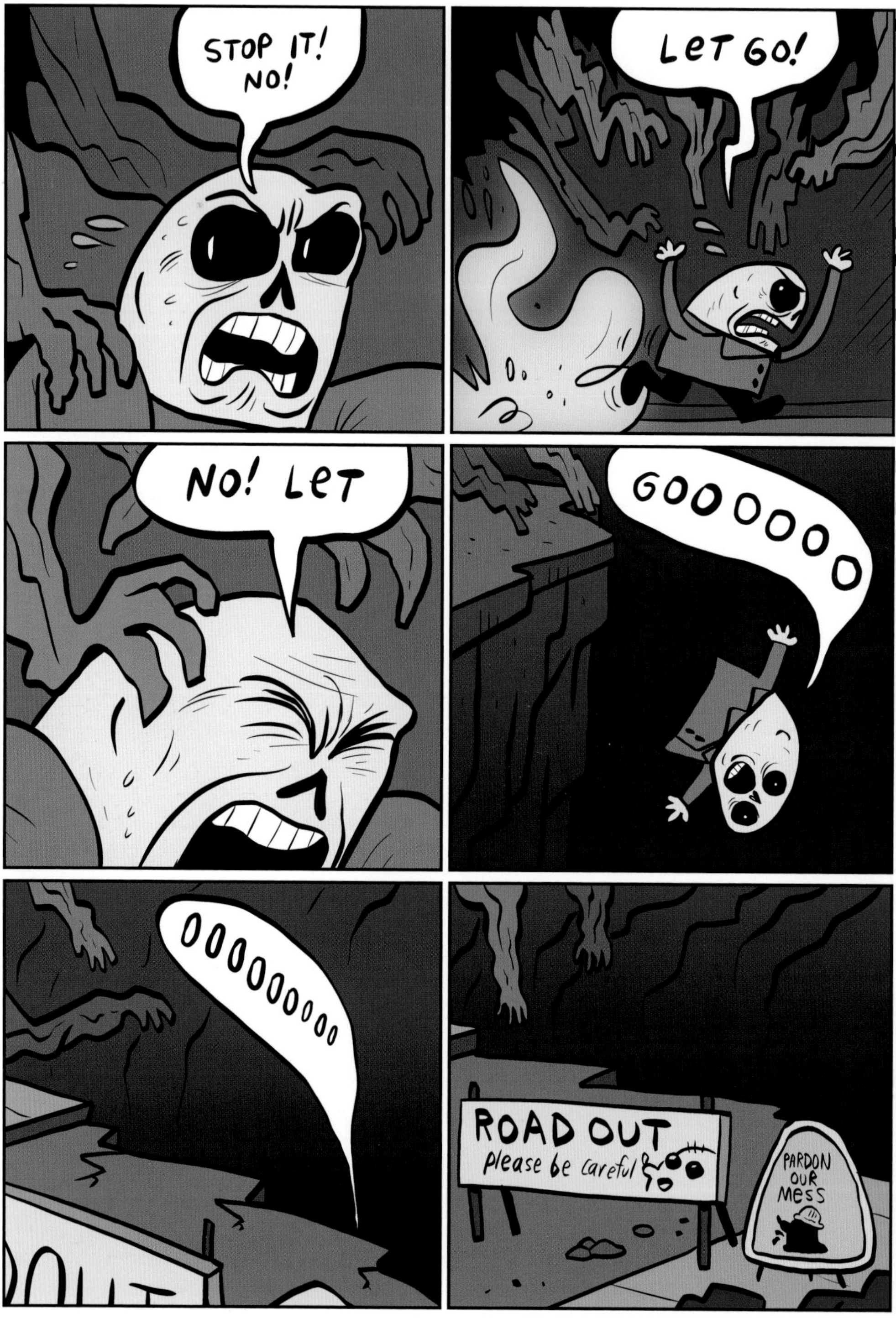
STOP IT! NO!
LET GO!
NO! LET
GOO OOOO
OOOOOOOOOO
ROAD OUT
please be careful
PARDON OUR MESS

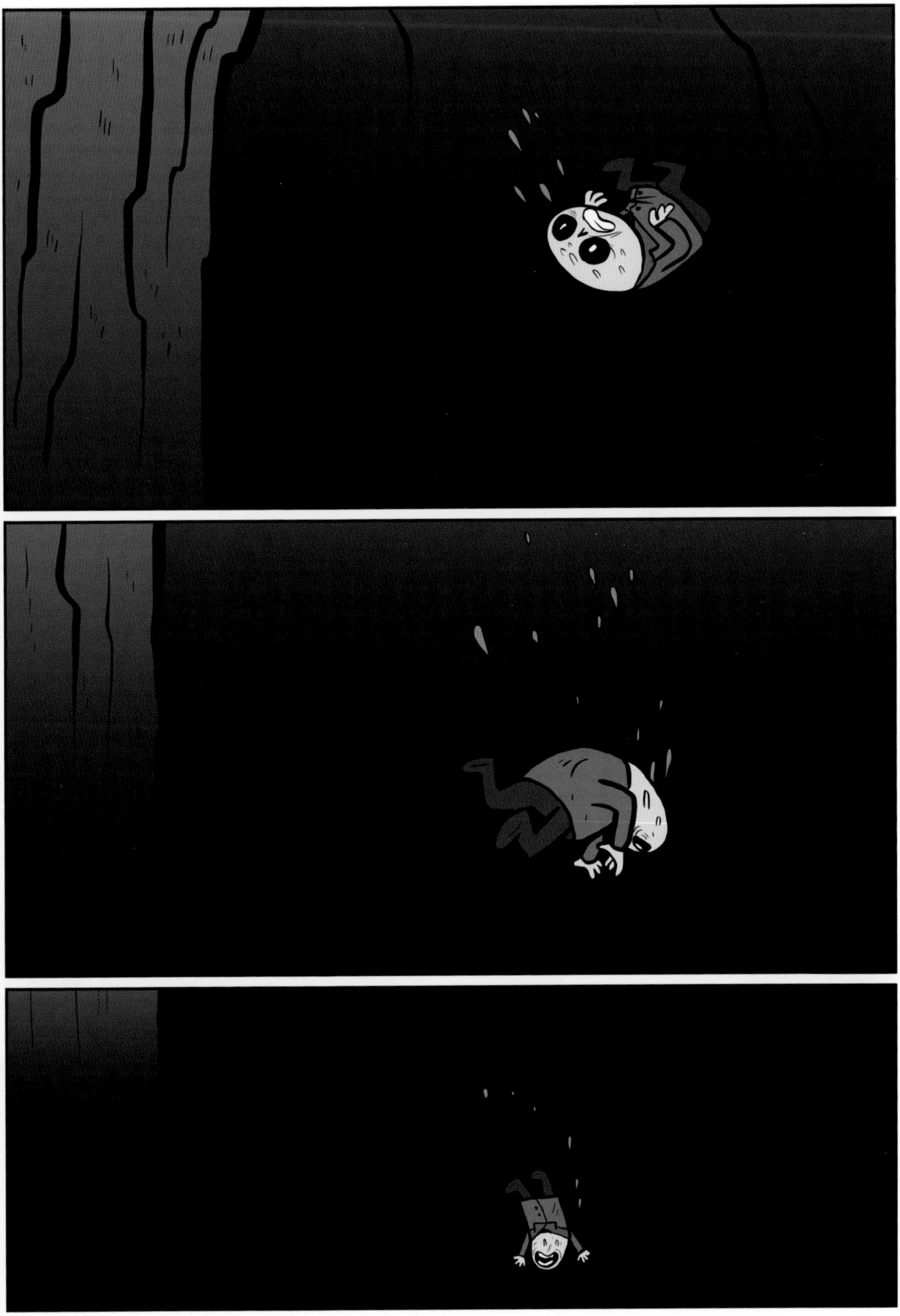

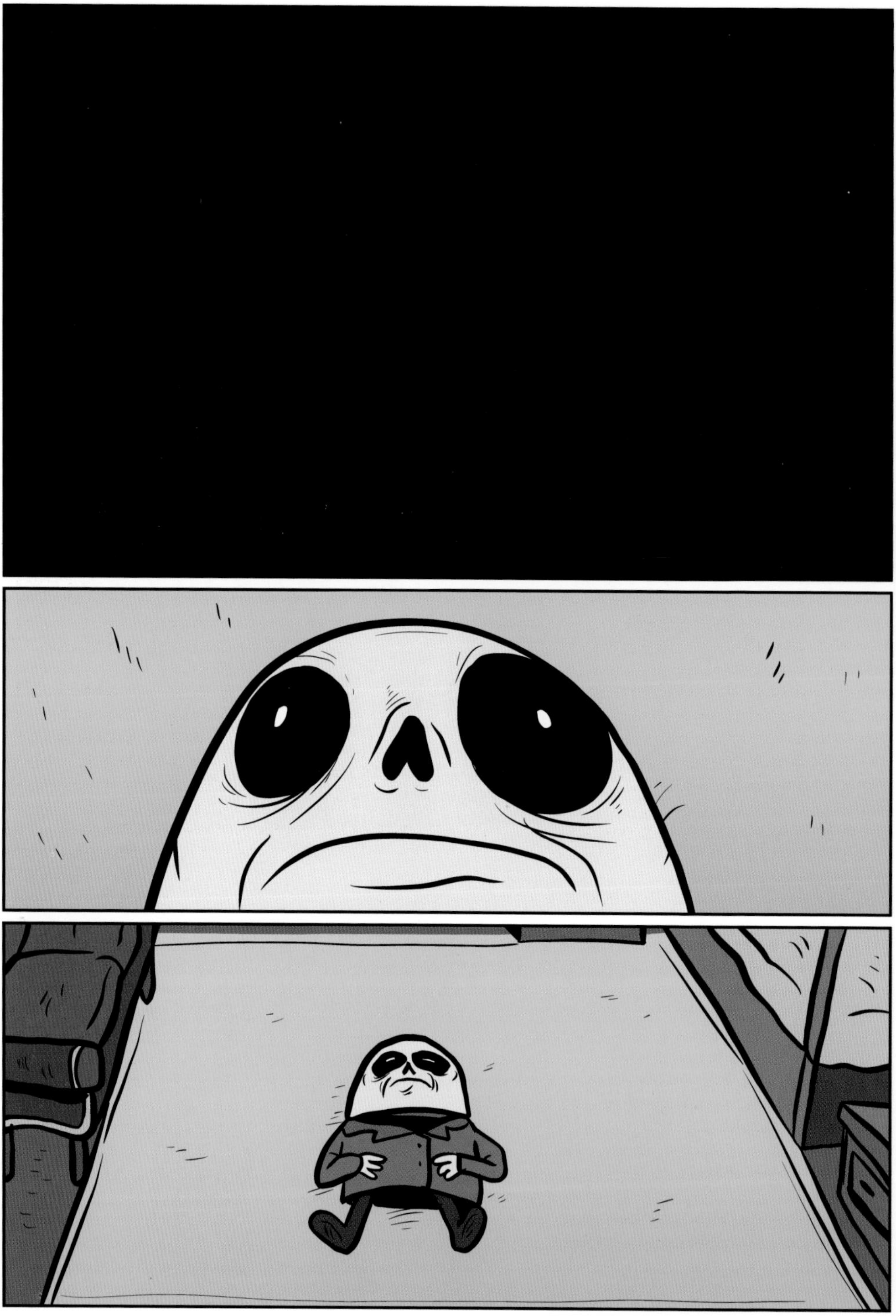

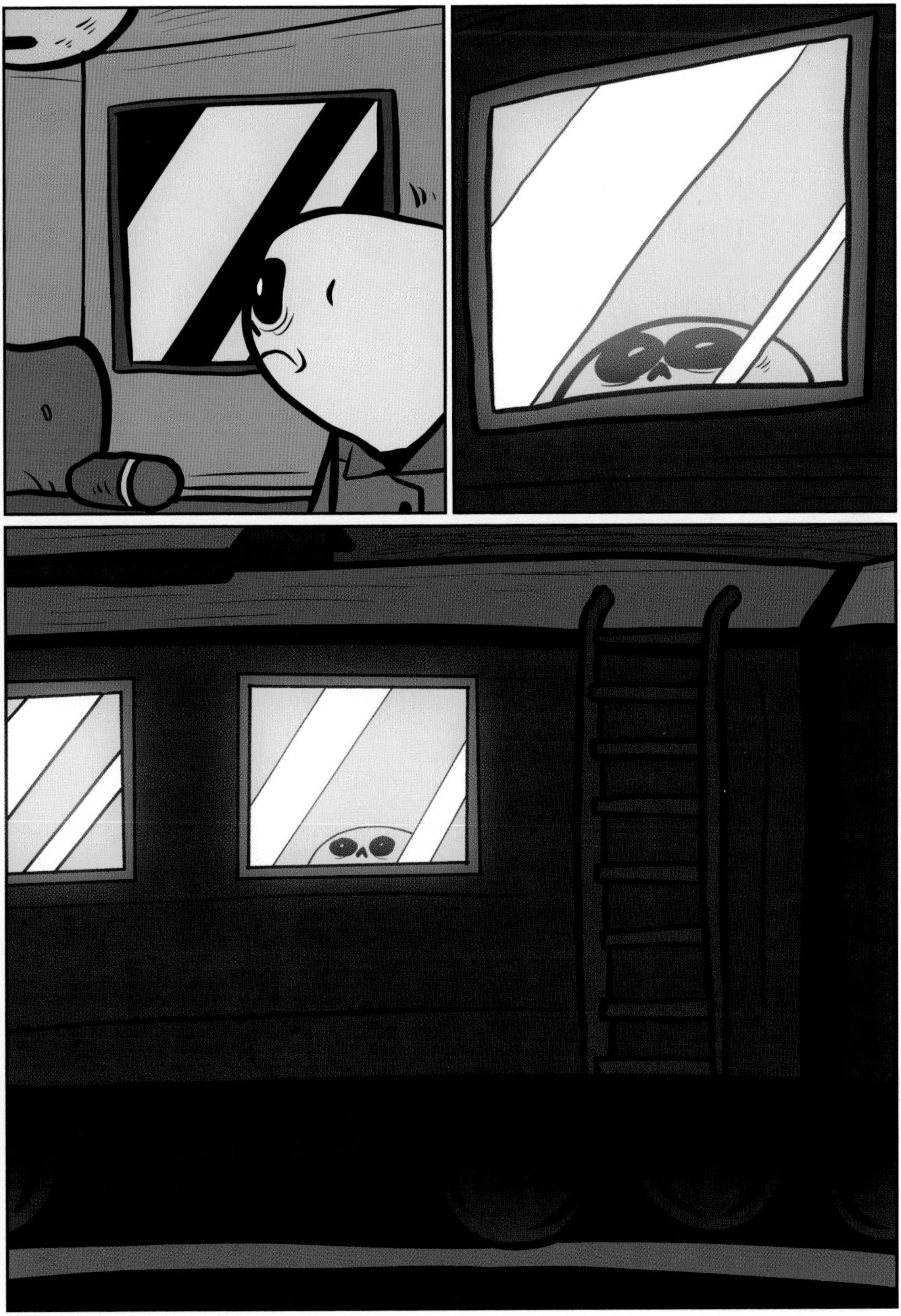

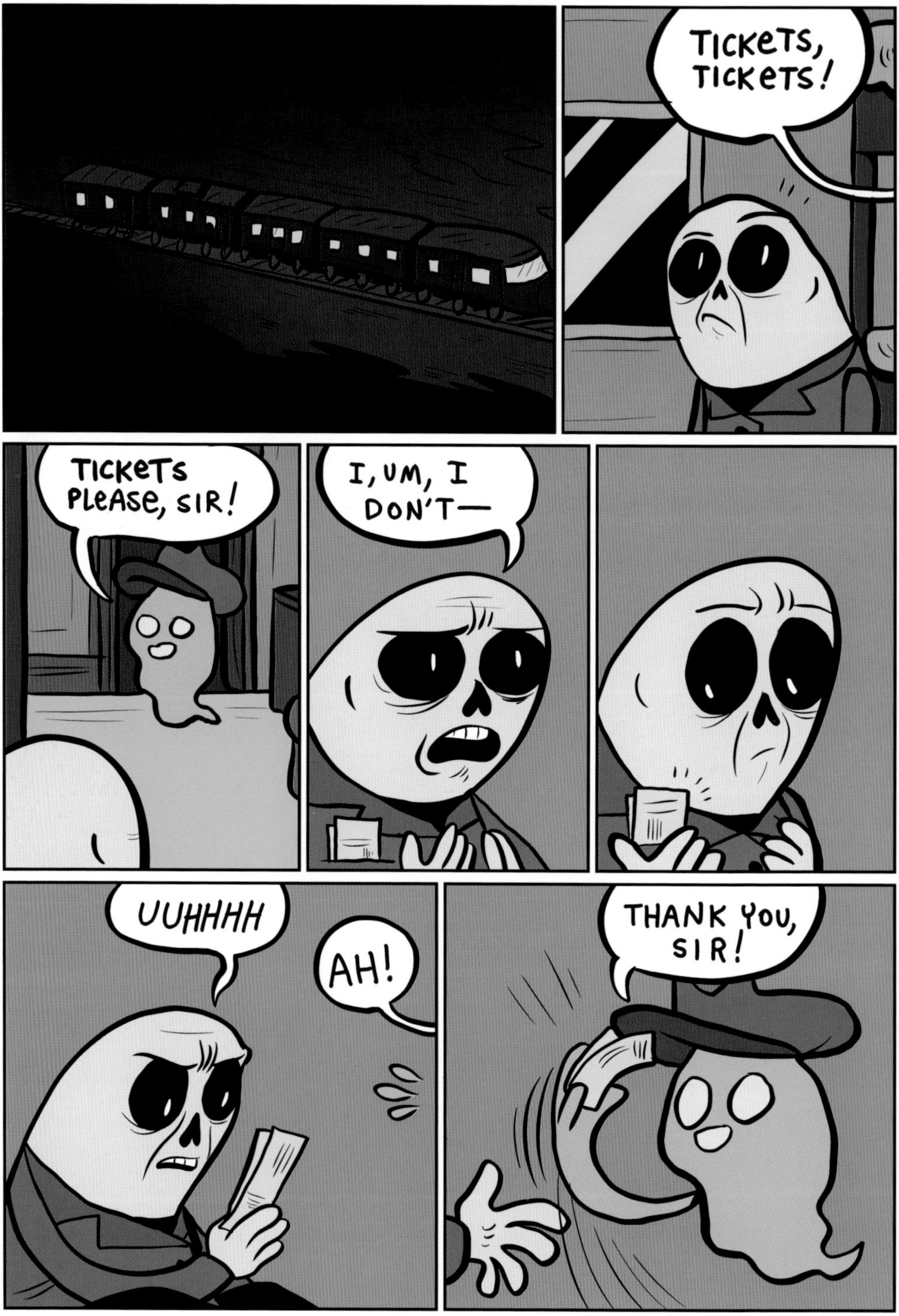
TICKETS, TICKETS!
TICKETS PLEASE, SIR!
I, UM, I DON'T—
UUHHHH
AH!
THANK YOU, SIR!

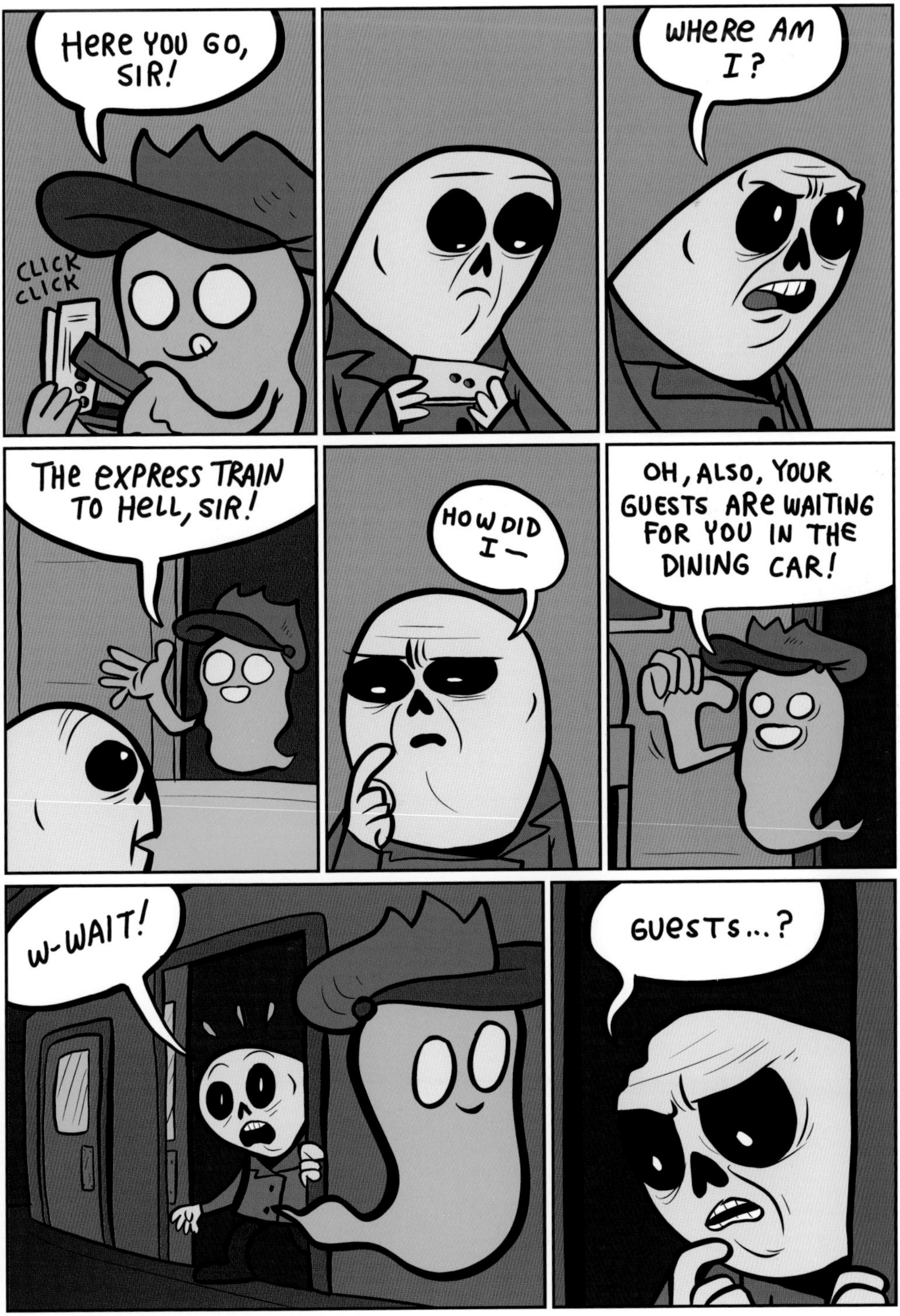
HERE YOU GO, SIR!
CLICK CLICK
WHERE AM I?
THE EXPRESS TRAIN TO HELL, SIR!
HOW DID I—
OH, ALSO, YOUR GUESTS ARE WAITING FOR YOU IN THE DINING CAR!
W-WAIT!
GUESTS...?

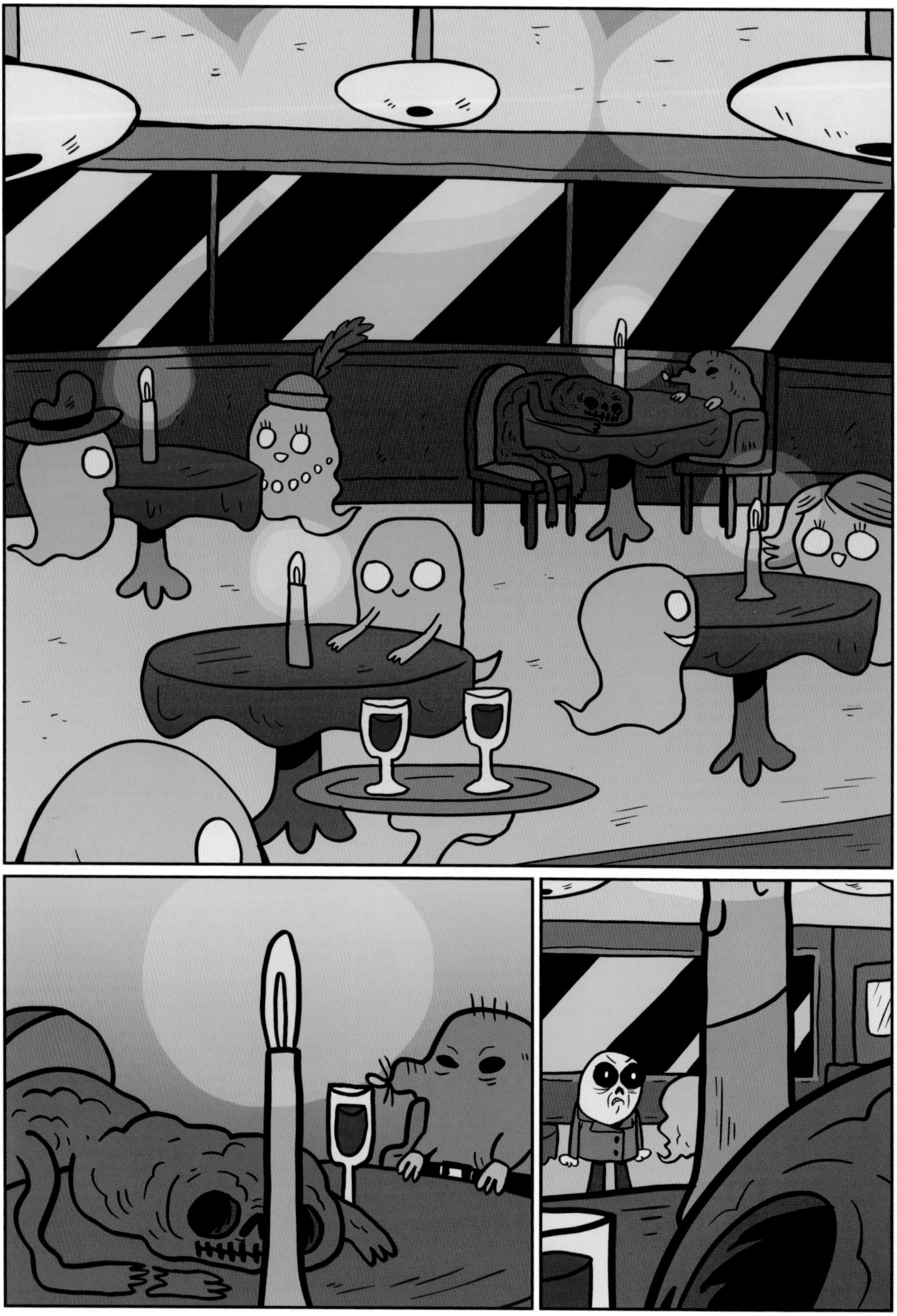

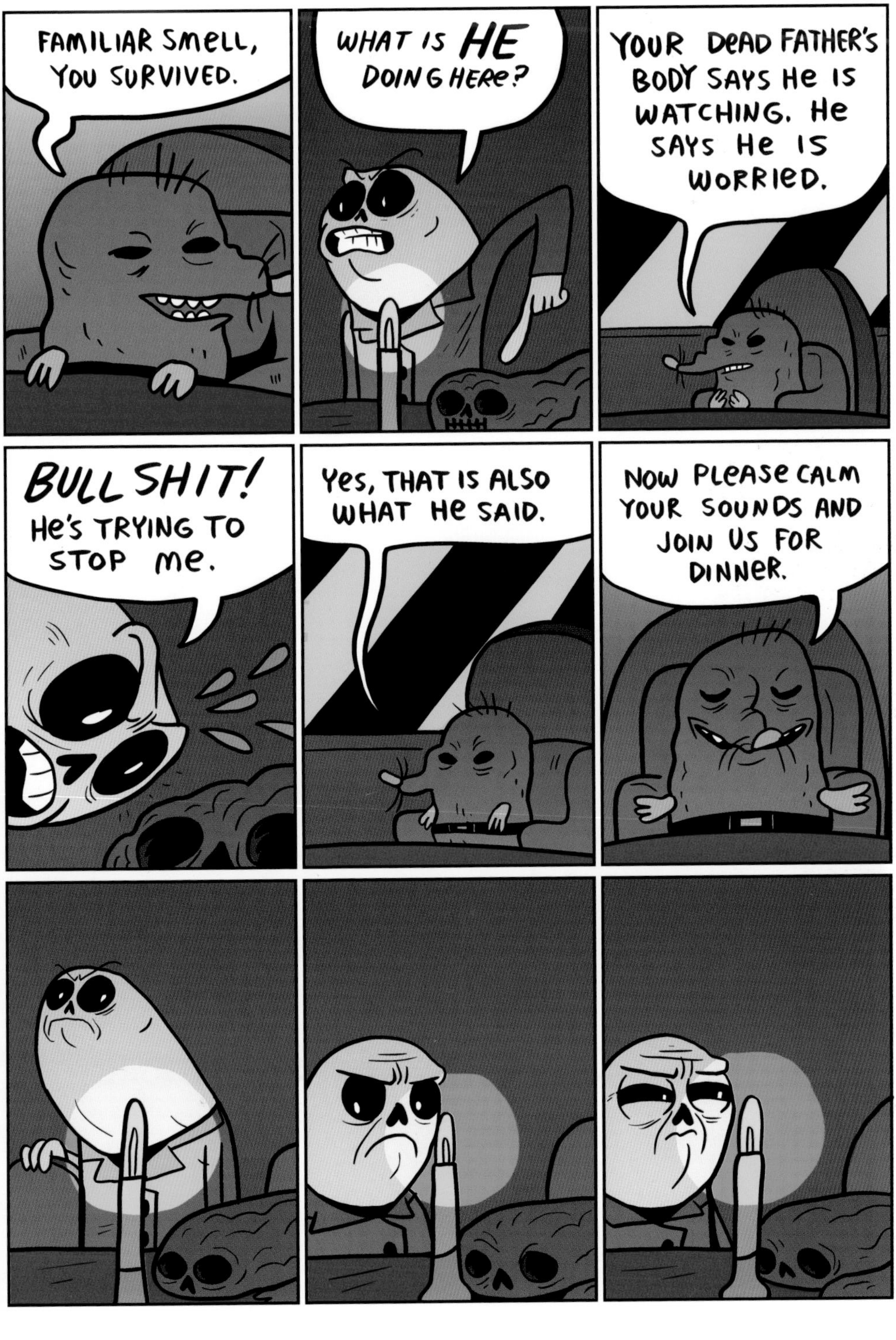
FAMILIAR SMELL, YOU SURVIVED.
WHAT IS HE DOING HERE?
YOUR DEAD FATHER'S BODY SAYS HE IS WATCHING. HE SAYS HE IS WORRIED.
BULLSHIT! HE'S TRYING TO STOP ME.
YES, THAT IS ALSO WHAT HE SAID.
NOW PLEASE CALM YOUR SOUNDS AND JOIN US FOR DINNER.

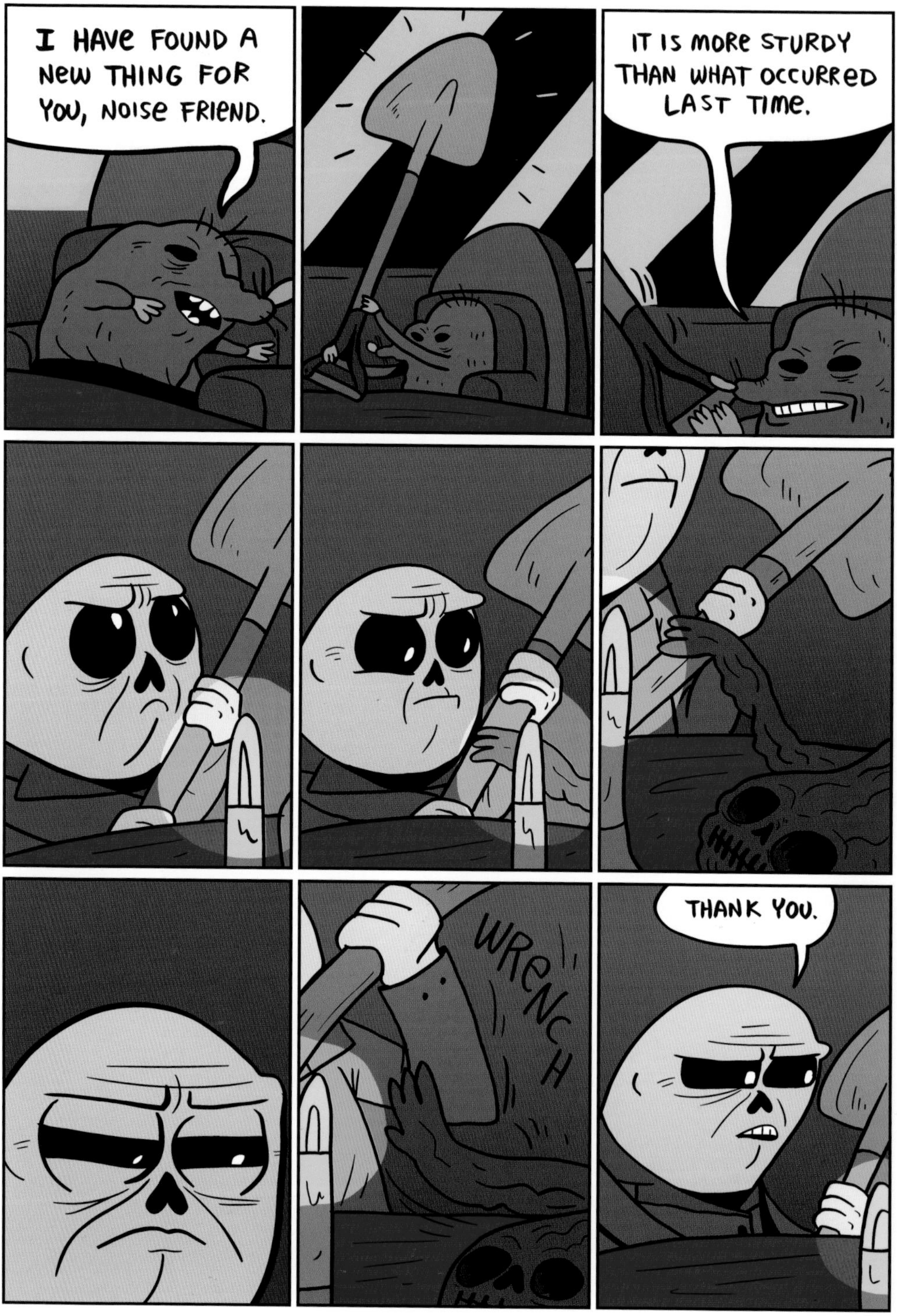
I HAVE FOUND A NEW THING FOR YOU, NOISE FRIEND.
IT IS MORE STURDY THAN WHAT OCCURRED LAST TIME.
WRENCH
THANK YOU.

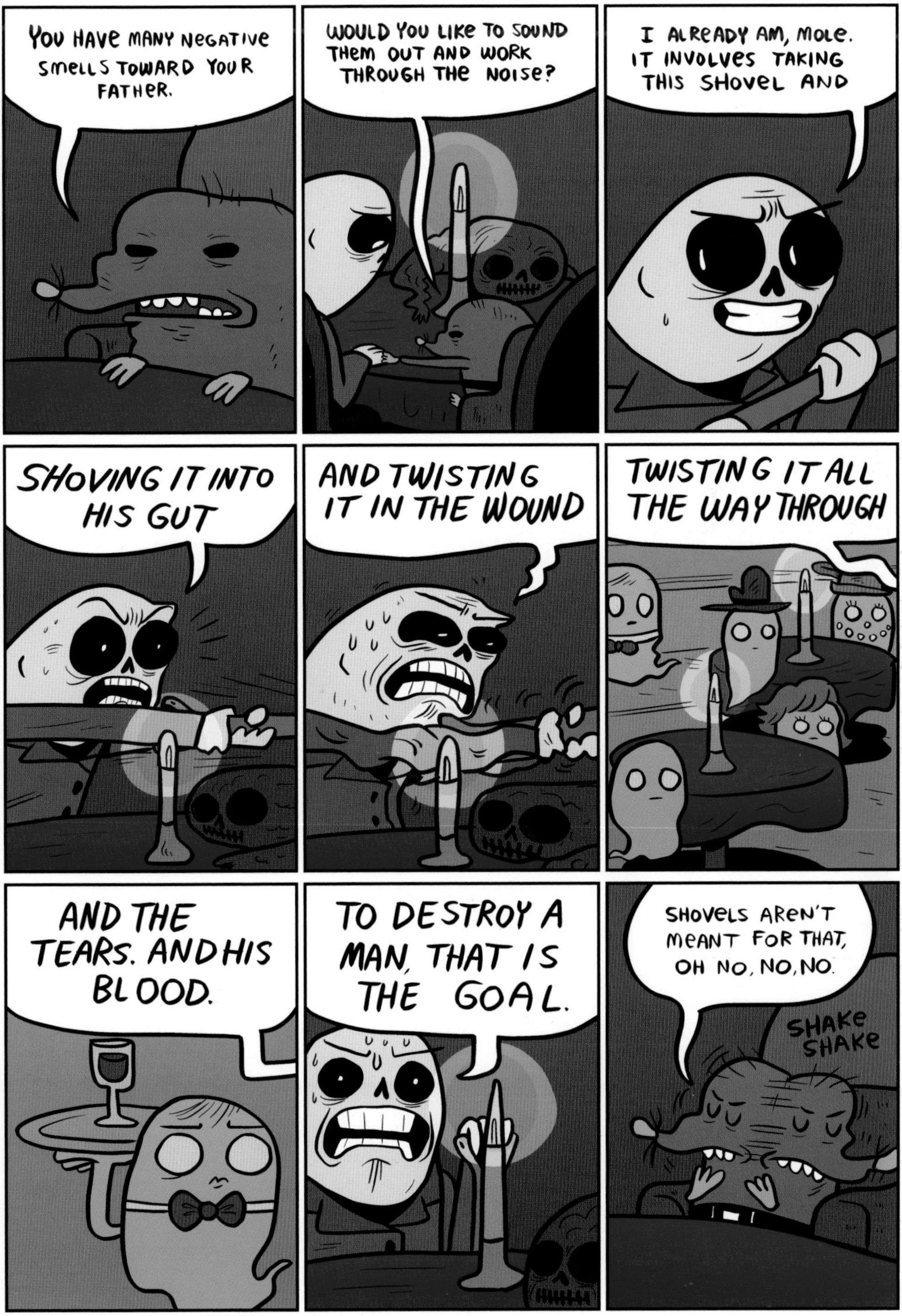
YOU HAVE MANY NEGATIVE SMELLS TOWARD YOUR FATHER.
WOULD YOU LIKE TO SOUND THEM OUT AND WORK THROUGH THE NOISE?
I ALREADY AM, MOLE. IT INVOLVES TAKING THIS SHOVEL AND
SHOVING IT INTO HIS GUT
AND TWISTING IT IN THE WOUND
TWISTING IT ALL THE WAY THROUGH
AND THE TEARS. AND HIS BLOOD.
TO DESTROY A MAN, THAT IS THE GOAL.
SHOVELS AREN'T MEANT FOR THAT, OH NO, NO, NO.
SHAKE SHAKE

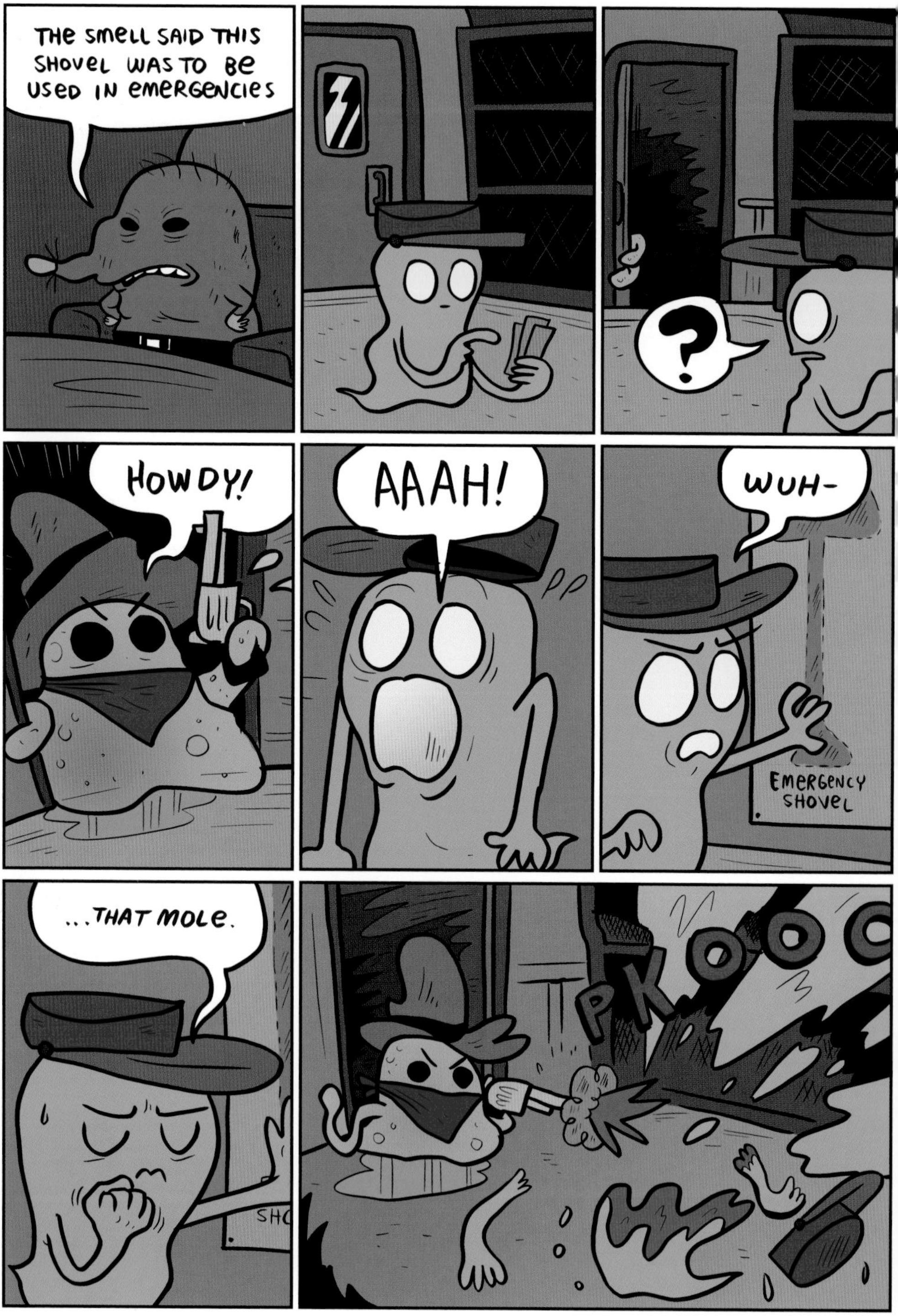
THE SMELL SAID THIS SHOVEL WAS TO BE USED IN EMERGENCIES
?
HOWDY!
AAAH!
WUH-
EMERGENCY SHOVEL
...THAT MOLE.
PKOOO

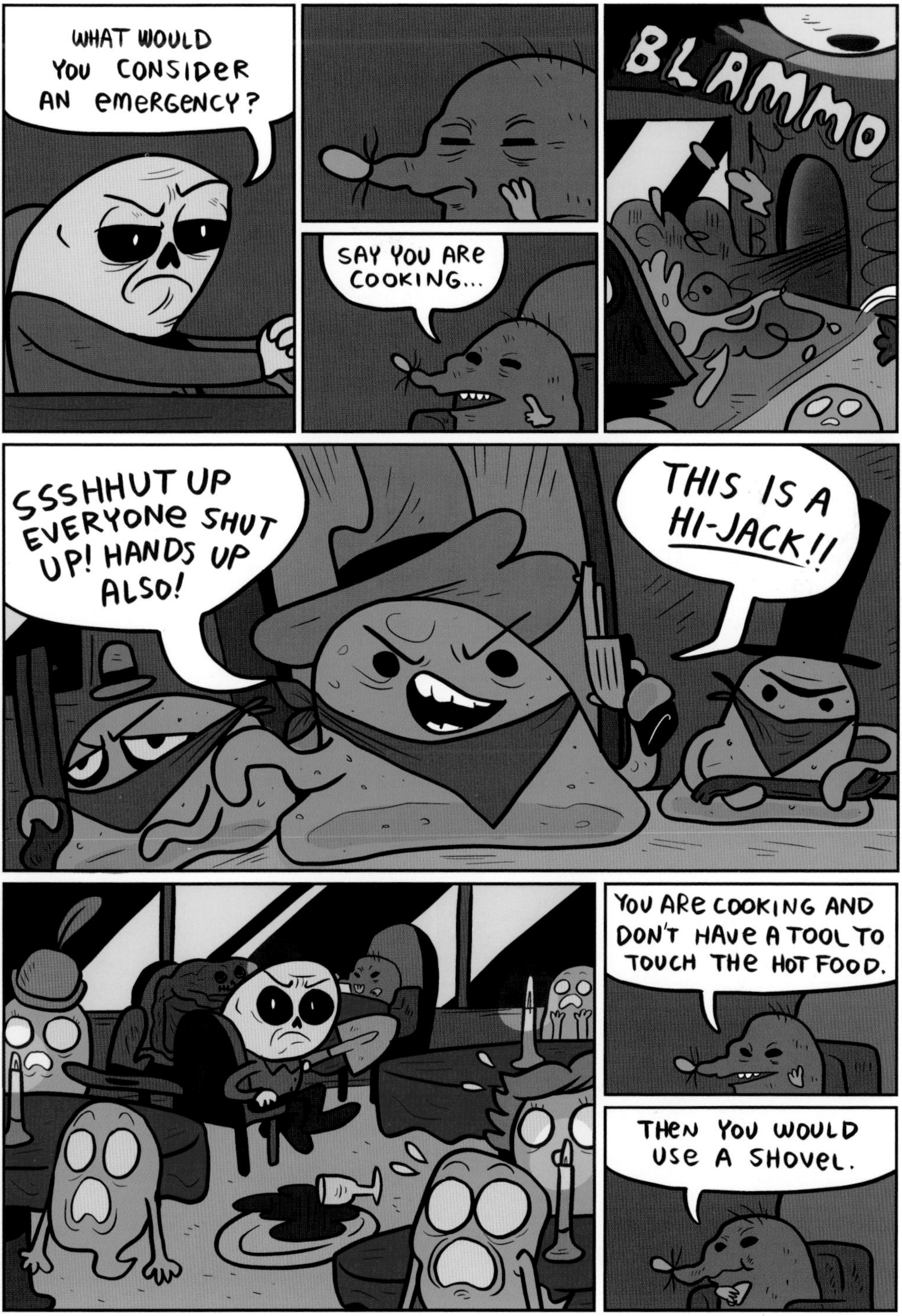
WHAT WOULD YOU CONSIDER AN EMERGENCY?
SAY YOU ARE COOKING...
BLAMMO
SSSHHUT UP EVERYONE SHUT UP! HANDS UP ALSO!
THIS IS A HI-JACK!!
YOU ARE COOKING AND DON'T HAVE A TOOL TO TOUCH THE HOT FOOD.
THEN YOU WOULD USE A SHOVEL.

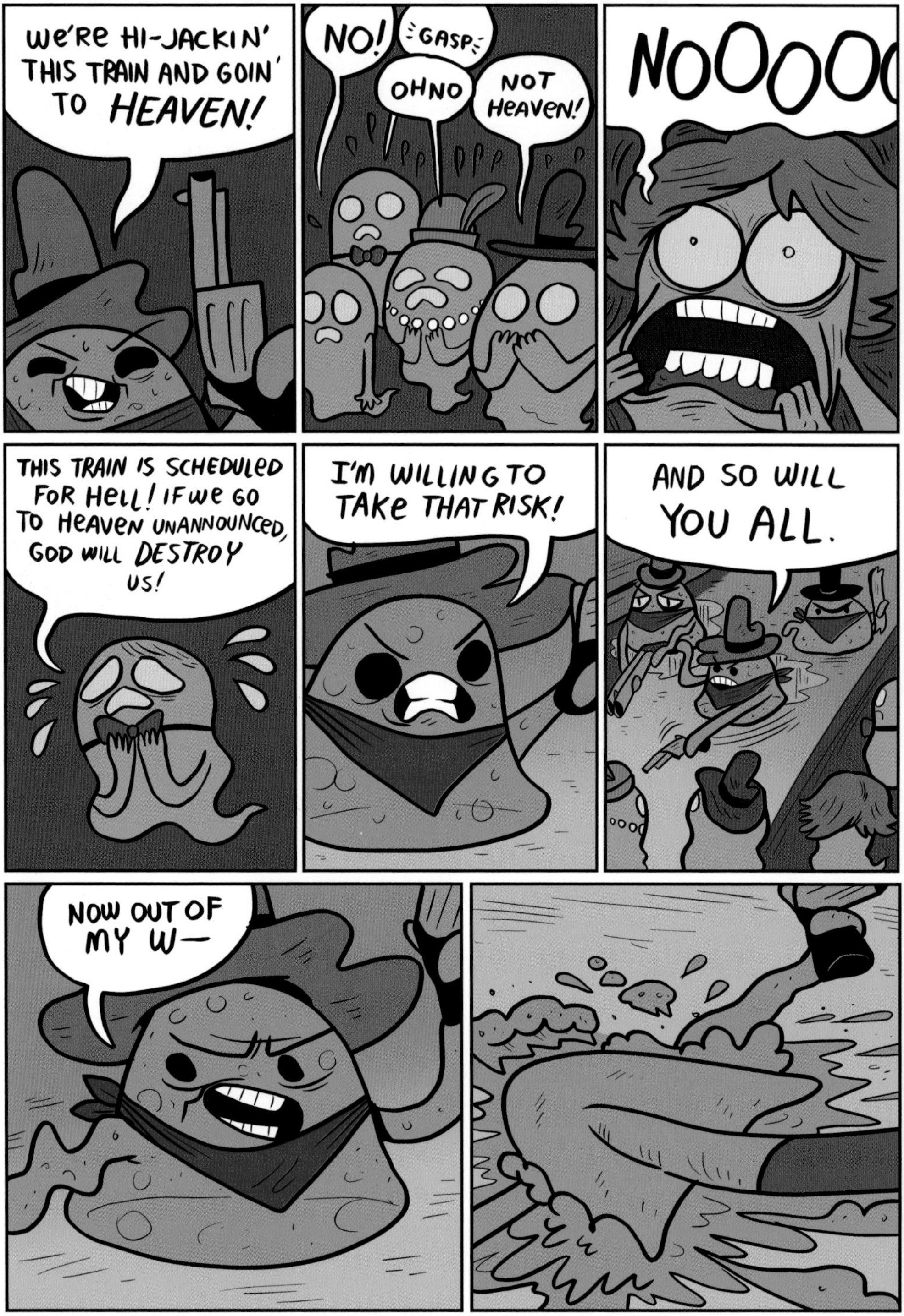
WE'RE HI-JACKIN' THIS TRAIN AND GOIN' TO HEAVEN!
NO!
GASP
OHNO
NOT HEAVEN!
NOOOOO
THIS TRAIN IS SCHEDULED FOR HELL! IF WE GO TO HEAVEN UNANNOUNCED, GOD WILL DESTROY US!
I'M WILLING TO TAKE THAT RISK!
AND SO WILL YOU ALL.
NOW OUT OF MY W—

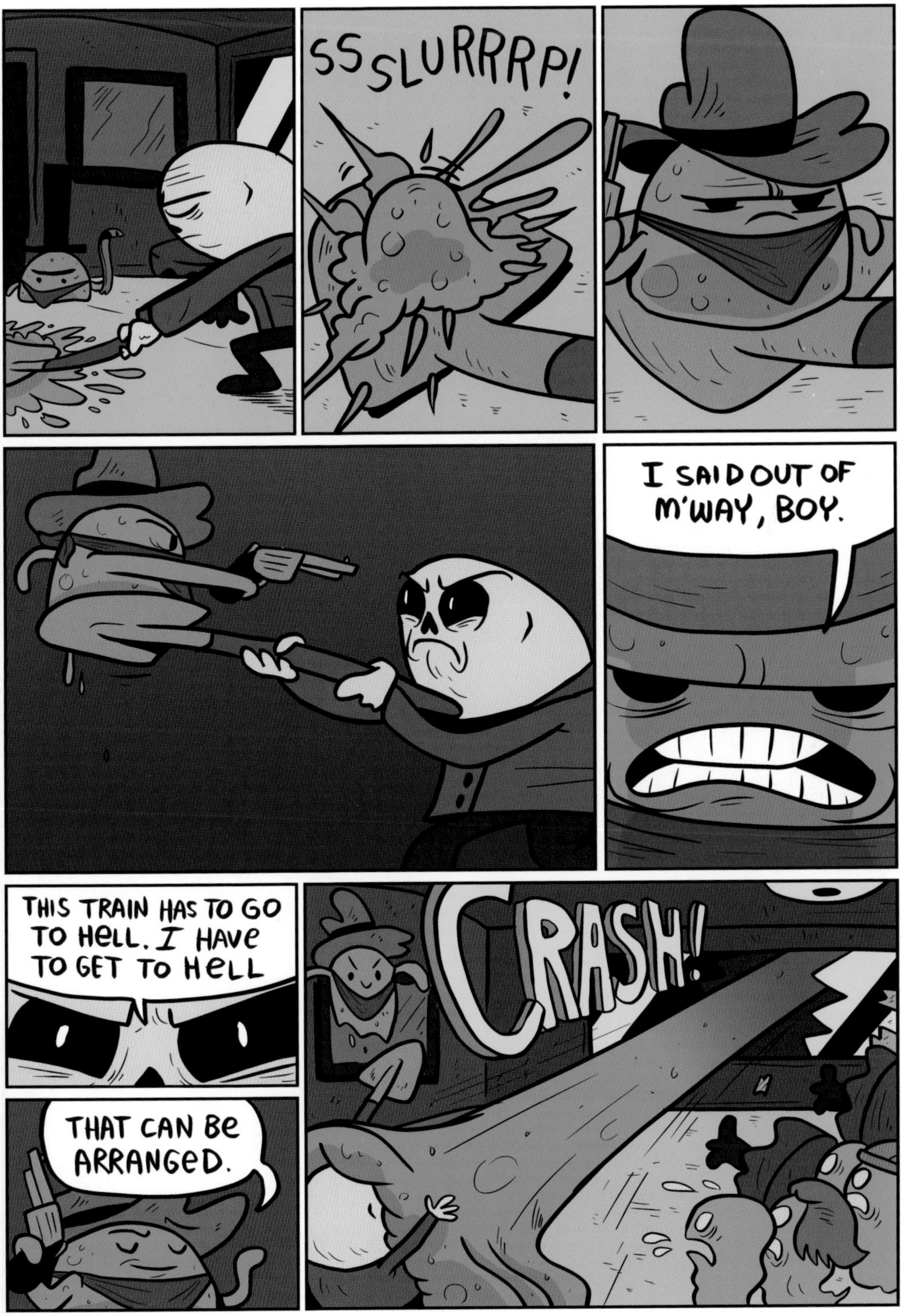

SSSLURRRRP!
I SAID OUT OF M'WAY, BOY.
THIS TRAIN HAS TO GO TO HELL. I HAVE TO GET TO HELL
THAT CAN BE ARRANGED.
CRASH!

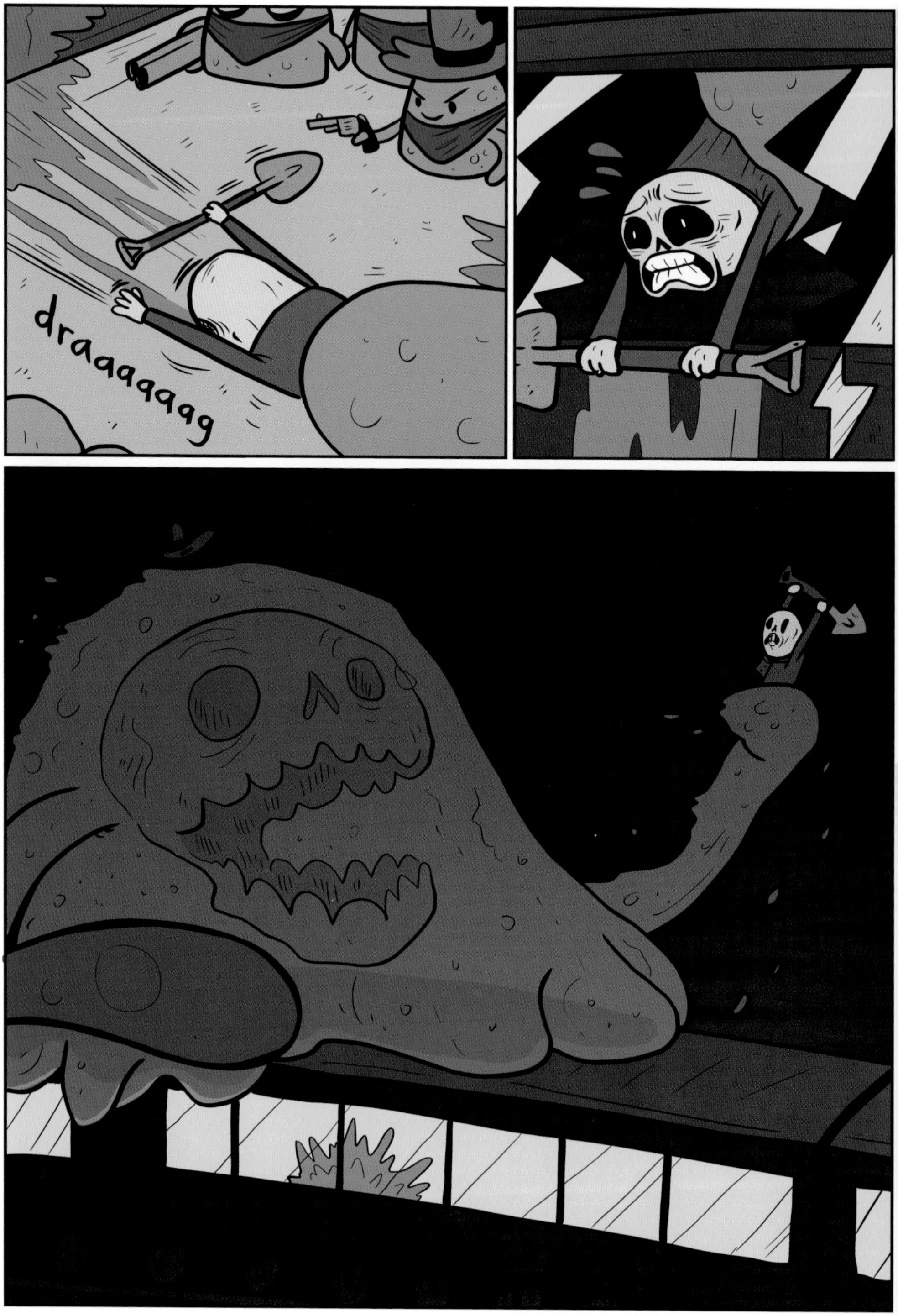
draaaaaag

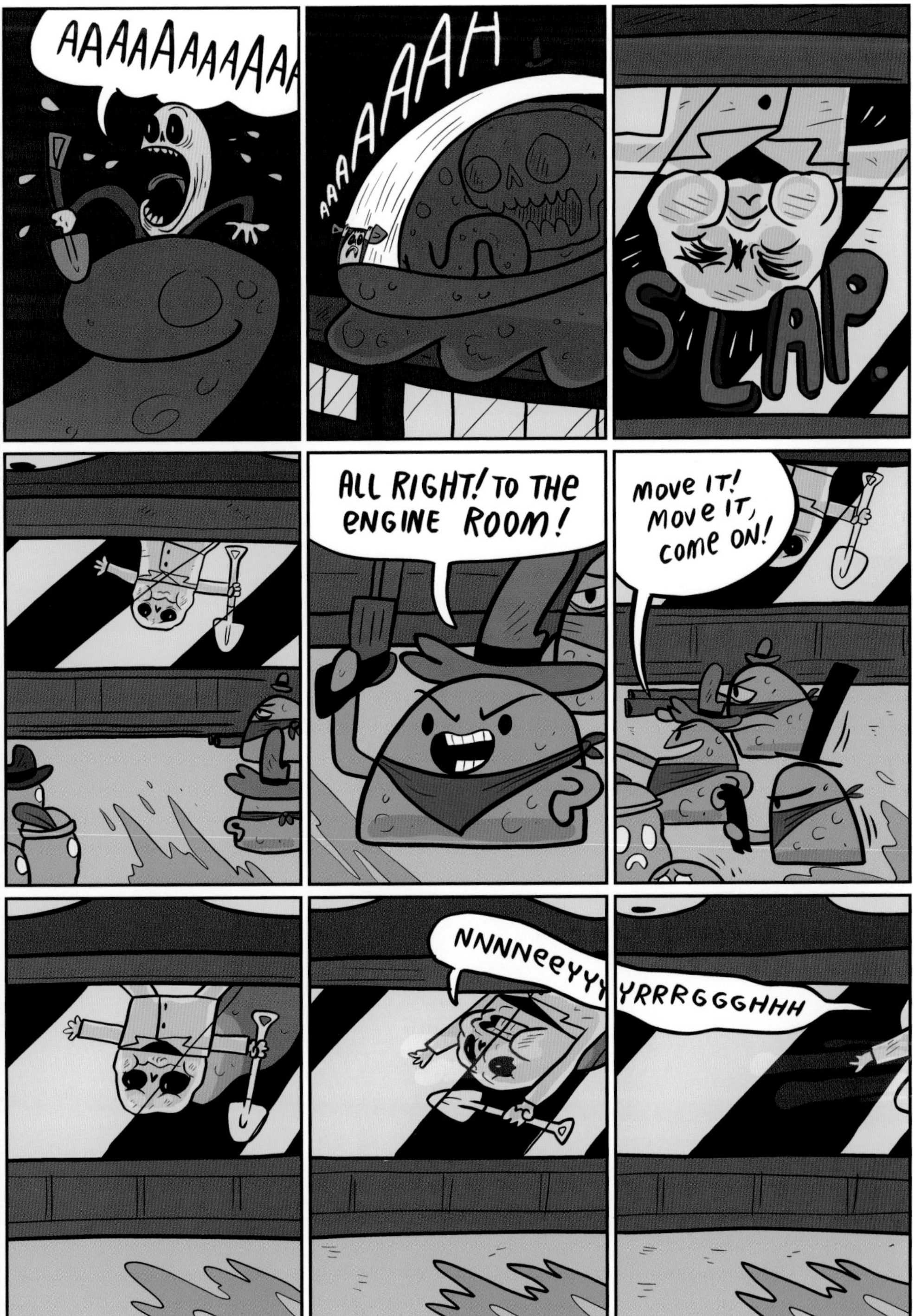
AAAAAAAAAAA
AAAAAAAAH
SLAP
ALL RIGHT! TO THE ENGINE ROOM!
MOVE IT! MOVE IT, COME ON!
NNNNeeYYYYRRRRGGGHHH

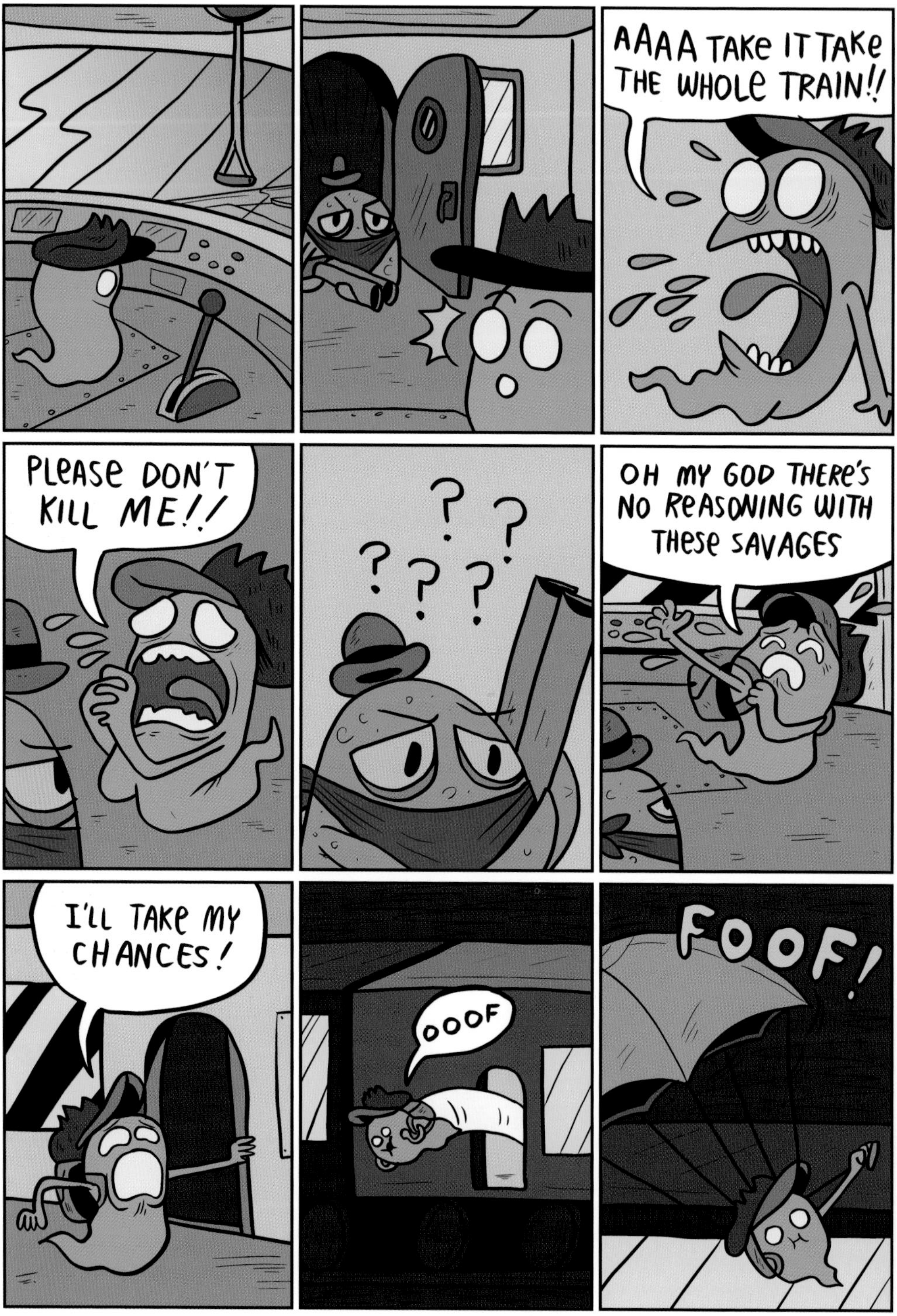
AAAA TAKE IT TAKE THE WHOLE TRAIN!!
PLEASE DON'T KILL ME!!
? ? ? ? ?
OH MY GOD THERE'S NO REASONING WITH THESE SAVAGES
I'LL TAKE MY CHANCES!
OOOF
FOOF!

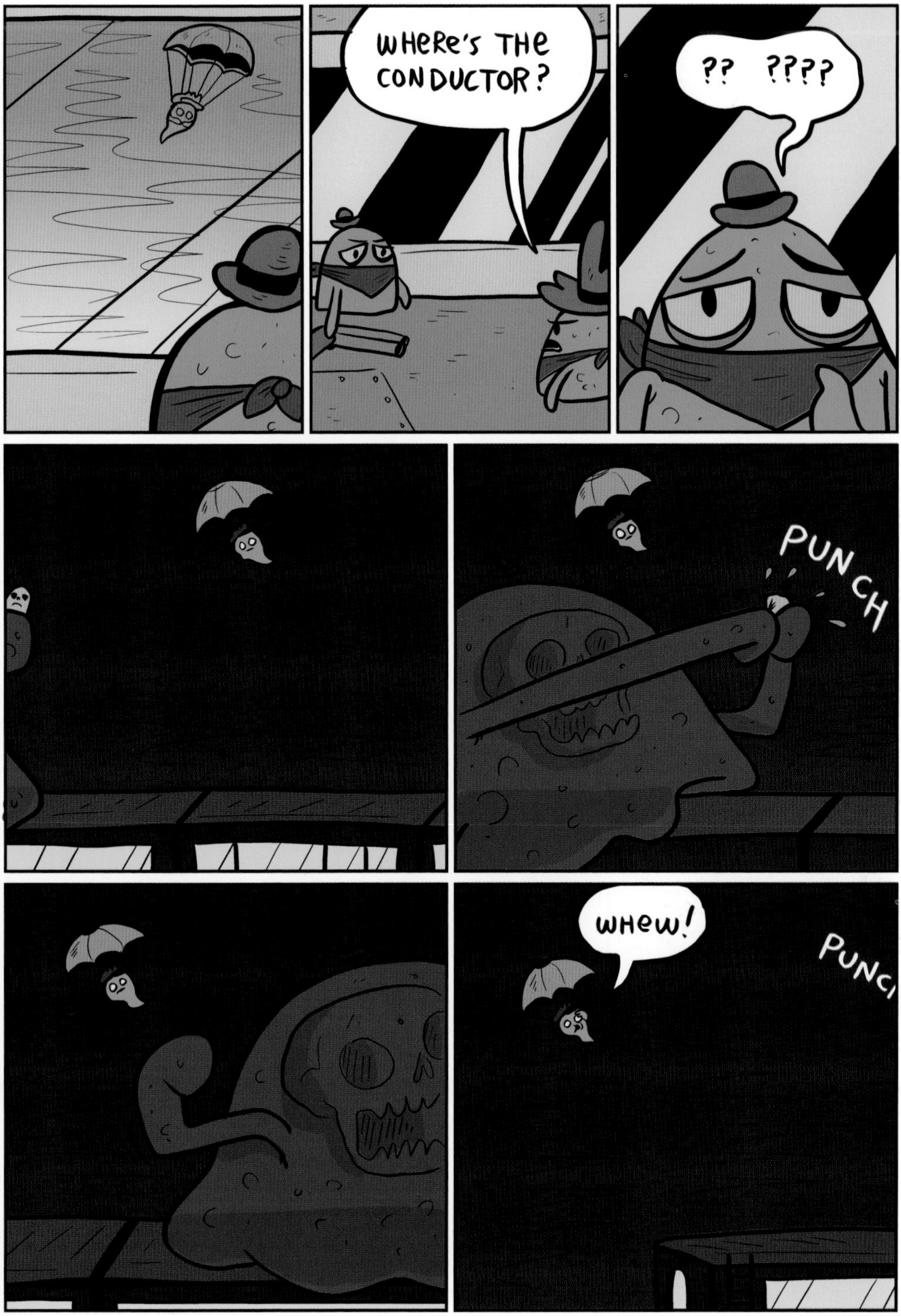
WHERE'S THE CONDUCTOR?
?? ????
PUNCH
WHEW!
PUNC

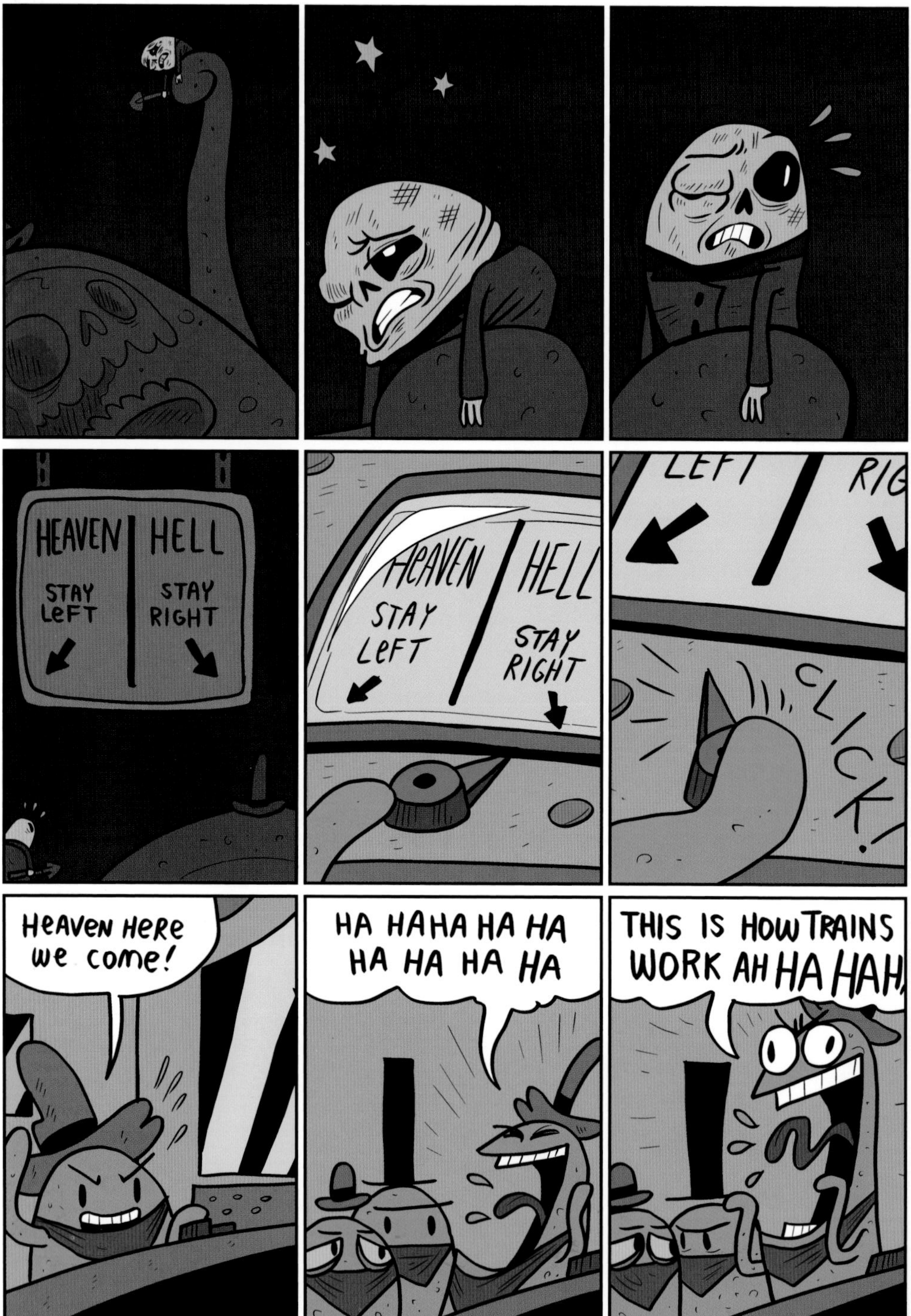
HEAVEN
HELL
STAY LEFT
STAY RIGHT
HEAVEN
HELL
STAY LEFT
STAY RIGHT
LEFT
CLICK!
Heaven Here we come!
HA HAHA HA HA HA HA HA HA HA
THIS IS HOW TRAINS WORK AH HA HAH

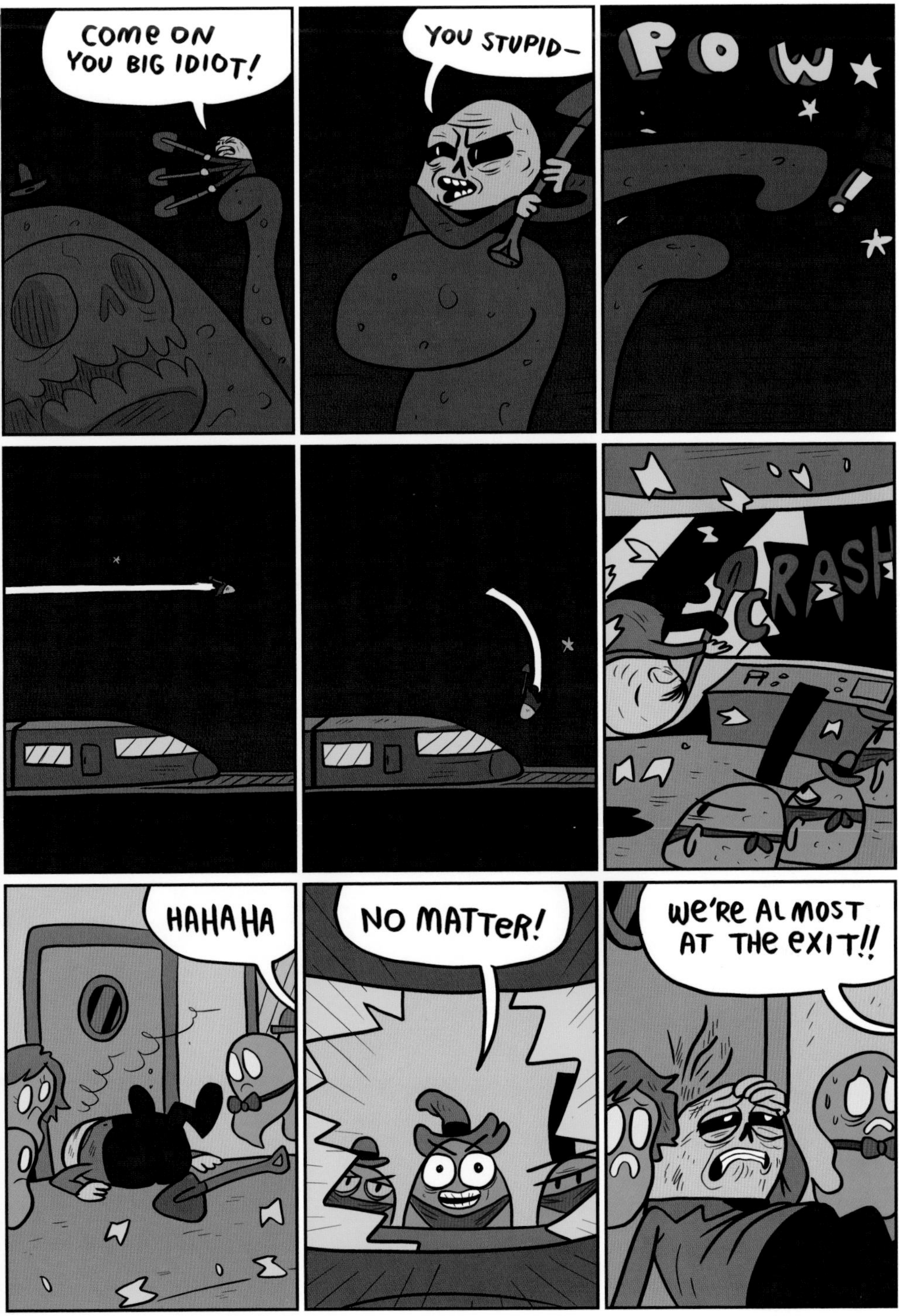

COME ON YOU BIG IDIOT!
YOU STUPID–
POW!
CRASH
HAHAHA
NO MATTER!
WE'RE ALMOST AT THE EXIT!!

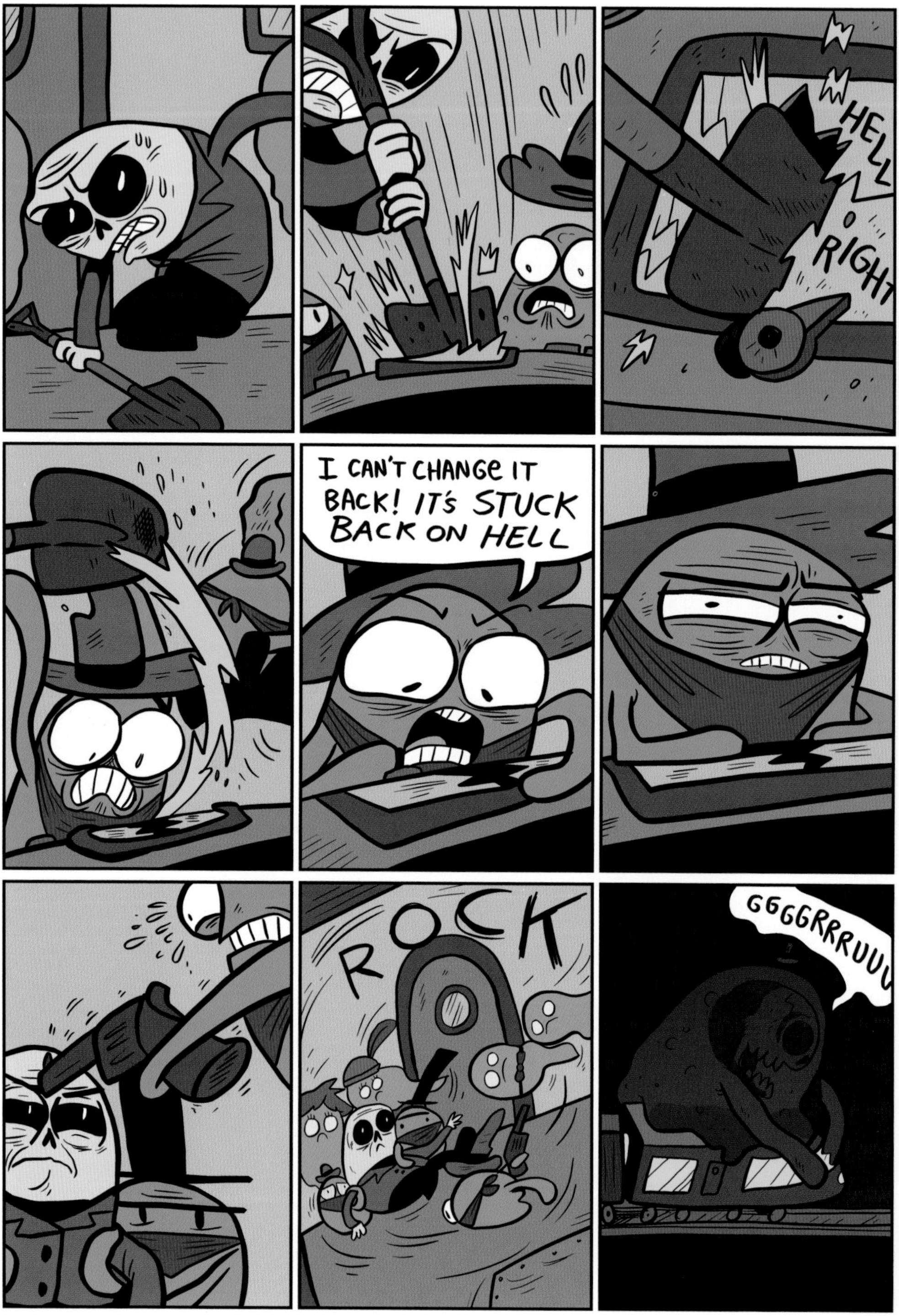
HELL
O
RIGHT
I CAN'T CHANGE IT BACK! IT'S STUCK BACK ON HELL
ROCK
GGGGRRRUUU

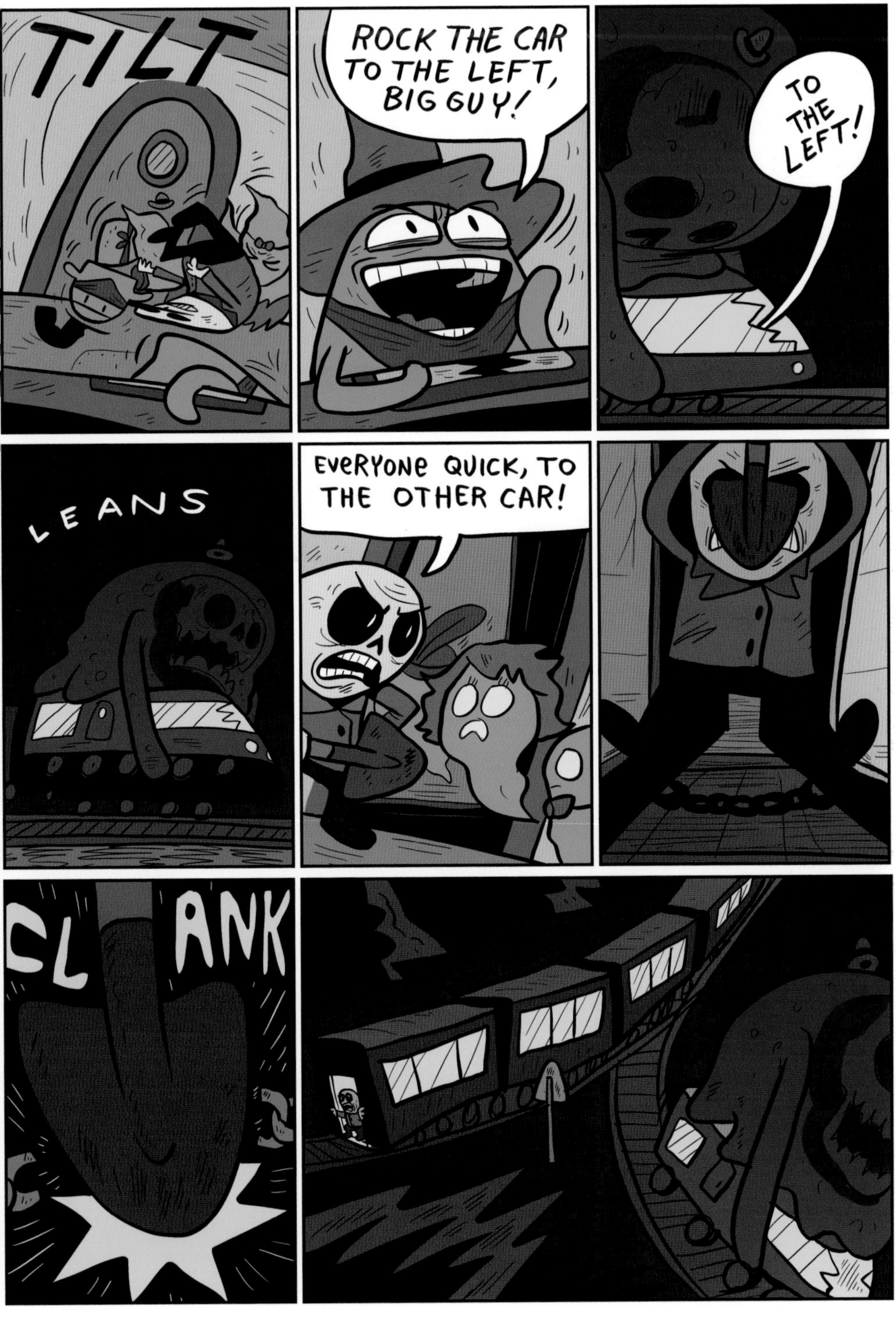
TILT
ROCK THE CAR TO THE LEFT, BIG GUY!
TO THE LEFT!
LEANS
EVERYONE QUICK, TO THE OTHER CAR!
CL ANK

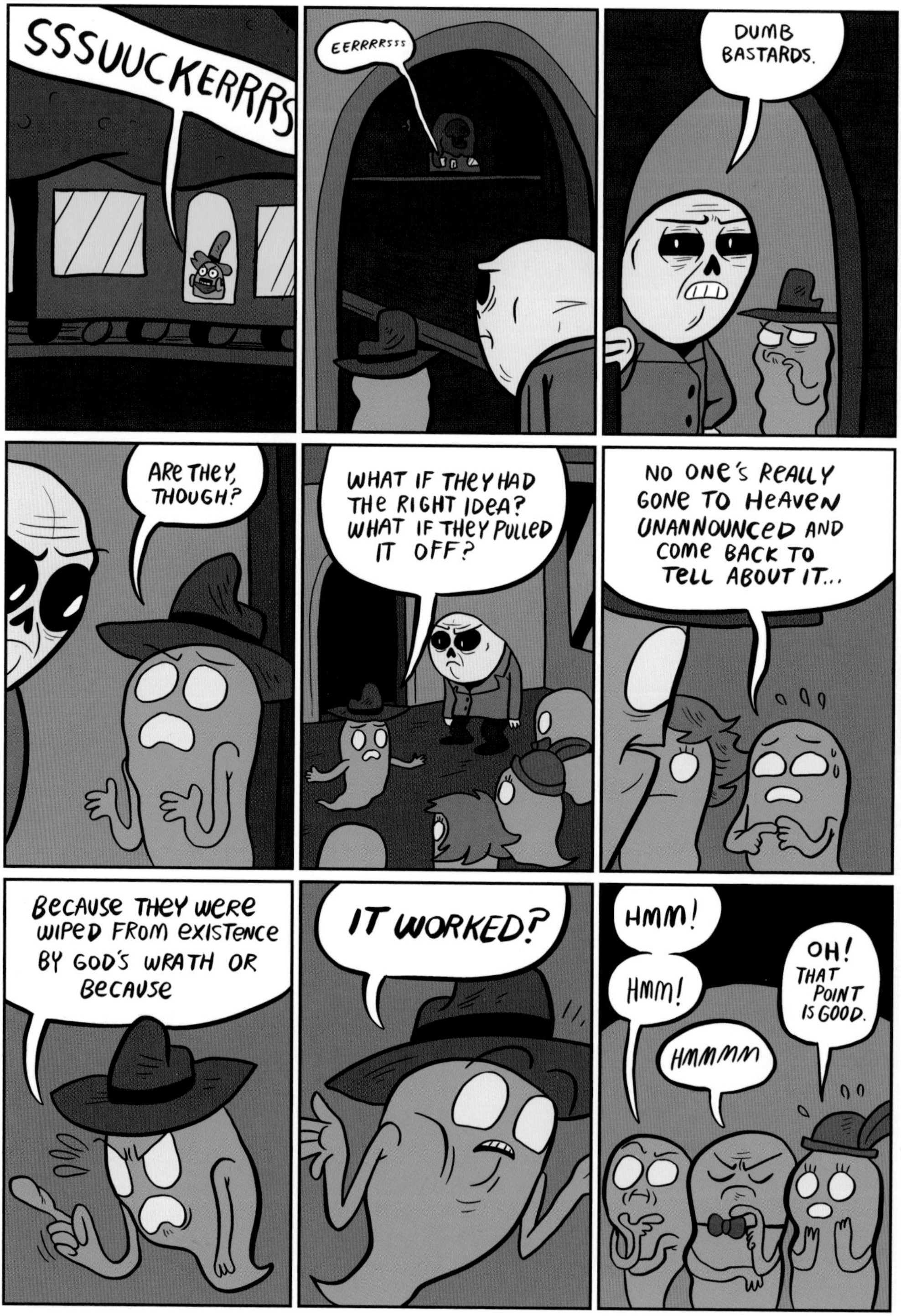
SSSUUCKERRRS
EERRRRSSS
DUMB BASTARDS.
ARE THEY, THOUGH?
WHAT IF THEY HAD THE RIGHT IDEA? WHAT IF THEY PULLED IT OFF?
NO ONE'S REALLY GONE TO HEAVEN UNANNOUNCED AND COME BACK TO TELL ABOUT IT...
BECAUSE THEY WERE WIPED FROM EXISTENCE BY GOD'S WRATH OR BECAUSE
IT WORKED?
HMM!
HMM!
HMMMM
OH! THAT POINT IS GOOD.

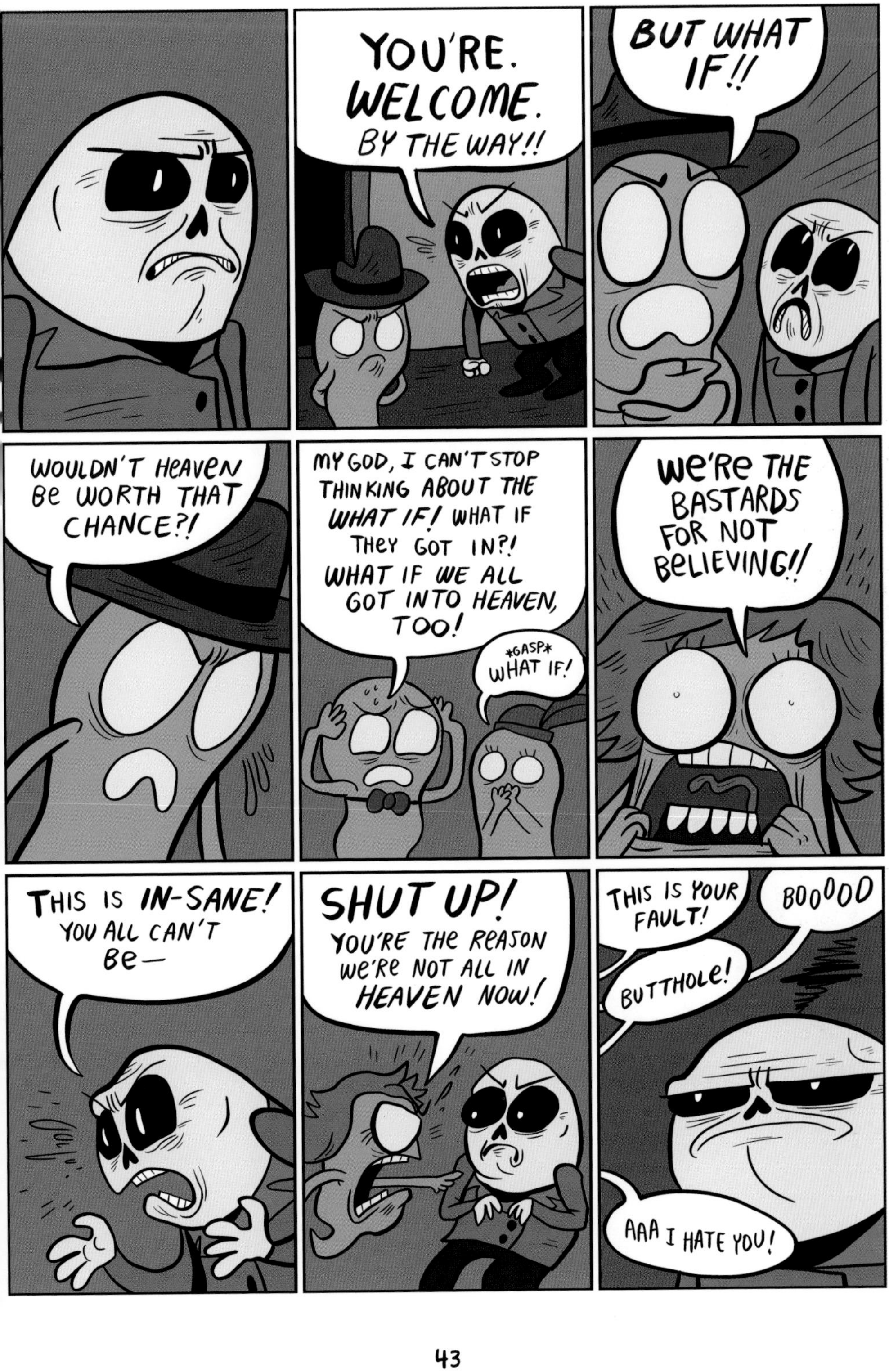
YOU'RE. WELCOME. BY THE WAY!!
BUT WHAT IF!!
WOULDN'T HEAVEN BE WORTH THAT CHANCE?!
MY GOD, I CAN'T STOP THINKING ABOUT THE WHAT IF! WHAT IF THEY GOT IN?! WHAT IF WE ALL GOT INTO HEAVEN, TOO!
GASP WHAT IF!
WE'RE THE BASTARDS FOR NOT BELIEVING!!
THIS IS IN-SANE! YOU ALL CAN'T BE—
SHUT UP! YOU'RE THE REASON WE'RE NOT ALL IN HEAVEN NOW!
THIS IS YOUR FAULT!
BOOOOOO
BUTTHOLE!
AAA I HATE YOU!

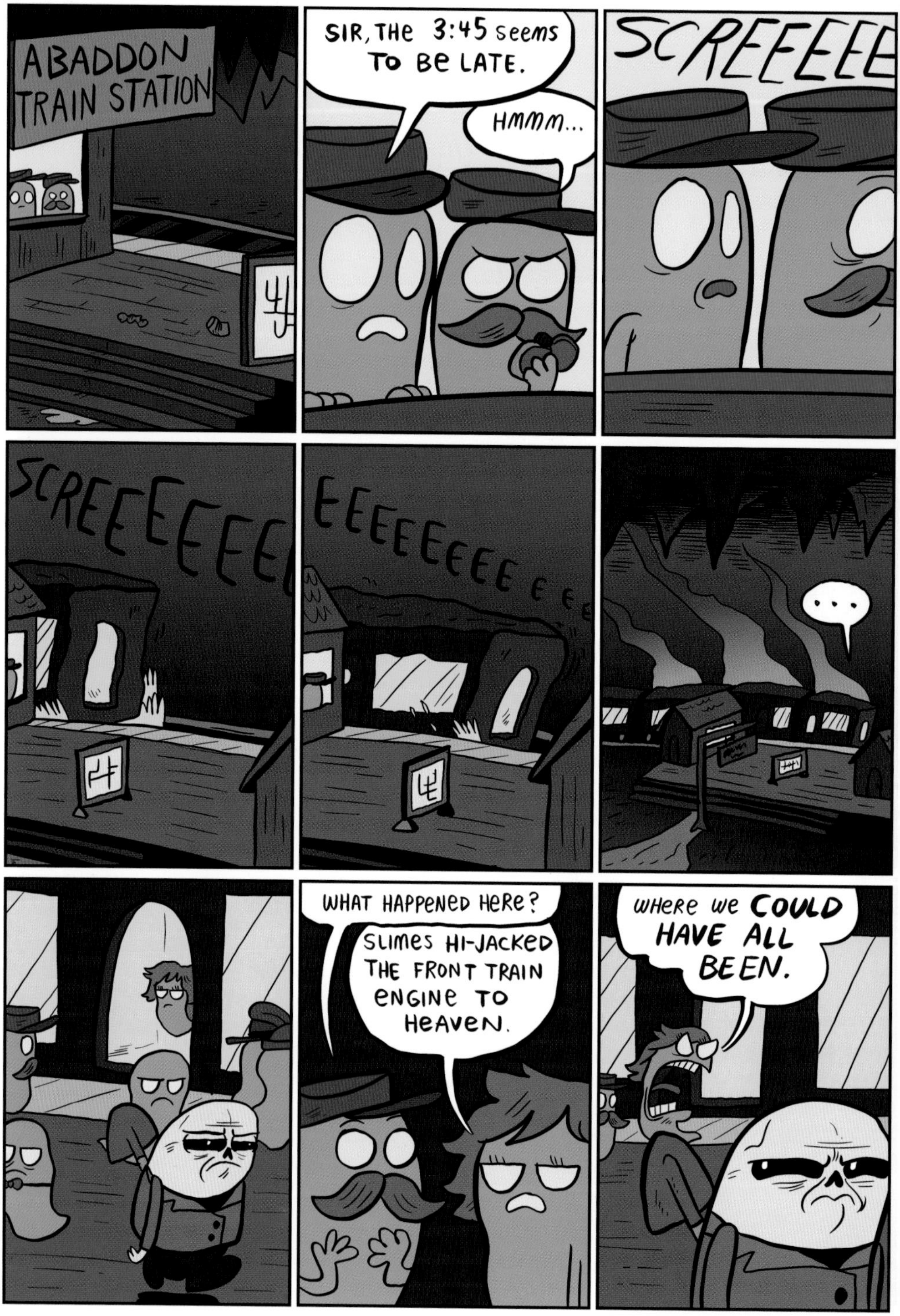
ABADDON TRAIN STATION
SIR, THE 3:45 seems TO Be LATE.
HMMM...
SCREEEEE
SCREEEEEEE
EEEEEEEEEE E E
...
WHAT HAPPENED HERE?
SLIMES HI-JACKED THE FRONT TRAIN ENGINE TO HEAVEN.
WHERE WE COULD HAVE ALL BEEN.

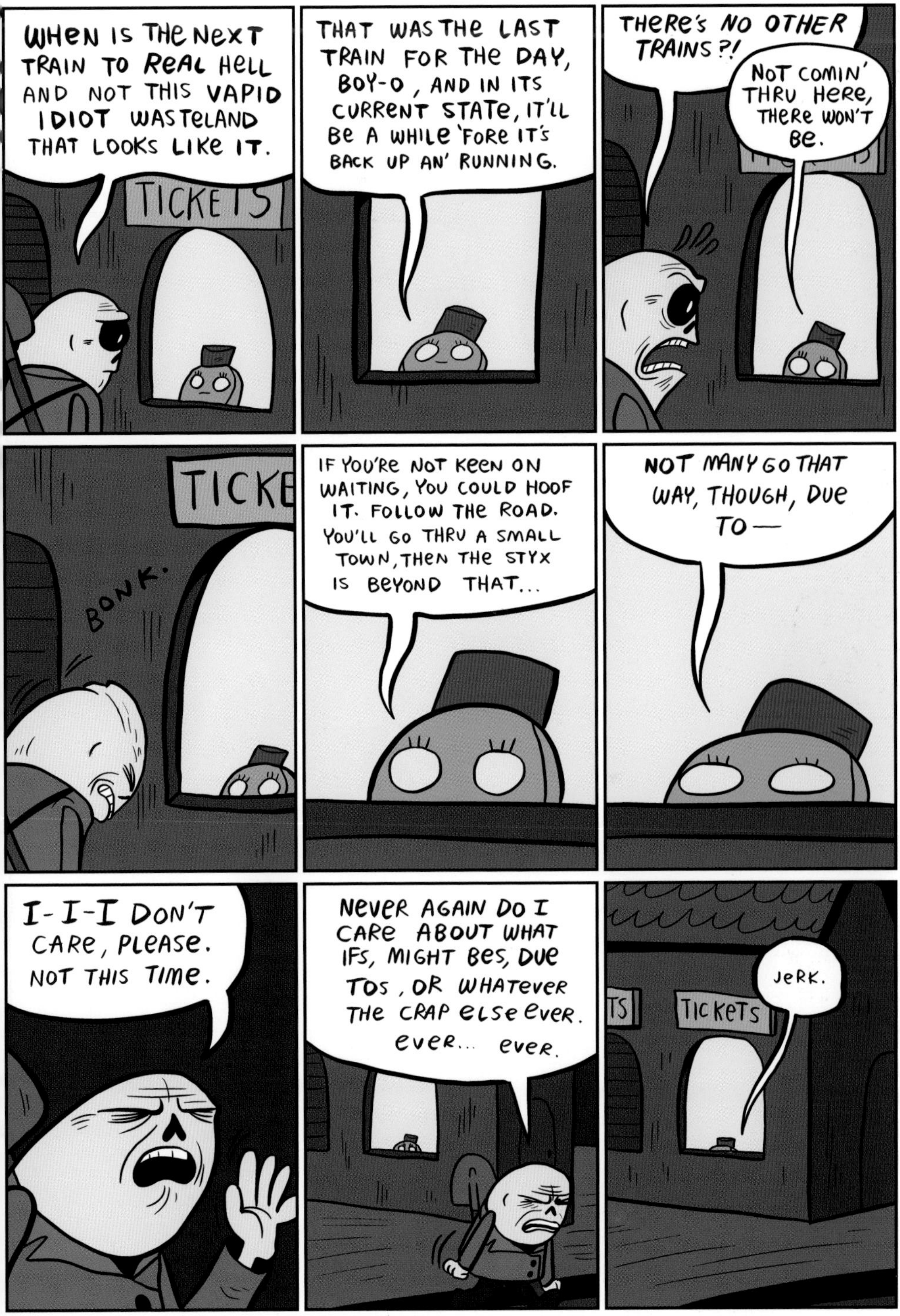
WHEN IS THE NEXT TRAIN TO REAL HELL AND NOT THIS VAPID IDIOT WASTELAND THAT LOOKS LIKE IT.
TICKETS
THAT WAS THE LAST TRAIN FOR THE DAY, BOY-O, AND IN ITS CURRENT STATE, IT'LL BE A WHILE 'FORE IT'S BACK UP AN' RUNNING.
THERE'S NO OTHER TRAINS?!
NOT COMIN' THRU HERE, THERE WON'T BE.
TICKE
BONK.
IF YOU'RE NOT KEEN ON WAITING, YOU COULD HOOF IT. FOLLOW THE ROAD. YOU'LL GO THRU A SMALL TOWN, THEN THE STYX IS BEYOND THAT...
NOT MANY GO THAT WAY, THOUGH, DUE TO—
I-I-I DON'T CARE, PLEASE. NOT THIS TIME.
NEVER AGAIN DO I CARE ABOUT WHAT IFS, MIGHT BES, DUE TOS, OR WHATEVER THE CRAP ELSE EVER. EVER... EVER.
TS
TICKETS
JERK.

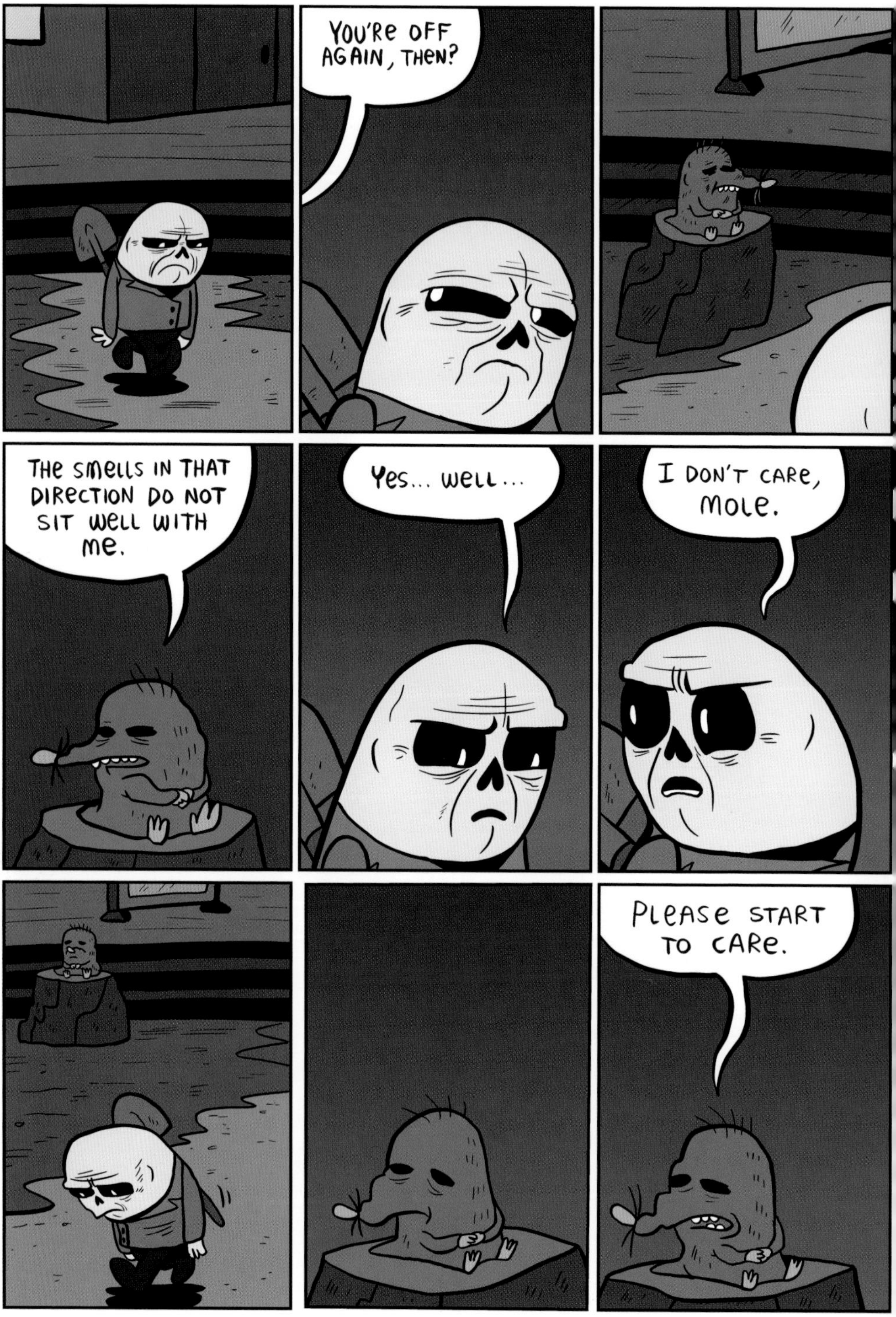
YOU'RE OFF AGAIN, THEN?
THE SMELLS IN THAT DIRECTION DO NOT SIT WELL WITH ME.
YES... WELL...
I DON'T CARE, MOLE.
PLEASE START TO CARE.

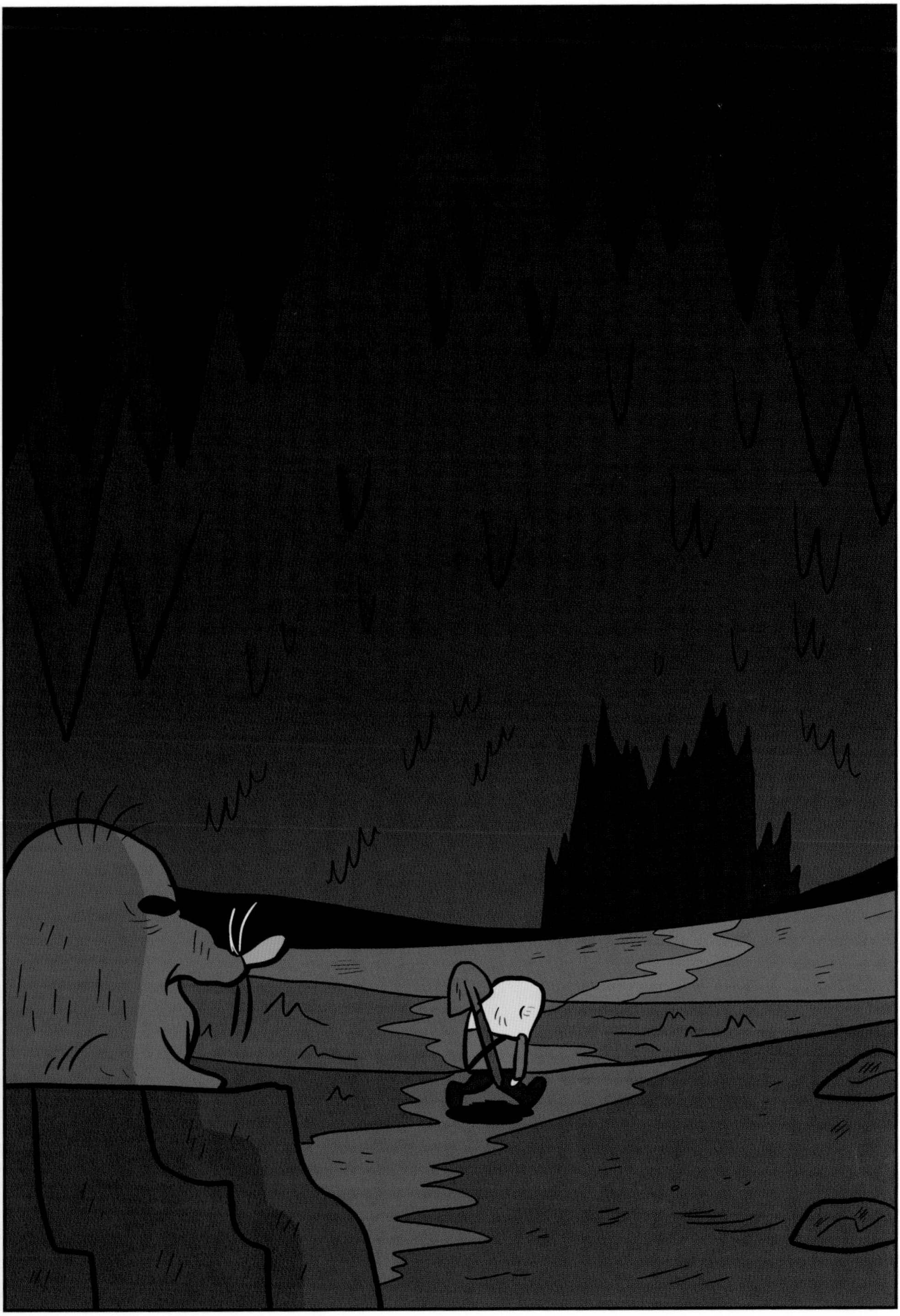

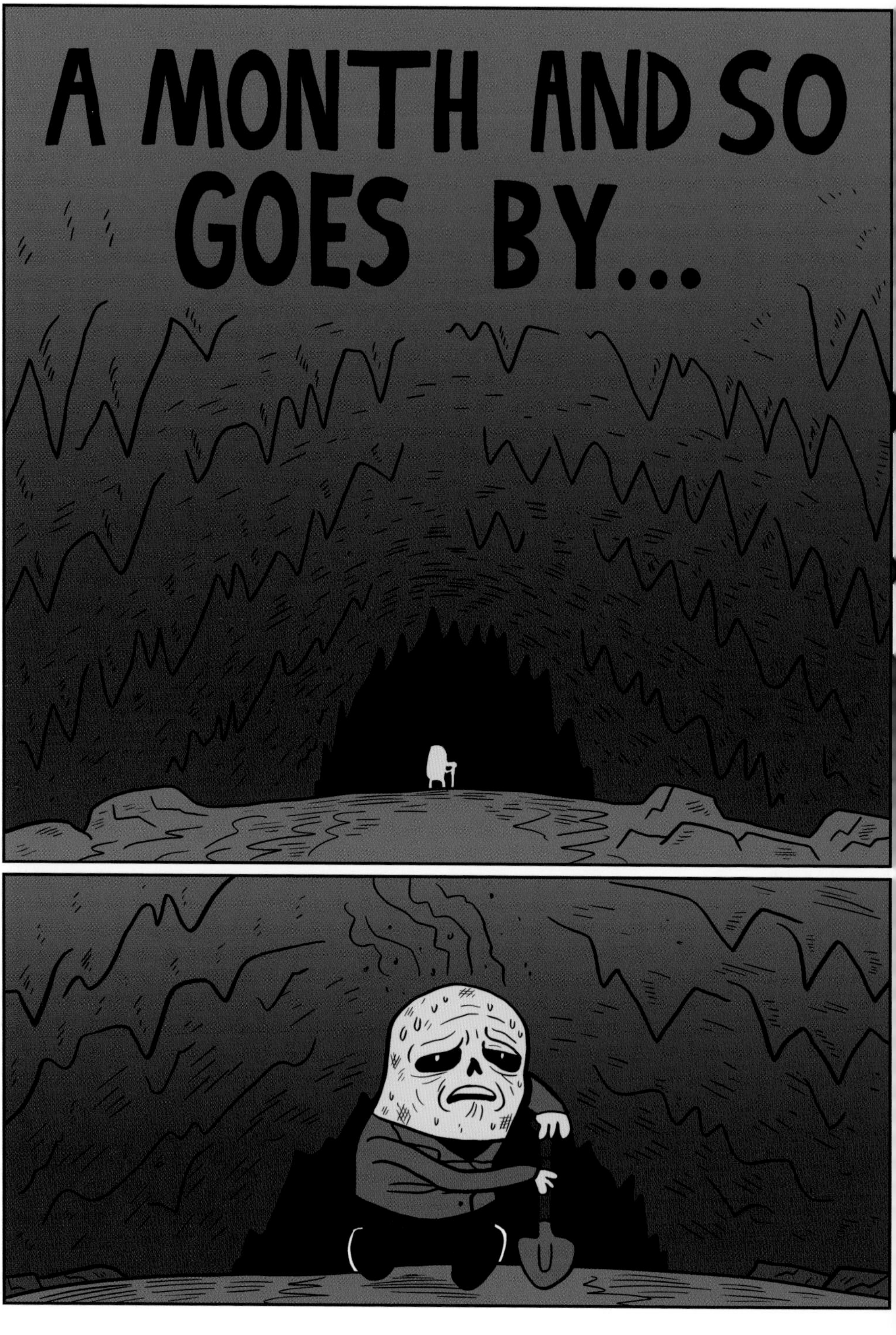
A MONTH AND SO GOES BY...

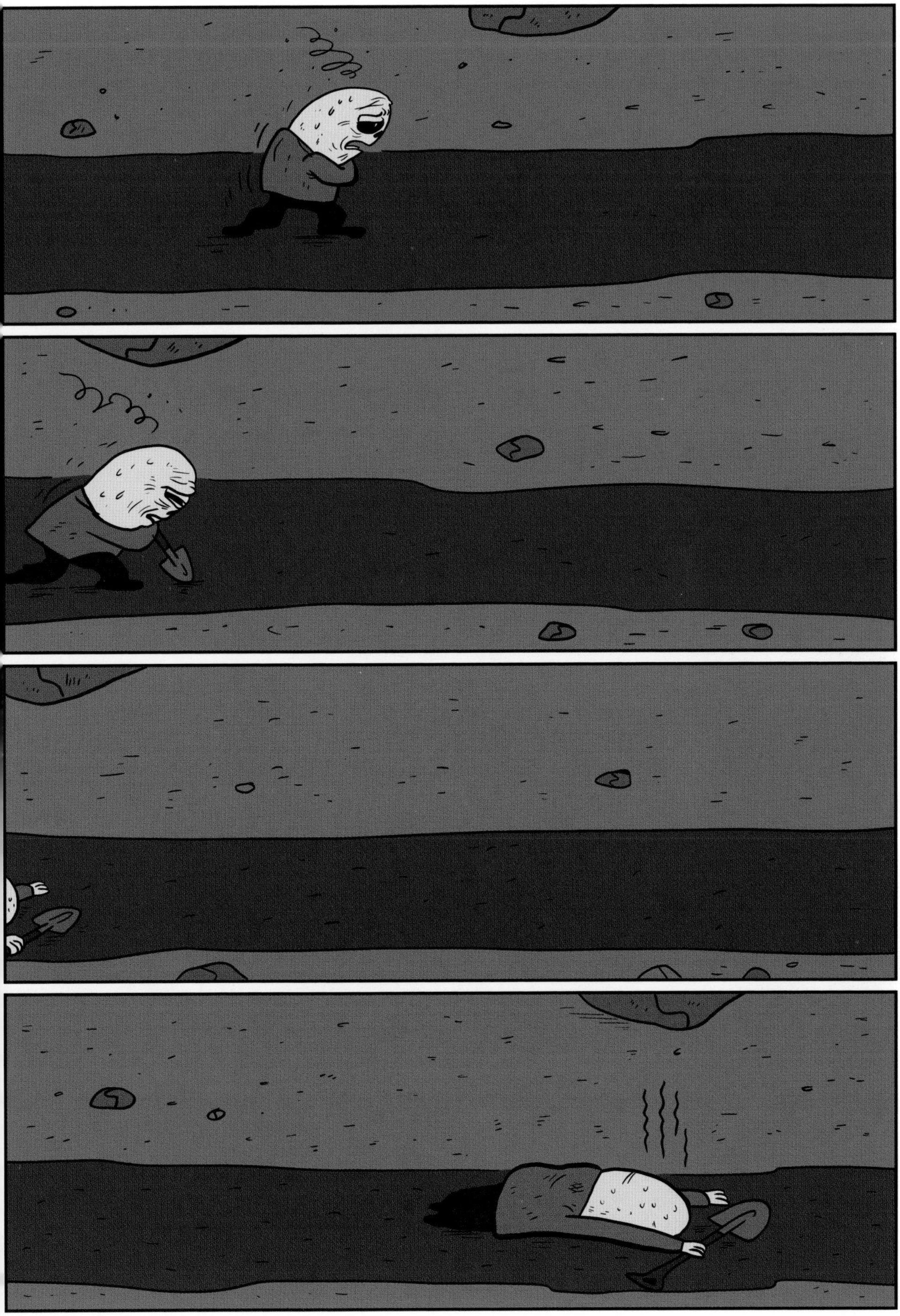

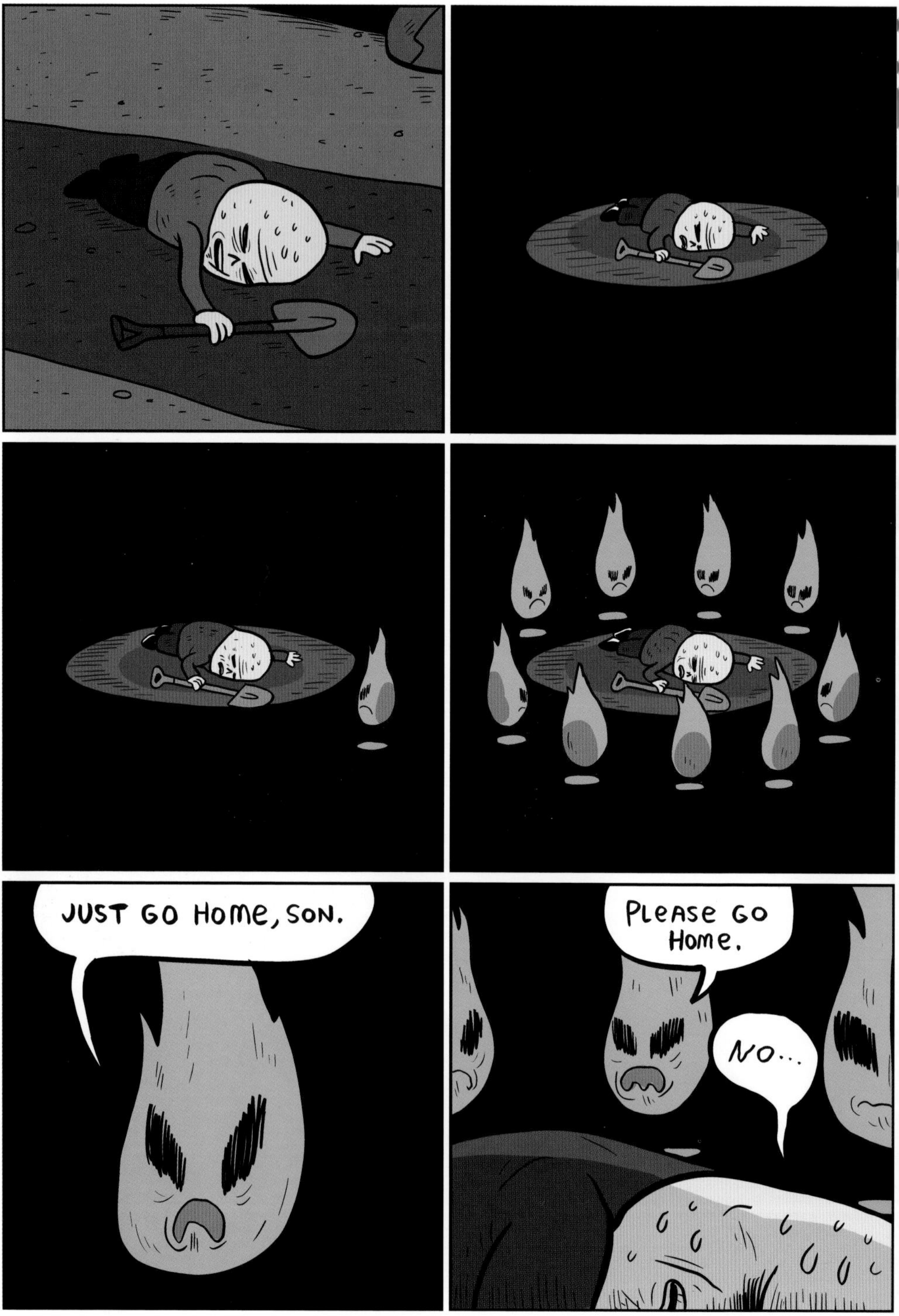
JUST GO HOME, SON.
PLEASE GO HOME.
NO...

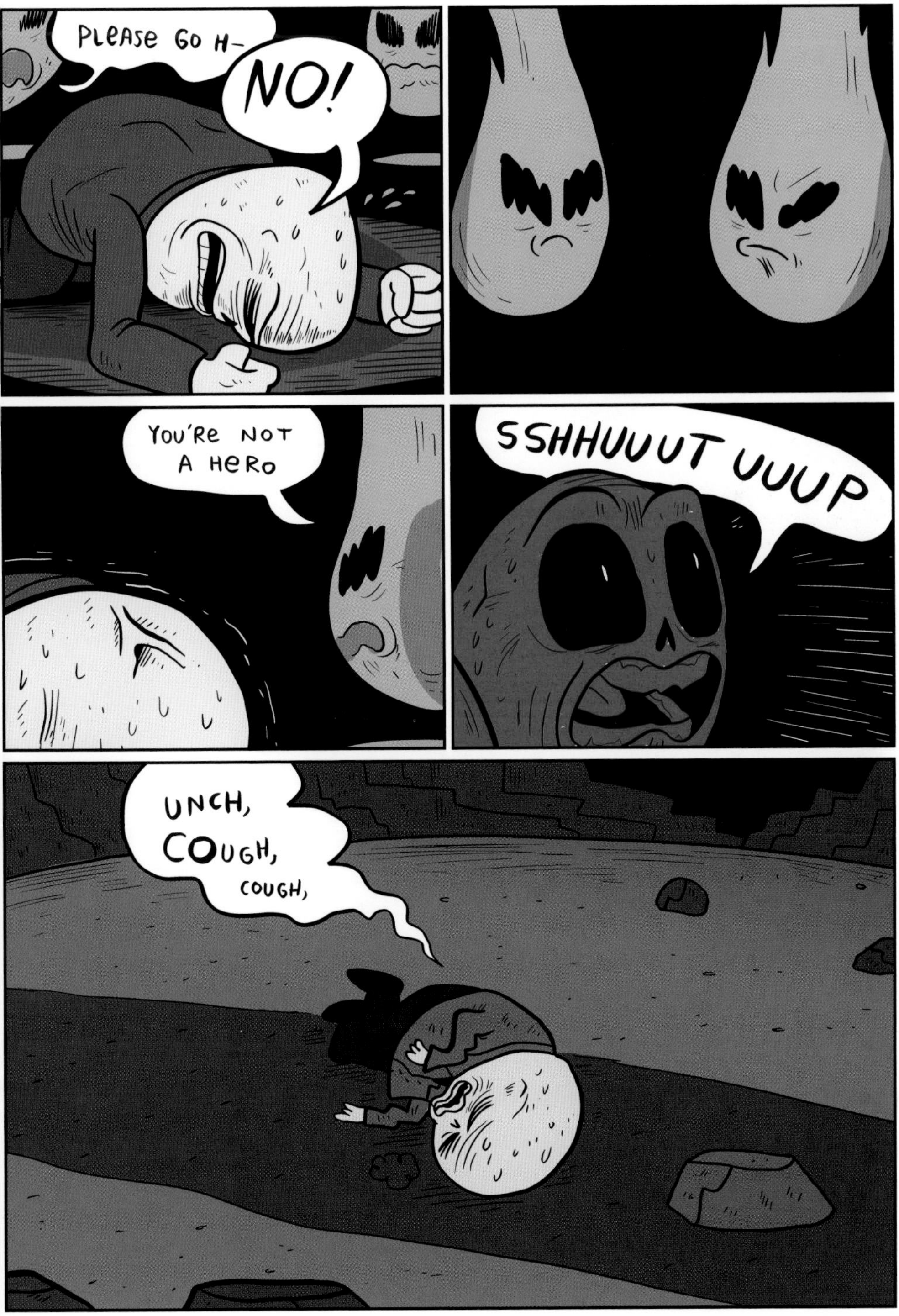
PLEASE GO H-
NO!
YOU'RE NOT A HERO
SSHHUUUT UUUP
UNCH, COUGH, COUGH,

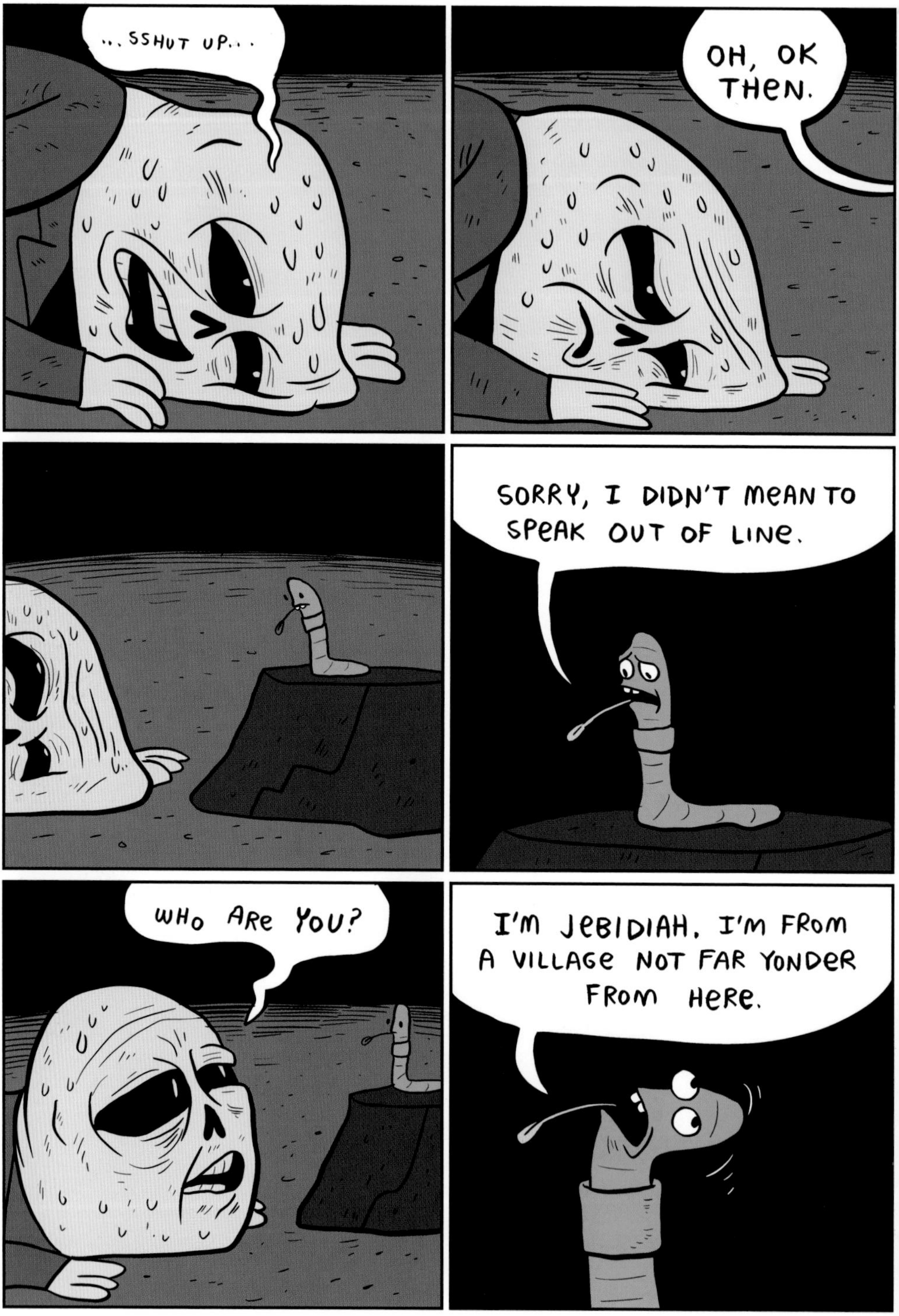
...SSHUT UP...
OH, OK THEN.
SORRY, I DIDN'T MEAN TO SPEAK OUT OF LINE.
WHO ARE YOU?
I'M JEBIDIAH. I'M FROM A VILLAGE NOT FAR YONDER FROM HERE.

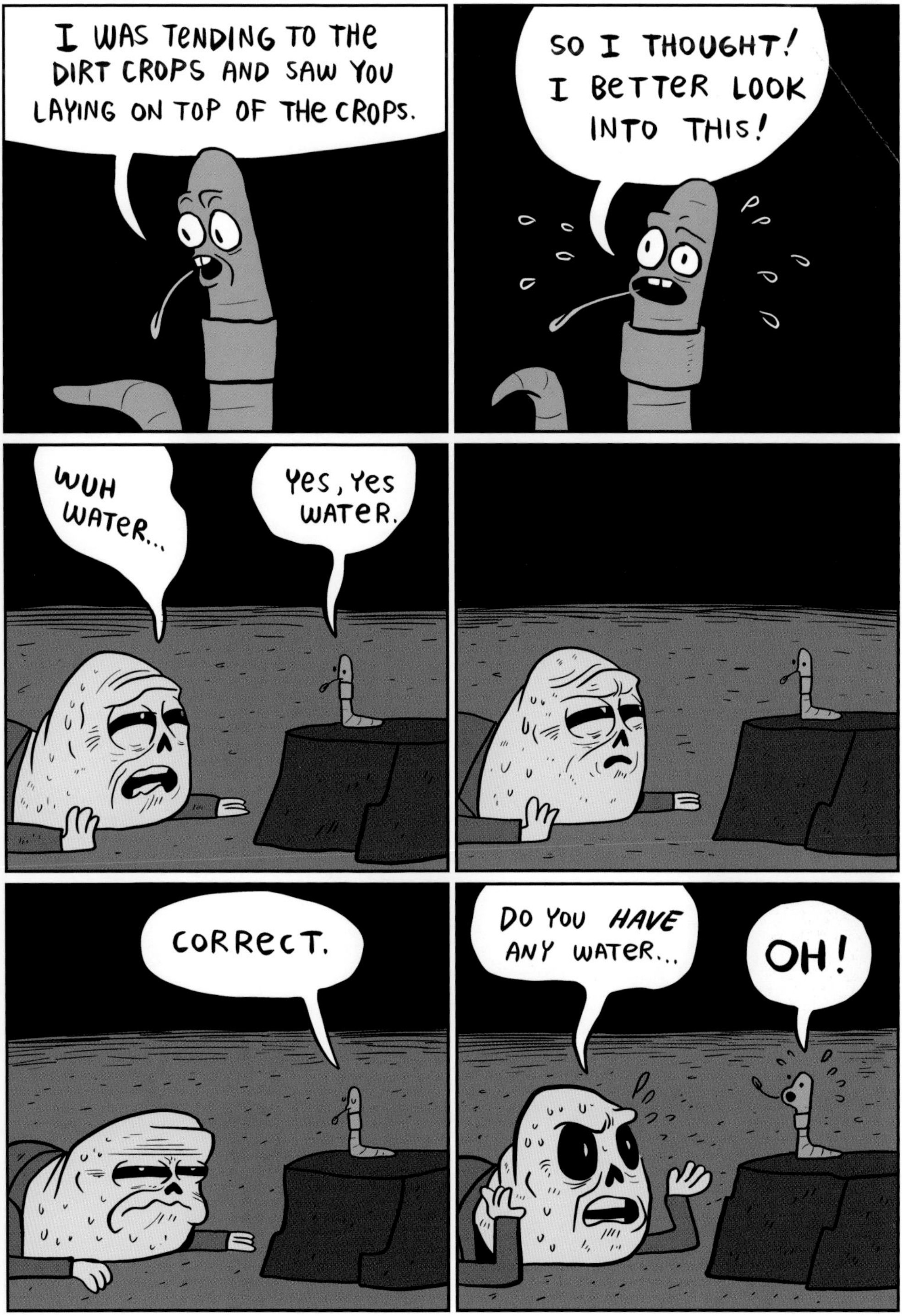
I WAS TENDING TO THE DIRT CROPS AND SAW YOU LAYING ON TOP OF THE CROPS.
SO I THOUGHT! I BETTER LOOK INTO THIS!
WUH WATER...
YES, YES WATER.
CORRECT.
DO YOU HAVE ANY WATER...
OH!

MORE WATER FOR OUR BIGGER GUESTS.
GLUG!
THAT'S A MIGHTY SHOVEL YOU GOT THERE, FRIEND! WHAT BUSINESS YOU IN?
I'M, UH...
Please Please Bury these. we are afraid. signed - Police
I'M A GRAVEDIGGER.
A GRAVE DIGGER! OH MY GOD! GREAT LORDY! A GRAVE DIGGER!

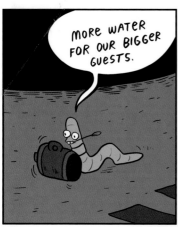

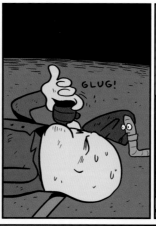

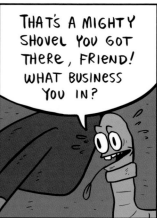

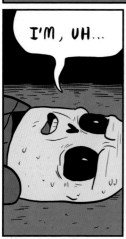

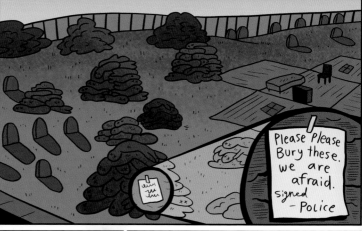

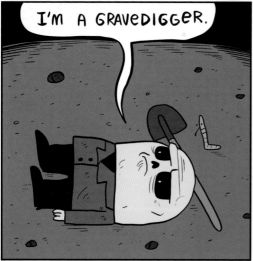

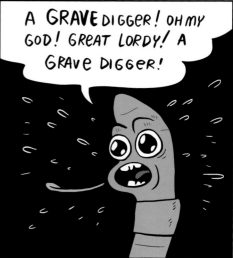

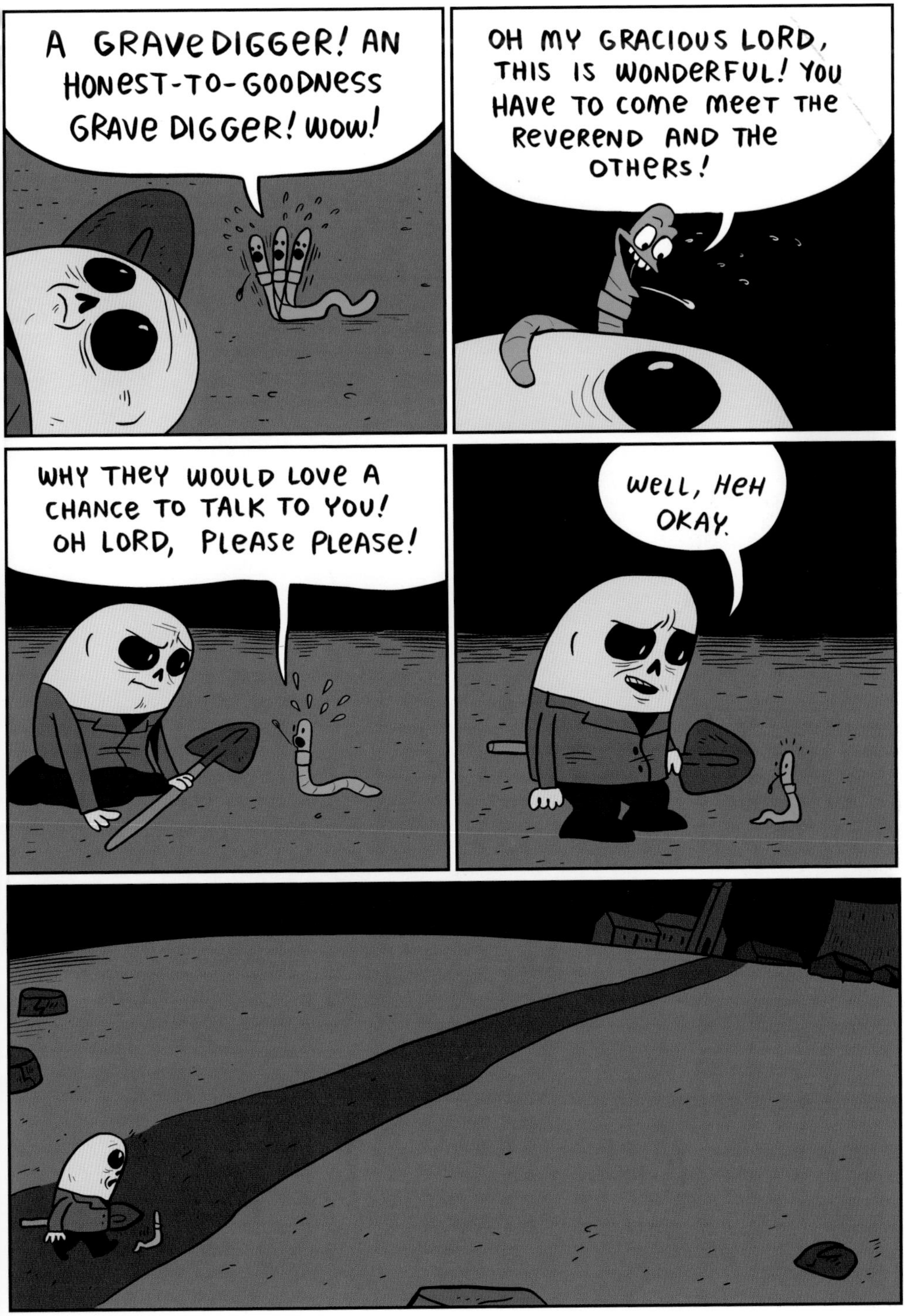
A GRAVEDIGGER! AN HONEST-TO-GOODNESS GRAVE DIGGER! WOW!
OH MY GRACIOUS LORD, THIS IS WONDERFUL! YOU HAVE TO COME MEET THE REVEREND AND THE OTHERS!
WHY THEY WOULD LOVE A CHANCE TO TALK TO YOU! OH LORD, PLEASE PLEASE!
WELL, HEH OKAY.

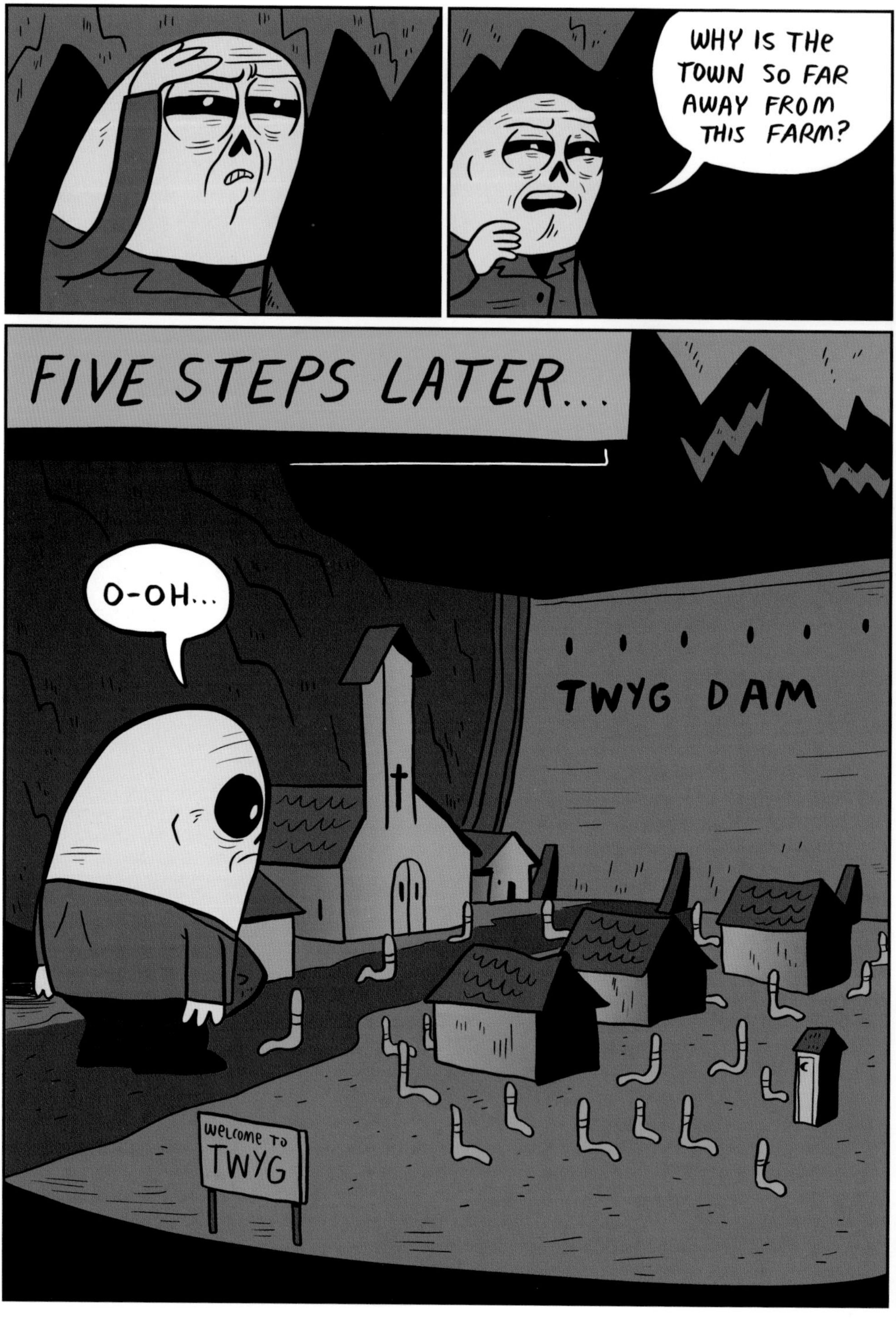
WHY IS THE TOWN SO FAR AWAY FROM THIS FARM?
FIVE STEPS LATER...
O-OH...
TWYG DAM
WELCOME TO TWYG

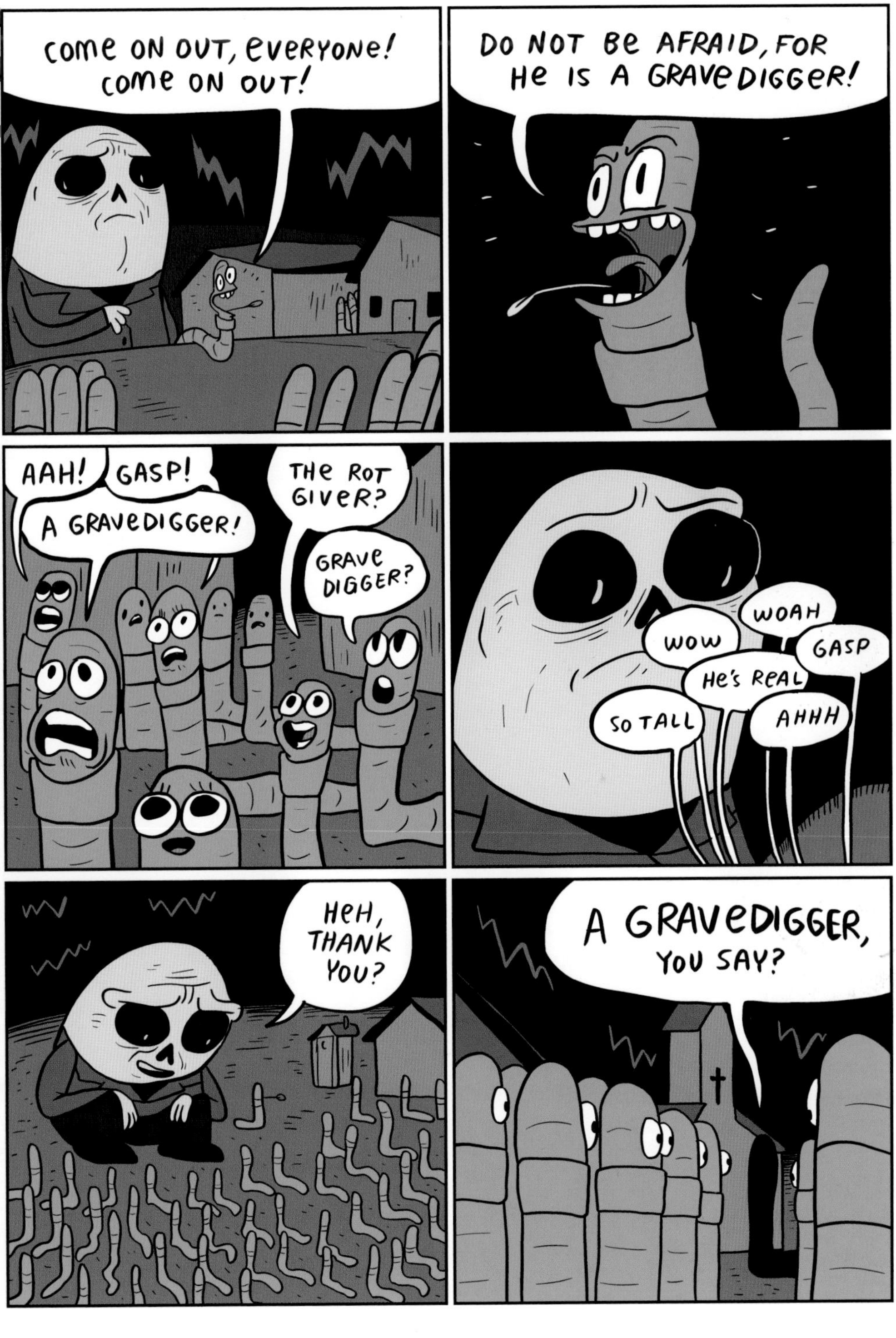
COME ON OUT, EVERYONE!
COME ON OUT!
DO NOT BE AFRAID, FOR
HE IS A GRAVEDIGGER!
AAH!
GASP!
A GRAVEDIGGER!
THE ROT
GIVER?
GRAVE
DIGGER?
WOAH
WOW
GASP
HE'S REAL
SO TALL
AHHH
HEH,
THANK
YOU?
A GRAVEDIGGER,
YOU SAY?

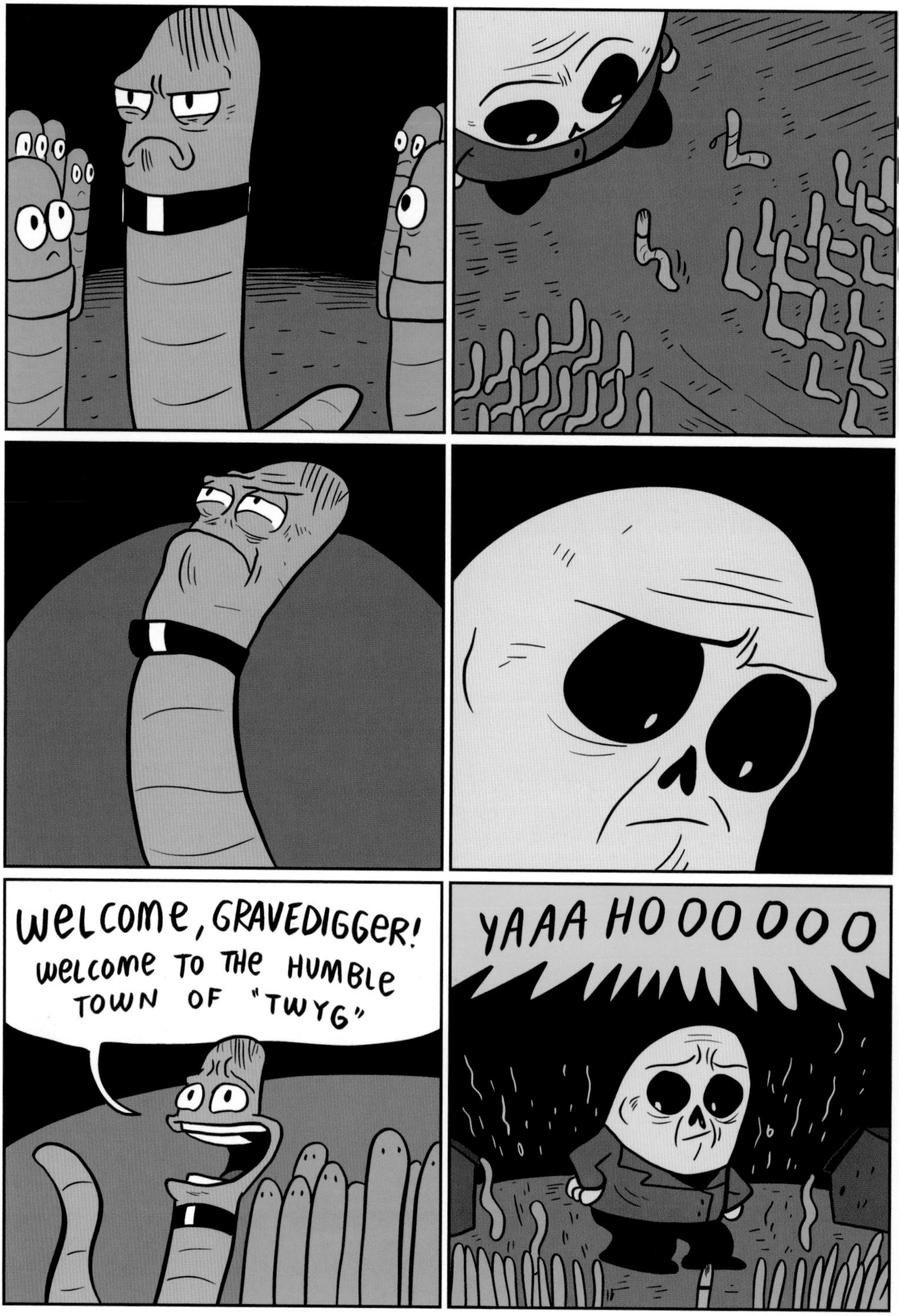
WELCOME, GRAVEDIGGER!
WELCOME TO THE HUMBLE TOWN OF "TWYG"
YAAA HOOOOOOO

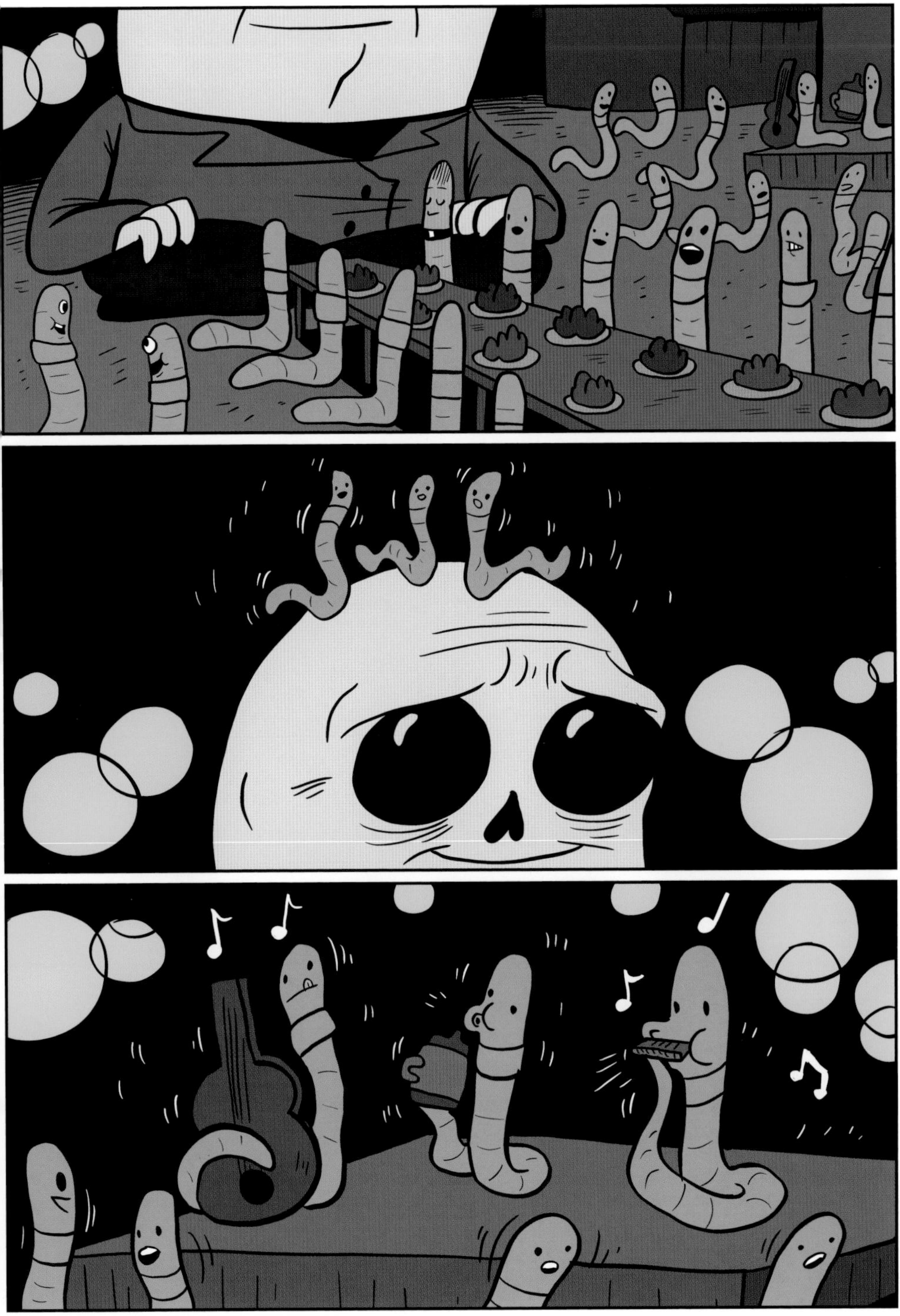

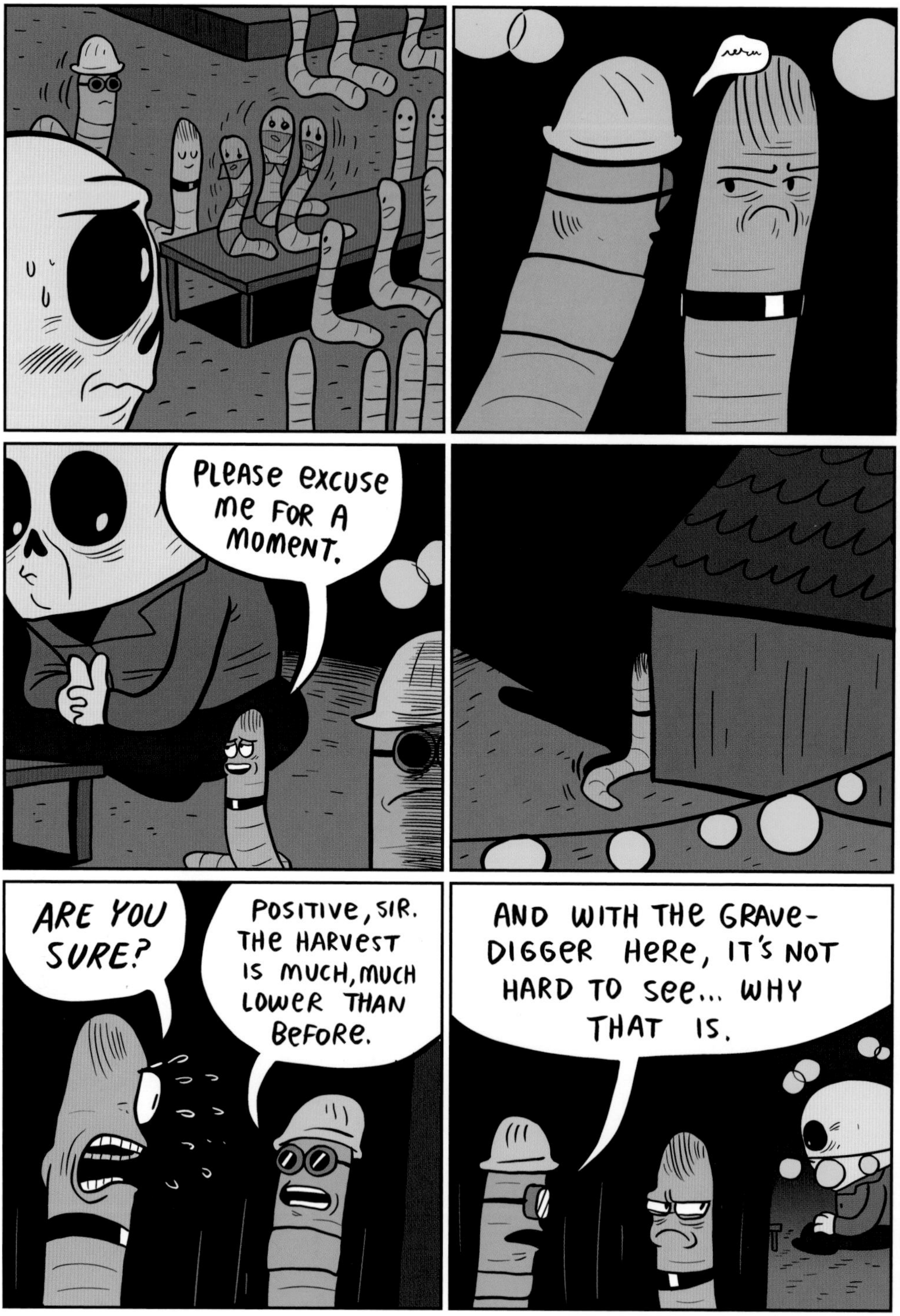
PLEASE EXCUSE ME FOR A MOMENT.
ARE YOU SURE?
POSITIVE, SIR. THE HARVEST IS MUCH, MUCH LOWER THAN BEFORE.
AND WITH THE GRAVE-DIGGER HERE, IT'S NOT HARD TO SEE... WHY THAT IS.

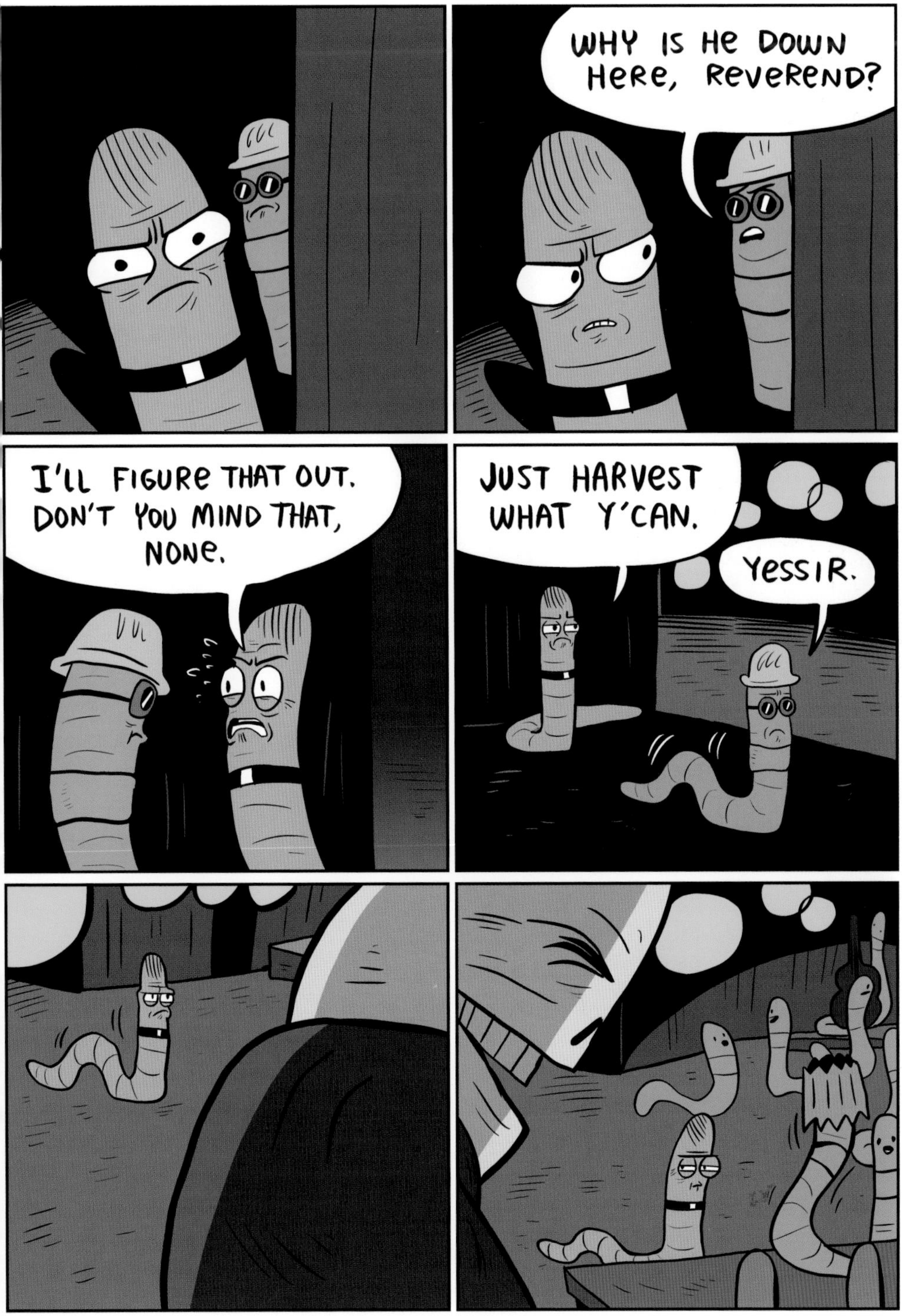
WHY IS HE DOWN HERE, REVEREND?
I'LL FIGURE THAT OUT. DON'T YOU MIND THAT, NONE.
JUST HARVEST WHAT Y'CAN.
YESSIR.

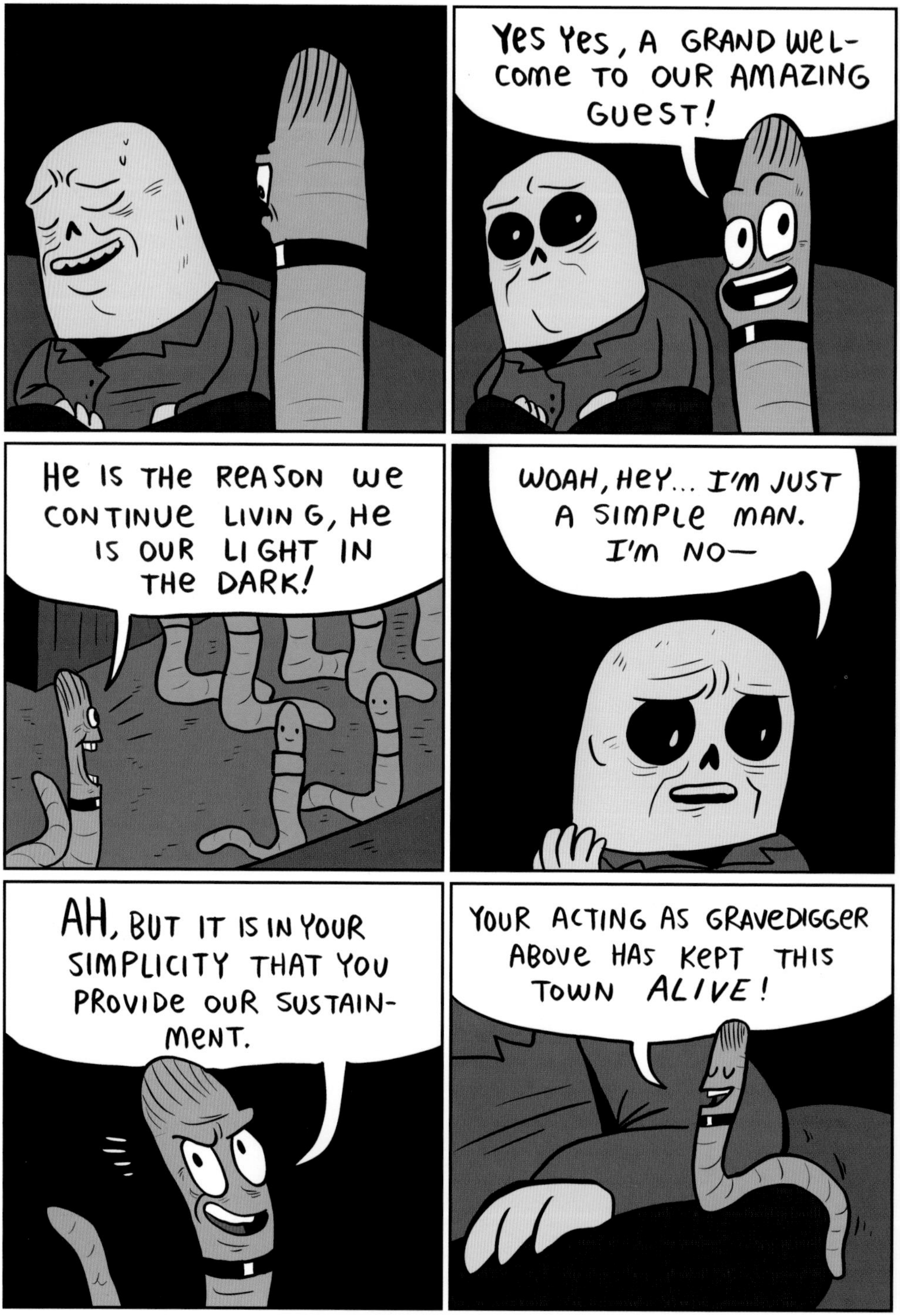
YES YES, A GRAND WEL-COME TO OUR AMAZING GUEST!
HE IS THE REASON WE CONTINUE LIVING, HE IS OUR LIGHT IN THE DARK!
WOAH, HEY... I'M JUST A SIMPLE MAN. I'M NO—
AH, BUT IT IS IN YOUR SIMPLICITY THAT YOU PROVIDE OUR SUSTAIN-MENT.
YOUR ACTING AS GRAVEDIGGER ABOVE HAS KEPT THIS TOWN ALIVE!

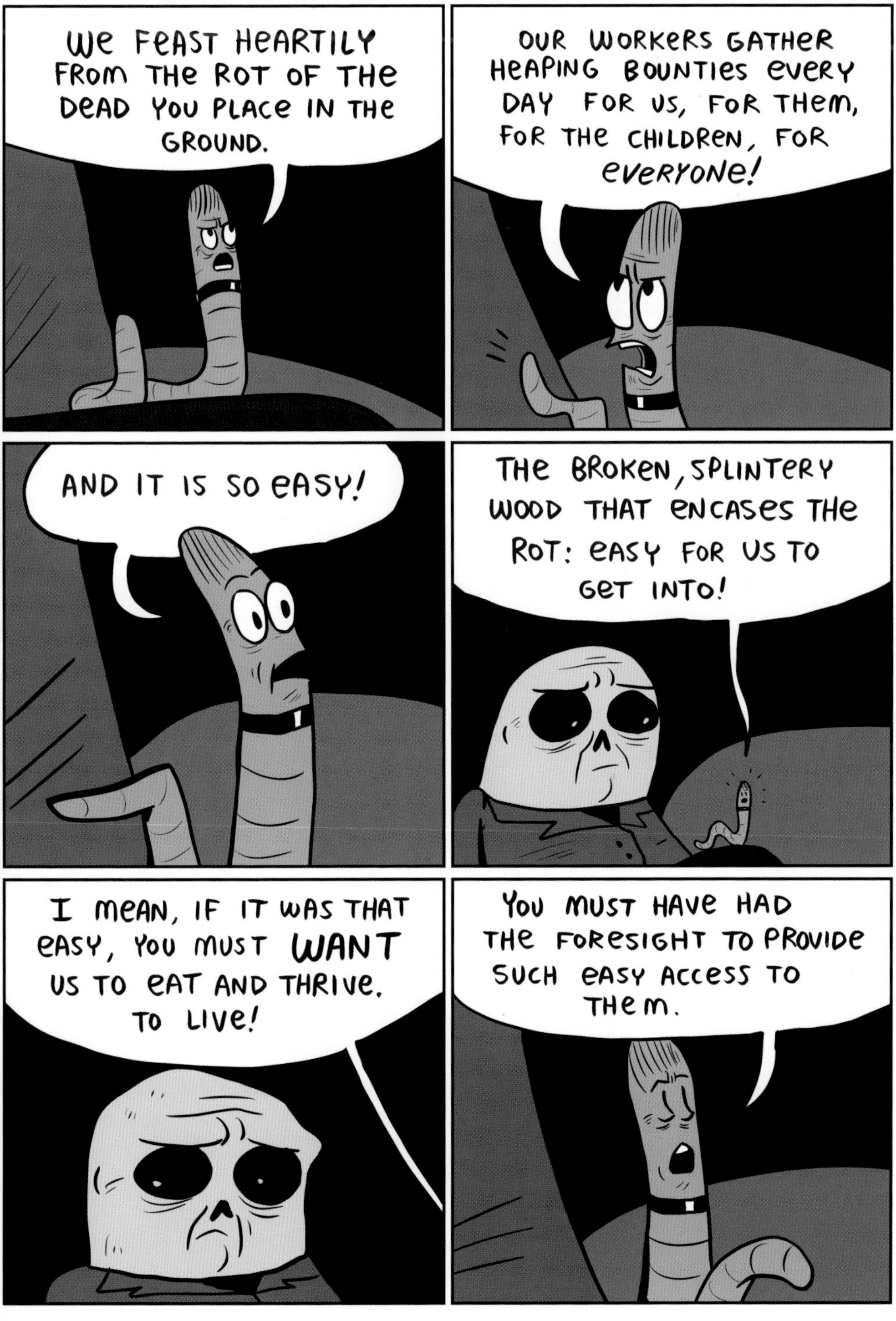
WE FEAST HEARTILY FROM THE ROT OF THE DEAD YOU PLACE IN THE GROUND.
OUR WORKERS GATHER HEAPING BOUNTIES EVERY DAY FOR US, FOR THEM, FOR THE CHILDREN, FOR EVERYONE!
AND IT IS SO EASY!
THE BROKEN, SPLINTERY WOOD THAT ENCASES THE ROT: EASY FOR US TO GET INTO!
I MEAN, IF IT WAS THAT EASY, YOU MUST WANT US TO EAT AND THRIVE. TO LIVE!
YOU MUST HAVE HAD THE FORESIGHT TO PROVIDE SUCH EASY ACCESS TO THEM.

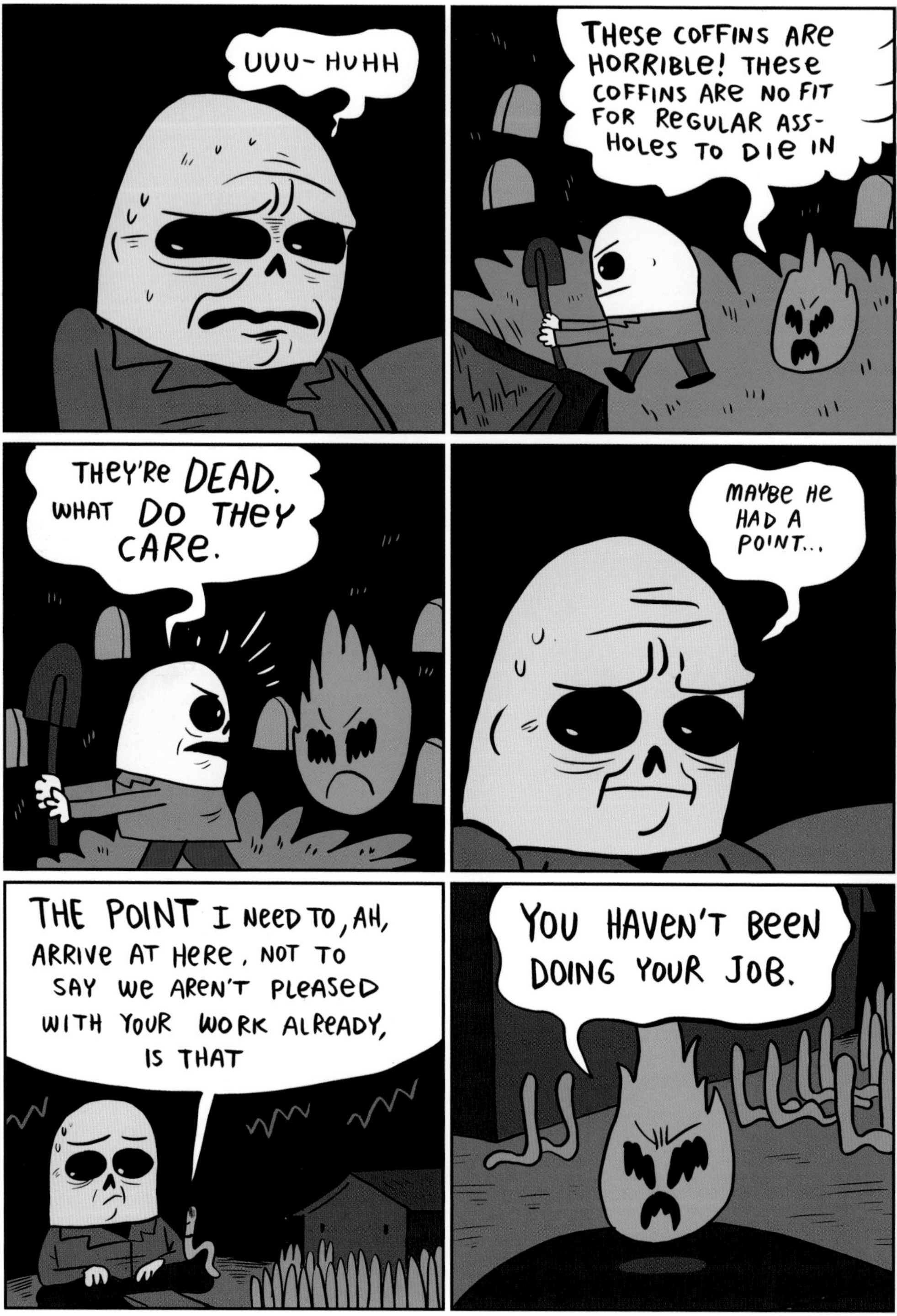
UUU-HUHH
THESE COFFINS ARE HORRIBLE! THESE COFFINS ARE NO FIT FOR REGULAR ASS-HOLES TO DIE IN
THEY'RE DEAD. WHAT DO THEY CARE.
MAYBE HE HAD A POINT...
THE POINT I NEED TO, AH, ARRIVE AT HERE, NOT TO SAY WE AREN'T PLEASED WITH YOUR WORK ALREADY, IS THAT
YOU HAVEN'T BEEN DOING YOUR JOB.

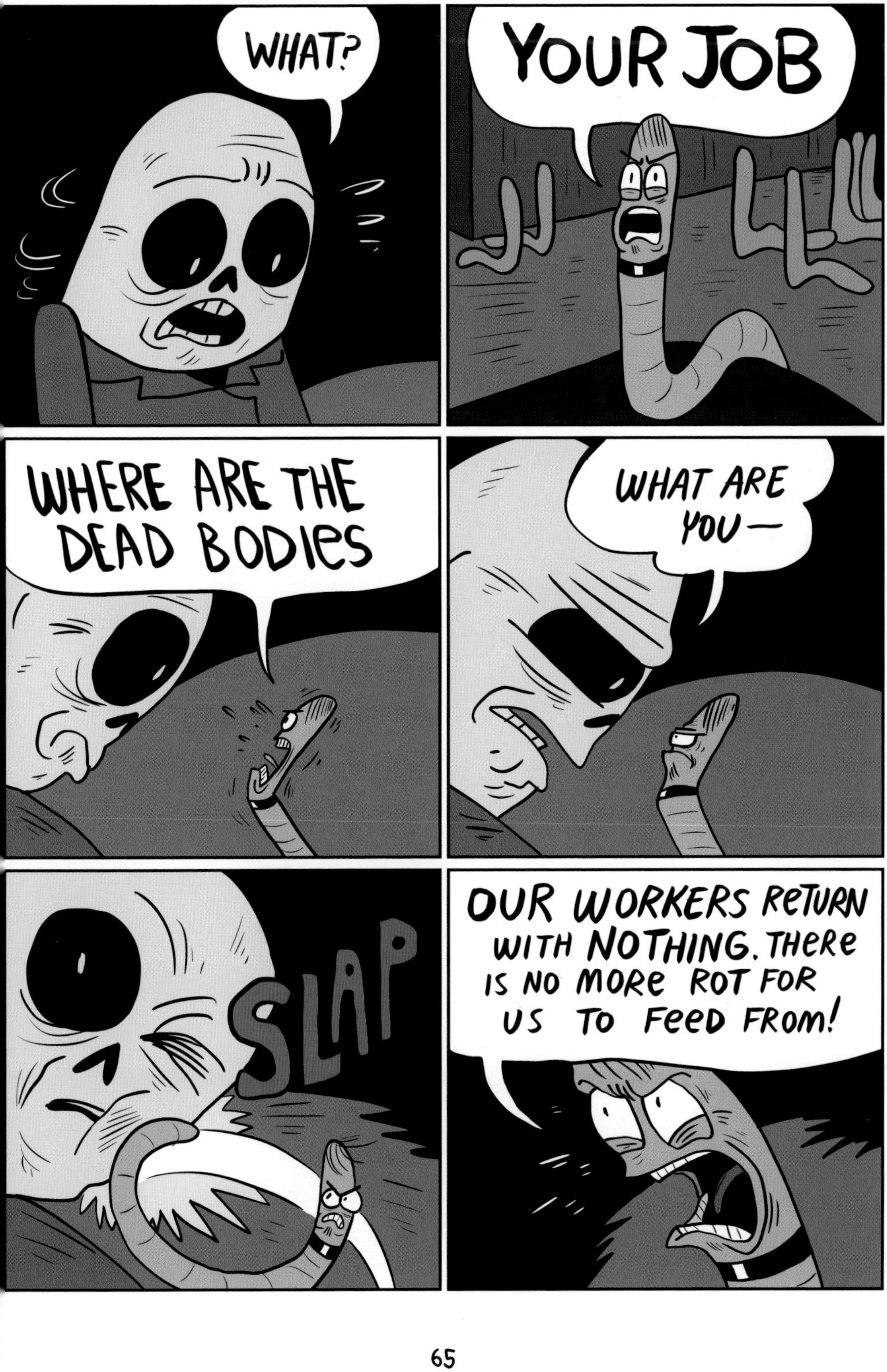
WHAT?
YOUR JOB
WHERE ARE THE DEAD BODIES
WHAT ARE YOU—
SLAP
OUR WORKERS RETURN WITH NOTHING. THERE IS NO MORE ROT FOR US TO FEED FROM!

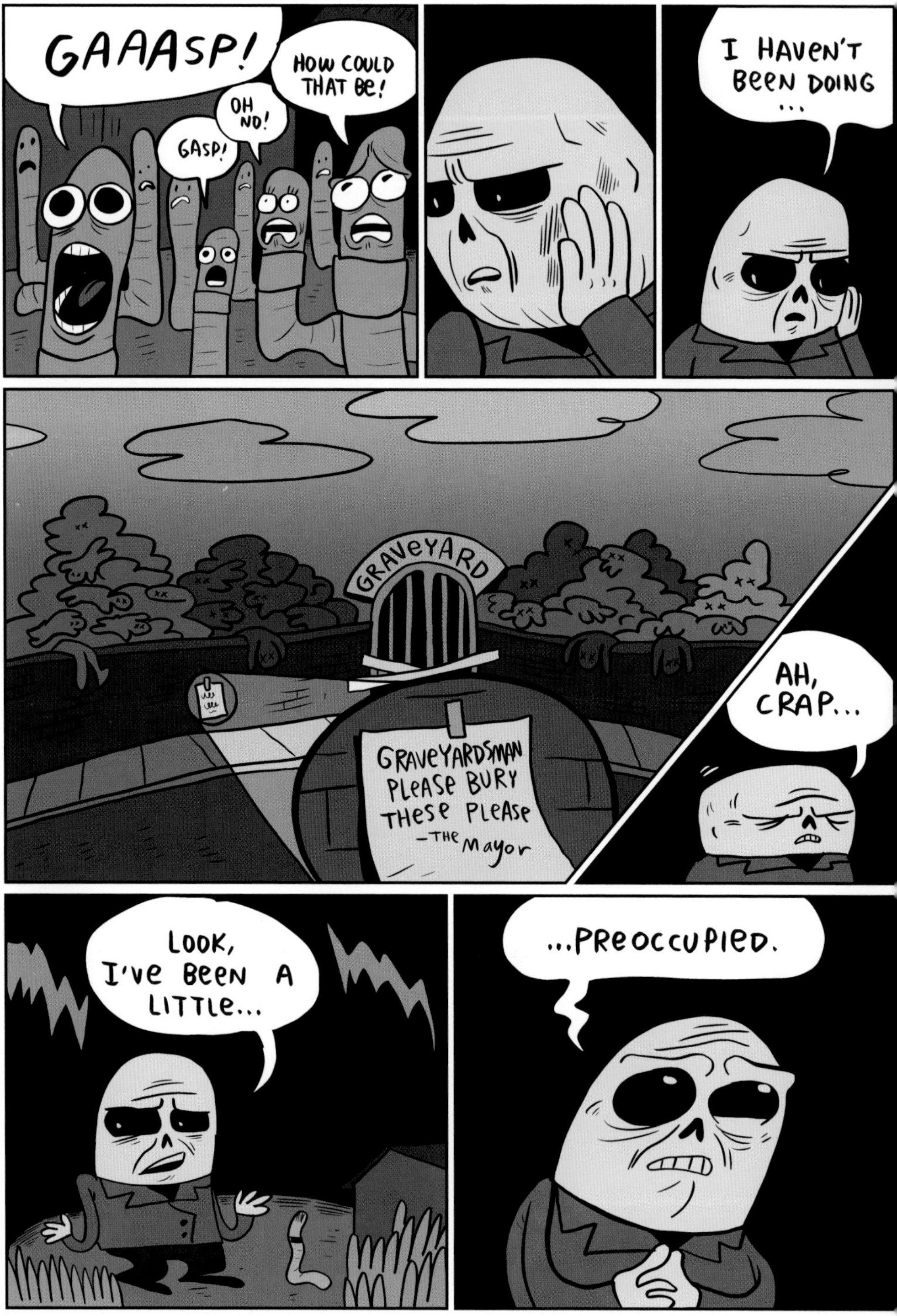
GAAASP!
GASP!
OH NO!
HOW COULD THAT BE!
I HAVEN'T BEEN DOING ...
GRAVEYARD
GRAVEYARDSMAN PLEASE BURY THESE PLEASE —THE Mayor
AH, CRAP...
LOOK, I'VE BEEN A LITTLE...
...PREOCCUPIED.

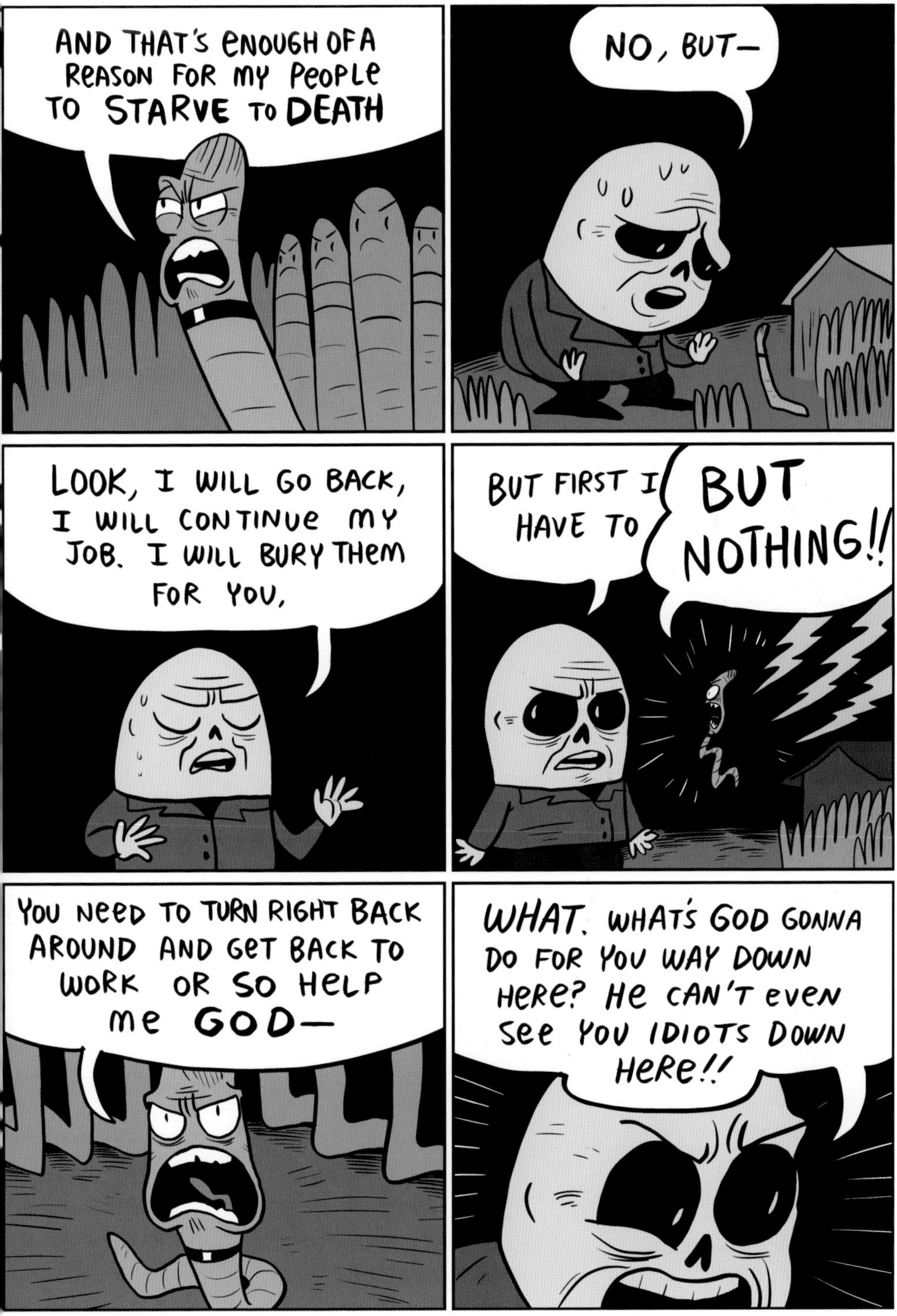
AND THAT'S ENOUGH OF A REASON FOR MY PEOPLE TO STARVE TO DEATH
NO, BUT—
LOOK, I WILL GO BACK, I WILL CONTINUE MY JOB. I WILL BURY THEM FOR YOU,
BUT FIRST I HAVE TO
BUT NOTHING!!
YOU NEED TO TURN RIGHT BACK AROUND AND GET BACK TO WORK OR SO HELP ME GOD—
WHAT. WHAT'S GOD GONNA DO FOR YOU WAY DOWN HERE? HE CAN'T EVEN SEE YOU IDIOTS DOWN HERE!!

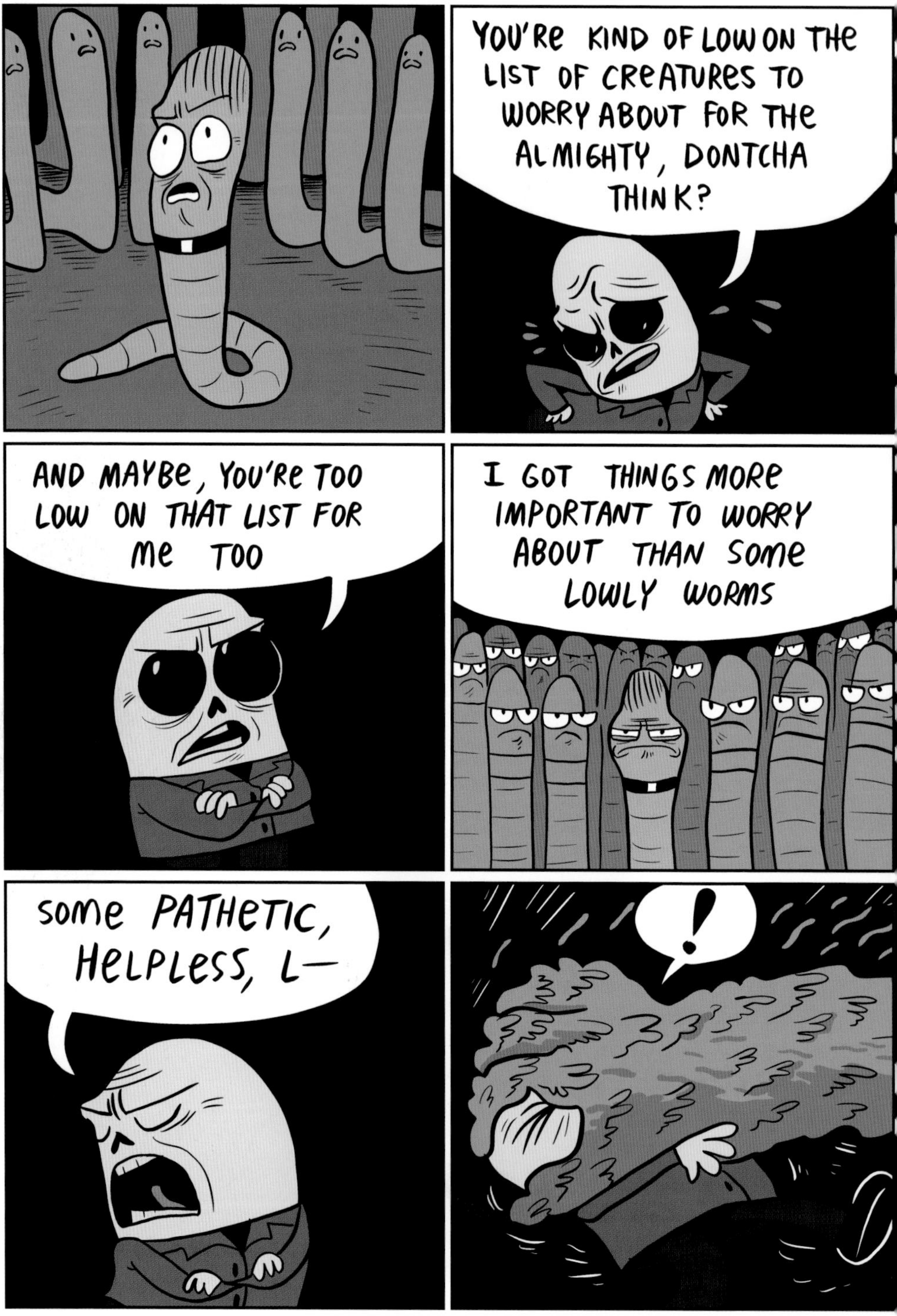
YOU'RE KIND OF LOW ON THE LIST OF CREATURES TO WORRY ABOUT FOR THE ALMIGHTY, DONTCHA THINK?
AND MAYBE, YOU'RE TOO LOW ON THAT LIST FOR ME TOO
I GOT THINGS MORE IMPORTANT TO WORRY ABOUT THAN SOME LOWLY WORMS
SOME PATHETIC, HELPLESS, L—
!

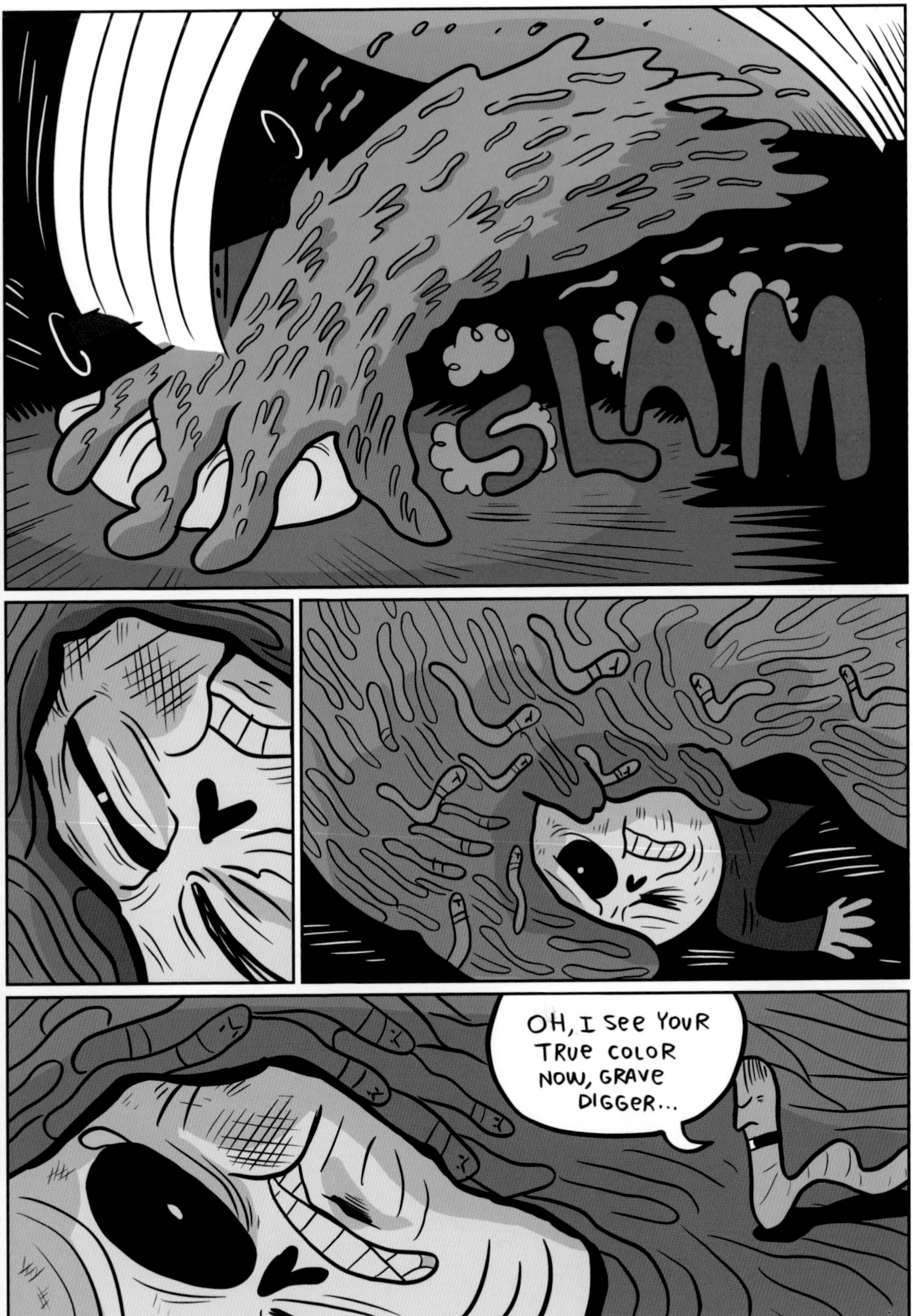
SLAM
OH, I see YOUR TRUE COLOR NOW, GRAVE DIGGER...

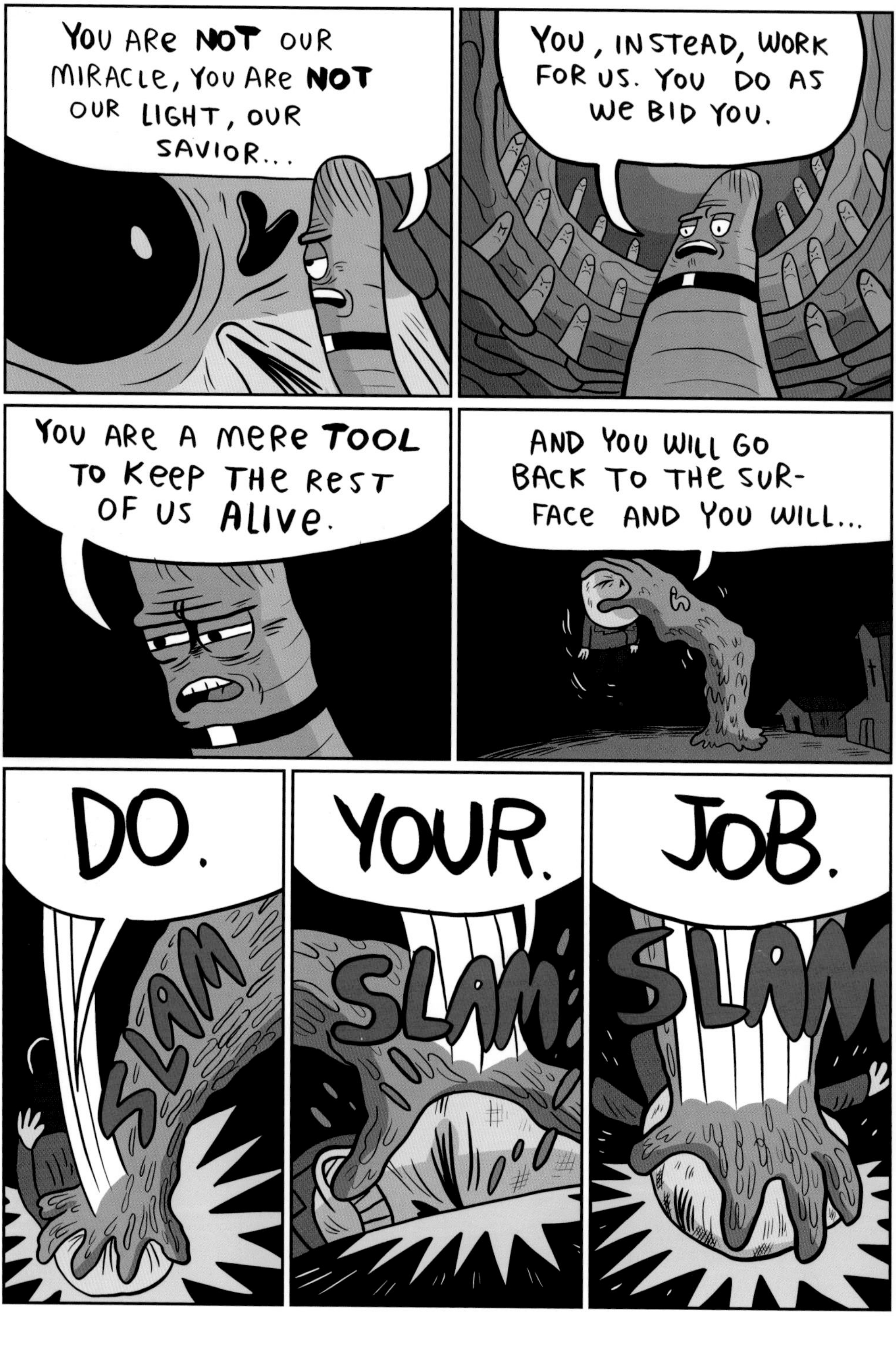
YOU ARE NOT OUR MIRACLE, YOU ARE NOT OUR LIGHT, OUR SAVIOR...
YOU, INSTEAD, WORK FOR US. YOU DO AS WE BID YOU.
YOU ARE A MERE TOOL TO KEEP THE REST OF US ALIVE.
AND YOU WILL GO BACK TO THE SUR-FACE AND YOU WILL...
DO.
SLAM
YOUR.
SLAM
JOB.
SLAM

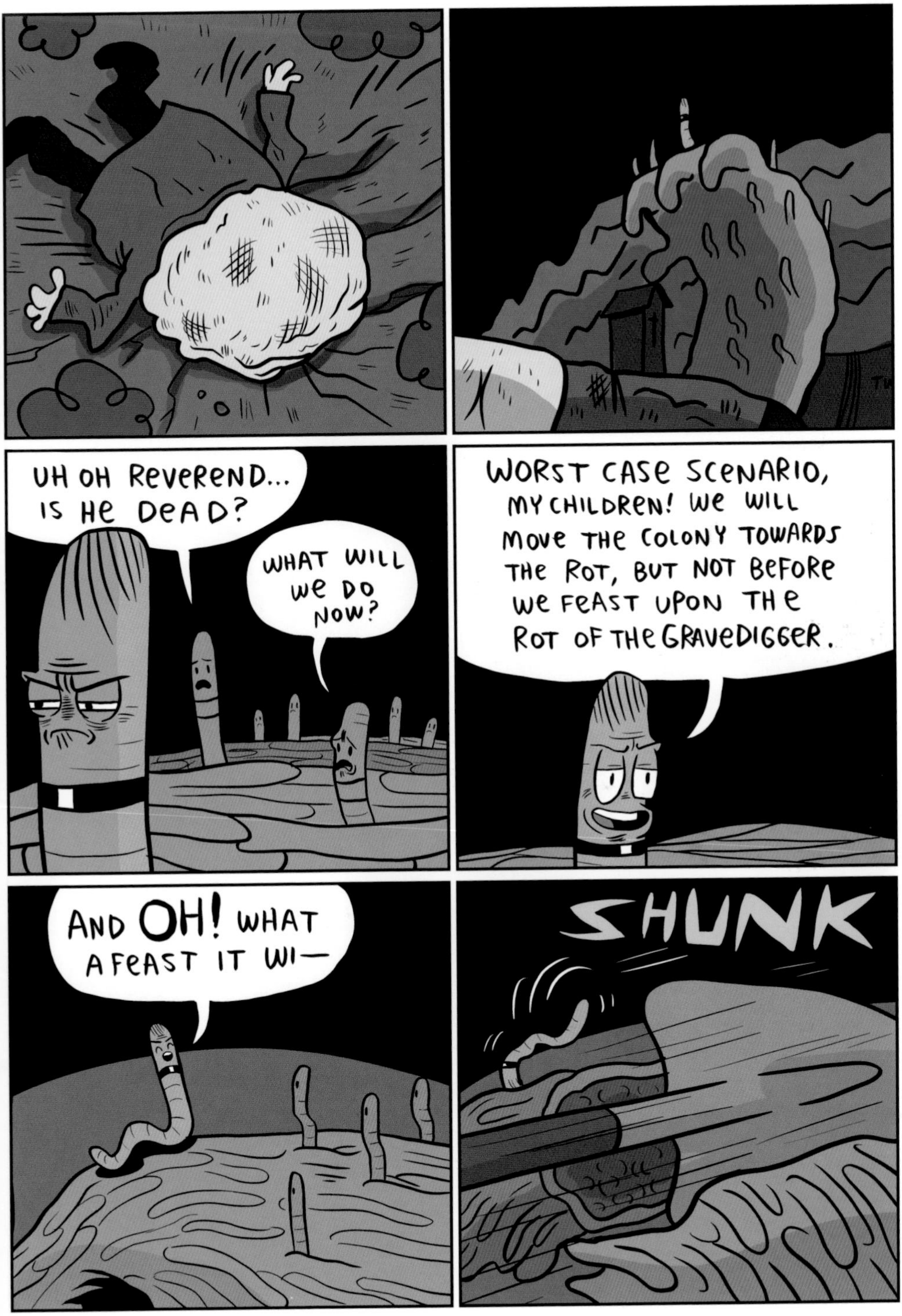
UH OH REVEREND... IS HE DEAD?
WHAT WILL WE DO NOW?
WORST CASE SCENARIO, MY CHILDREN! WE WILL MOVE THE COLONY TOWARDS THE ROT, BUT NOT BEFORE WE FEAST UPON THE ROT OF THE GRAVEDIGGER.
AND OH! WHAT A FEAST IT WI—
SHUNK

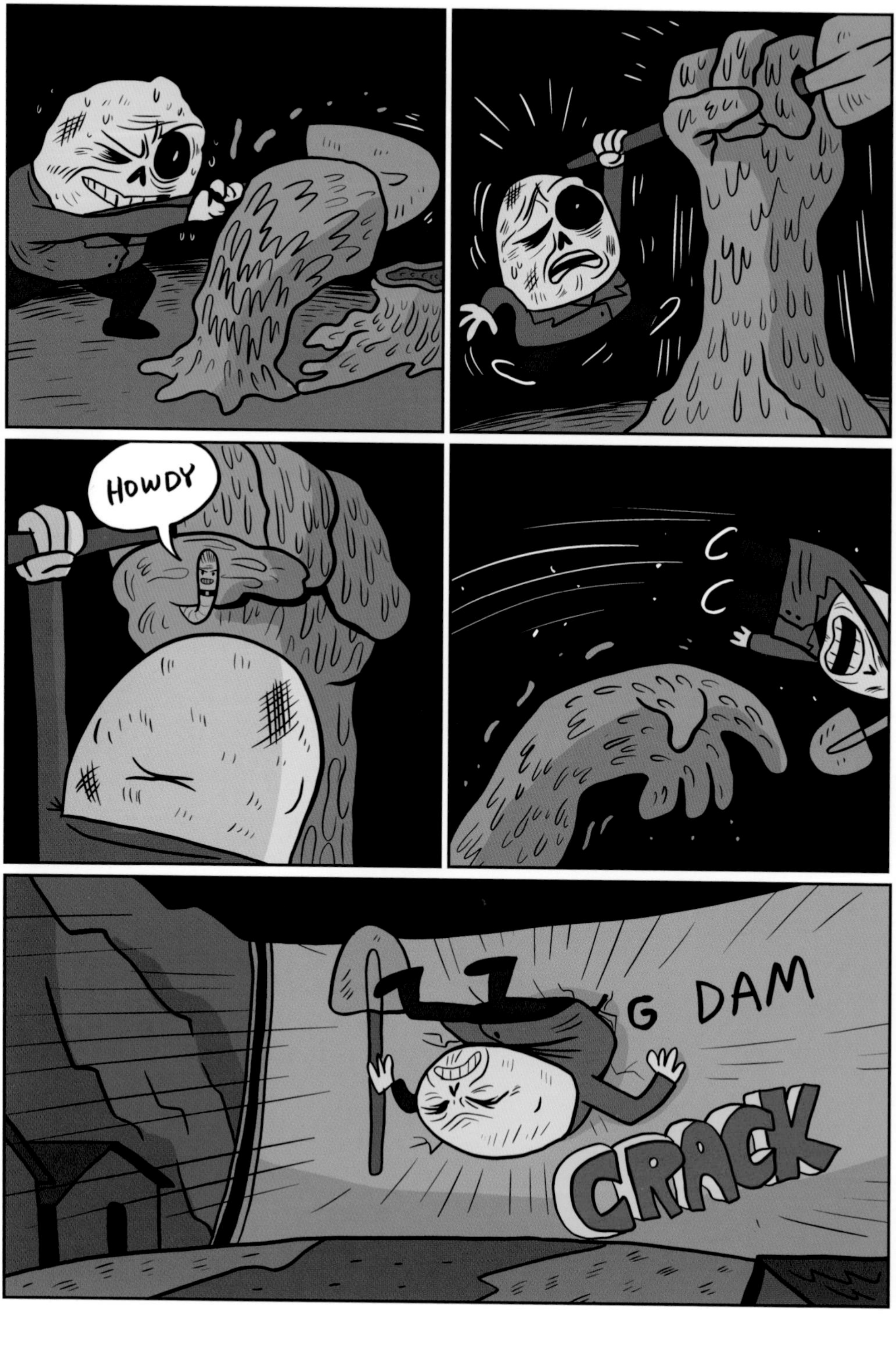
HOWDY
G DAM
CRACK

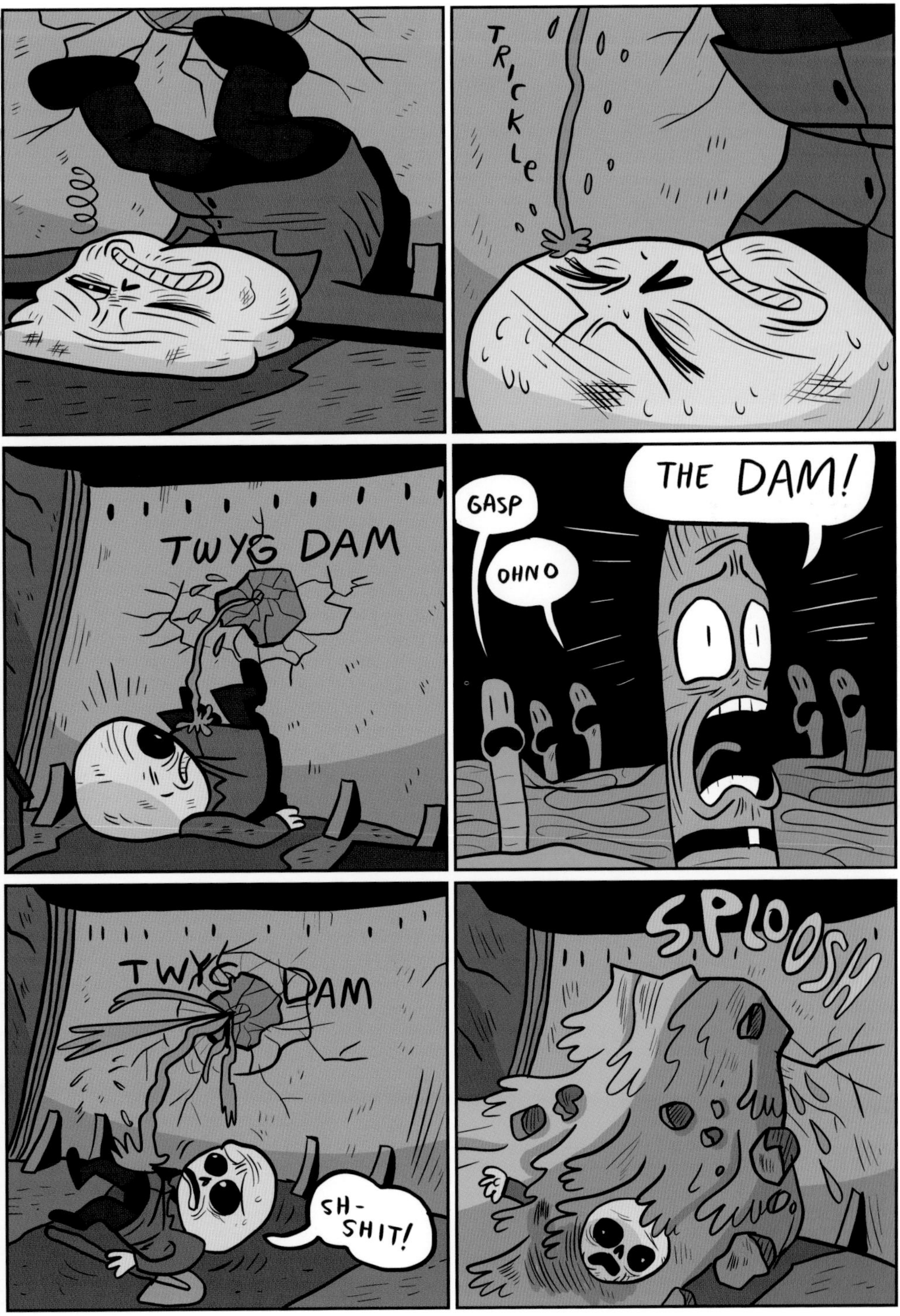
TRICKLE
TWYG DAM
GASP
OHNO
THE DAM!
TWYG DAM
SH-SHIT!
SPLOOSH

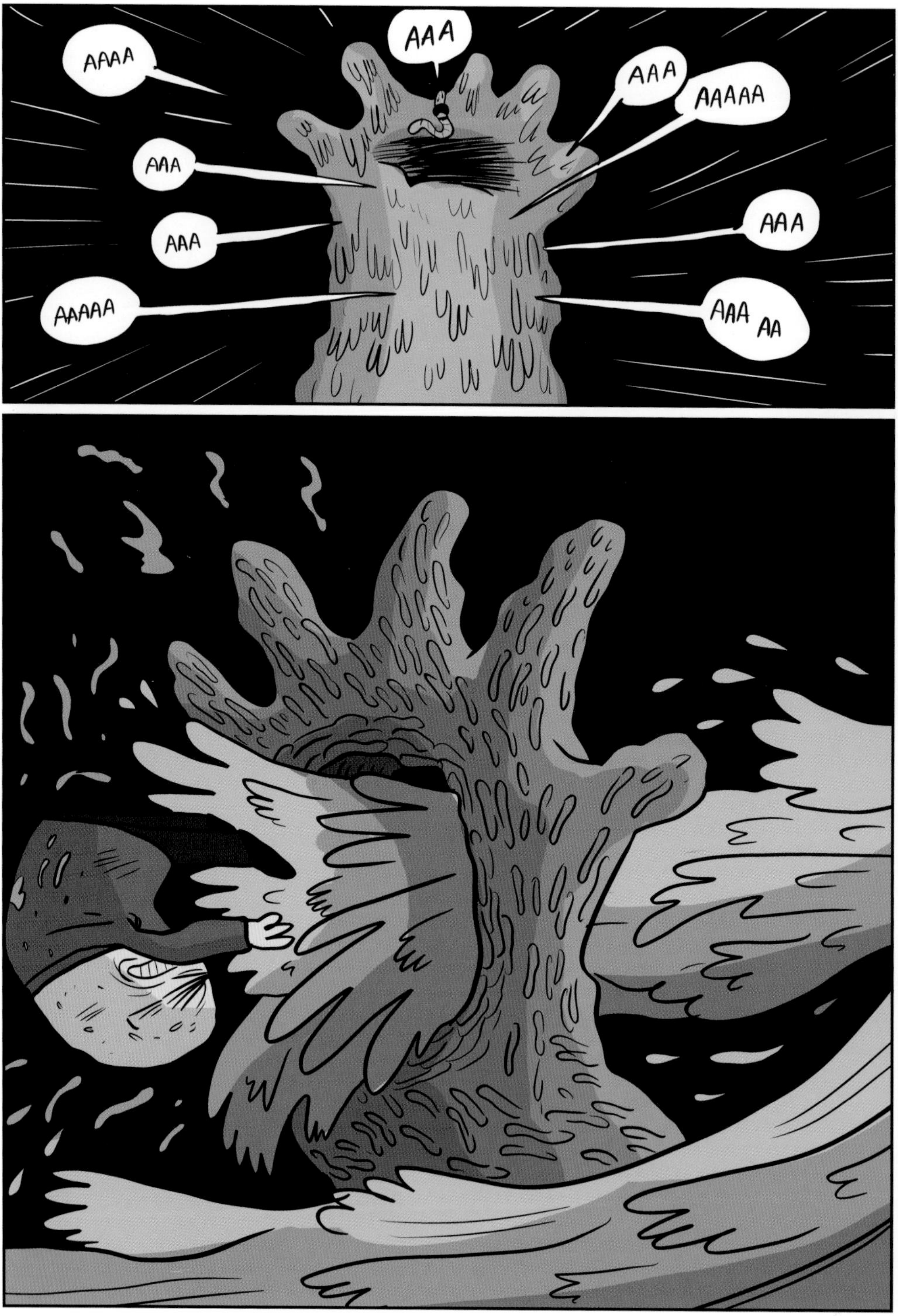
AAA
AAAA
AAA
AAAAA
AAA
AAA
AAA
AAAAA
AAAAA
AAA AA

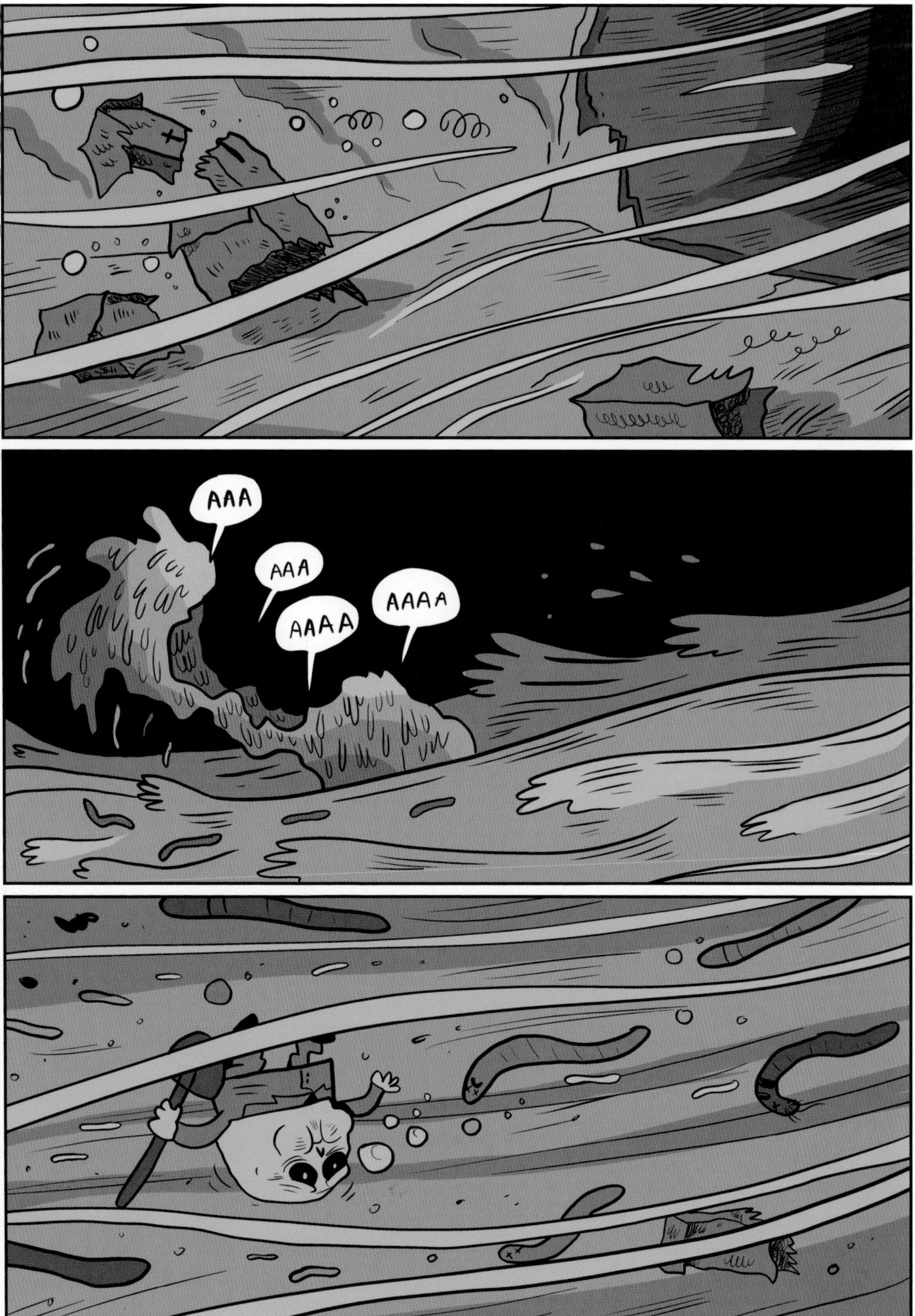
AAA
AAA
AAAA
AAAA

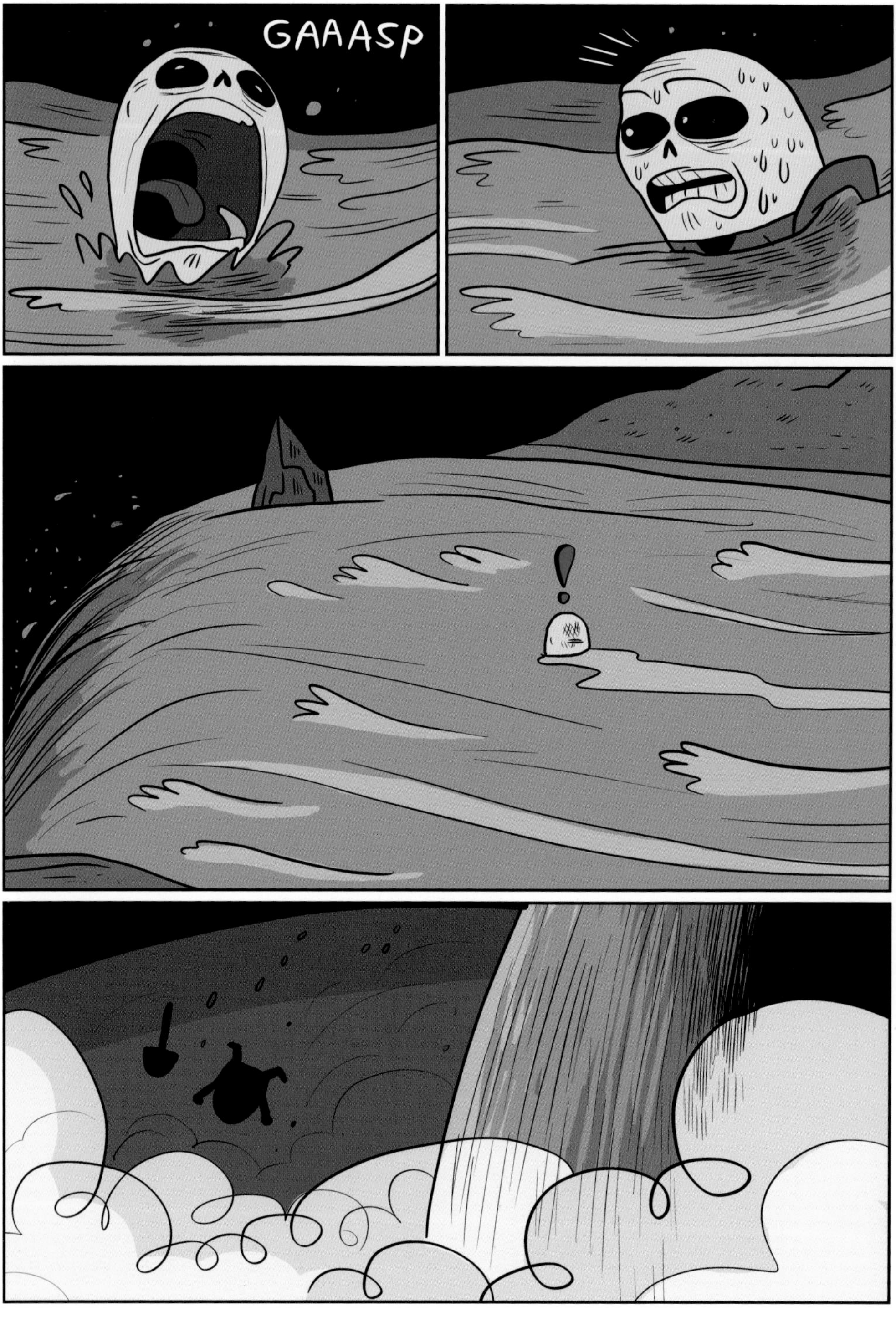
GAAASP
!

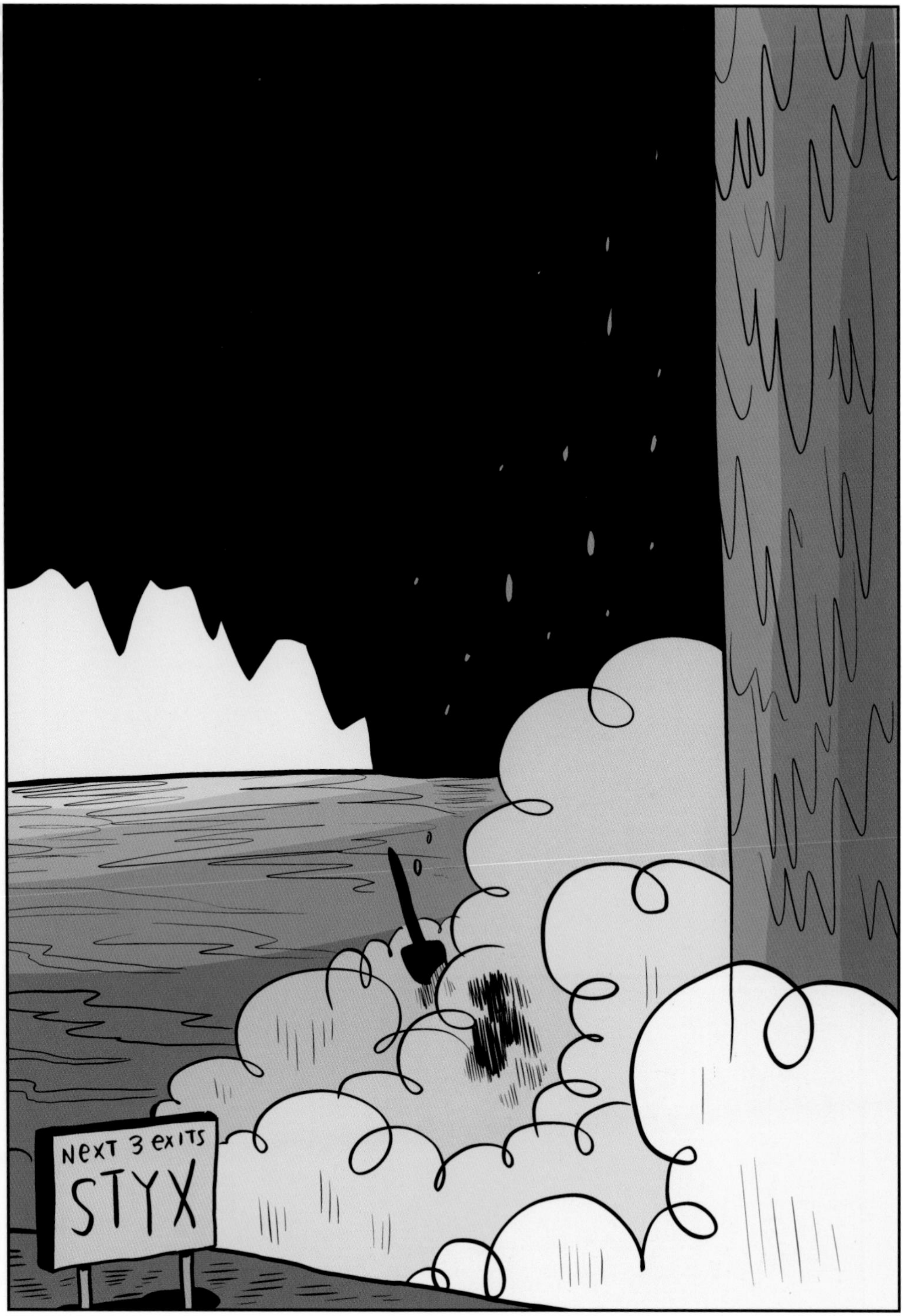
NEXT 3 EXITS
STYX

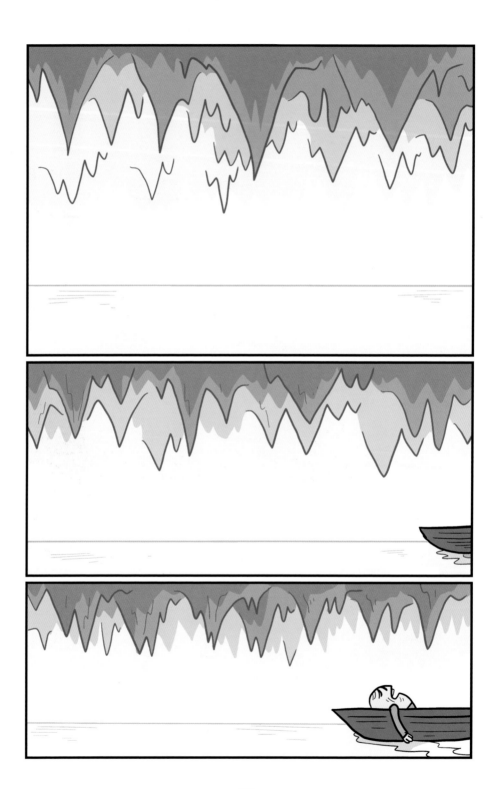

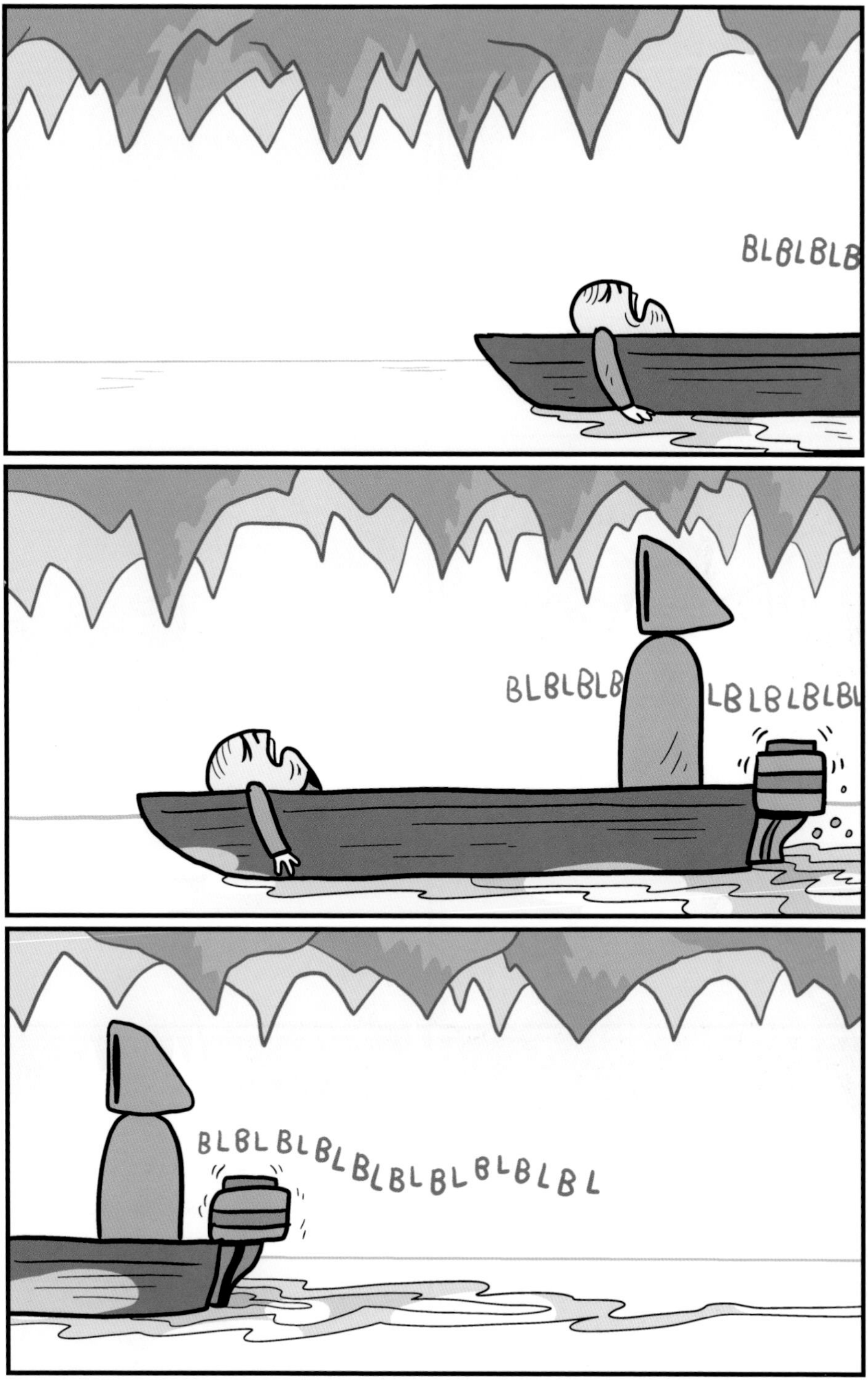
BLBLBLB
BLBLBLB
LBLBLBLBL
BLBLBLBLBLBLBLBLBLBLBL

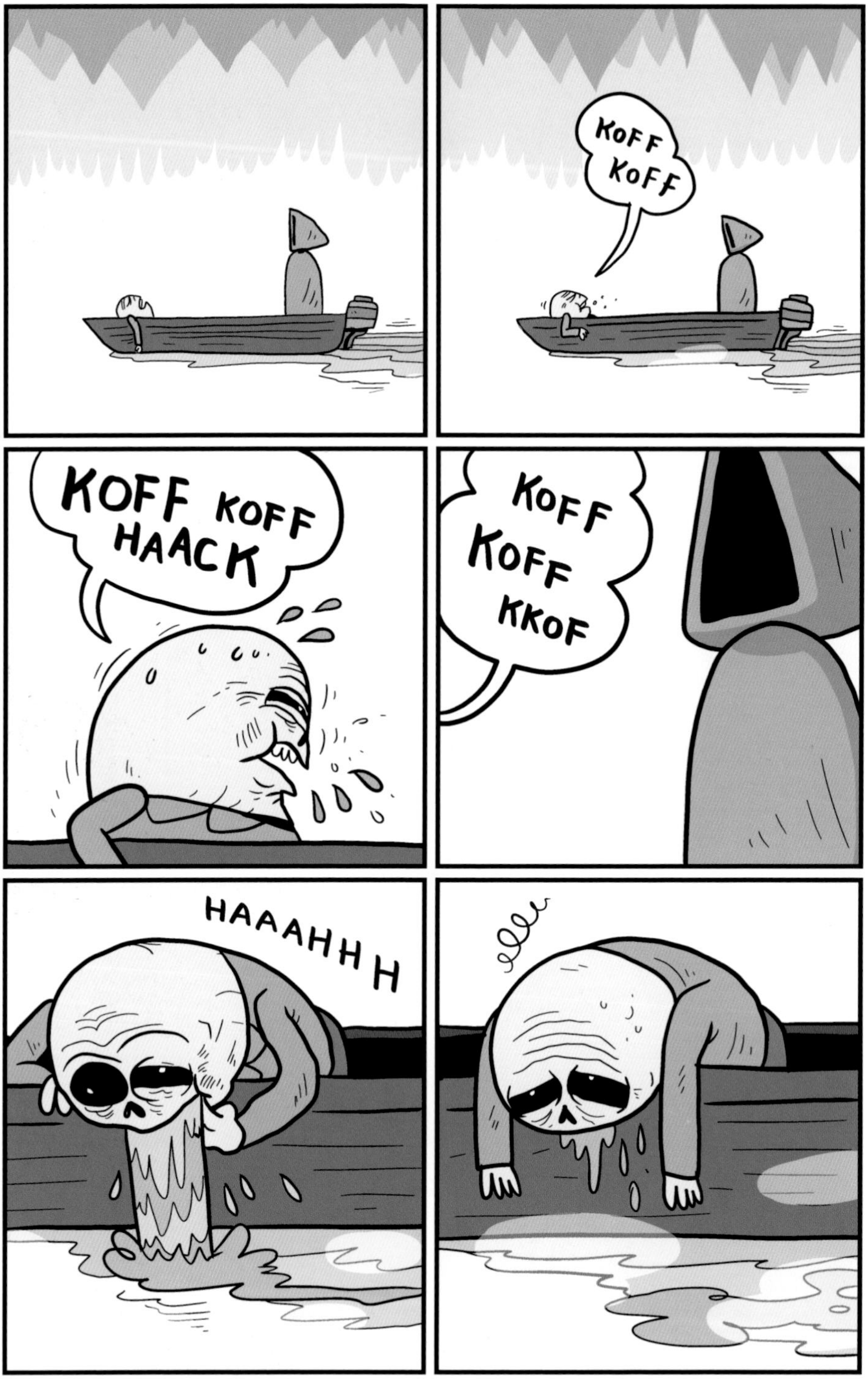

KOFF KOFF
KOFF KOFF HAACK
KOFF KOFF KKOF
HAAAHHHH

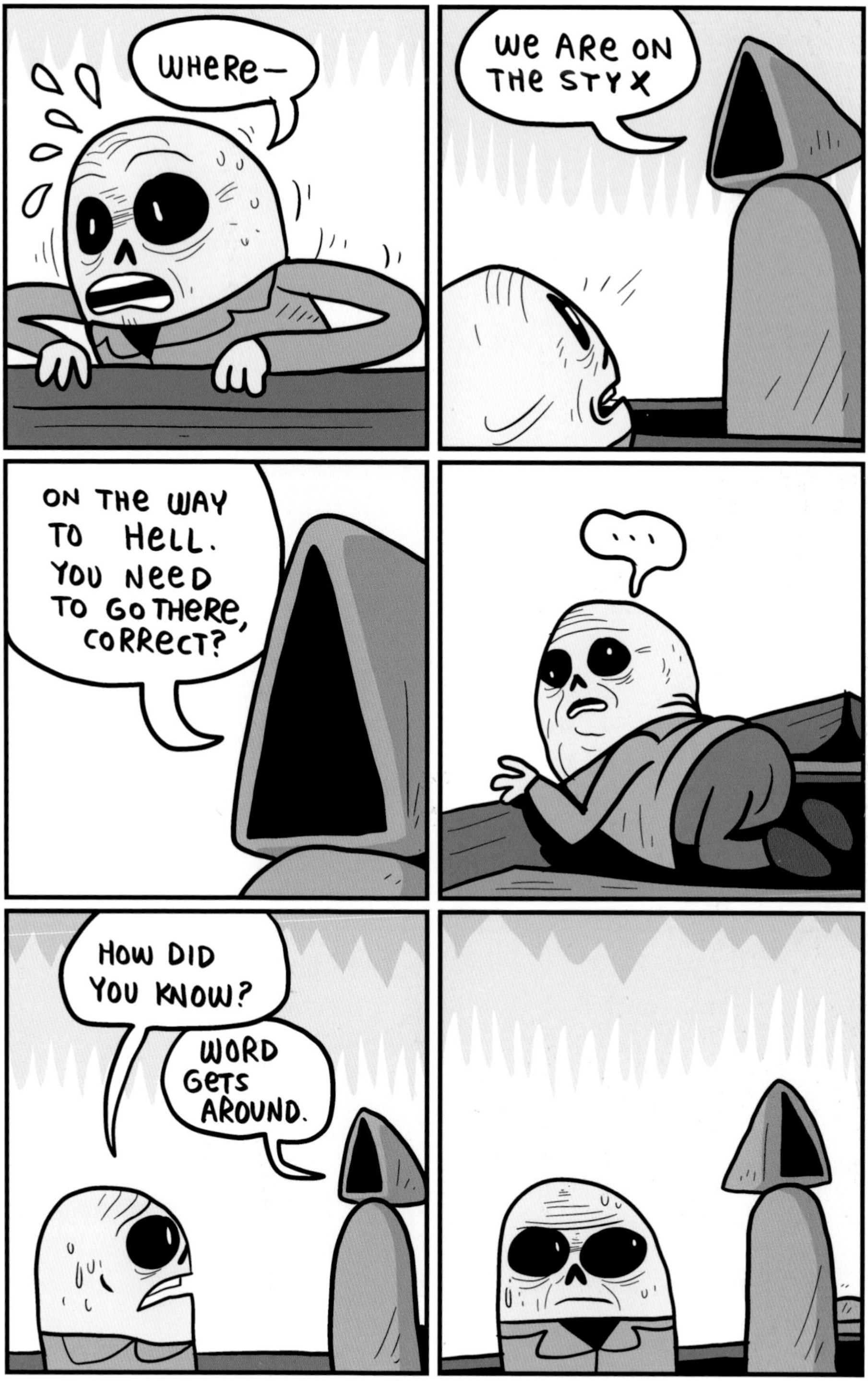
WHERE—
WE ARE ON THE STYX
ON THE WAY TO HELL. YOU NEED TO GO THERE, CORRECT?
...
HOW DID YOU KNOW?
WORD GETS AROUND.

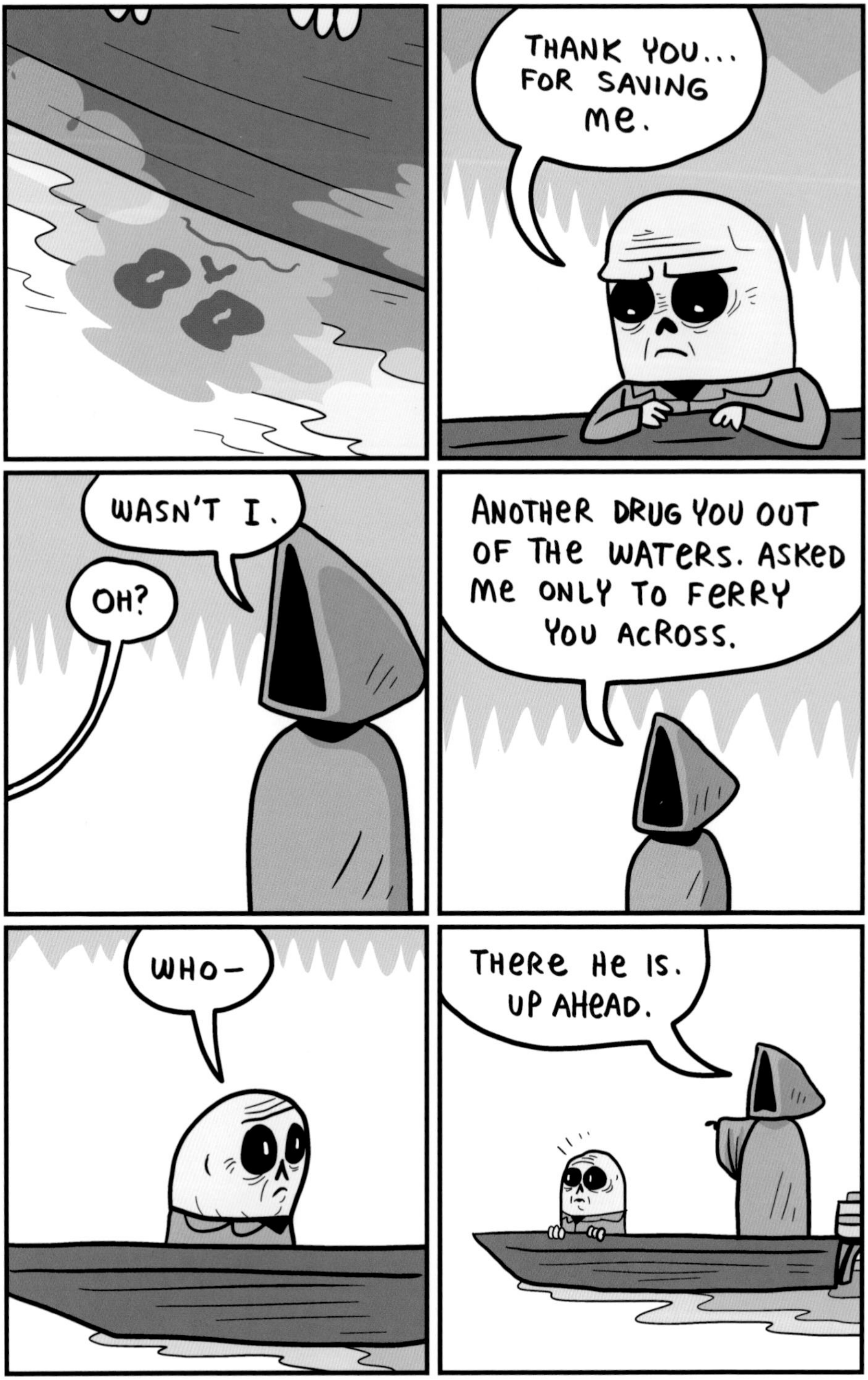
THANK YOU... FOR SAVING me.
WASN'T I.
OH?
ANOTHER DRUG YOU OUT OF THE WATERS. ASKED ME ONLY TO FERRY YOU ACROSS.
WHO-
THERE HE IS. UP AHEAD.

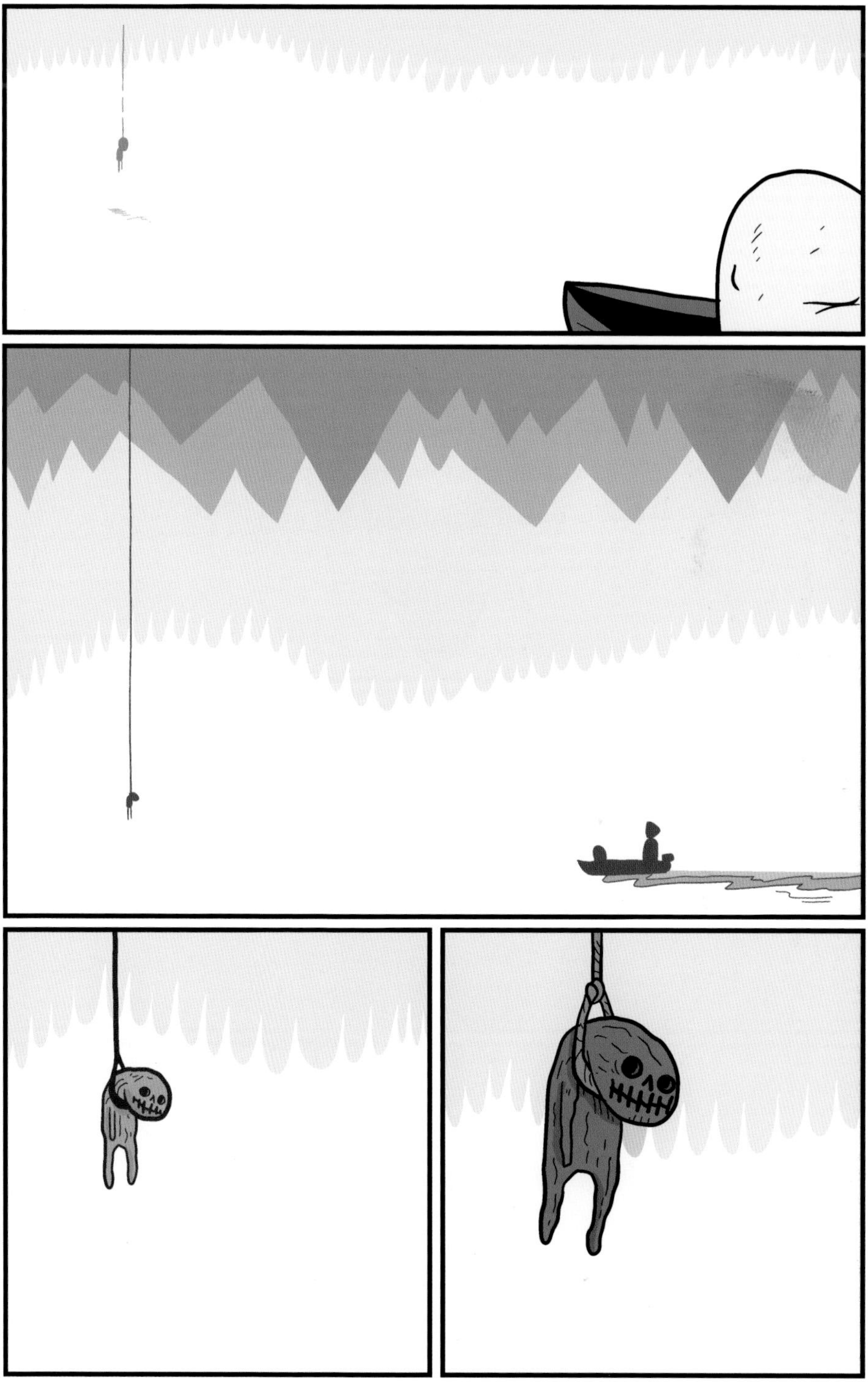

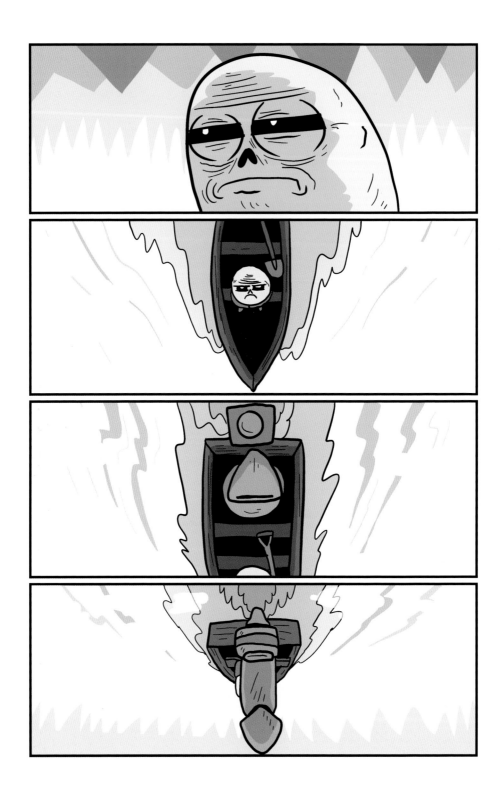

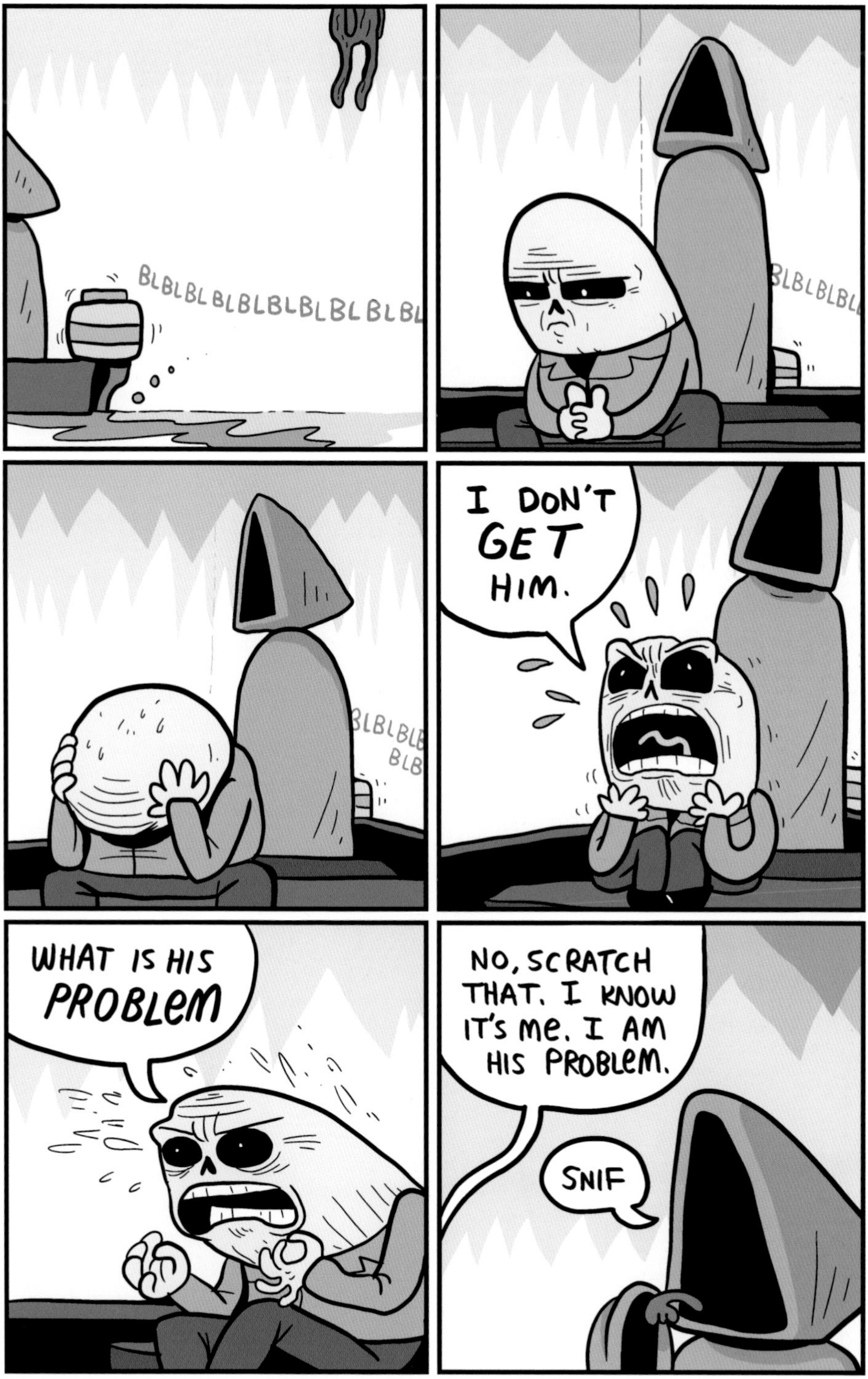
BLBLBLBLBLBLBLBLBLBLBL
BLBLBLBL
BLBLBLBL
BLB
I DON'T GET HIM.
WHAT IS HIS PROBLEM
NO, SCRATCH THAT. I KNOW IT'S ME. I AM HIS PROBLEM.
SNIF

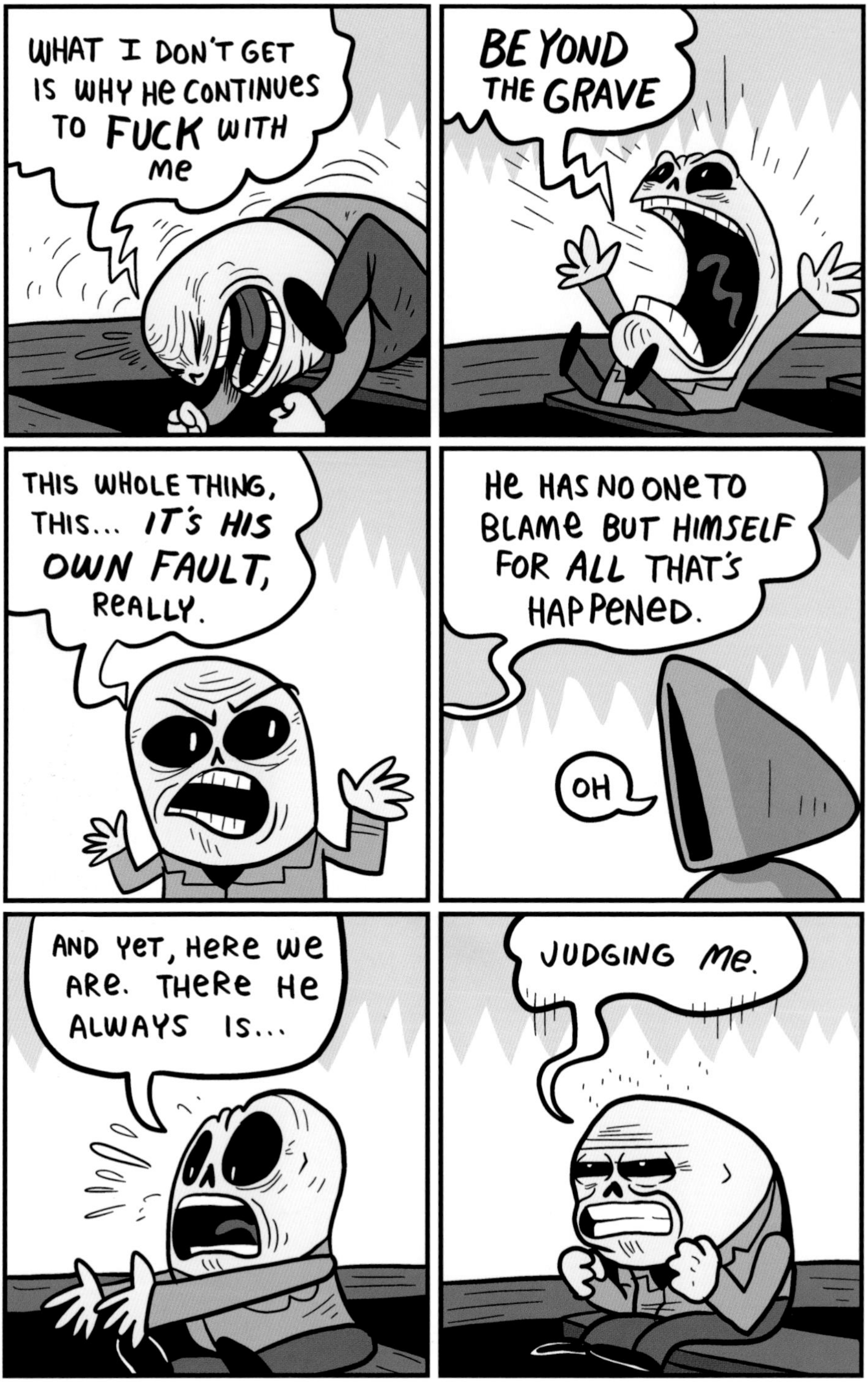
WHAT I DON'T GET IS WHY HE CONTINUES TO FUCK WITH ME
BEYOND THE GRAVE
THIS WHOLE THING, THIS... IT'S HIS OWN FAULT, REALLY.
HE HAS NO ONE TO BLAME BUT HIMSELF FOR ALL THAT'S HAPPENED.
OH
AND YET, HERE WE ARE. THERE HE ALWAYS IS...
JUDGING ME.

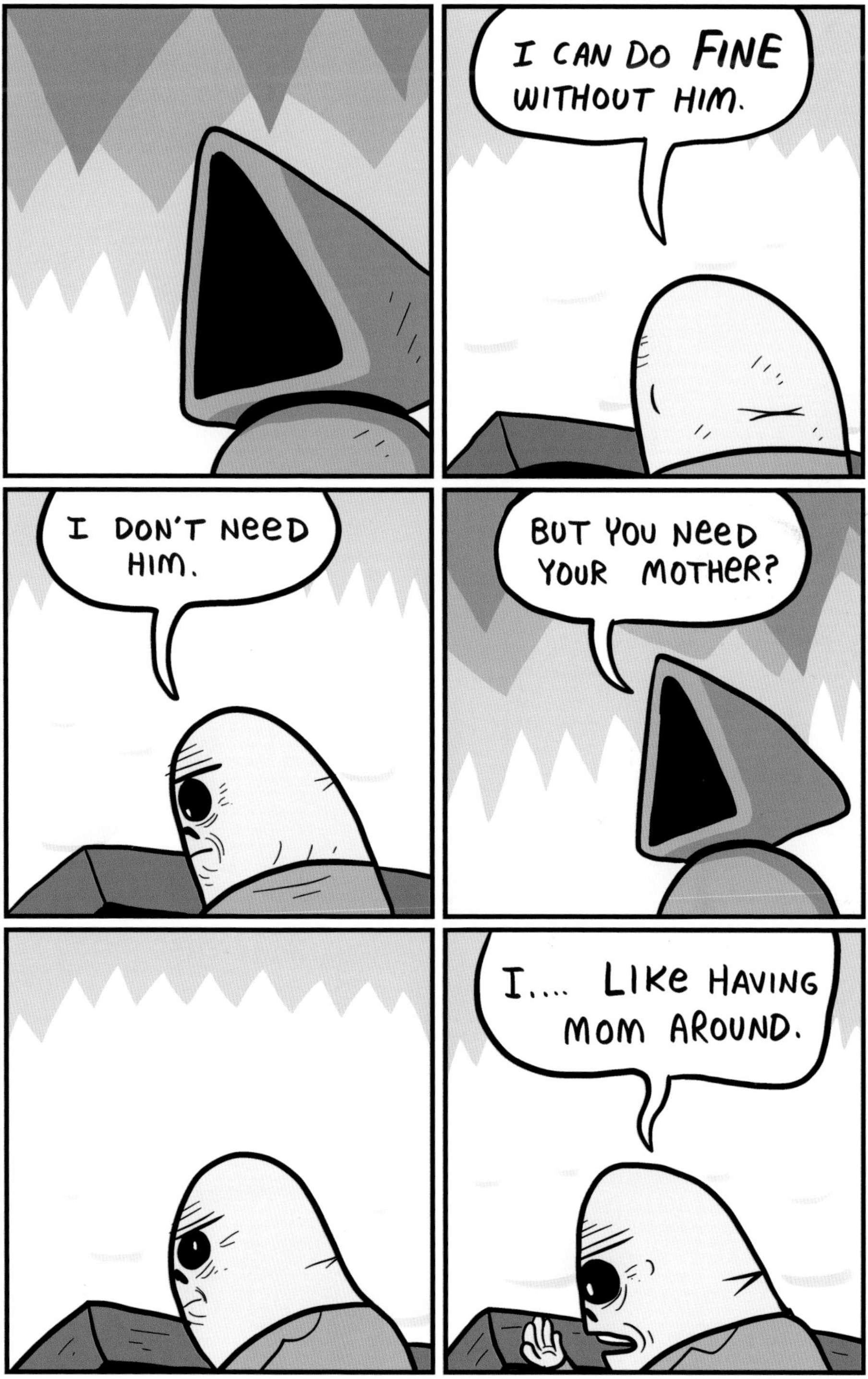
I CAN DO FINE WITHOUT HIM.
I DON'T NEED HIM.
BUT YOU NEED YOUR MOTHER?
I.... LIKE HAVING MOM AROUND.

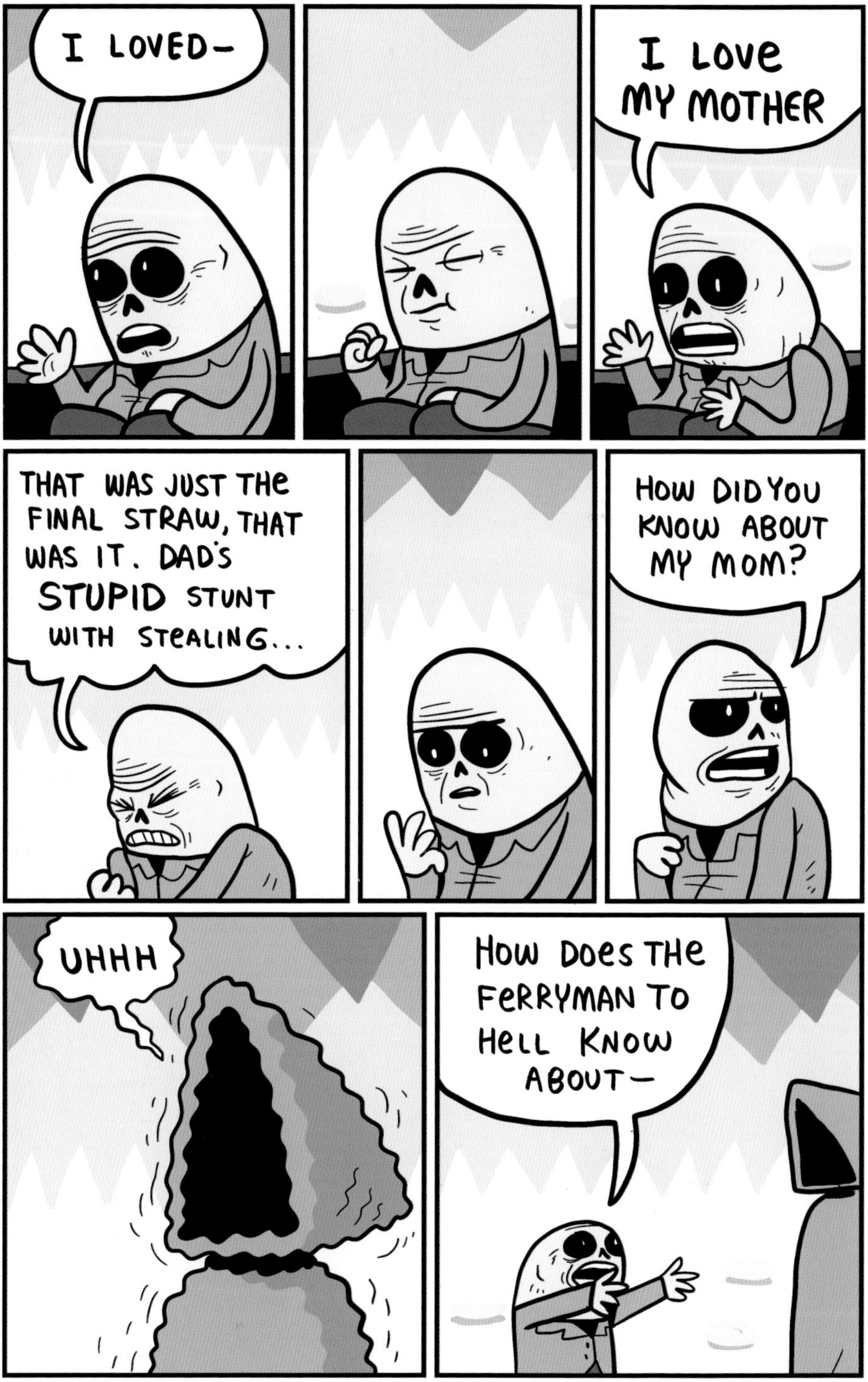
I LOVED-
I LOVE MY MOTHER
THAT WAS JUST THE FINAL STRAW, THAT WAS IT. DAD'S STUPID STUNT WITH STEALING...
HOW DID YOU KNOW ABOUT MY MOM?
UHHH
HOW DOES THE FERRYMAN TO HELL KNOW ABOUT-

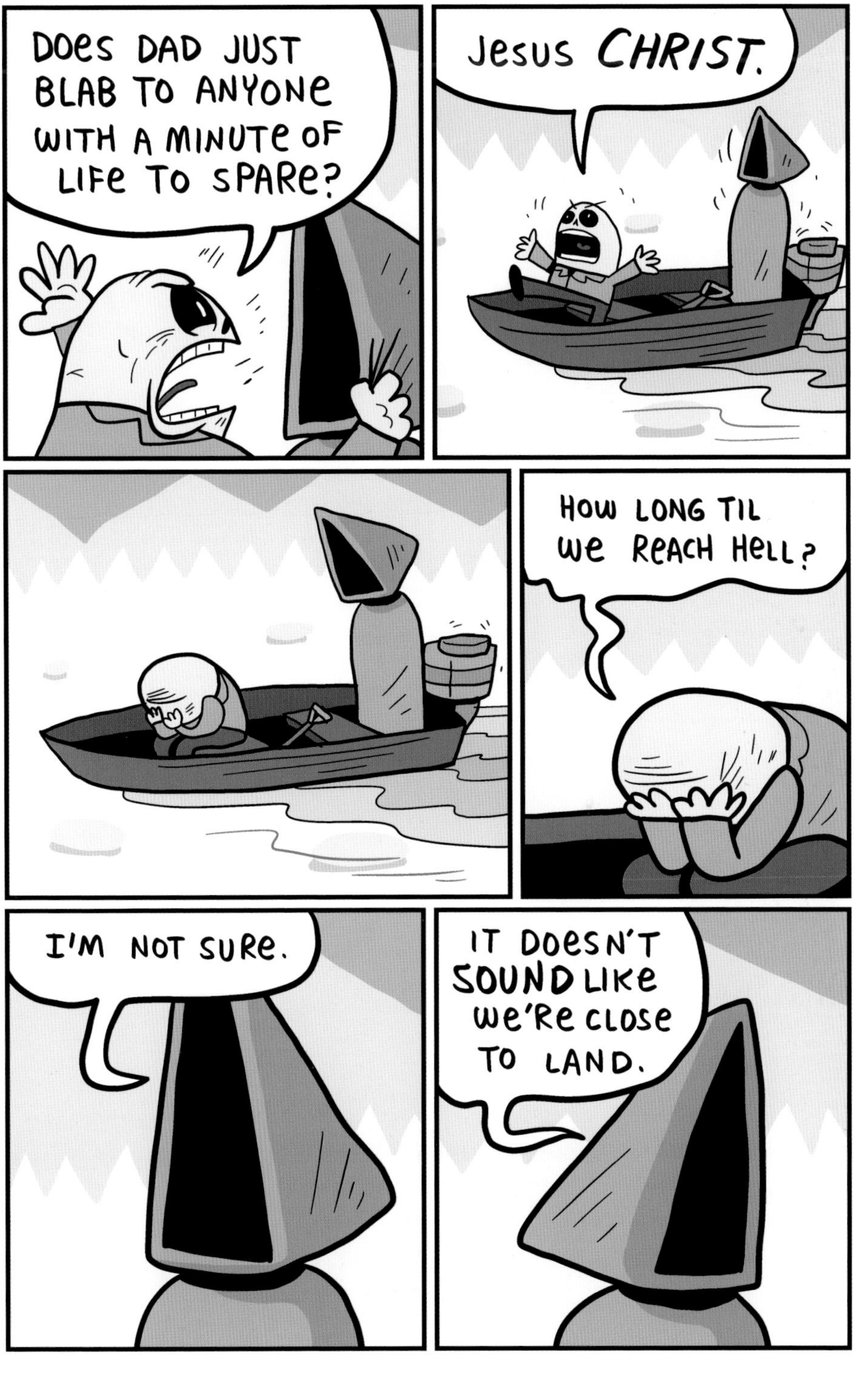
DOES DAD JUST BLAB TO ANYONE WITH A MINUTE OF LIFE TO SPARE?
JESUS CHRIST.
HOW LONG TIL WE REACH HELL?
I'M NOT SURE.
IT DOESN'T SOUND LIKE WE'RE CLOSE TO LAND.

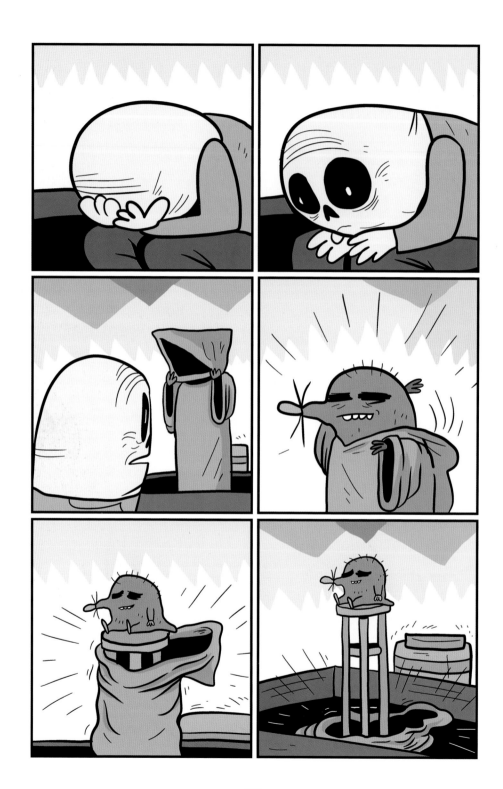

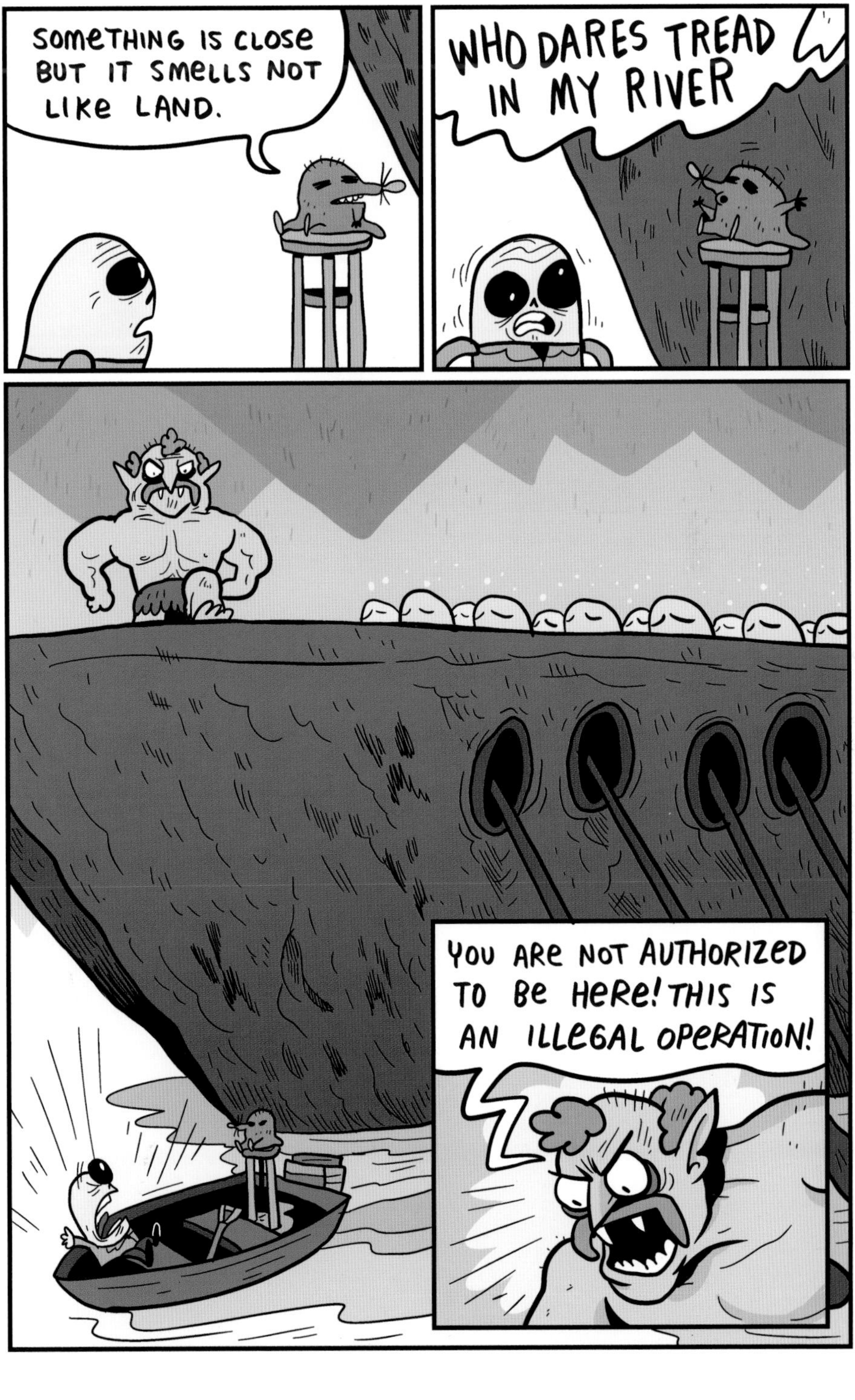
SOMETHING IS CLOSE BUT IT SMELLS NOT LIKE LAND.
WHO DARES TREAD IN MY RIVER
YOU ARE NOT AUTHORIZED TO BE HERE! THIS IS AN ILLEGAL OPERATION!

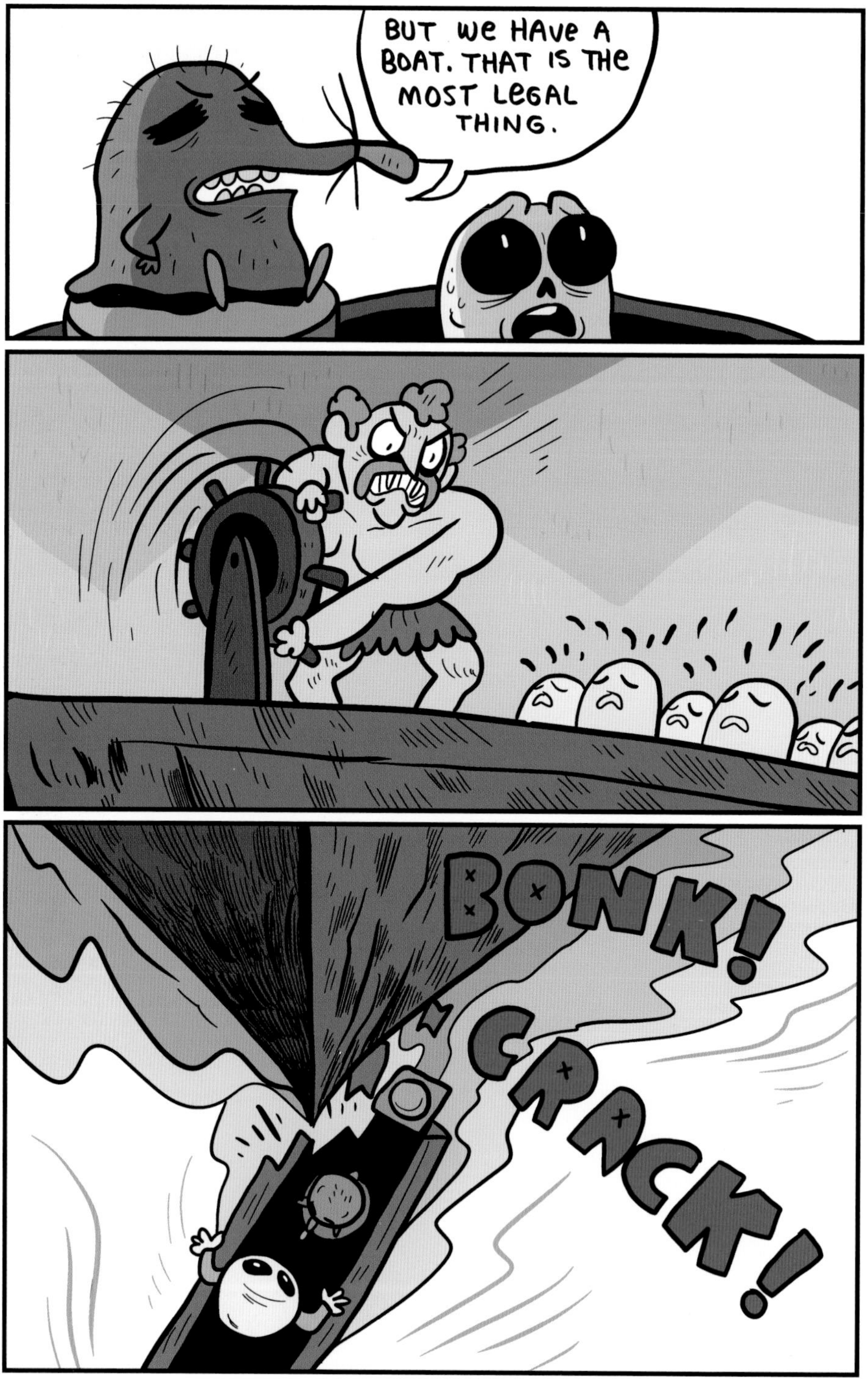
BUT WE HAVE A BOAT. THAT IS THE MOST LEGAL THING.
BONK!
CRACK!

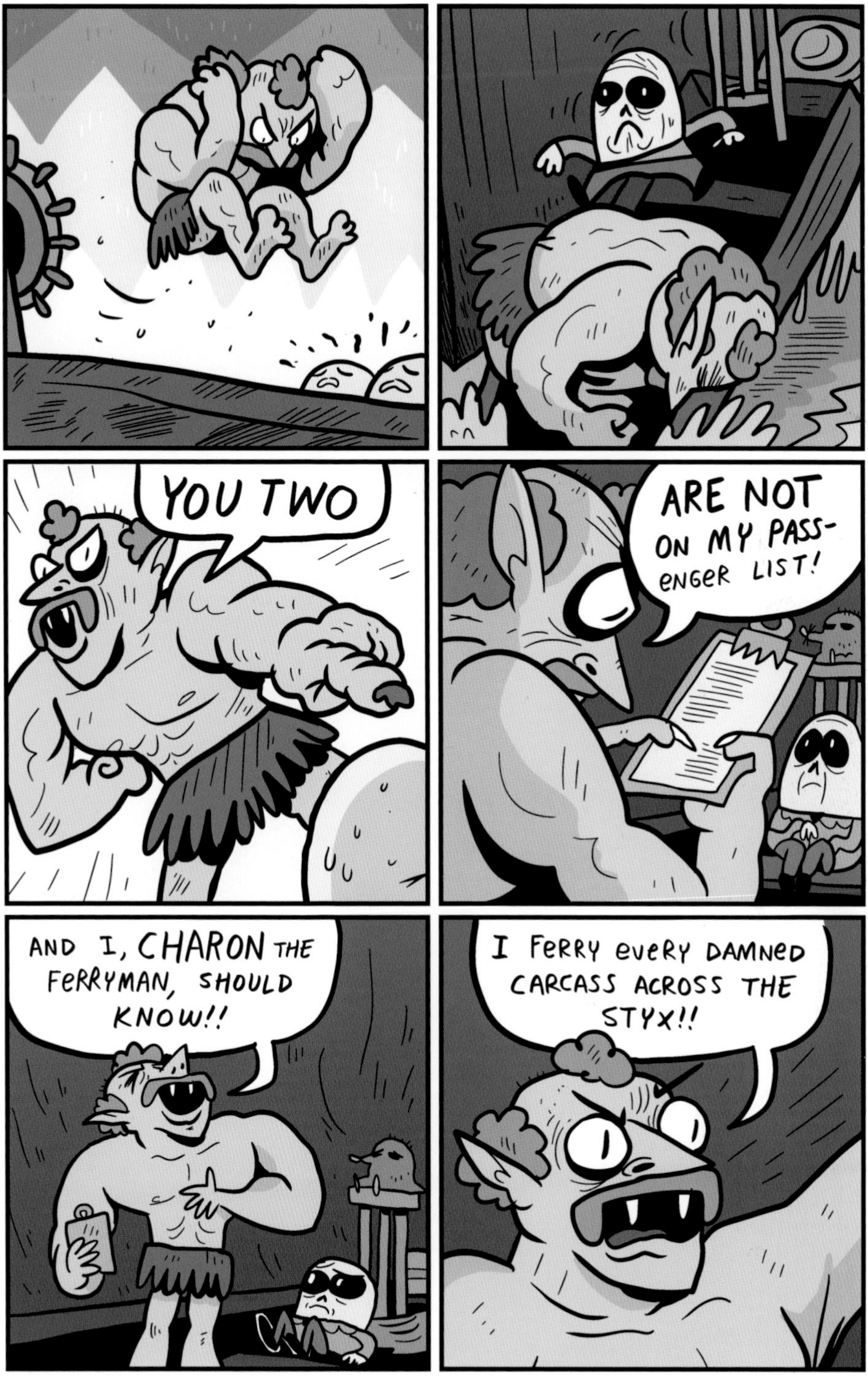
YOU TWO
ARE NOT ON MY PASS-ENGER LIST!
AND I, CHARON THE FERRYMAN, SHOULD KNOW!!
I FERRY EVERY DAMNED CARCASS ACROSS THE STYX!!

NEITHER OF YOU LOOK PARTICULARLY CARCASSY OR ROTTEN

LOOK AT YOU, SON!

FIT AS THE DEVIL'S FIDDLE!!

FUMP

THE PICTURE OF HEALTH

AND THIS ONE!!

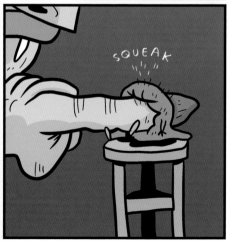

SQUEAK

94

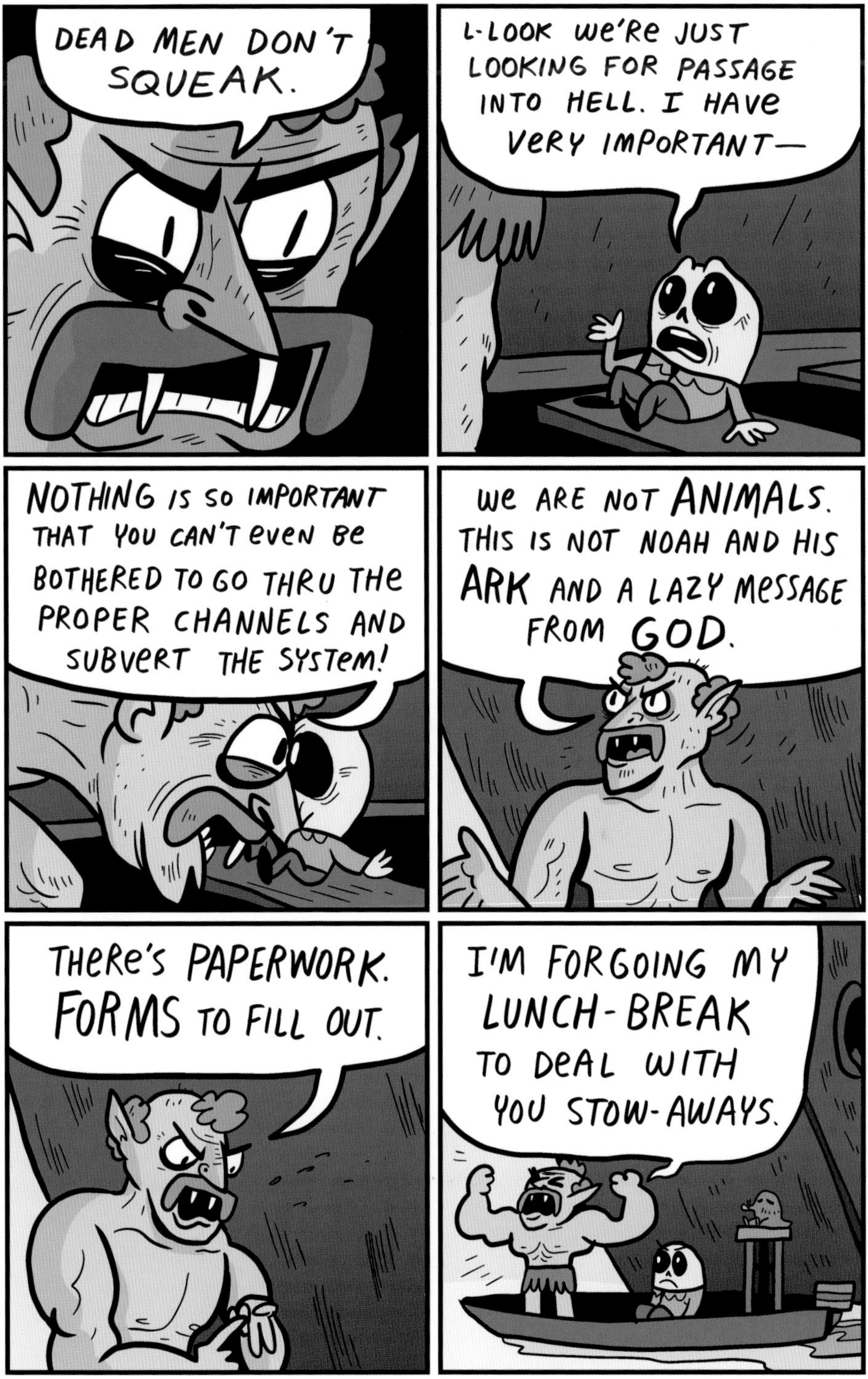
DEAD MEN DON'T SQUEAK.
L-LOOK WE'RE JUST LOOKING FOR PASSAGE INTO HELL. I HAVE VERY IMPORTANT—
NOTHING IS SO IMPORTANT THAT YOU CAN'T EVEN BE BOTHERED TO GO THRU THE PROPER CHANNELS AND SUBVERT THE SYSTEM!
WE ARE NOT ANIMALS. THIS IS NOT NOAH AND HIS ARK AND A LAZY MESSAGE FROM GOD.
THERE'S PAPERWORK. FORMS TO FILL OUT.
I'M FORGOING MY LUNCH-BREAK TO DEAL WITH YOU STOW-AWAYS.

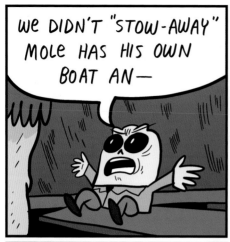

WE DIDN'T "STOW-AWAY" MOLE HAS HIS OWN BOAT AN—

THIS BOAT!! IS AN ILLEGAL OPERATION!!

SHUT IT DOWN, **NOW**.

WHAT THE HELL DO YOU exactly... WANT US TO DO?

I HAVE MADE MYSELF VERY CLEAR

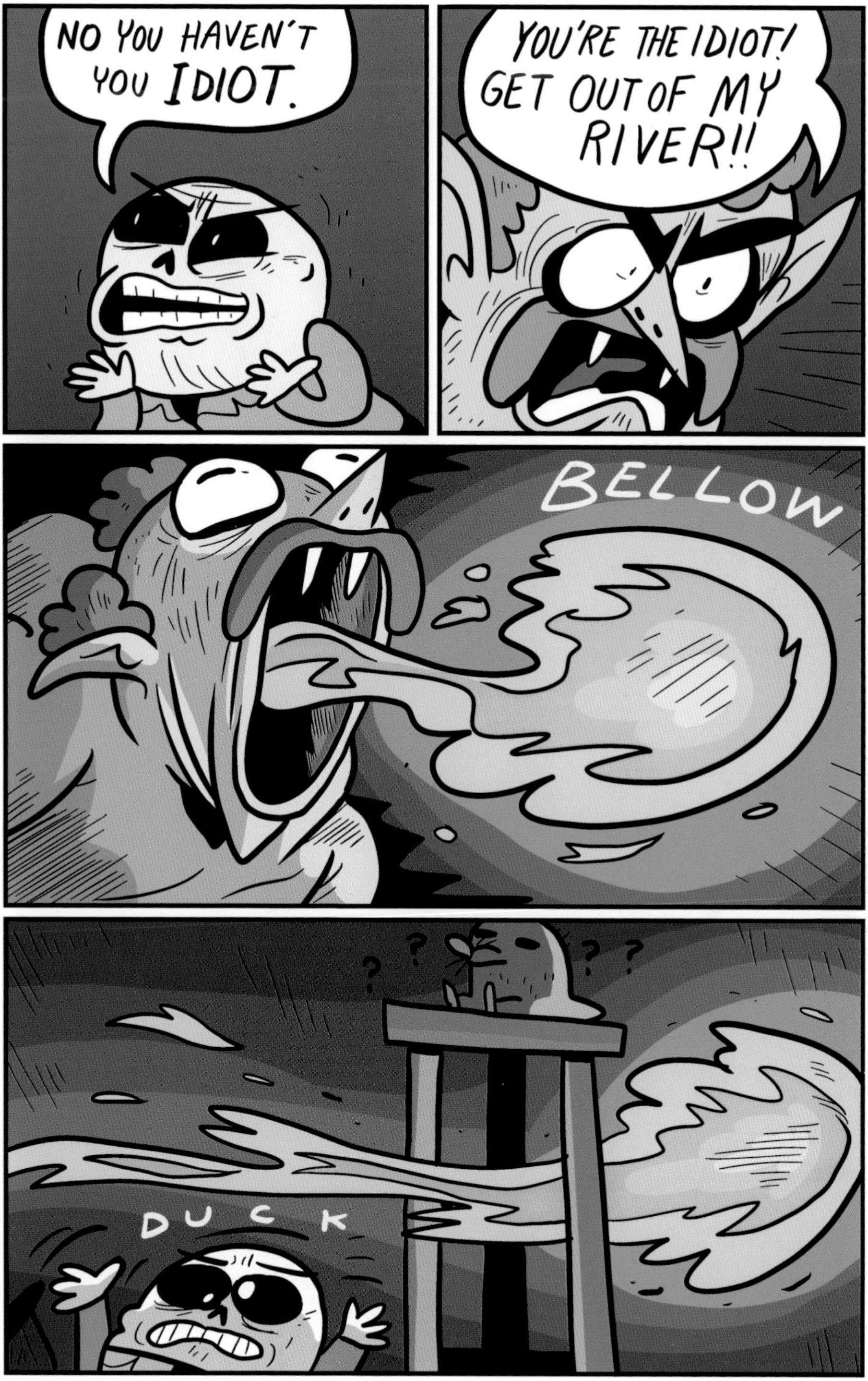
NO YOU HAVEN'T YOU IDIOT.
YOU'RE THE IDIOT! GET OUT OF MY RIVER!!
BELLOW
? ? ? ?
DUCK

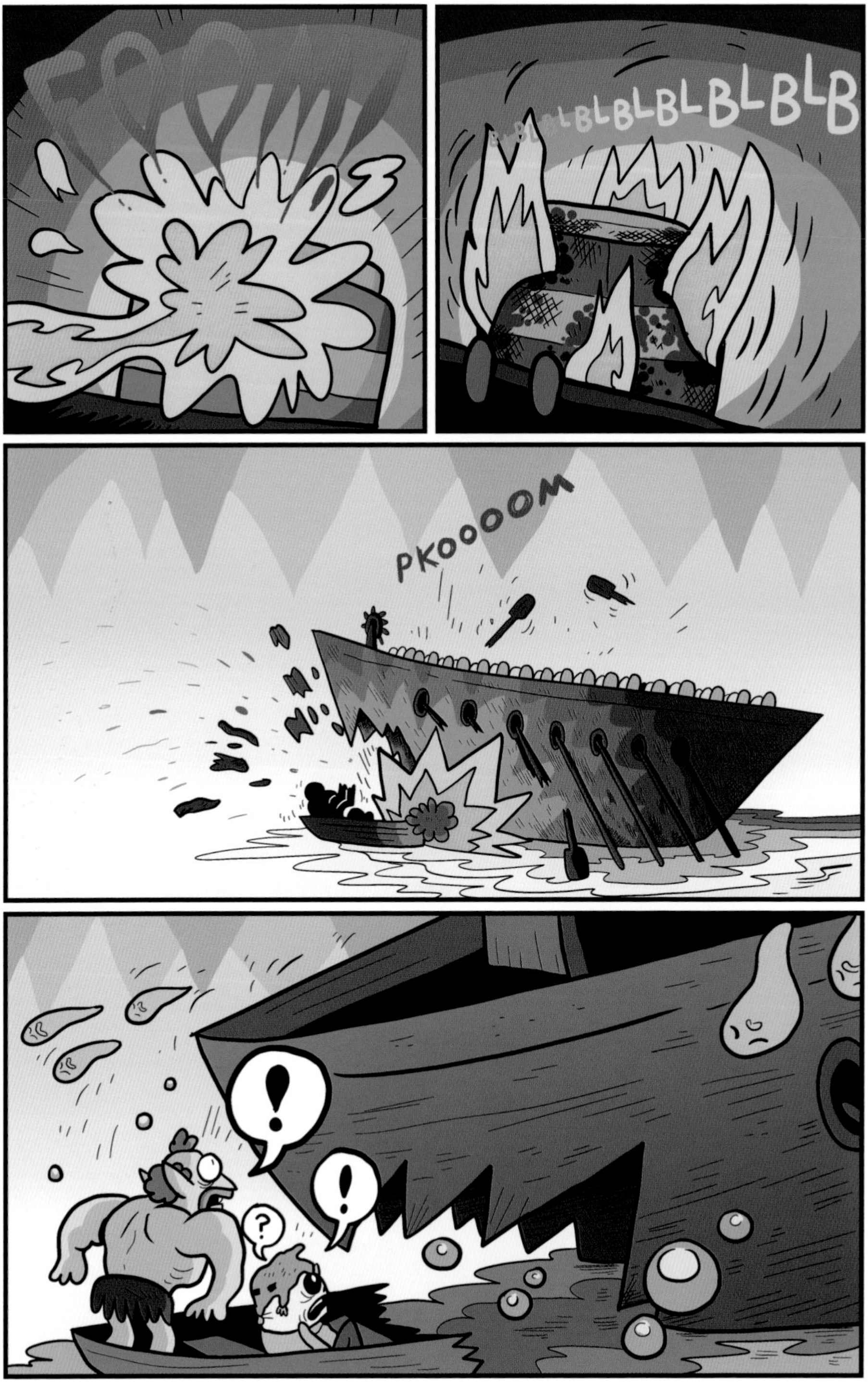

BLBLBLBLBLBLB
PKOOOOM
!
!
?

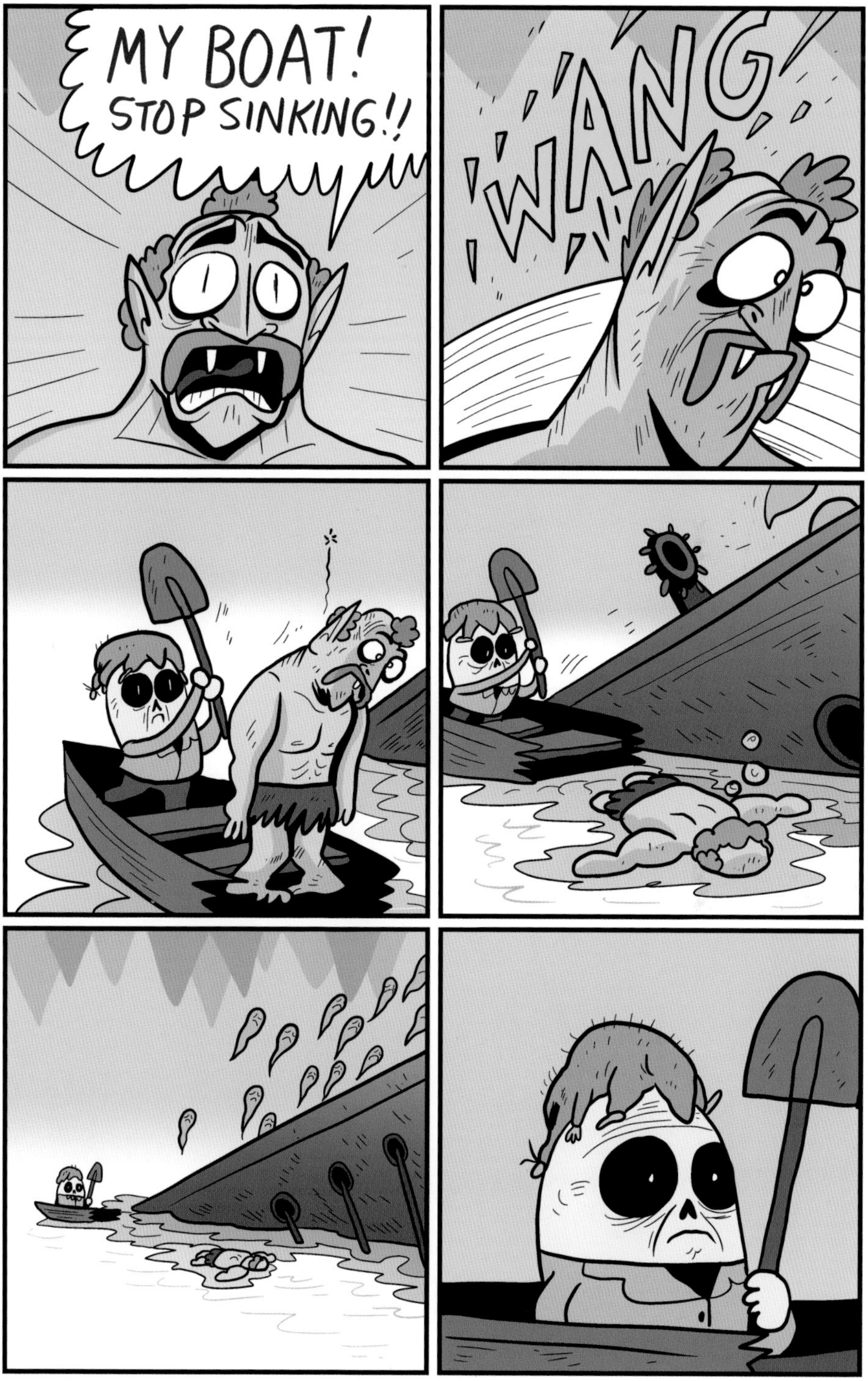
MY BOAT! STOP SINKING!!
WANG!

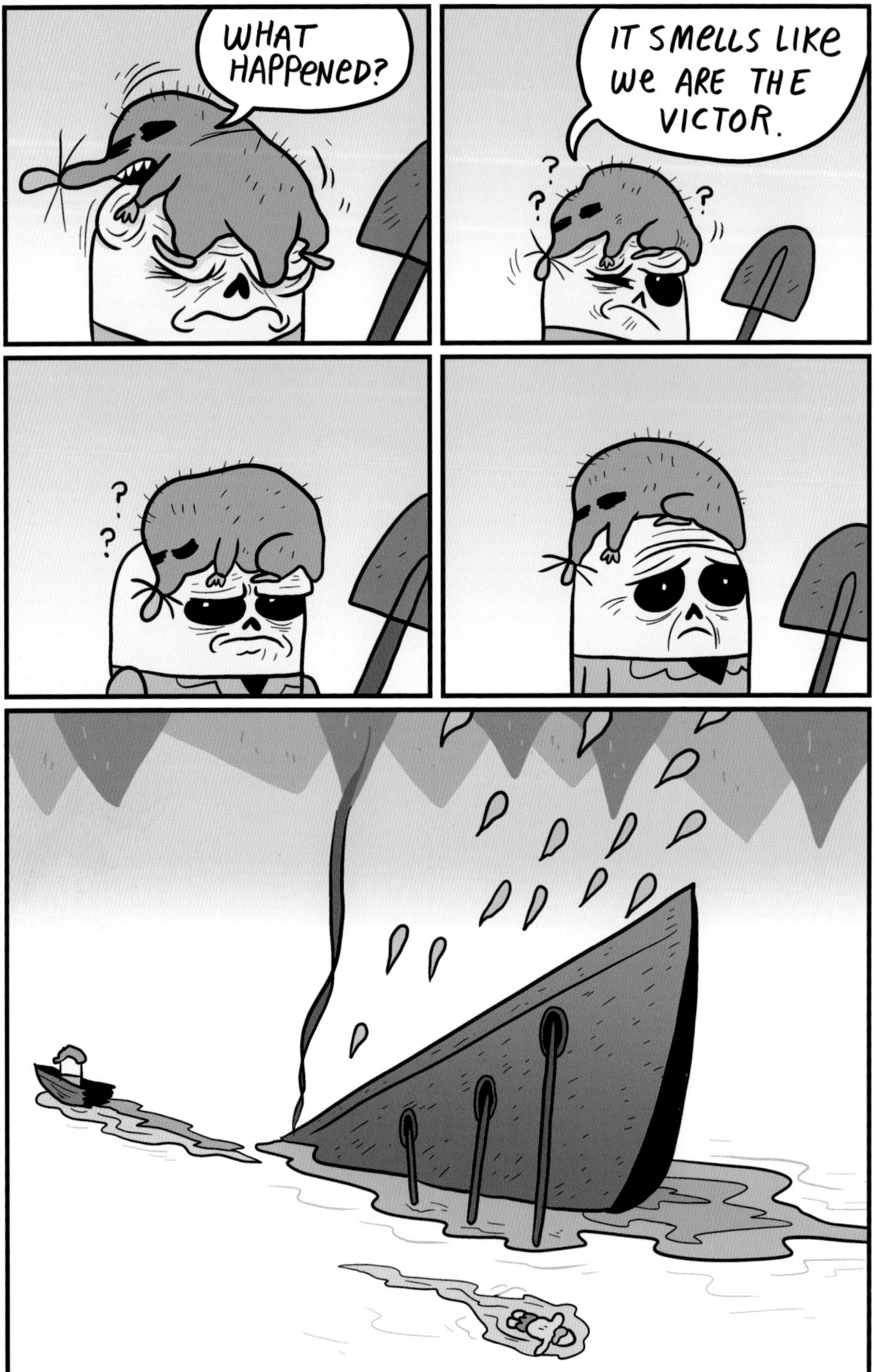
WHAT HAPPENED?
IT SMELLS LIKE WE ARE THE VICTOR.
?
?
?
?
?

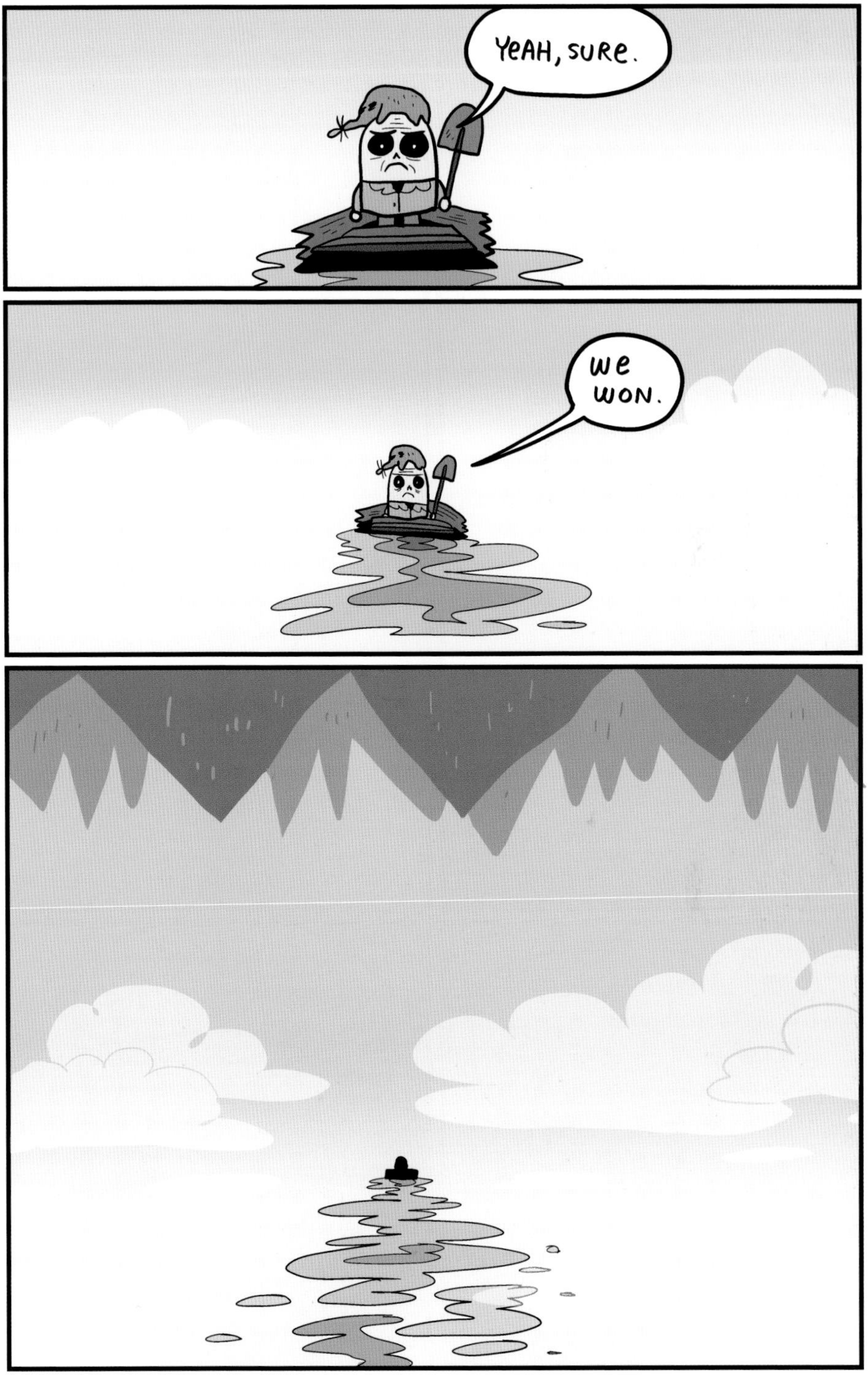
YEAH, SURE.
WE WON.

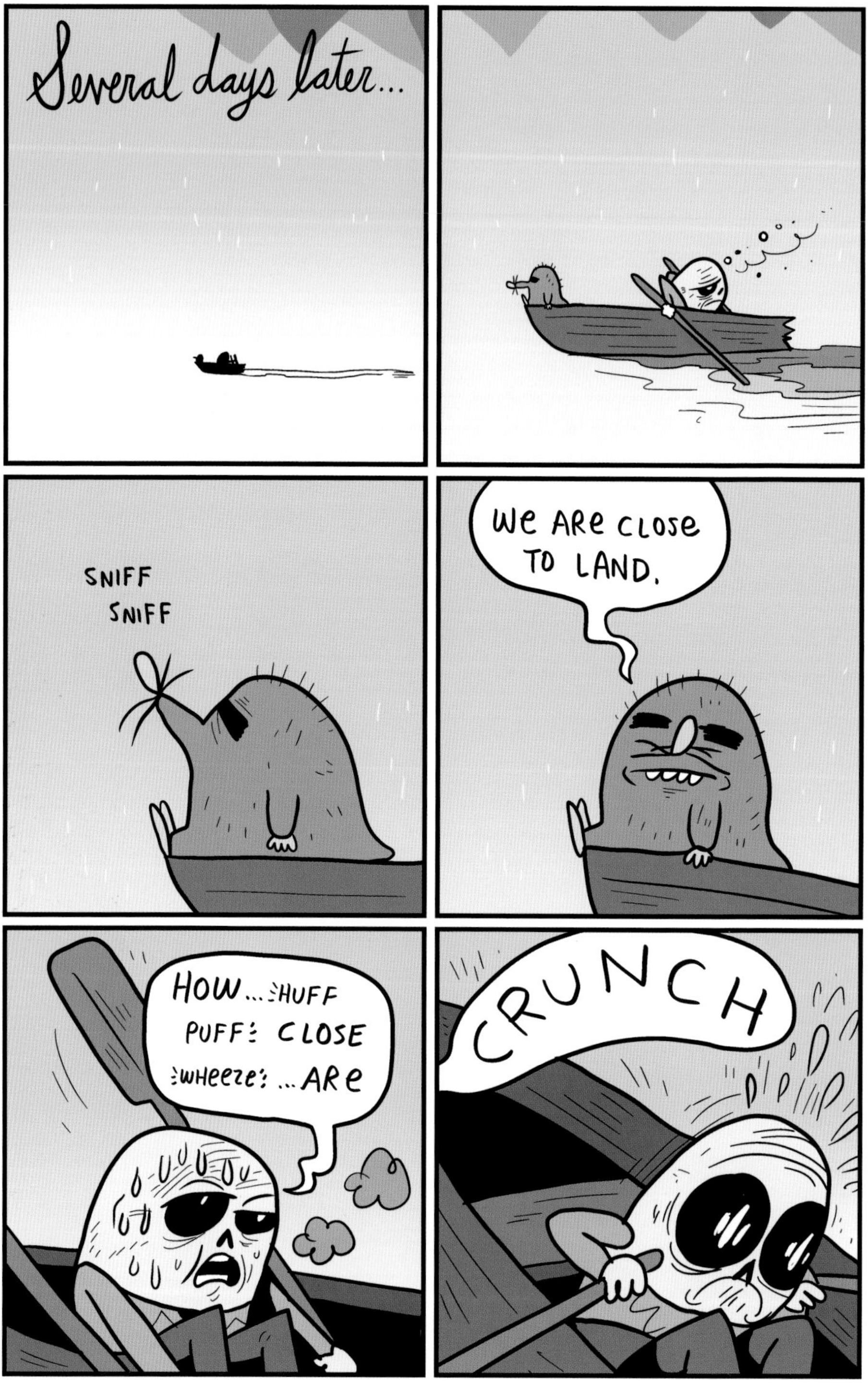
Several days later...
SNIFF
SNIFF
WE ARE CLOSE TO LAND.
HOW... HUFF PUFF CLOSE WHEEZE ...ARE
CRUNCH

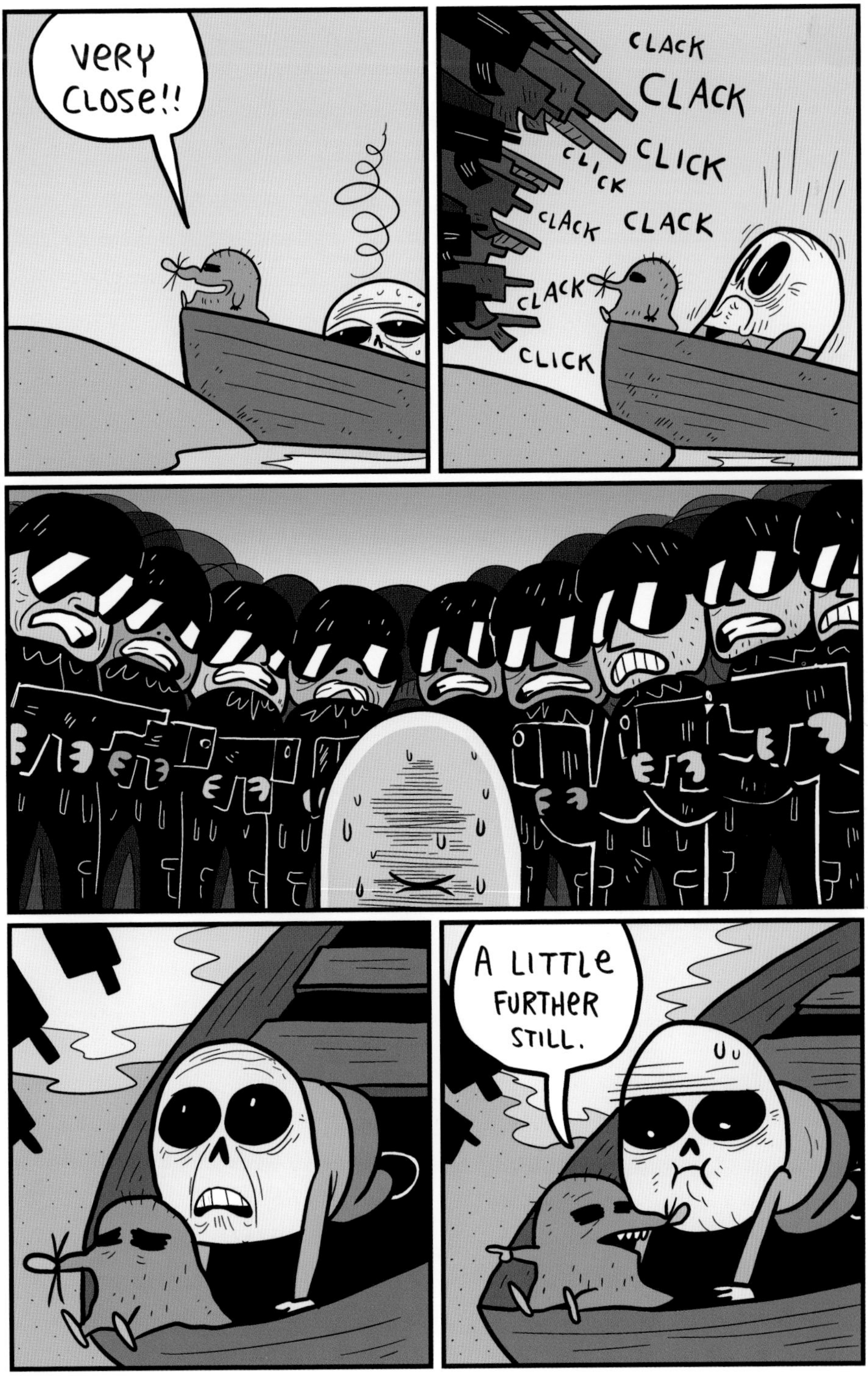
VERY CLOSE!!
CLACK
CLACK
CLICK
CLICK
CLACK
CLACK
CLACK
CLICK
A LITTLE FURTHER STILL.

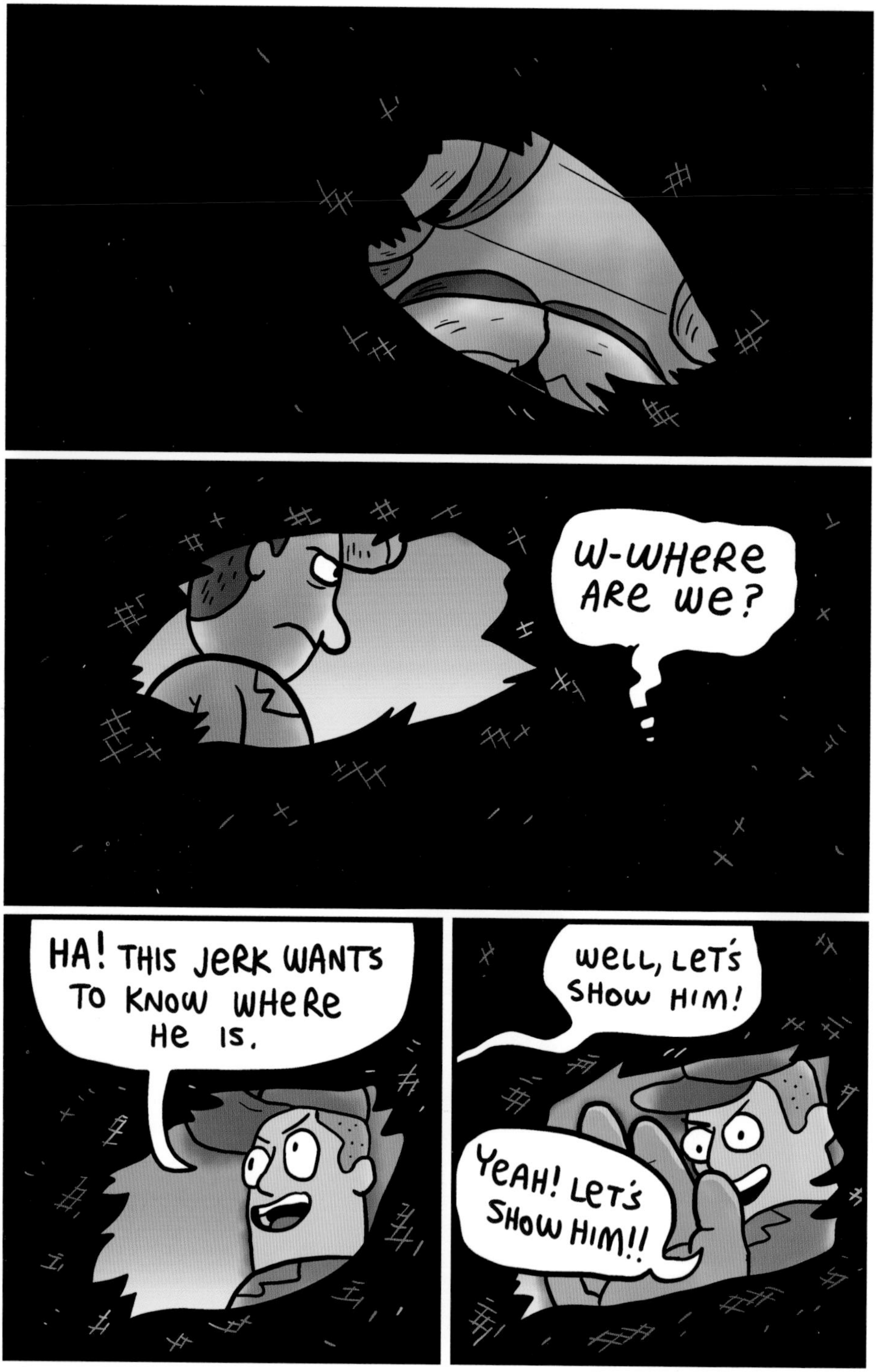
W-WHERE ARE WE?
HA! THIS JERK WANTS TO KNOW WHERE HE IS.
WELL, LET'S SHOW HIM!
YEAH! LET'S SHOW HIM!!

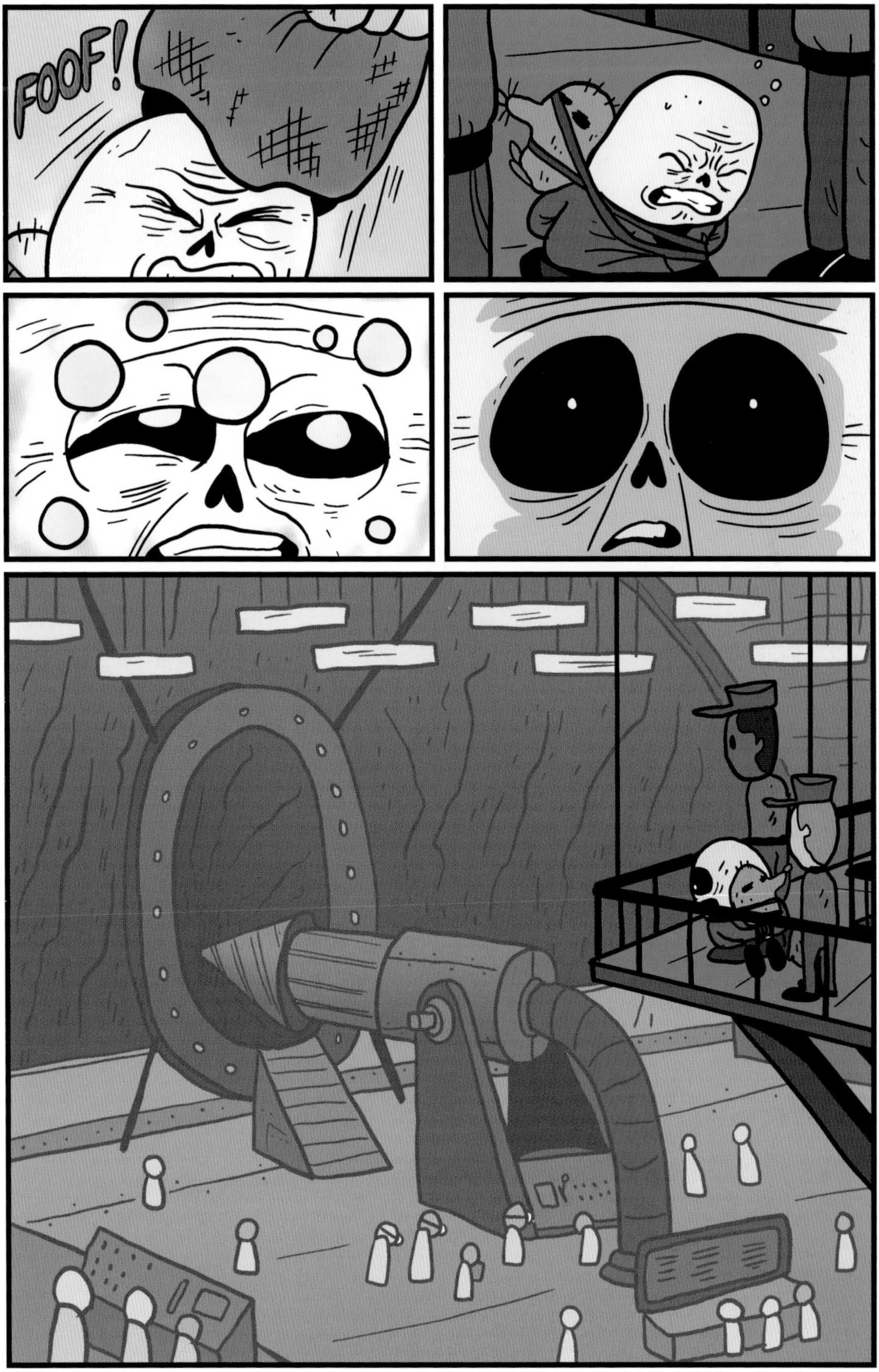
FOOF!

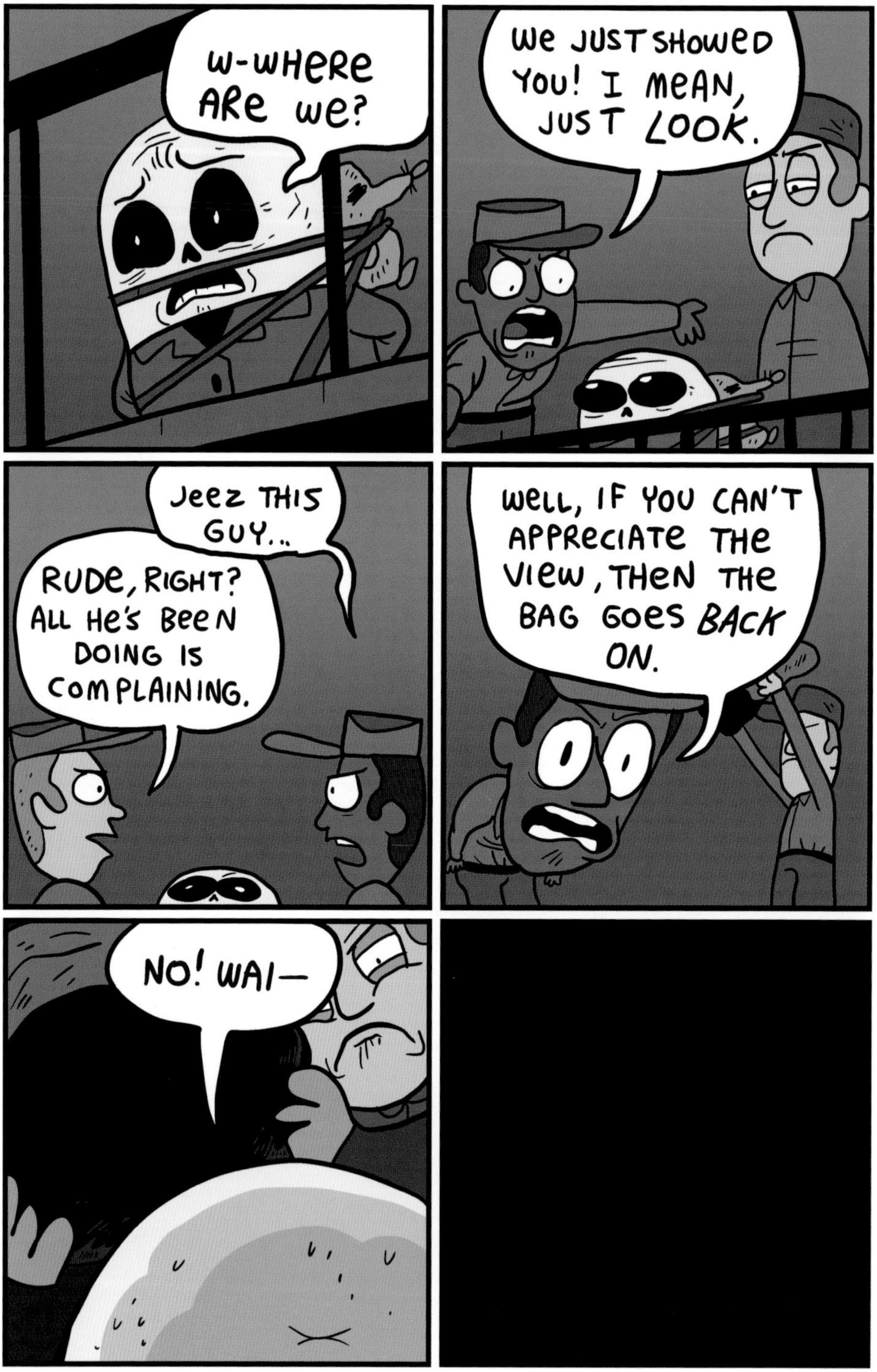
W-WHERE ARE WE?
WE JUST SHOWED YOU! I MEAN, JUST LOOK.
JEEZ THIS GUY...
RUDE, RIGHT? ALL HE'S BEEN DOING IS COMPLAINING.
WELL, IF YOU CAN'T APPRECIATE THE VIEW, THEN THE BAG GOES BACK ON.
NO! WAI—

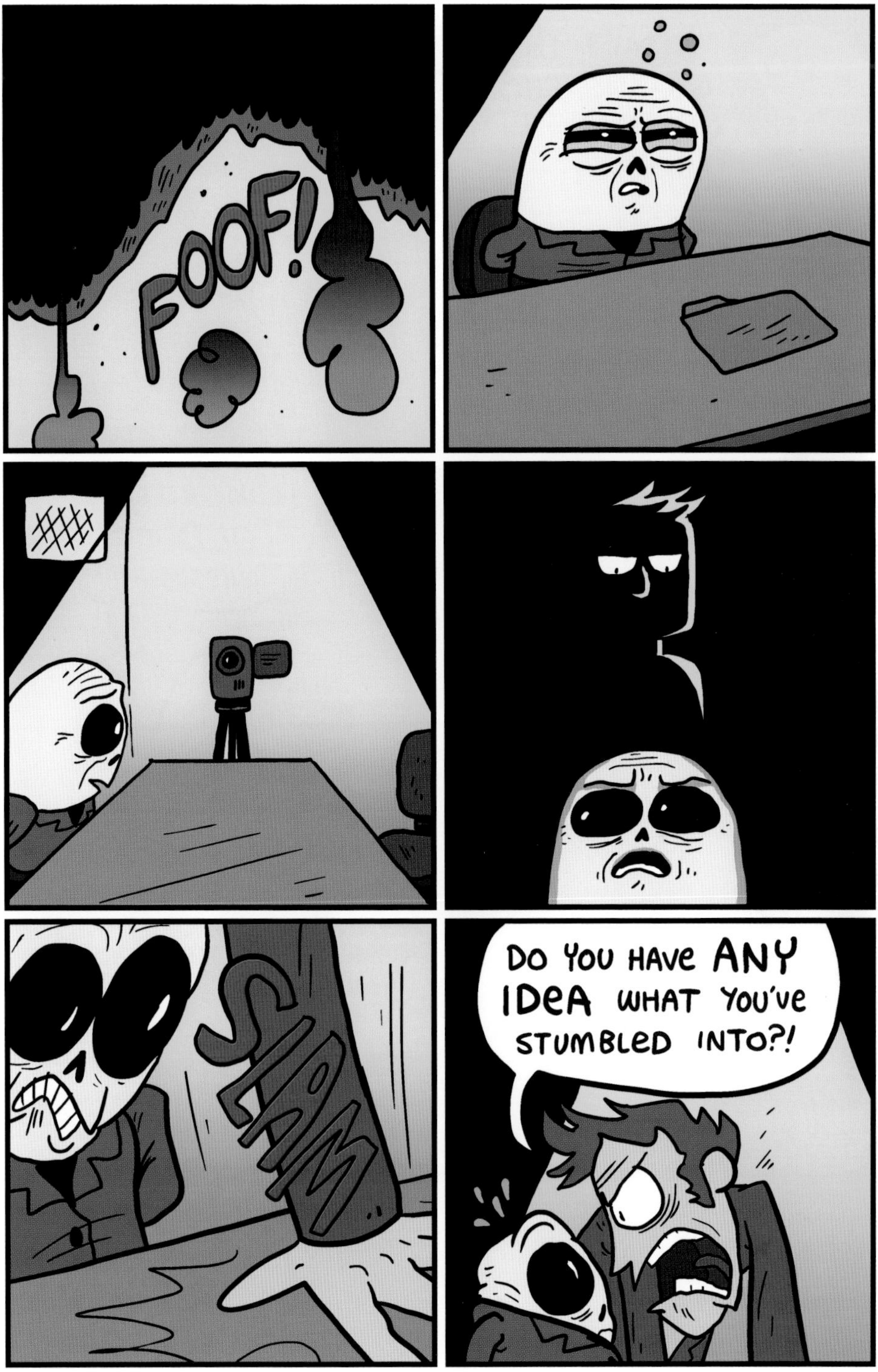
FOOF!
SLAM
DO YOU HAVE ANY IDEA WHAT YOU'VE STUMBLED INTO?!

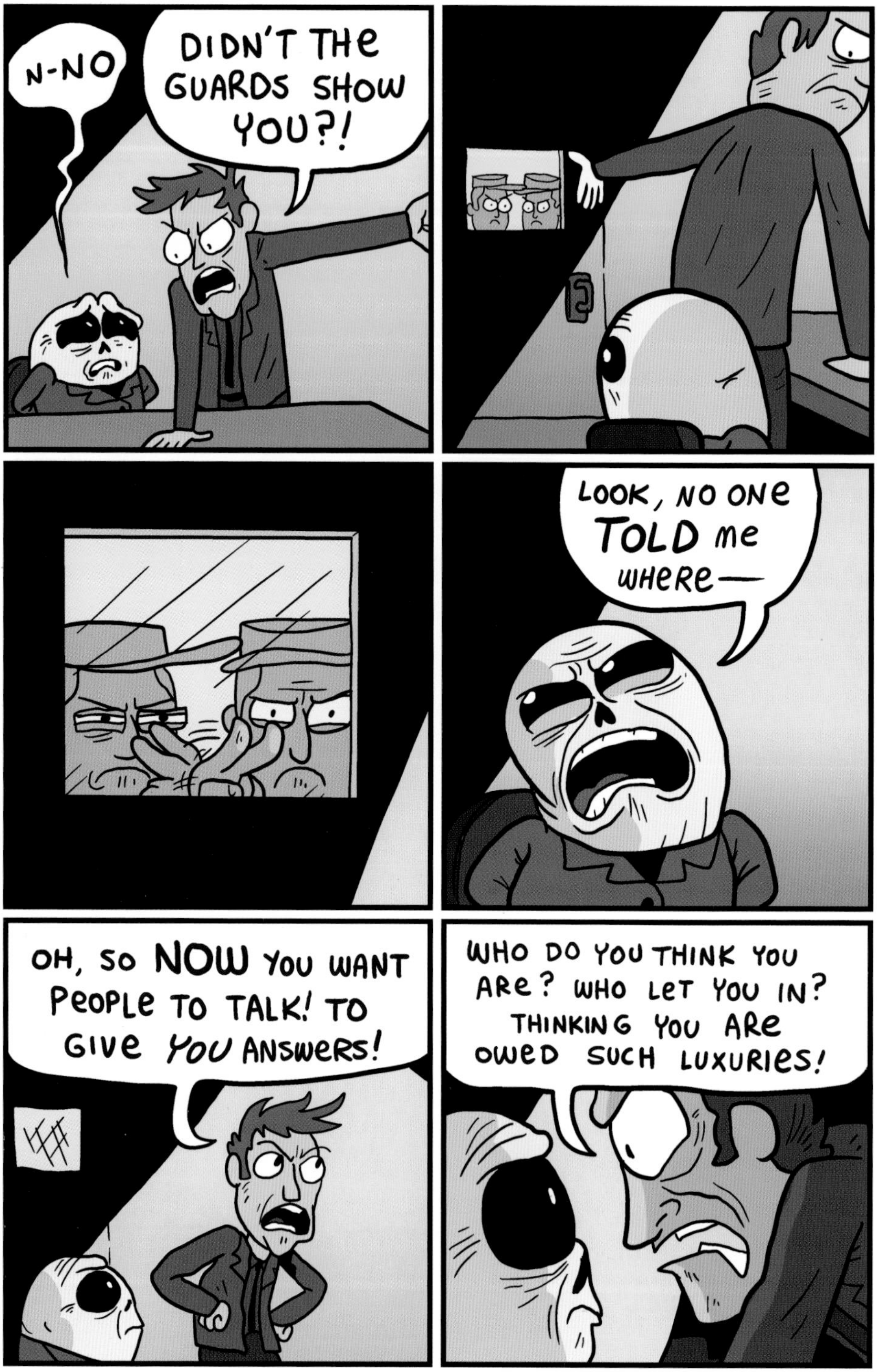
N-NO
DIDN'T THE GUARDS SHOW YOU?!
LOOK, NO ONE TOLD ME WHERE—
OH, SO NOW YOU WANT PEOPLE TO TALK! TO GIVE YOU ANSWERS!
WHO DO YOU THINK YOU ARE? WHO LET YOU IN? THINKING YOU ARE OWED SUCH LUXURIES!

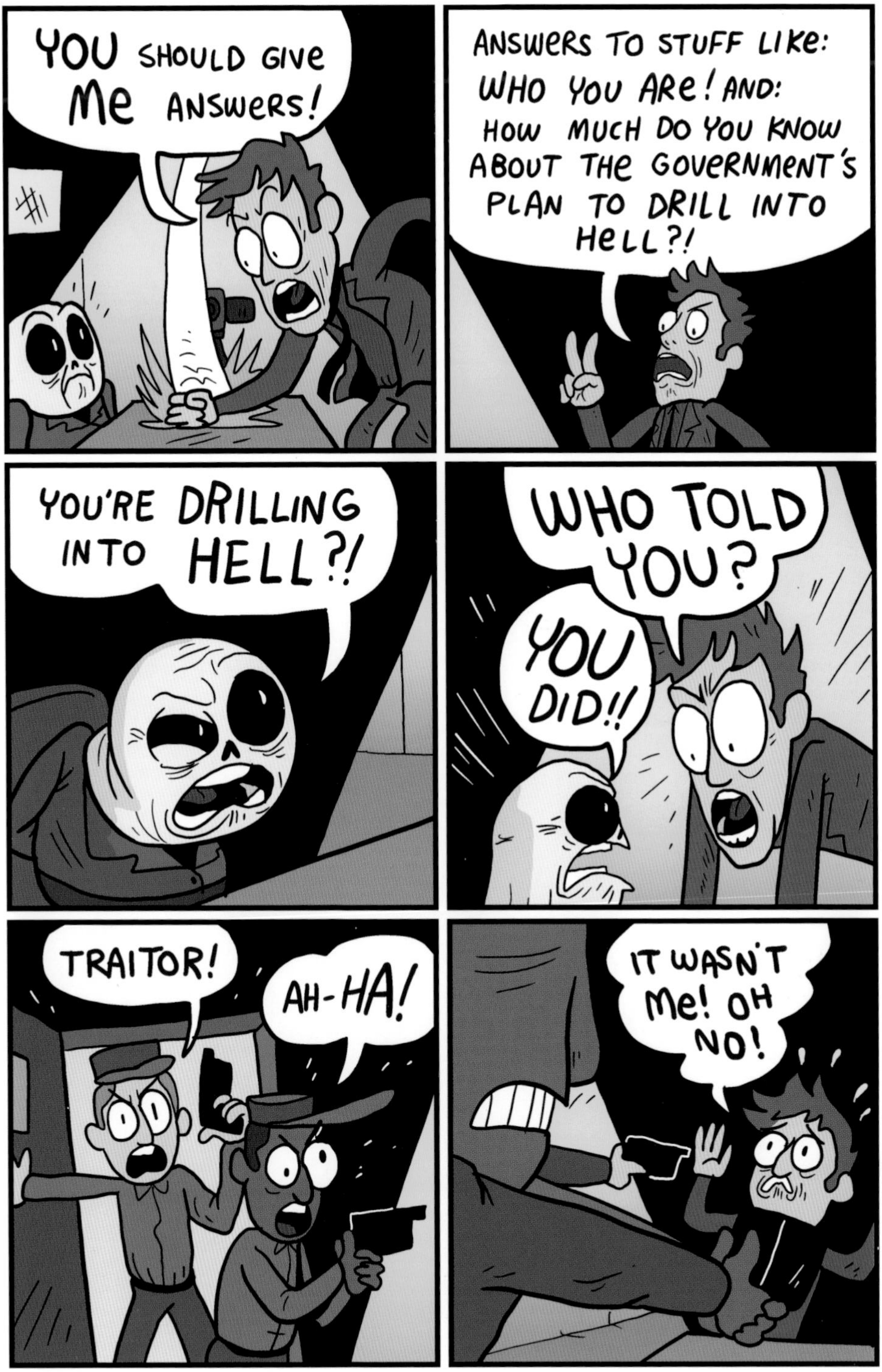
YOU SHOULD GIVE ME ANSWERS!
ANSWERS TO STUFF LIKE: WHO YOU ARE! AND: HOW MUCH DO YOU KNOW ABOUT THE GOVERNMENT'S PLAN TO DRILL INTO HELL?!
YOU'RE DRILLING INTO HELL?!
WHO TOLD YOU?
YOU DID!!
TRAITOR!
AH-HA!
IT WASN'T ME! OH NO!

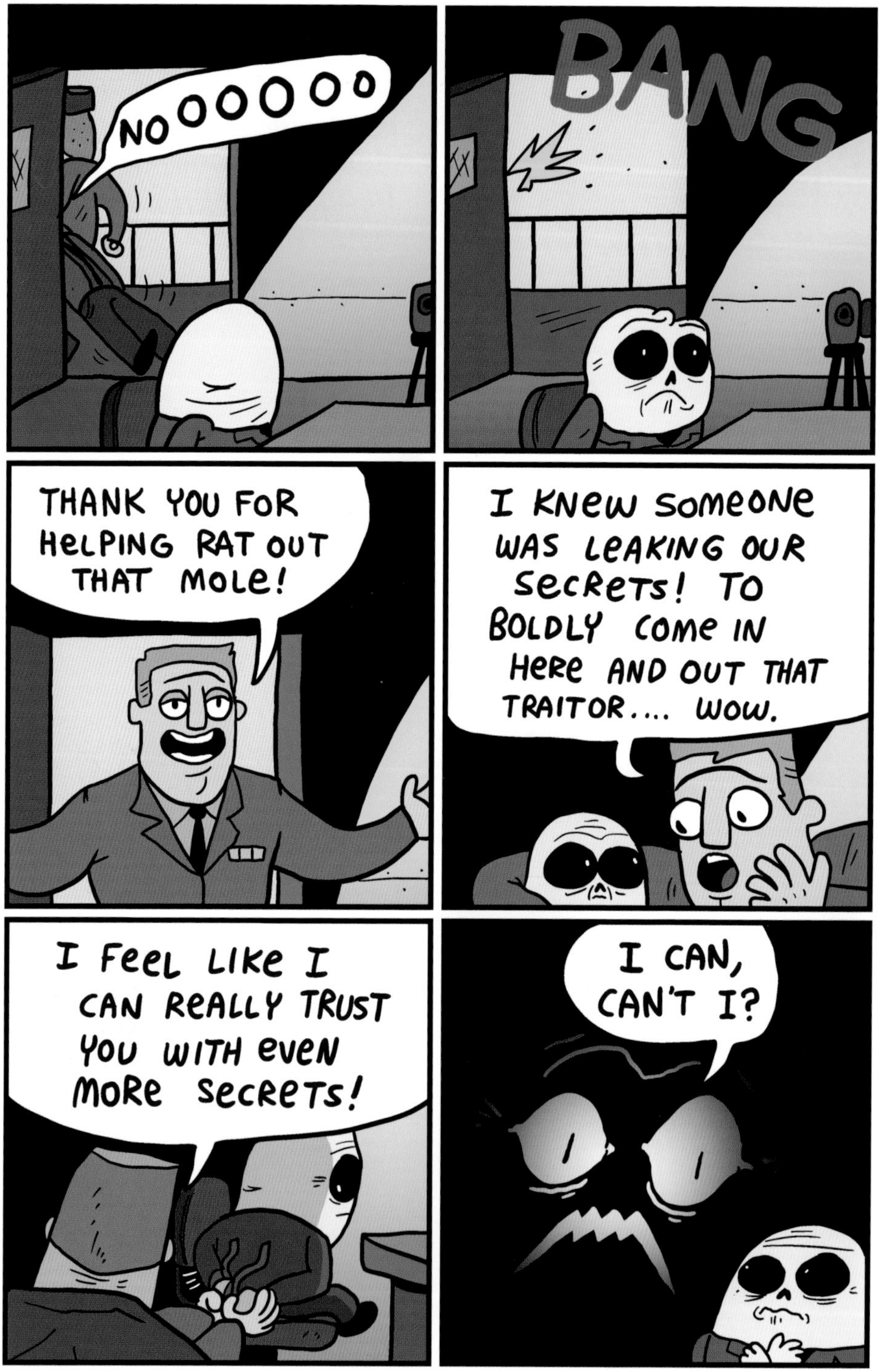
NOOOOOO
BANG
THANK YOU FOR HELPING RAT OUT THAT MOLE!
I KNEW SOMEONE WAS LEAKING OUR SECRETS! TO BOLDLY COME IN HERE AND OUT THAT TRAITOR.... WOW.
I FEEL LIKE I CAN REALLY TRUST YOU WITH EVEN MORE SECRETS!
I CAN, CAN'T I?

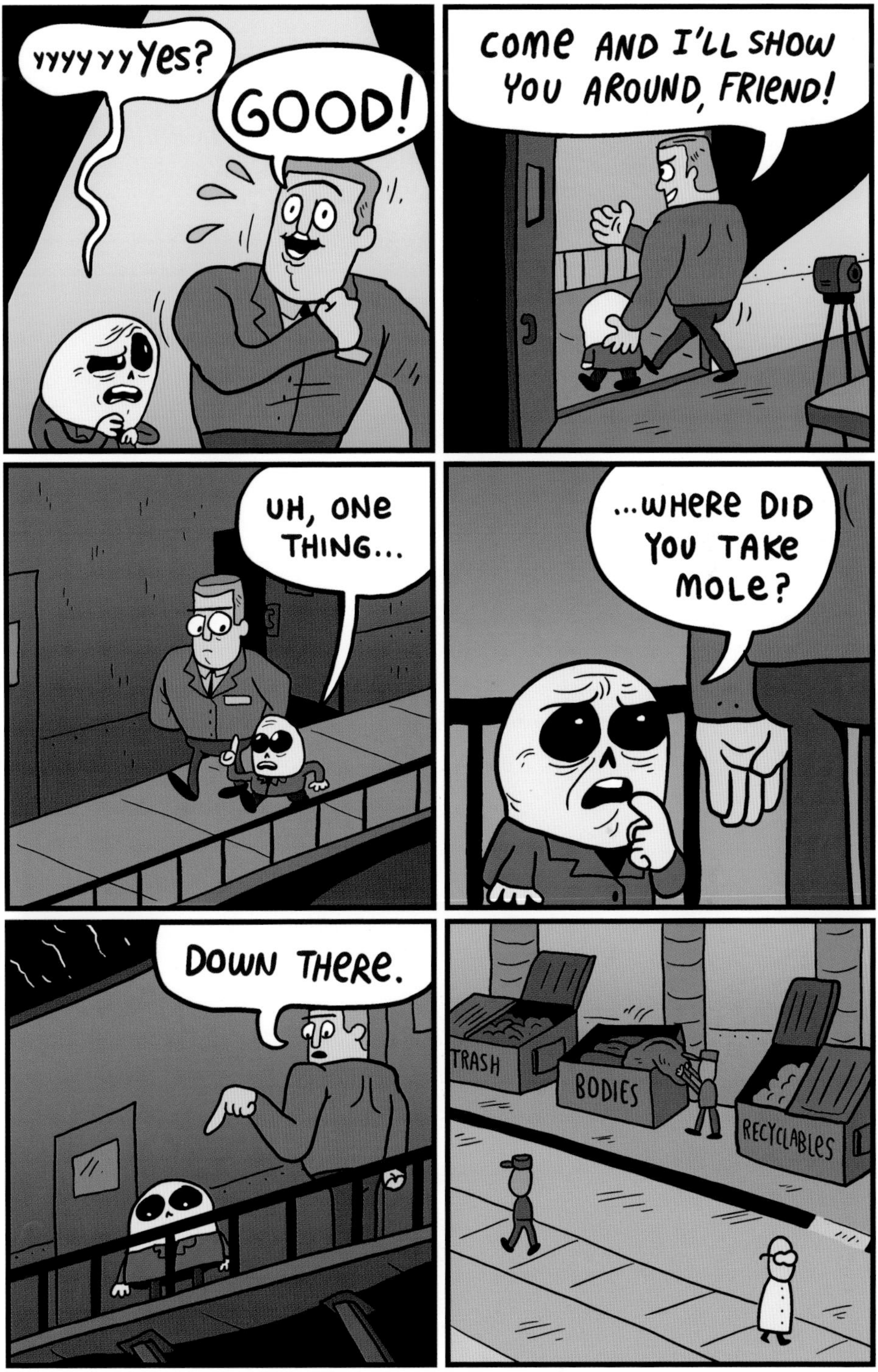
yyyyyyyYes?
GOOD!
COME AND I'LL SHOW YOU AROUND, FRIEND!
UH, ONE THING...
...WHERE DID YOU TAKE MOLE?
DOWN THERE.
TRASH
BODIES
RECYCLABLES

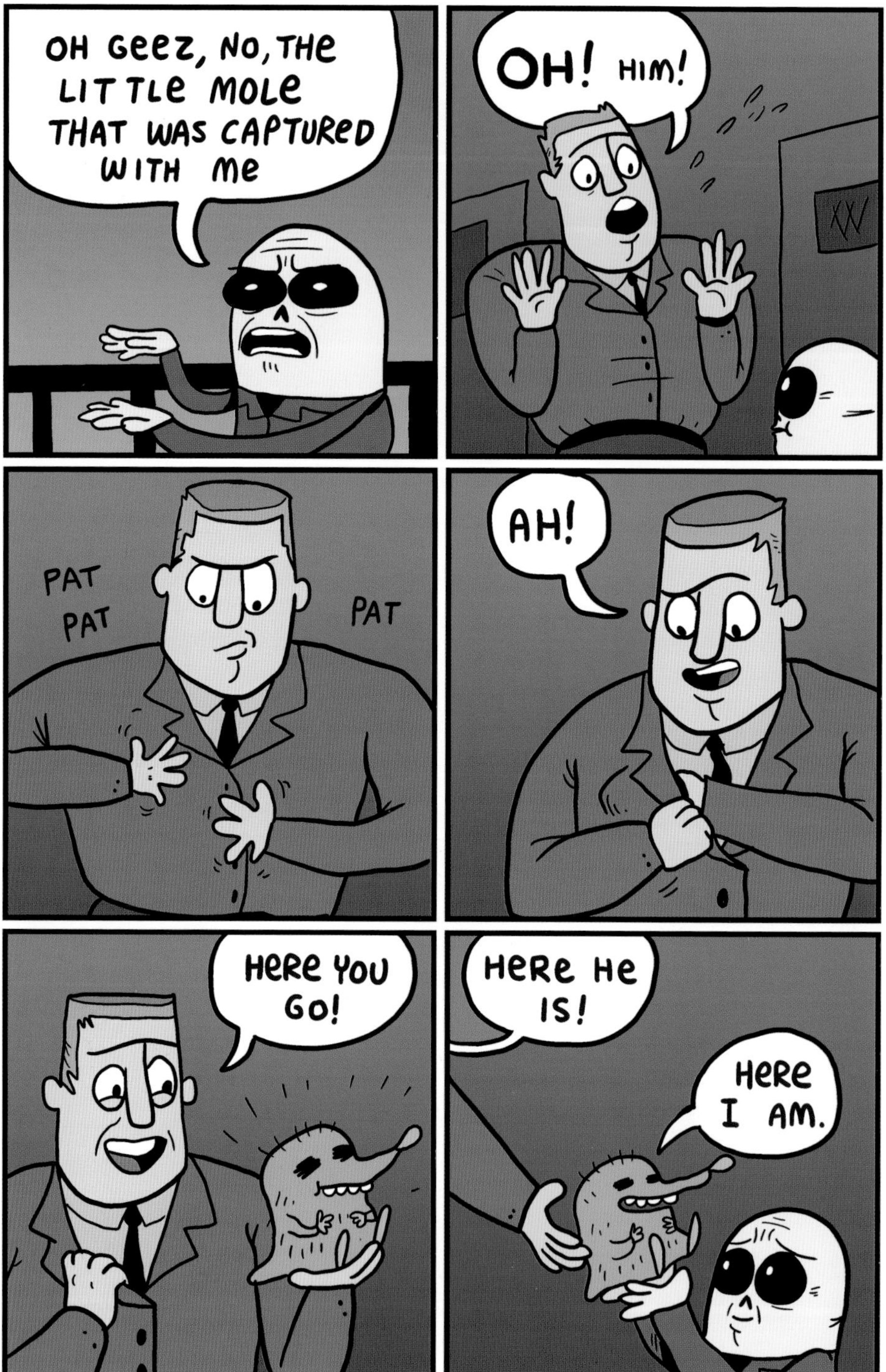
OH GEEZ, NO, THE LITTLE MOLE THAT WAS CAPTURED WITH ME
OH! HIM!
PAT PAT
PAT
AH!
HERE YOU GO!
HERE HE IS!
HERE I AM.

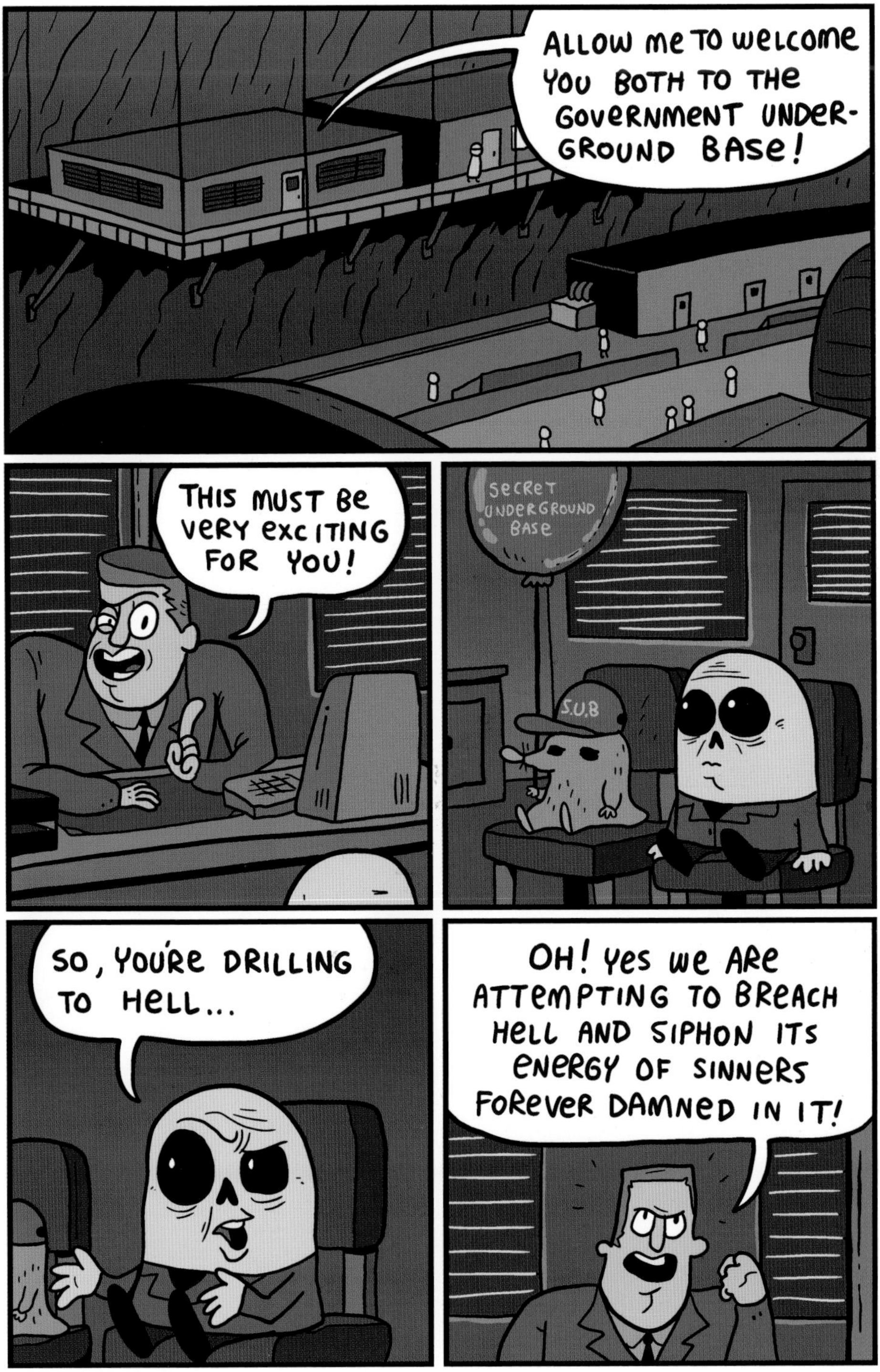
ALLOW ME TO WELCOME YOU BOTH TO THE GOVERNMENT UNDER-GROUND BASE!
THIS MUST BE VERY EXCITING FOR YOU!
SECRET UNDERGROUND BASE
S.U.B
SO, YOU'RE DRILLING TO HELL...
OH! YES WE ARE ATTEMPTING TO BREACH HELL AND SIPHON ITS ENERGY OF SINNERS FOREVER DAMNED IN IT!

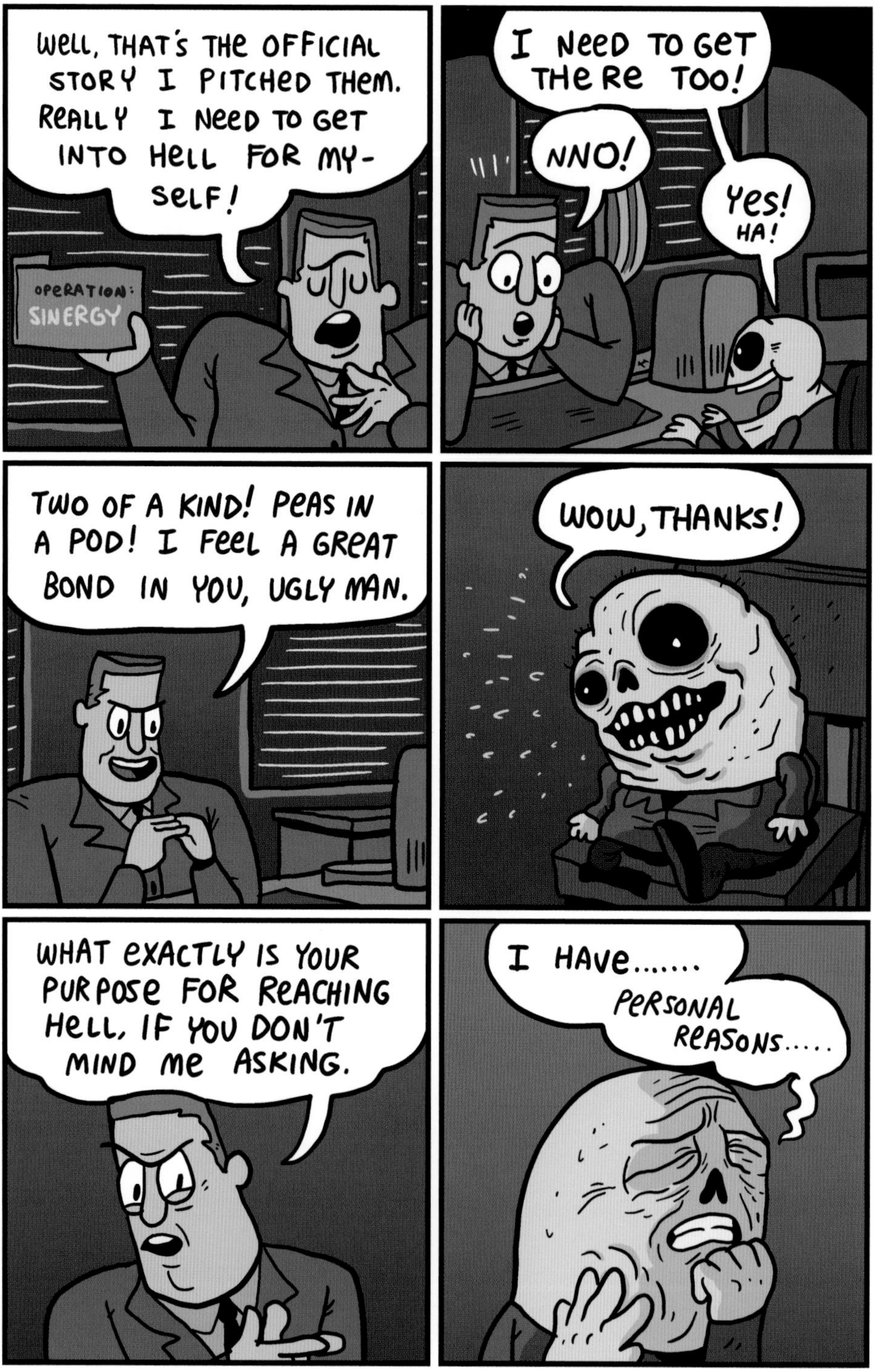
WELL, THAT'S THE OFFICIAL STORY I PITCHED THEM. REALLY I NEED TO GET INTO HELL FOR MY-SELF!
OPERATION: SINERGY
I NEED TO GET THERE TOO!
NNO!
YES! HA!
TWO OF A KIND! PEAS IN A POD! I FEEL A GREAT BOND IN YOU, UGLY MAN.
WOW, THANKS!
WHAT EXACTLY IS YOUR PURPOSE FOR REACHING HELL, IF YOU DON'T MIND ME ASKING.
I HAVE....... PERSONAL REASONS.....

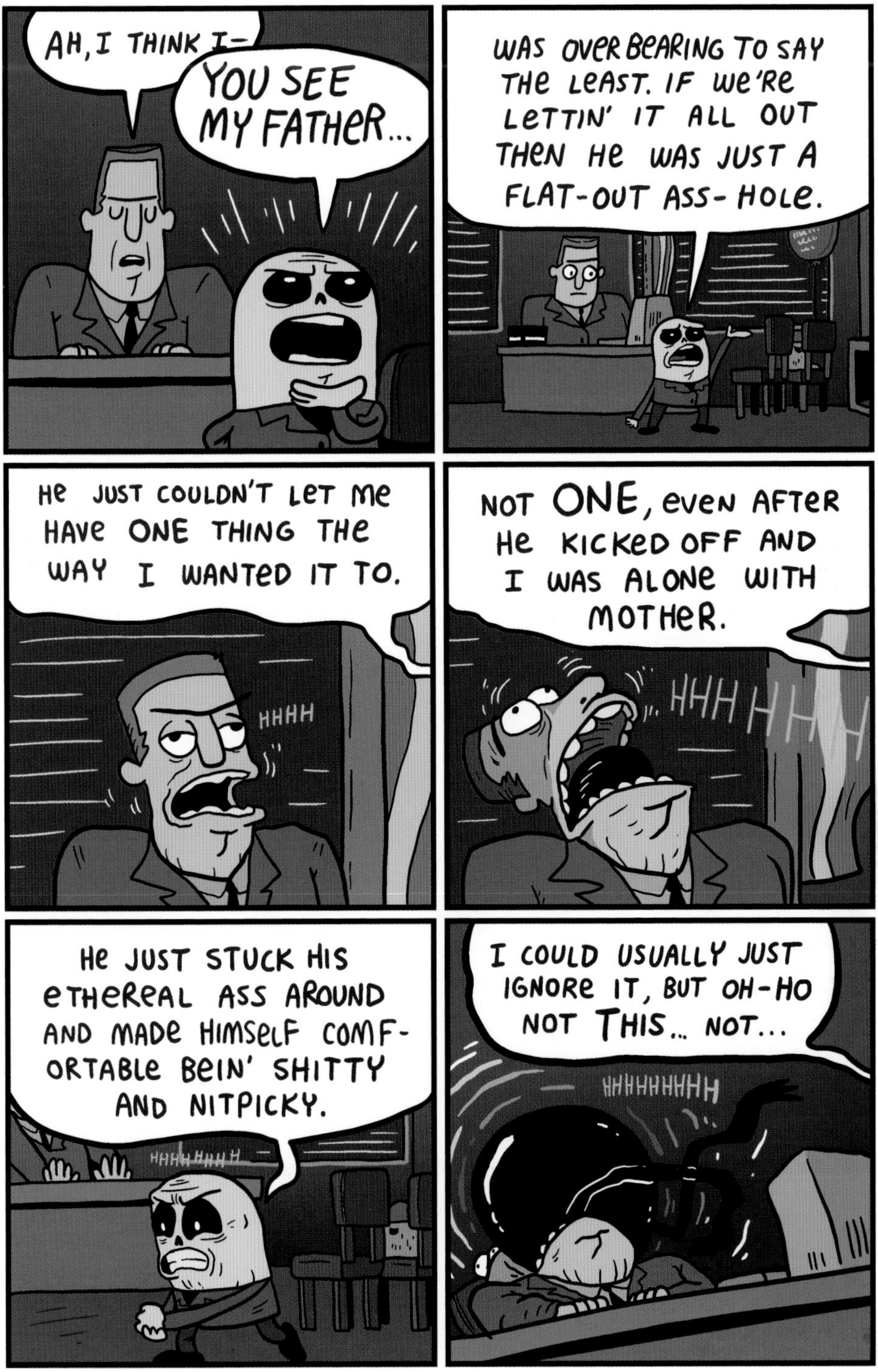
AH, I THINK I—
YOU SEE MY FATHER...
WAS OVERBEARING TO SAY THE LEAST. IF WE'RE LETTIN' IT ALL OUT THEN HE WAS JUST A FLAT-OUT ASS-HOLE.
HE JUST COULDN'T LET ME HAVE ONE THING THE WAY I WANTED IT TO.
HHHH
NOT ONE, EVEN AFTER HE KICKED OFF AND I WAS ALONE WITH MOTHER.
HHHHHH
HE JUST STUCK HIS ETHEREAL ASS AROUND AND MADE HIMSELF COMF-ORTABLE BEIN' SHITTY AND NITPICKY.
HHHHHHHH
I COULD USUALLY JUST IGNORE IT, BUT OH-HO NOT THIS... NOT...
HHHHHHHHH

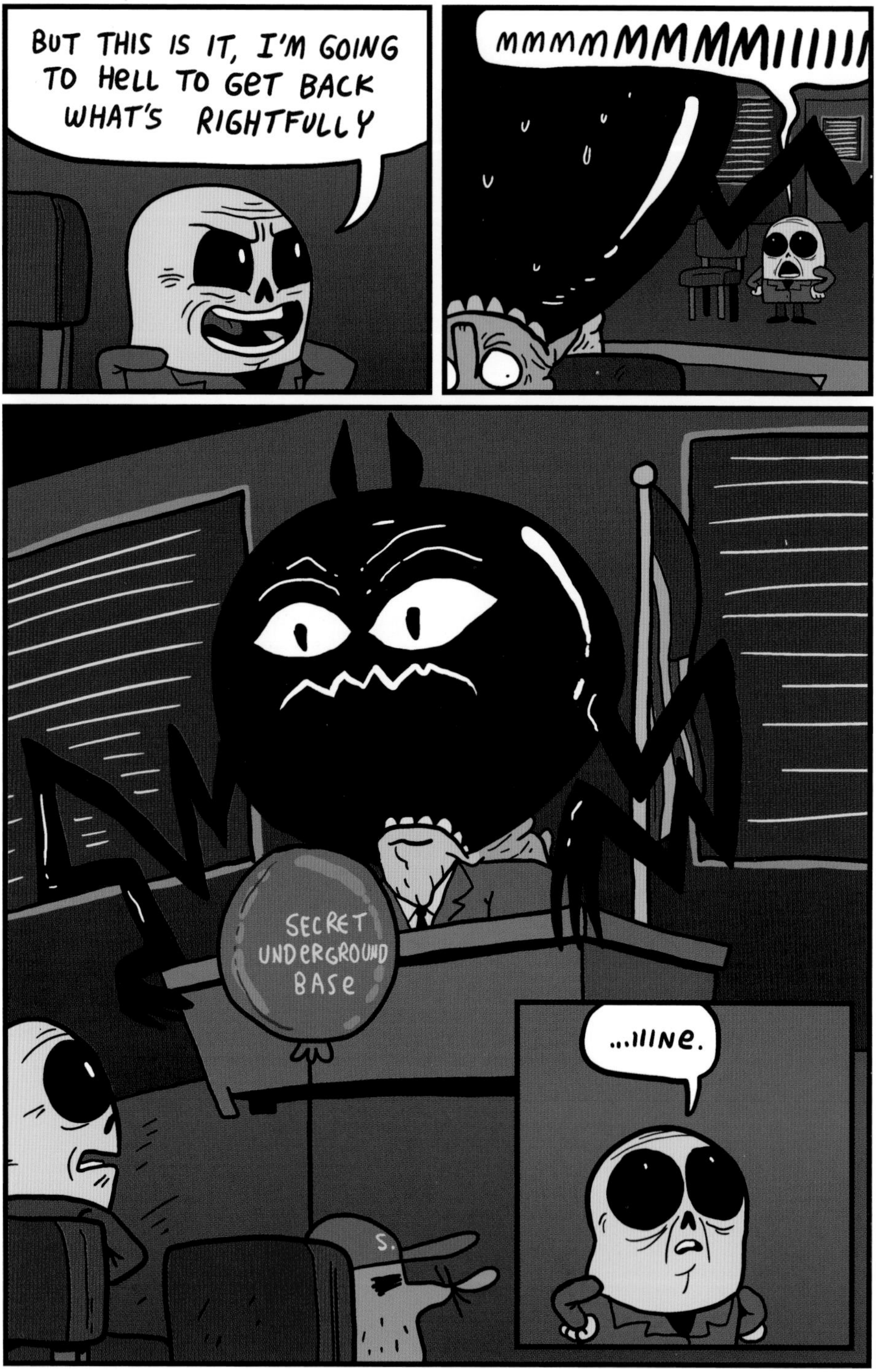
BUT THIS IS IT, I'M GOING TO HELL TO GET BACK WHAT'S RIGHTFULLY
MMMMMMMMIIIII
SECRET UNDERGROUND BASE
...IIINE.

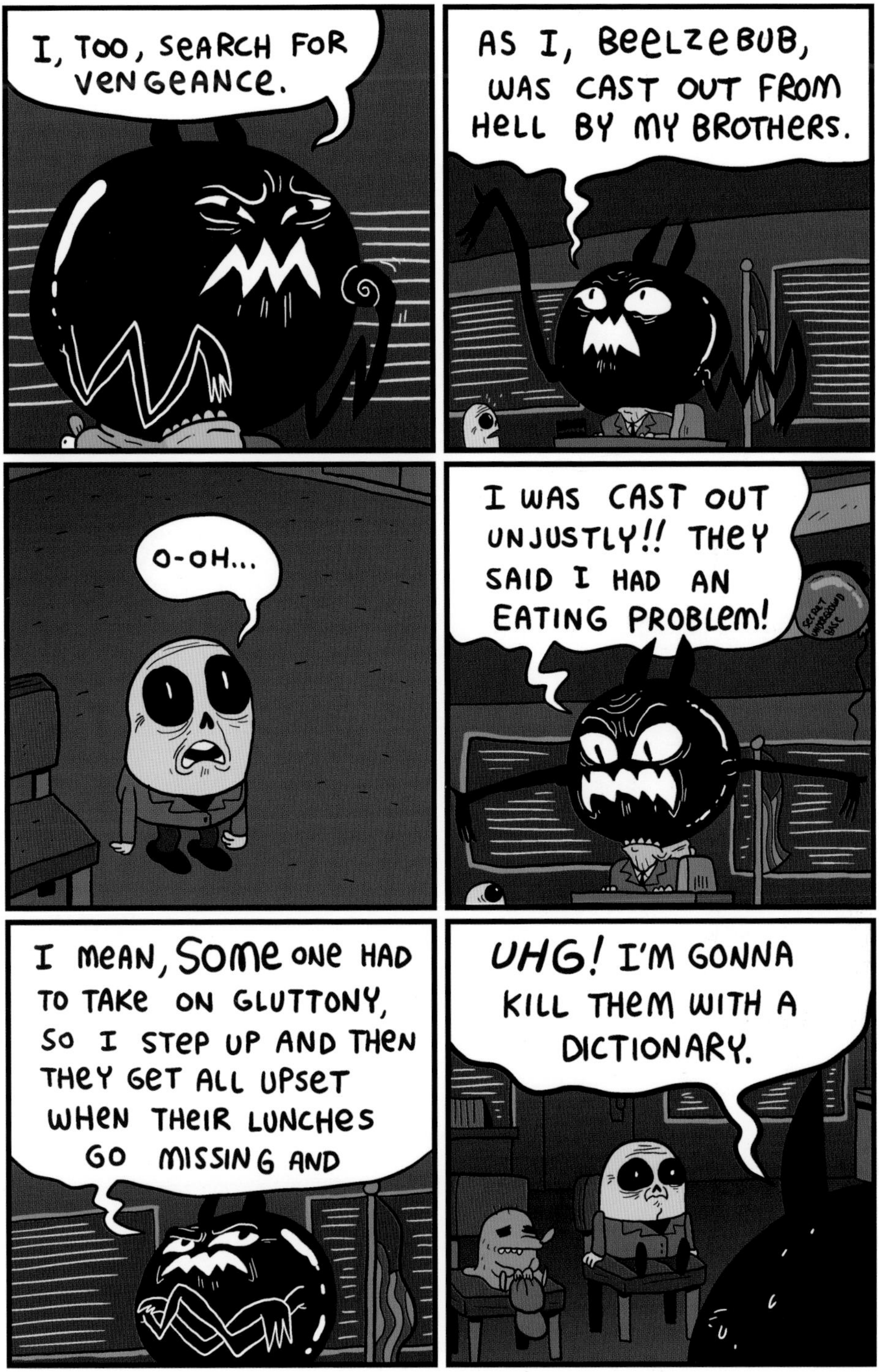
I, TOO, SEARCH FOR VENGEANCE.
AS I, BEELZEBUB, WAS CAST OUT FROM HELL BY MY BROTHERS.
O-OH...
I WAS CAST OUT UNJUSTLY!! THEY SAID I HAD AN EATING PROBLEM!
I MEAN, SOME ONE HAD TO TAKE ON GLUTTONY, SO I STEP UP AND THEN THEY GET ALL UPSET WHEN THEIR LUNCHES GO MISSING AND
UHG! I'M GONNA KILL THEM WITH A DICTIONARY.

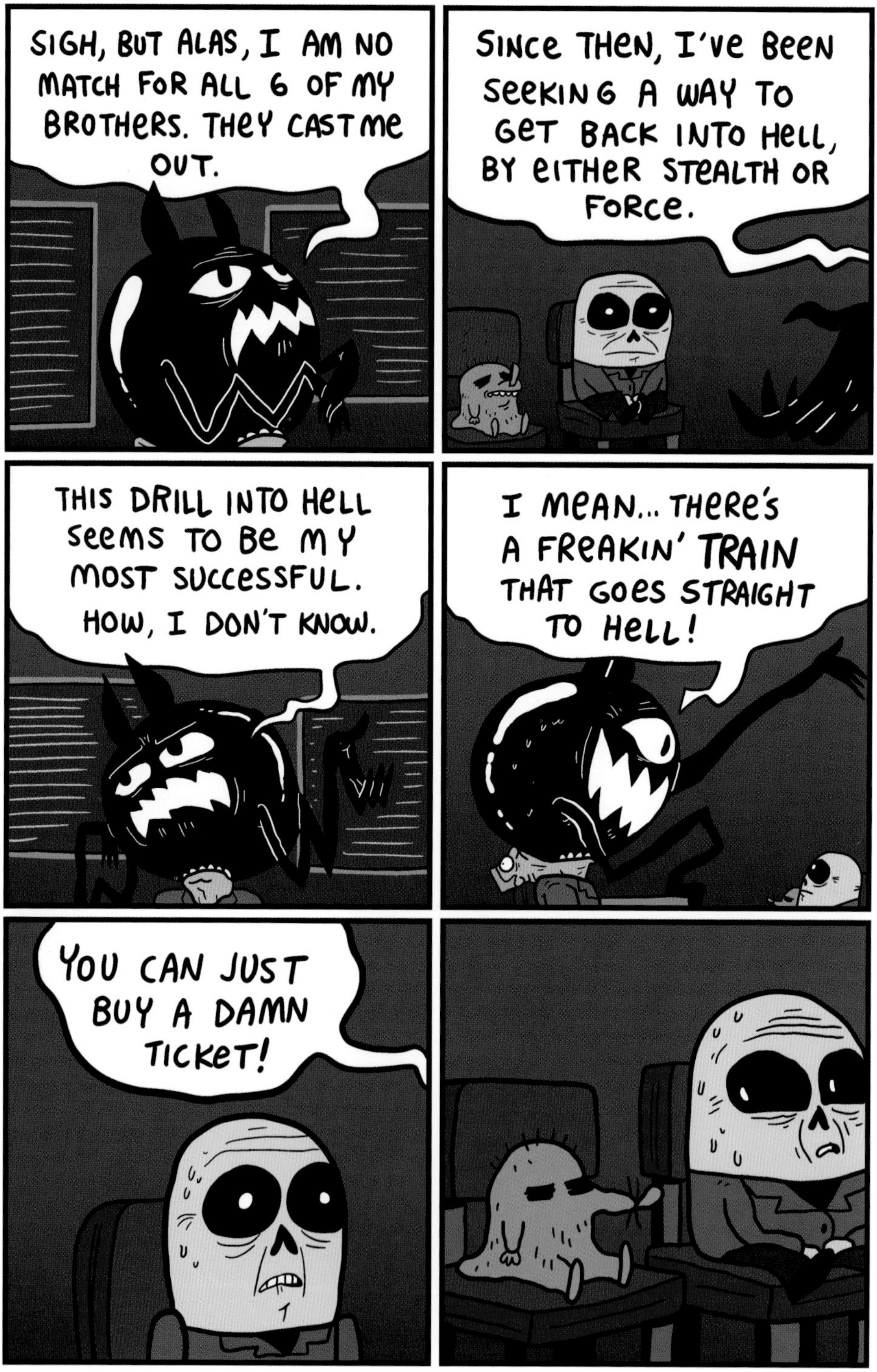
SIGH, BUT ALAS, I AM NO MATCH FOR ALL 6 OF MY BROTHERS. THEY CAST ME OUT.
SINCE THEN, I'VE BEEN SEEKING A WAY TO GET BACK INTO HELL, BY EITHER STEALTH OR FORCE.
THIS DRILL INTO HELL SEEMS TO BE MY MOST SUCCESSFUL. HOW, I DON'T KNOW.
I MEAN... THERE'S A FREAKIN' TRAIN THAT GOES STRAIGHT TO HELL!
YOU CAN JUST BUY A DAMN TICKET!

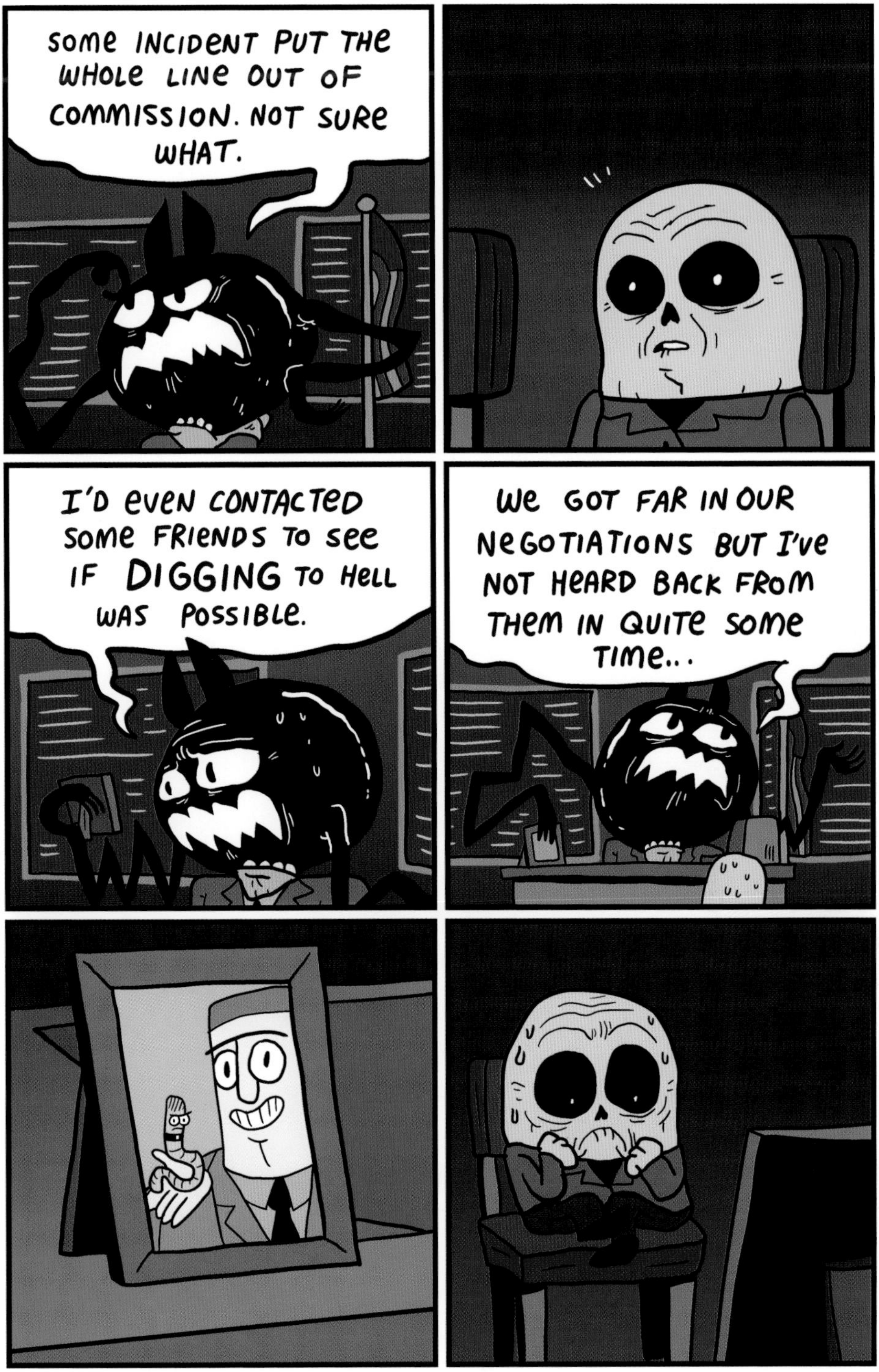
SOME INCIDENT PUT THE WHOLE LINE OUT OF COMMISSION. NOT SURE WHAT.
I'D EVEN CONTACTED SOME FRIENDS TO SEE IF DIGGING TO HELL WAS POSSIBLE.
WE GOT FAR IN OUR NEGOTIATIONS BUT I'VE NOT HEARD BACK FROM THEM IN QUITE SOME TIME...

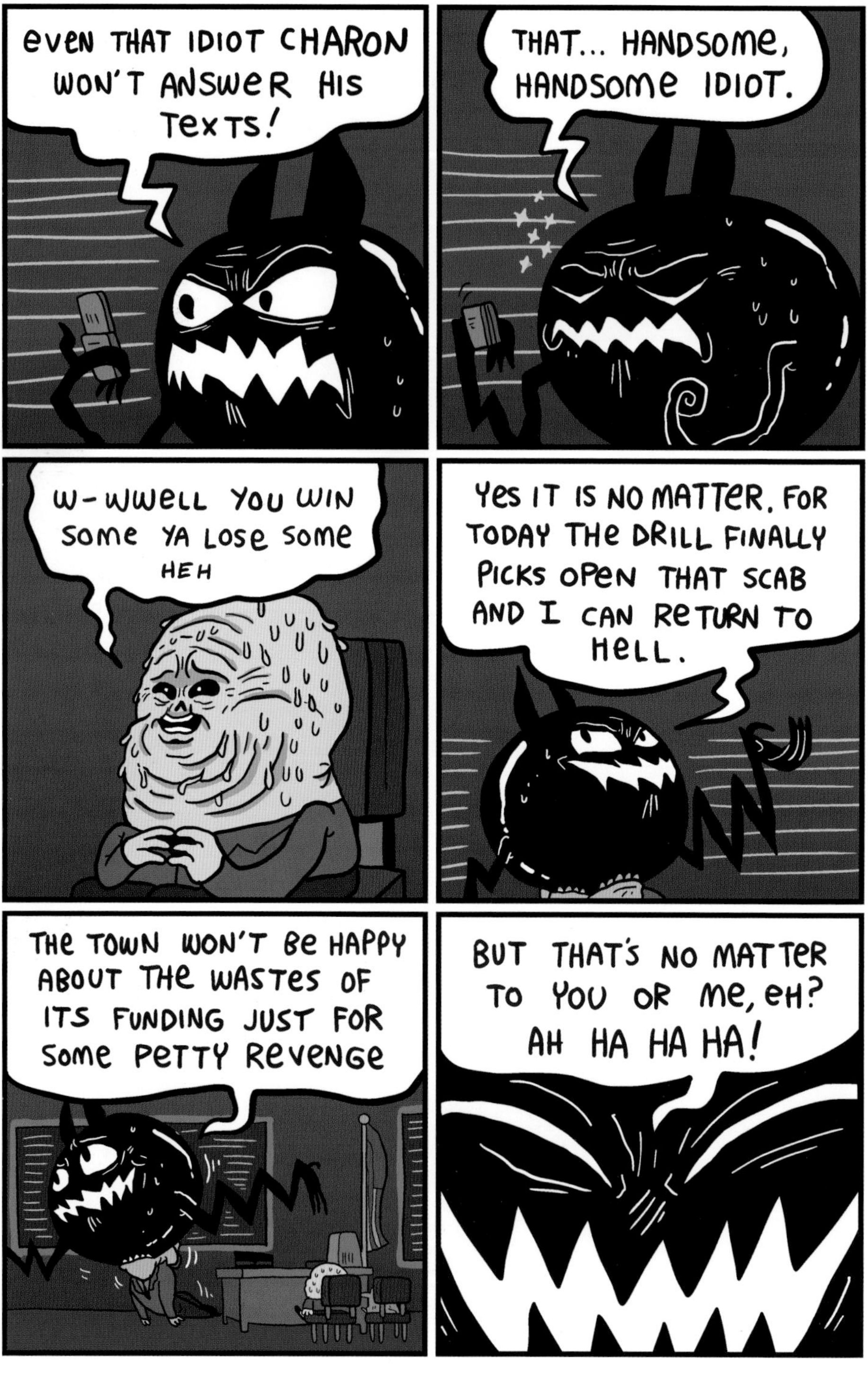
EVEN THAT IDIOT CHARON WON'T ANSWER HIS TEXTS!
THAT... HANDSOME, HANDSOME IDIOT.
W-WWELL YOU WIN SOME YA LOSE SOME HEH
YES IT IS NO MATTER. FOR TODAY THE DRILL FINALLY PICKS OPEN THAT SCAB AND I CAN RETURN TO HELL.
THE TOWN WON'T BE HAPPY ABOUT THE WASTES OF ITS FUNDING JUST FOR SOME PETTY REVENGE
BUT THAT'S NO MATTER TO YOU OR ME, EH? AH HA HA HA!

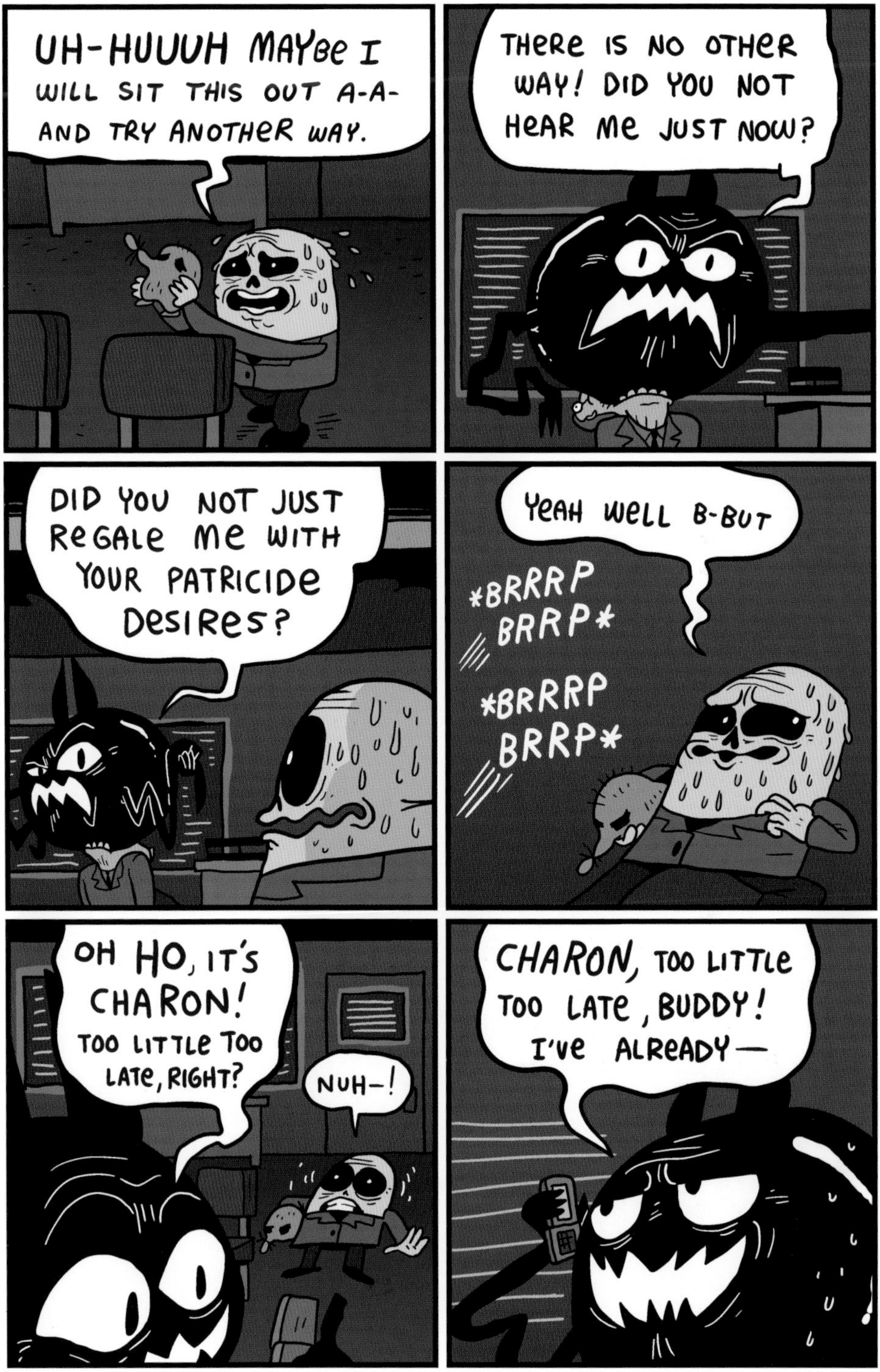
UH-HUUUH MAYBE I WILL SIT THIS OUT A-A-AND TRY ANOTHER WAY.
THERE IS NO OTHER WAY! DID YOU NOT HEAR ME JUST NOW?
DID YOU NOT JUST REGALE ME WITH YOUR PATRICIDE DESIRES?
YEAH WELL B-BUT
BRRRP BRRP
BRRRP BRRP
OH HO, IT'S CHARON! TOO LITTLE TOO LATE, RIGHT?
NUH-!
CHARON, TOO LITTLE TOO LATE, BUDDY! I'VE ALREADY—

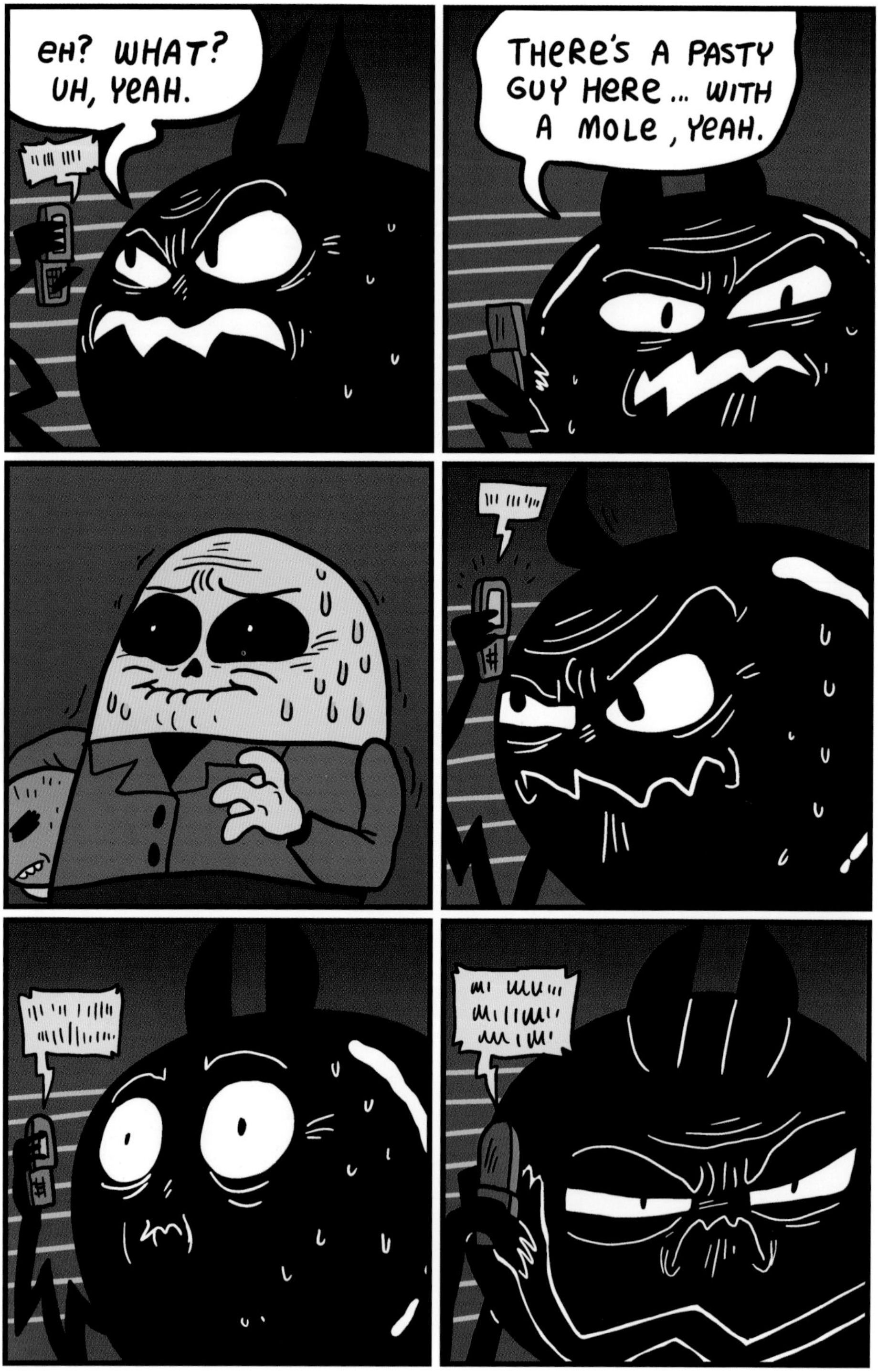
EH? WHAT? UH, YEAH.
THERE'S A PASTY GUY HERE... WITH A MOLE, YEAH.

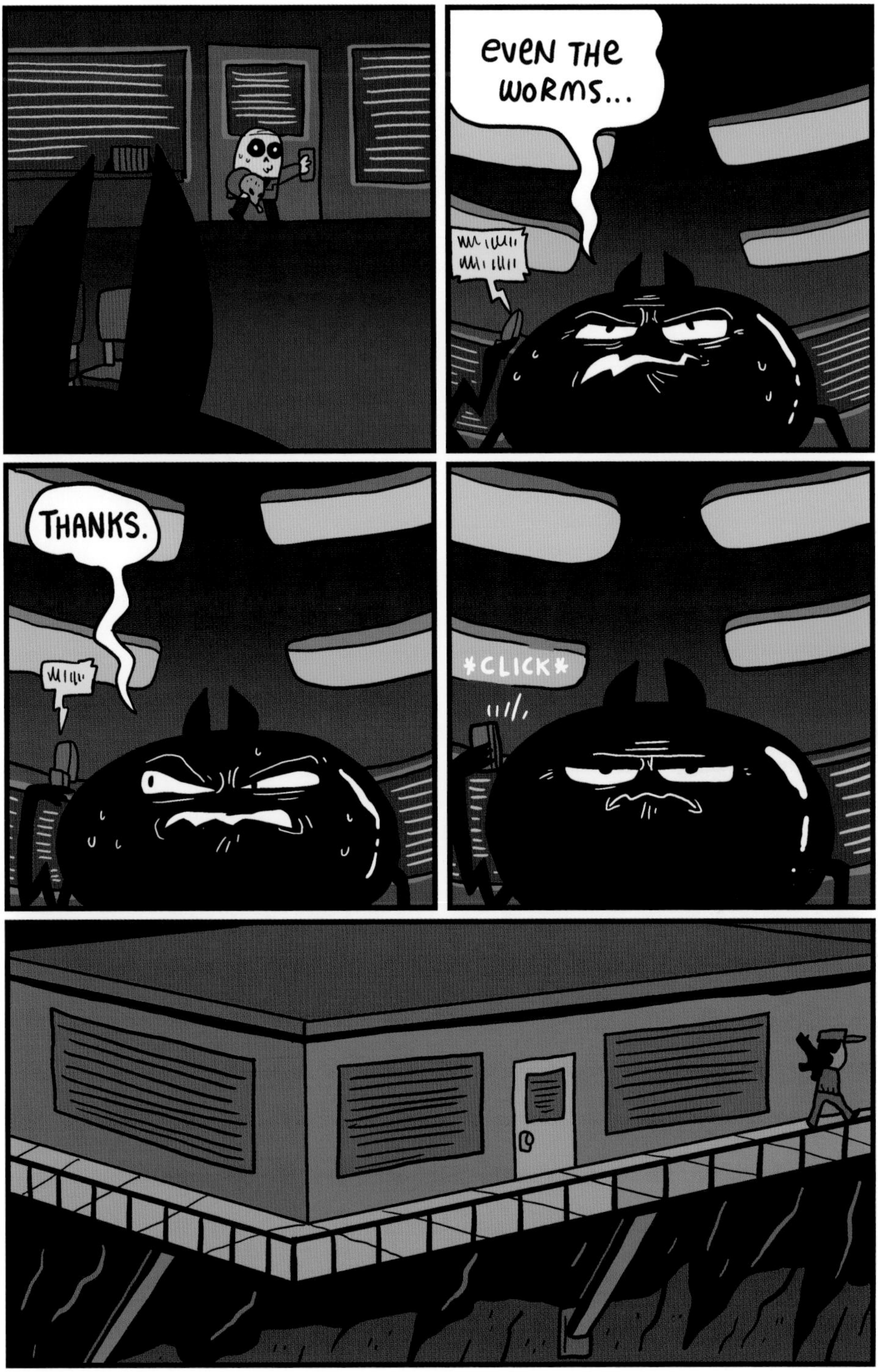
even THE WORMS...
THANKS.
CLICK

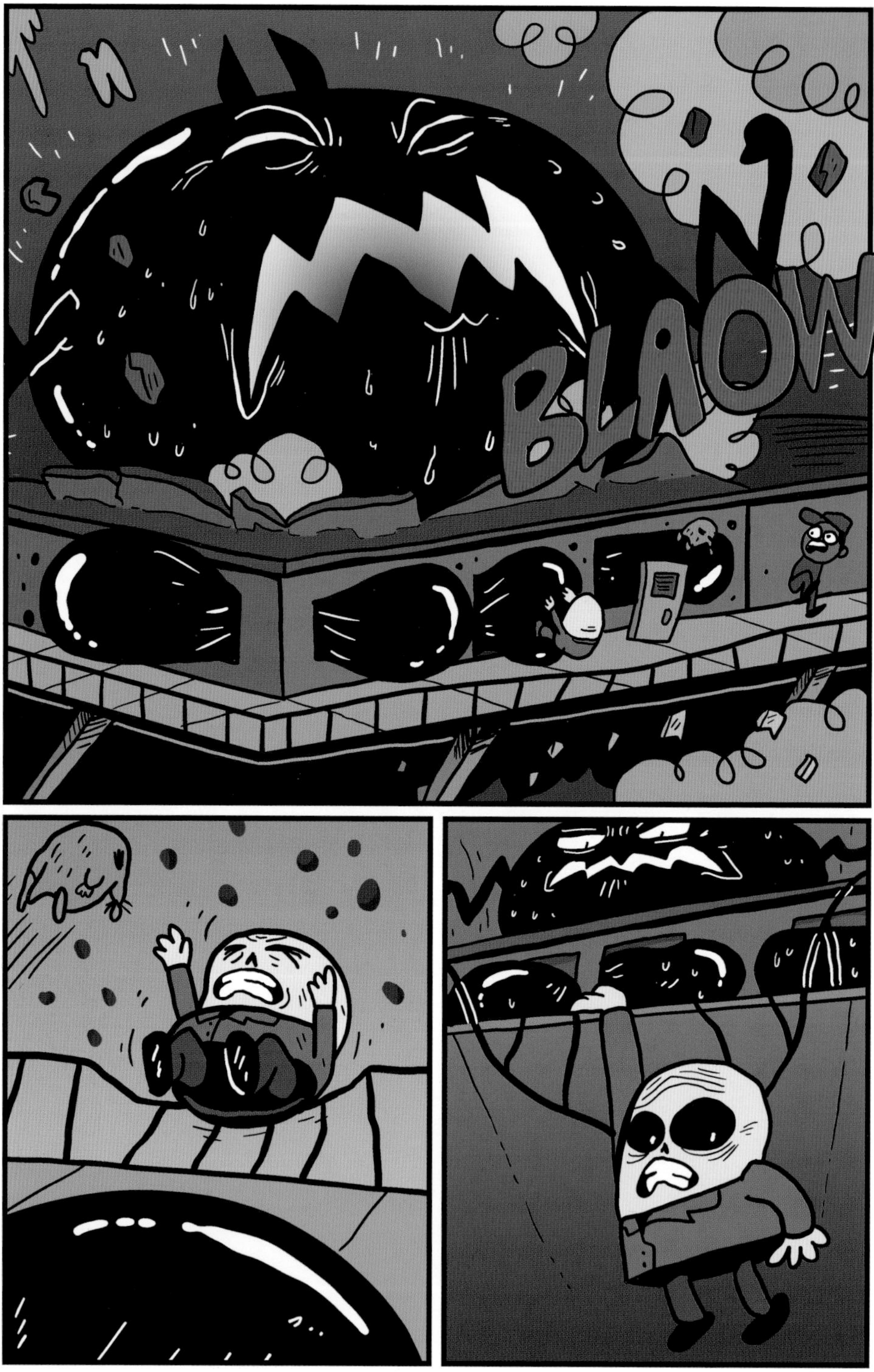
BLAOW

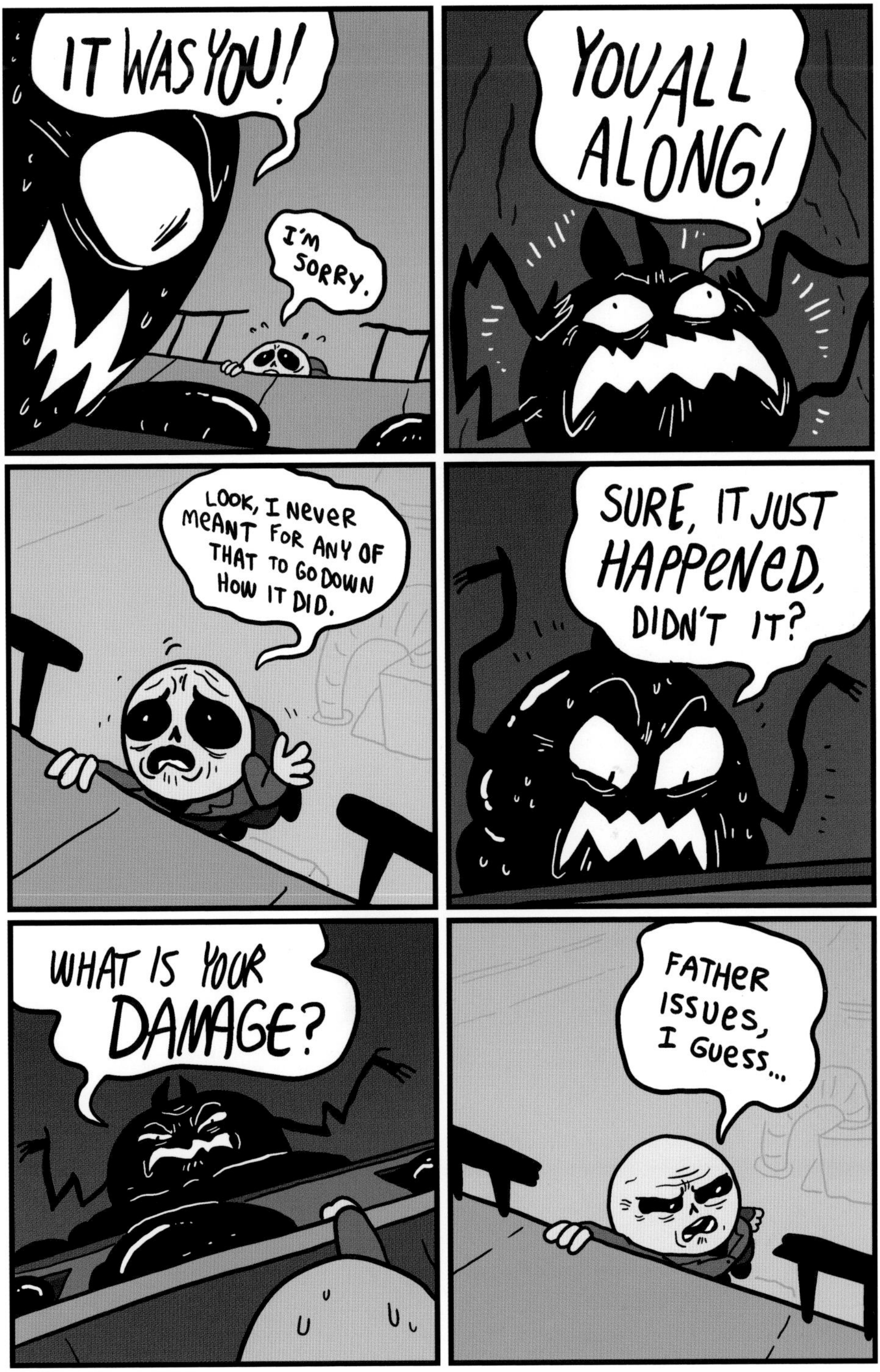
IT WAS YOU!
I'M SORRY.
YOU ALL ALONG!
LOOK, I NEVER MEANT FOR ANY OF THAT TO GO DOWN HOW IT DID.
SURE, IT JUST HAPPENED, DIDN'T IT?
WHAT IS YOUR DAMAGE?
FATHER ISSUES, I GUESS...

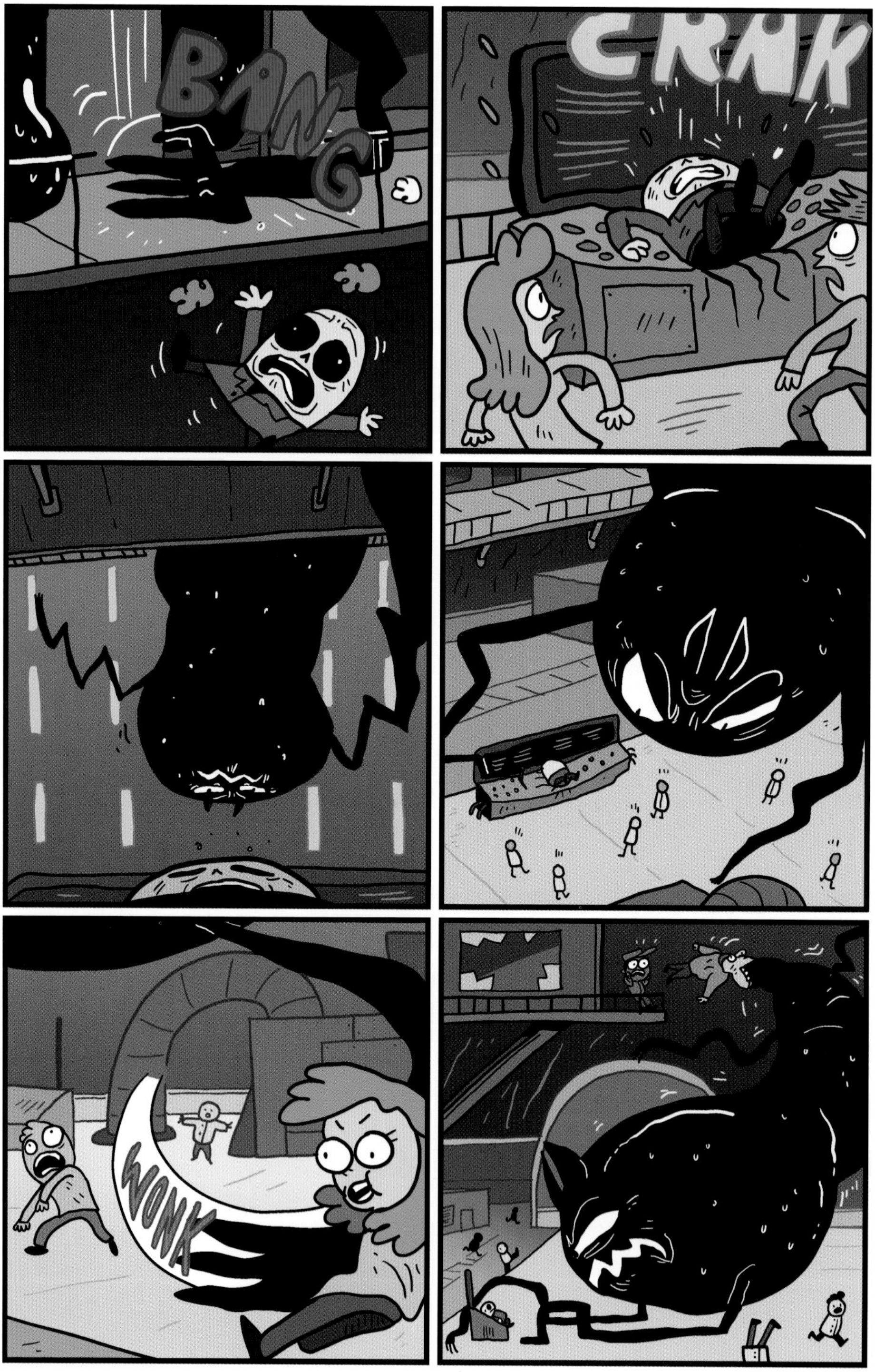
BANG
CRAK
WONK

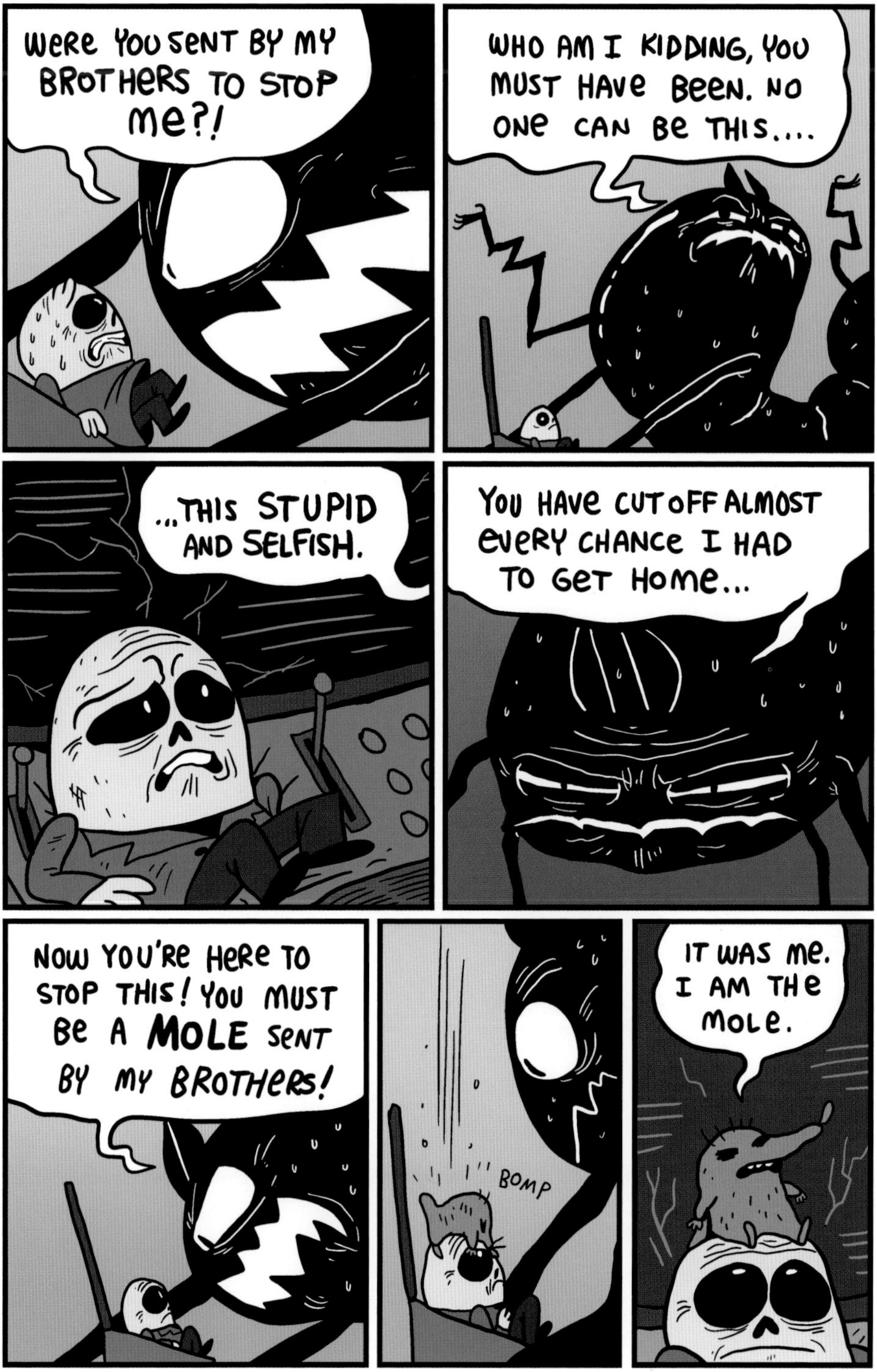
WERE YOU SENT BY MY BROTHERS TO STOP ME?!
WHO AM I KIDDING, YOU MUST HAVE BEEN. NO ONE CAN BE THIS....
...THIS STUPID AND SELFISH.
YOU HAVE CUT OFF ALMOST EVERY CHANCE I HAD TO GET HOME...
NOW YOU'RE HERE TO STOP THIS! YOU MUST BE A MOLE SENT BY MY BROTHERS!
BOMP
IT WAS ME. I AM THE MOLE.

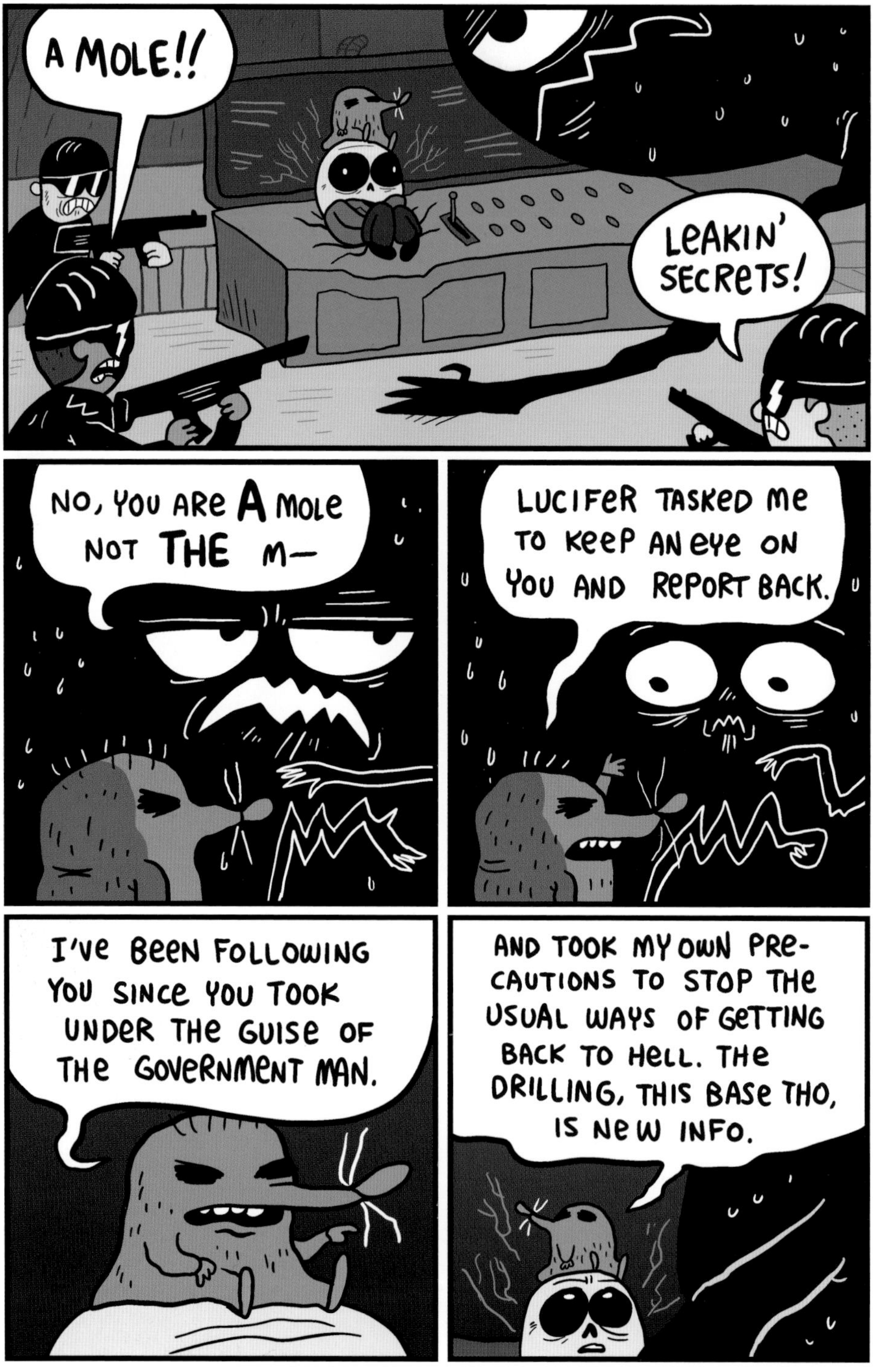
A MOLE!!
LEAKIN' SECRETS!
NO, YOU ARE A MOLE NOT THE M—
LUCIFER TASKED ME TO KEEP AN EYE ON YOU AND REPORT BACK.
I'VE BEEN FOLLOWING YOU SINCE YOU TOOK UNDER THE GUISE OF THE GOVERNMENT MAN.
AND TOOK MY OWN PRE-CAUTIONS TO STOP THE USUAL WAYS OF GETTING BACK TO HELL. THE DRILLING, THIS BASE THO, IS NEW INFO.

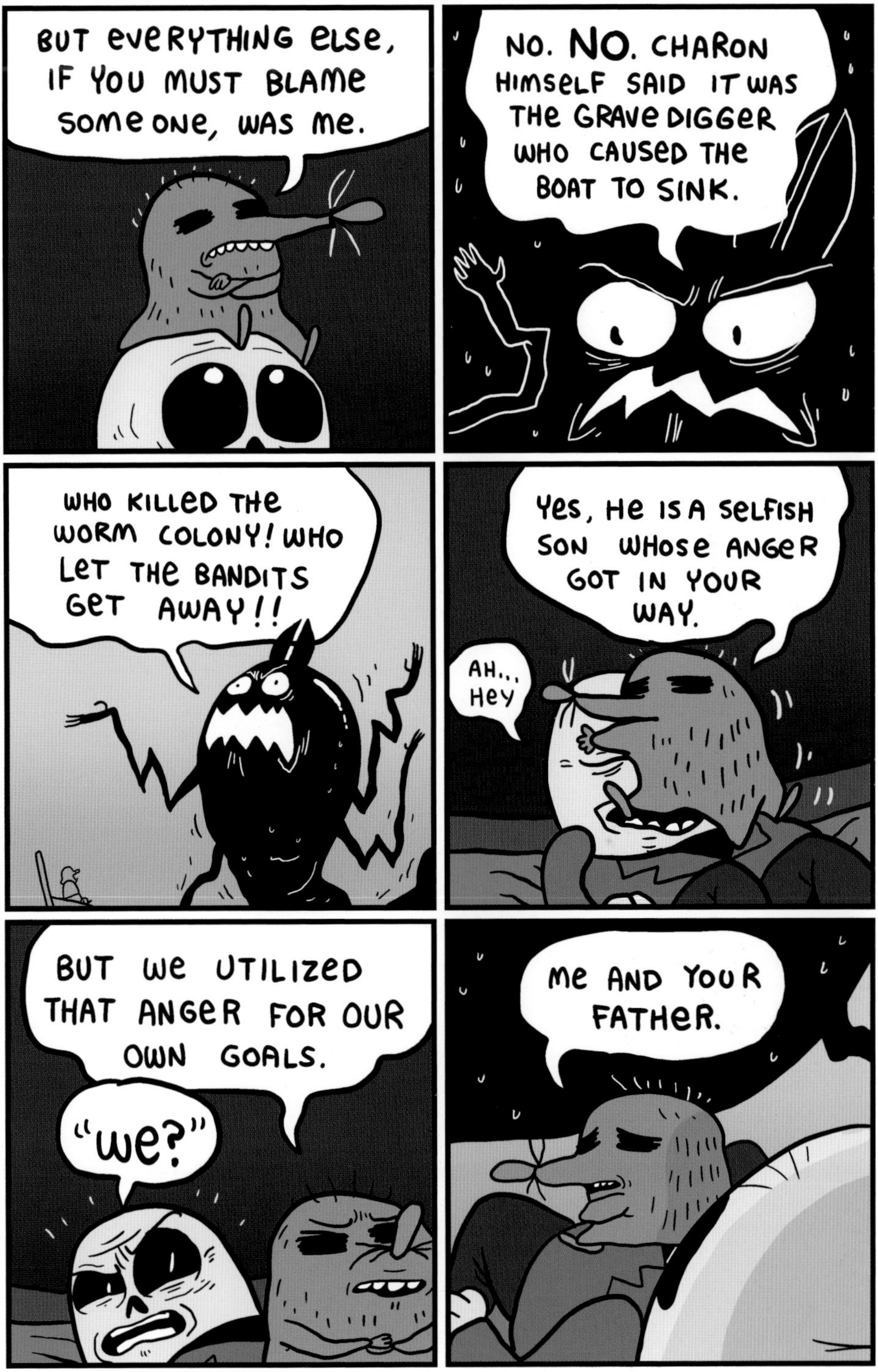
BUT EVERYTHING ELSE, IF YOU MUST BLAME SOMEONE, WAS ME.
NO. NO. CHARON HIMSELF SAID IT WAS THE GRAVE DIGGER WHO CAUSED THE BOAT TO SINK.
WHO KILLED THE WORM COLONY! WHO LET THE BANDITS GET AWAY!!
YES, HE IS A SELFISH SON WHOSE ANGER GOT IN YOUR WAY.
AH... HEY
BUT WE UTILIZED THAT ANGER FOR OUR OWN GOALS.
"WE?"
ME AND YOUR FATHER.

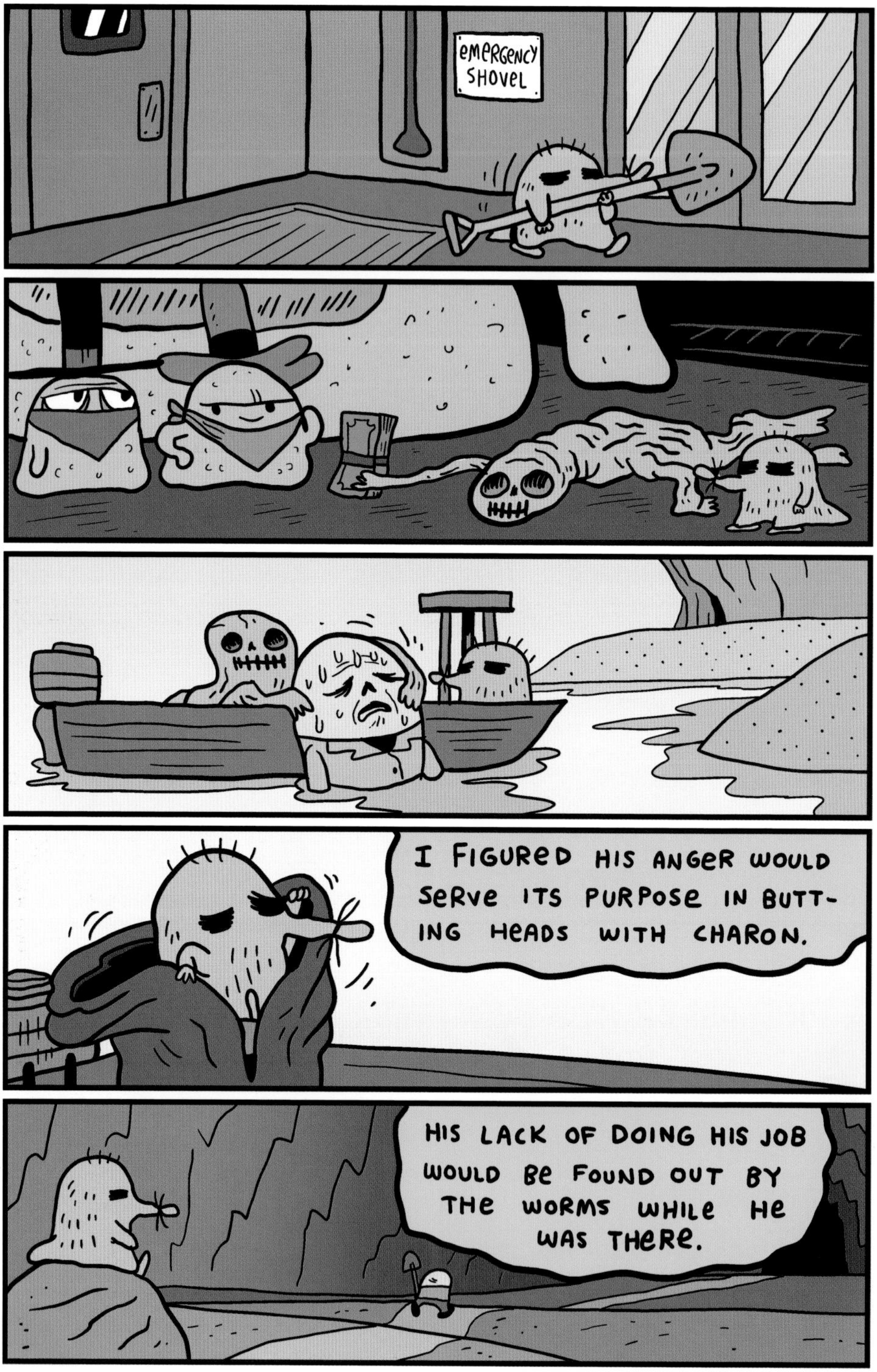
EMERGENCY SHOVEL
I FIGURED HIS ANGER WOULD SERVE ITS PURPOSE IN BUTT-ING HEADS WITH CHARON.
HIS LACK OF DOING HIS JOB WOULD BE FOUND OUT BY THE WORMS WHILE HE WAS THERE.

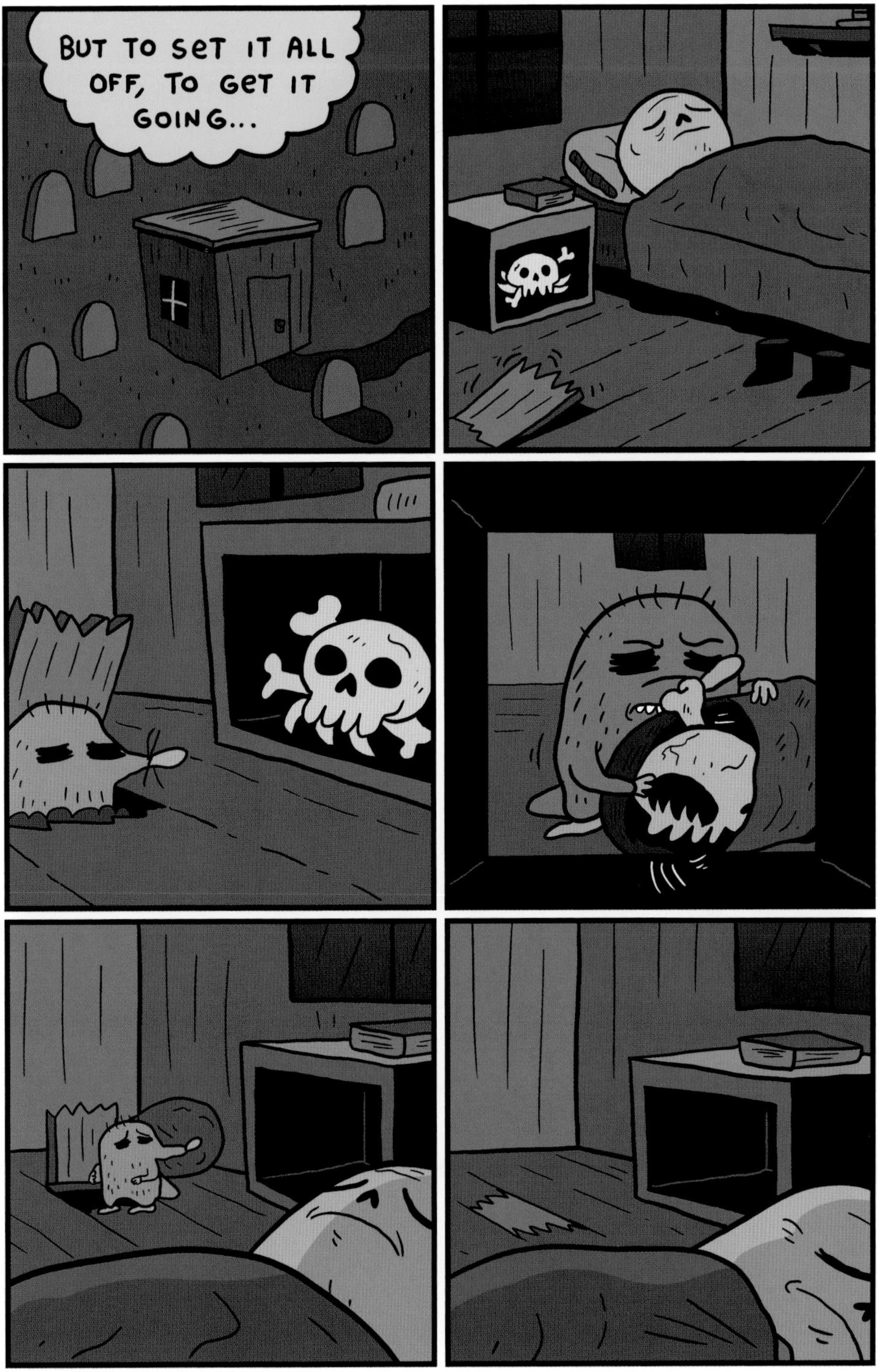
BUT TO SET IT ALL OFF, TO GET IT GOING...

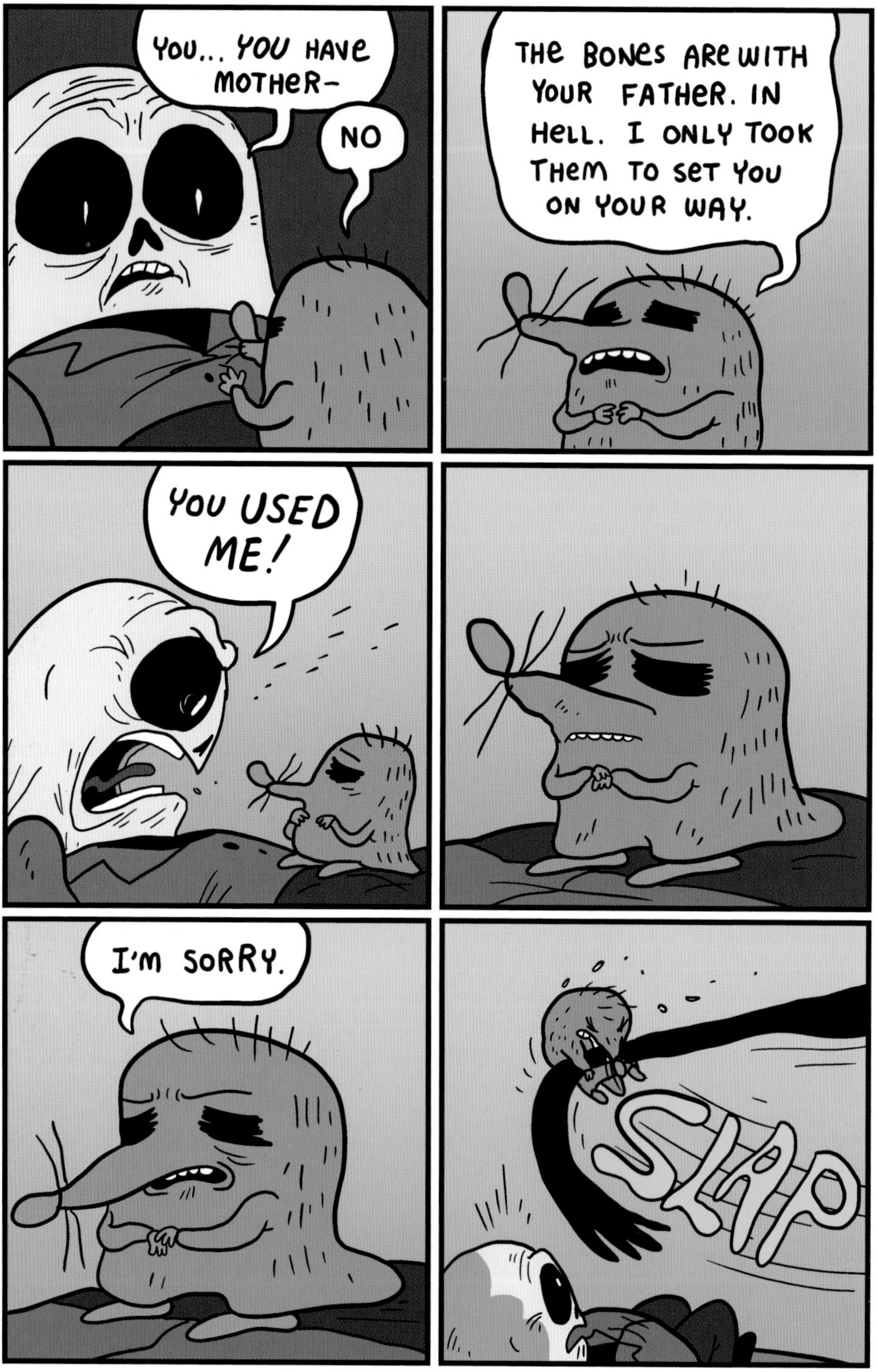
YOU... YOU HAVE MOTHER-
NO
THE BONES ARE WITH YOUR FATHER. IN HELL. I ONLY TOOK THEM TO SET YOU ON YOUR WAY.
YOU USED ME!
I'M SORRY.
SLAP

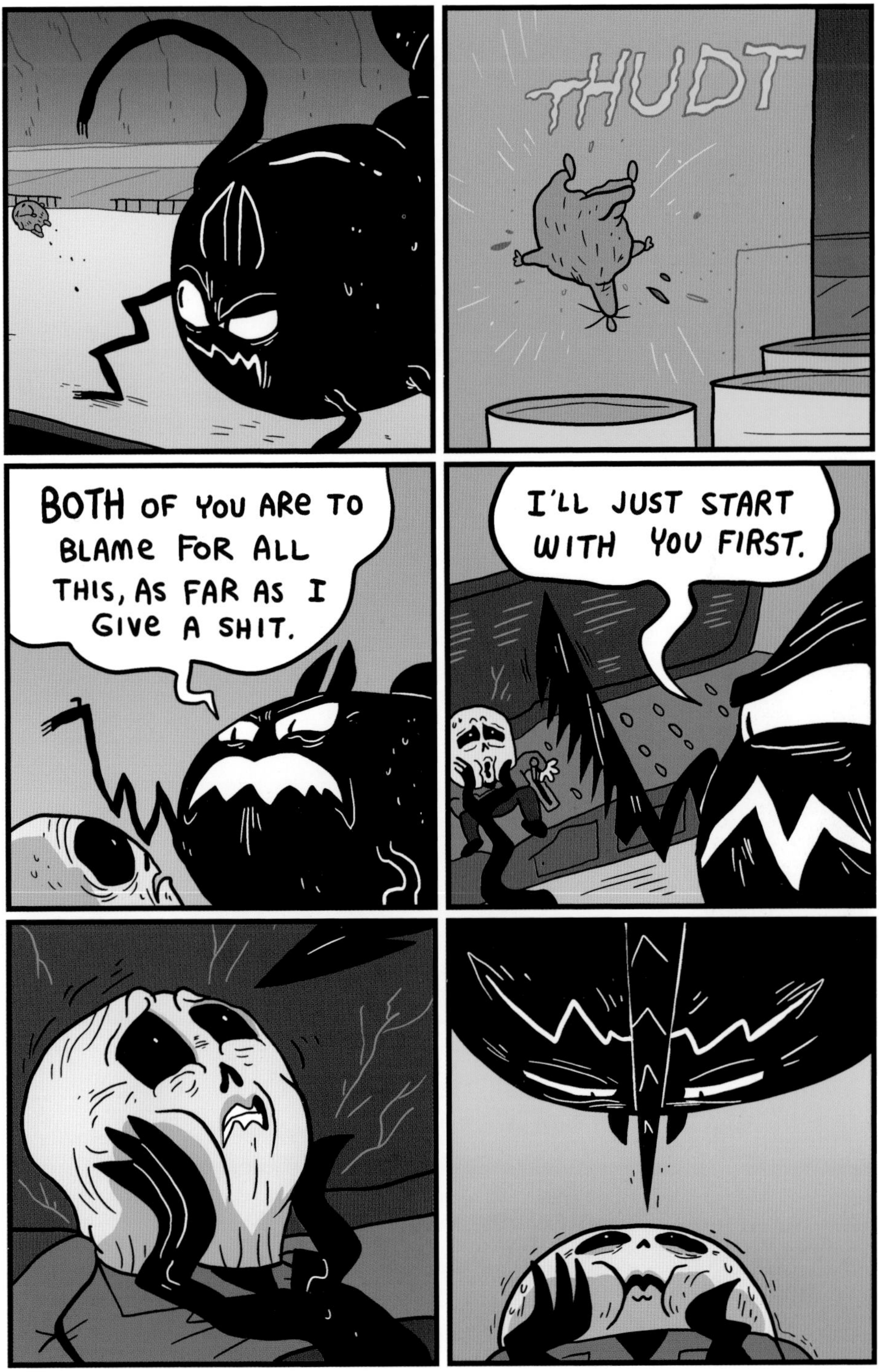
THUDT
BOTH OF YOU ARE TO BLAME FOR ALL THIS, AS FAR AS I GIVE A SHIT.
I'LL JUST START WITH YOU FIRST.

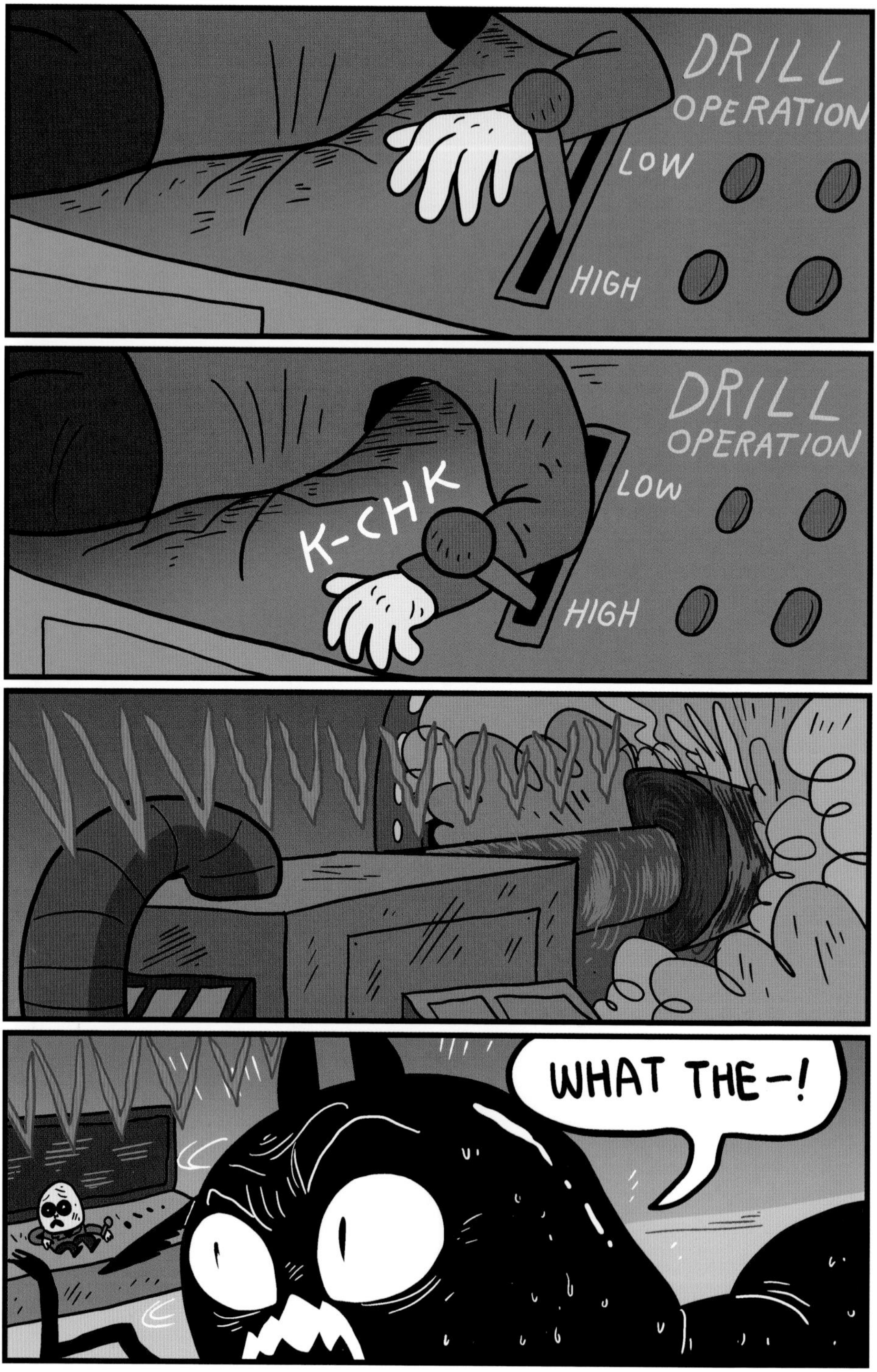
DRILL OPERATION
LOW
HIGH
DRILL OPERATION
LOW
HIGH
K-CHK
WHAT THE-!

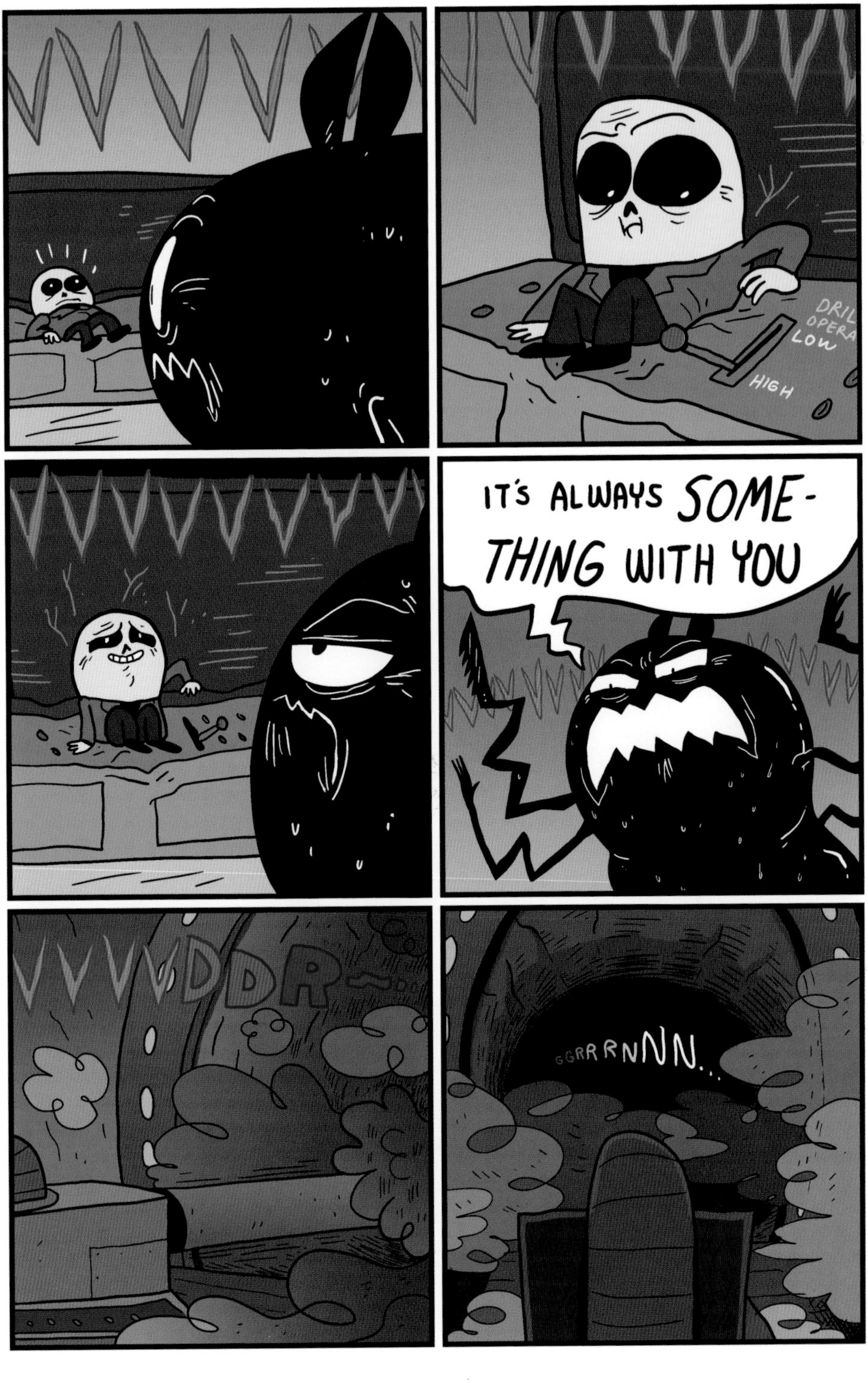
DRIL
OPERA
LOW
HIGH
IT'S ALWAYS SOME-THING WITH YOU
DDR~..
GGRRRNNN...

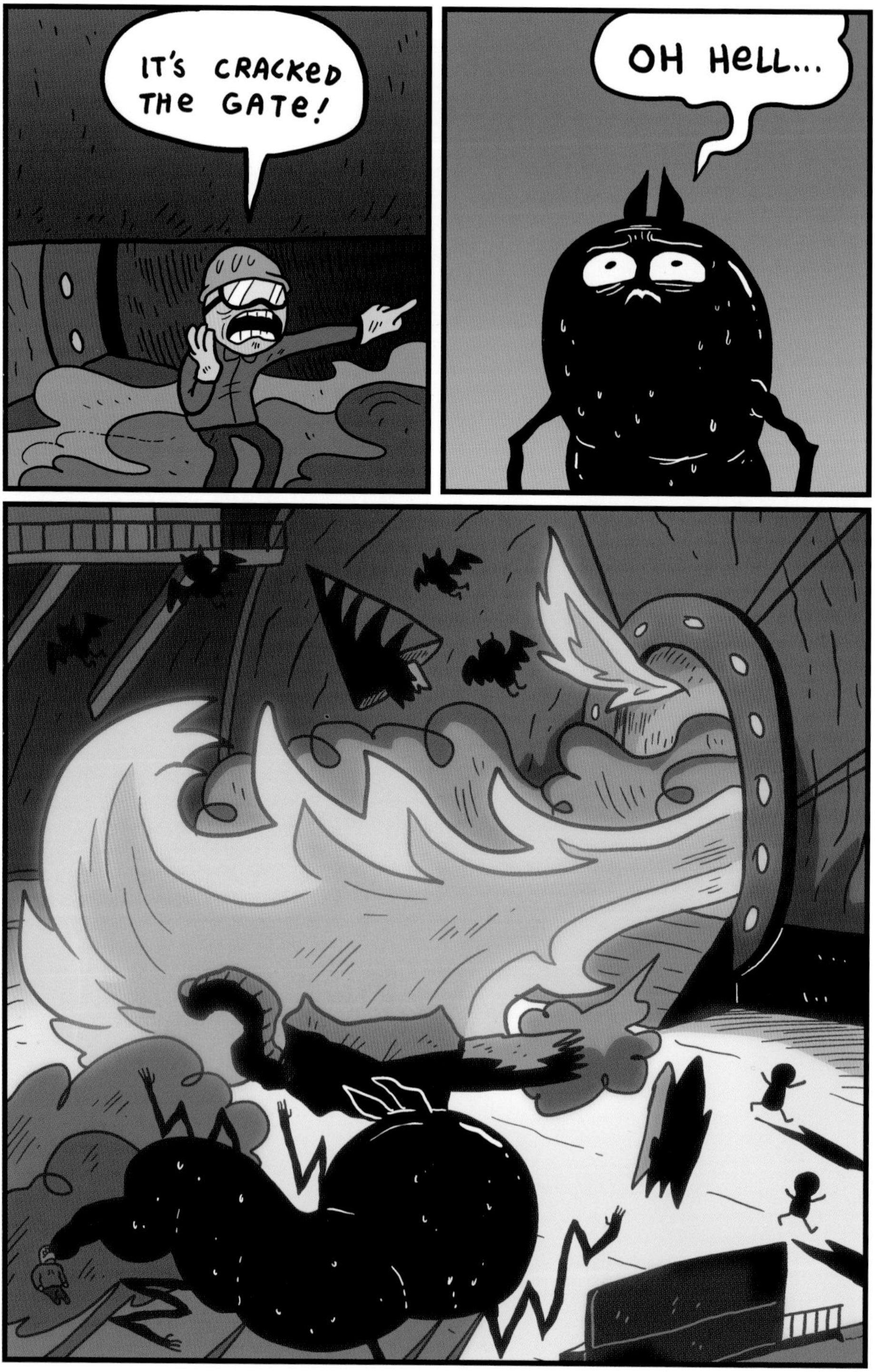
IT'S CRACKED THE GATE!
OH HELL...

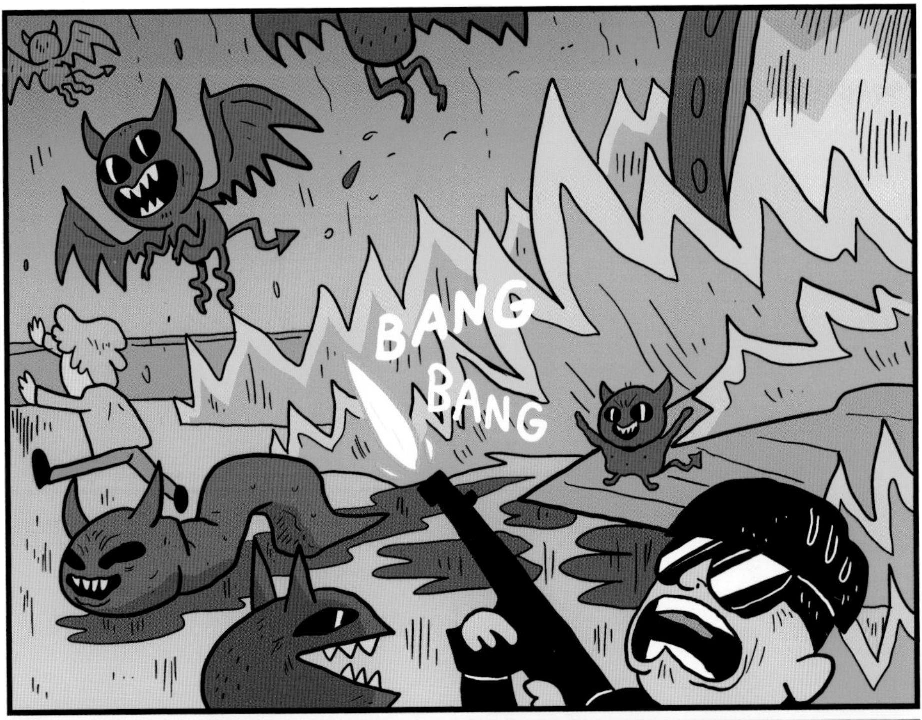
BANG
BANG

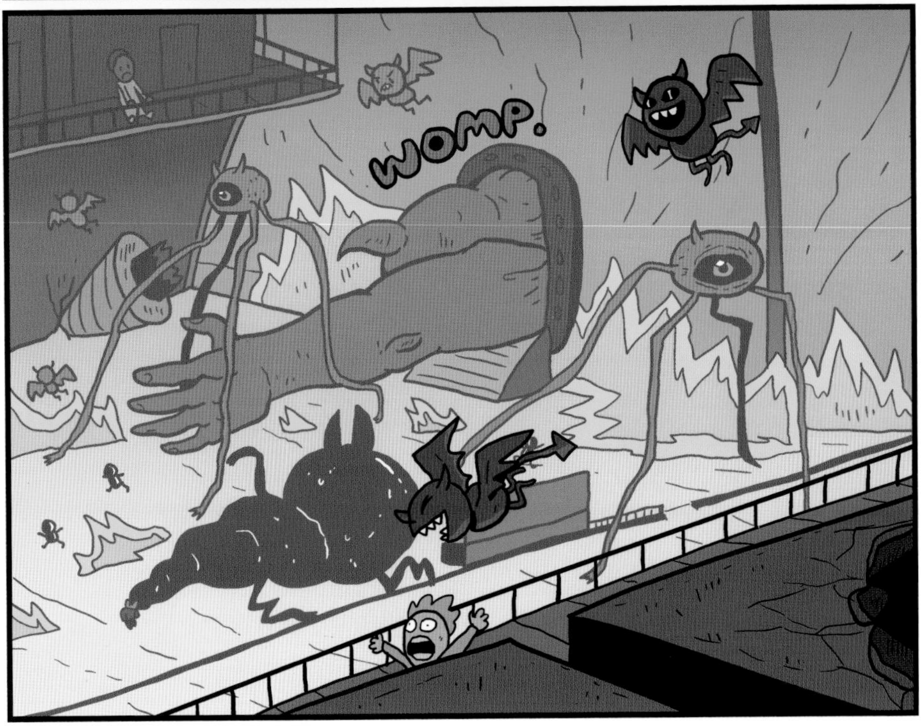
WOMP.

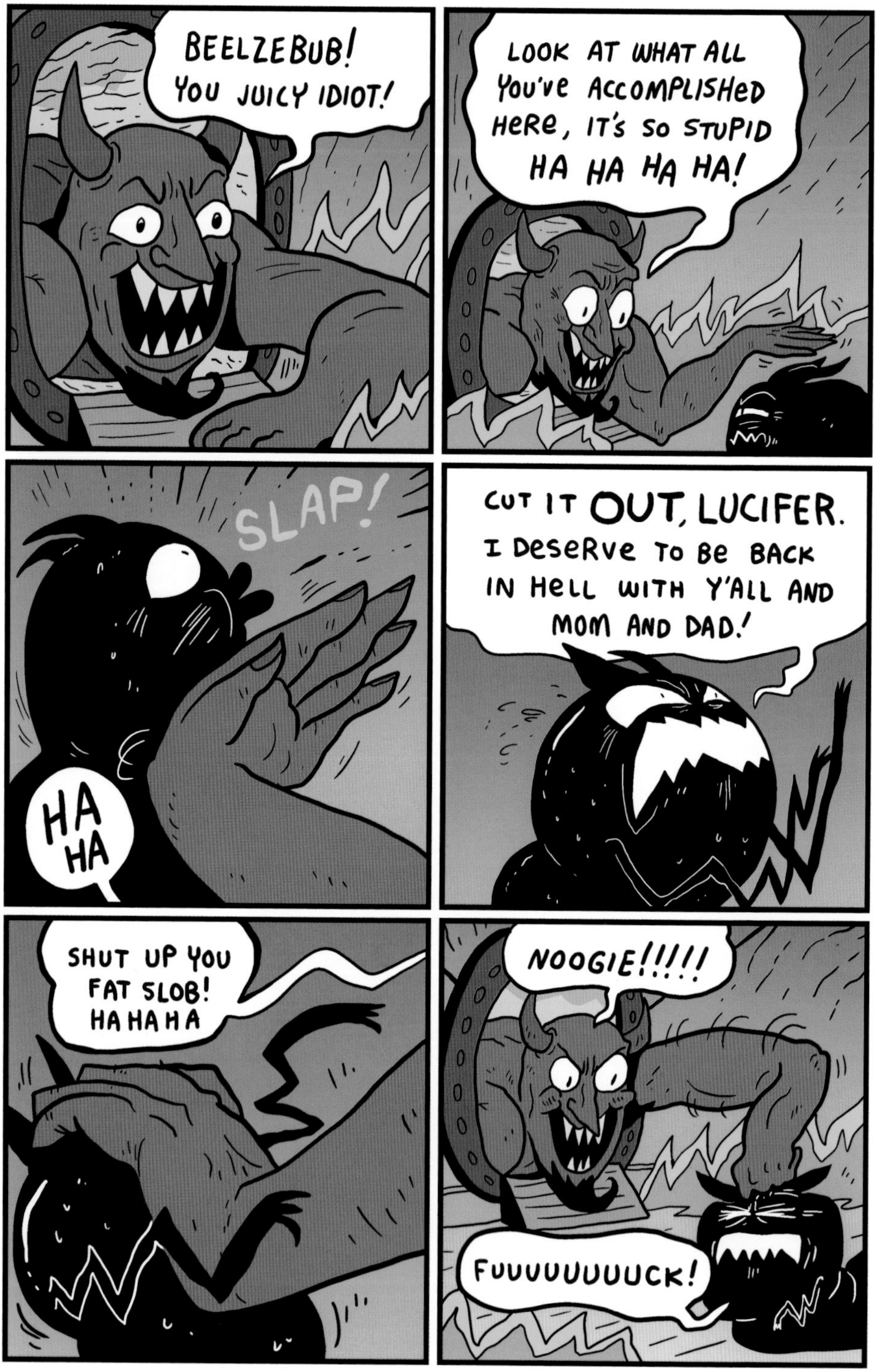
BEELZEBUB! YOU JUICY IDIOT!
LOOK AT WHAT ALL YOU'VE ACCOMPLISHED HERE, IT'S SO STUPID HA HA HA HA!
SLAP!
HA HA
CUT IT OUT, LUCIFER. I DESERVE TO BE BACK IN HELL WITH Y'ALL AND MOM AND DAD!
SHUT UP YOU FAT SLOB! HA HA HA
NOOGIE!!!!!
FUUUUUUUUCK!

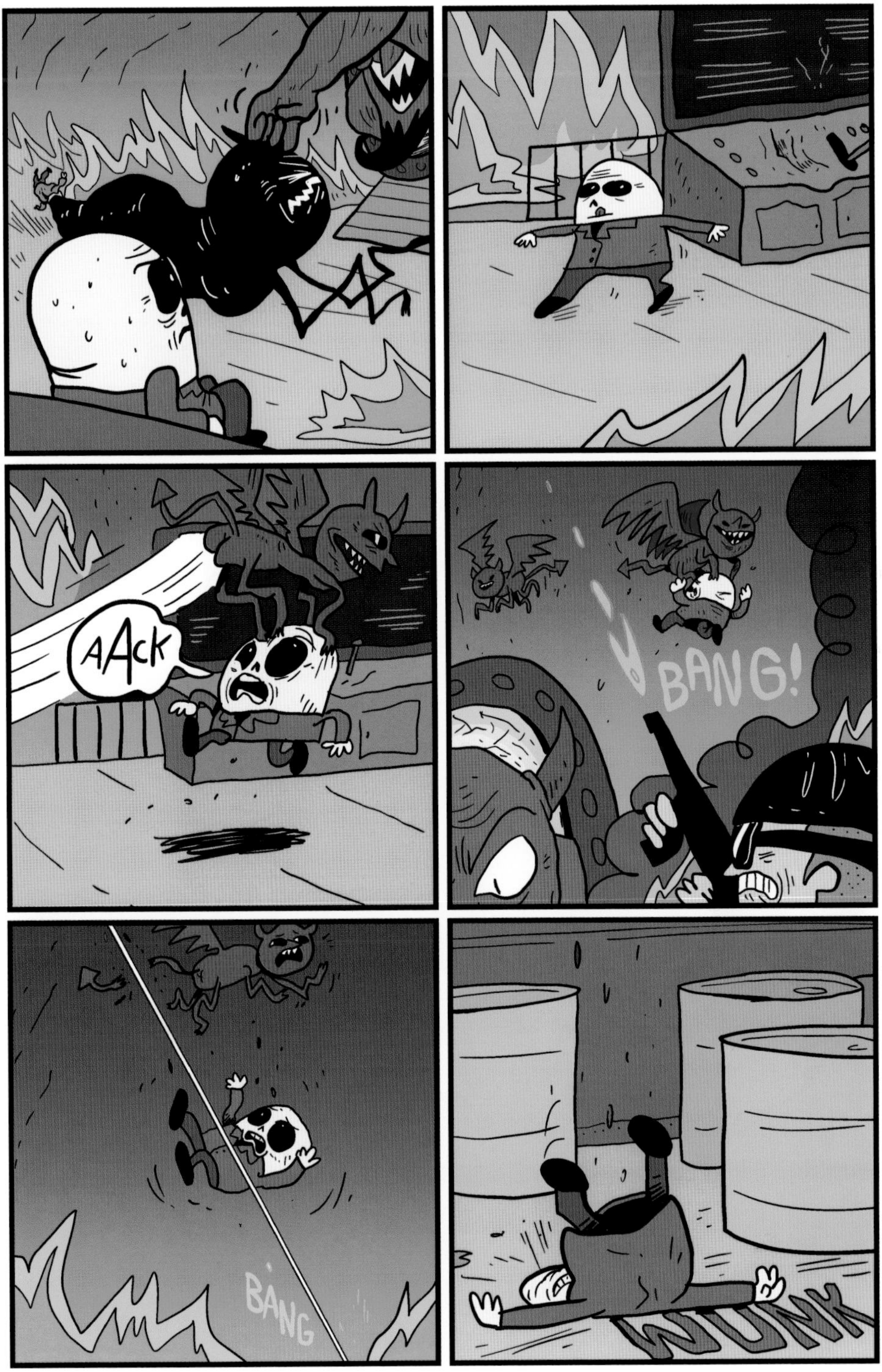
AACK
BANG!
BANG
WUNK

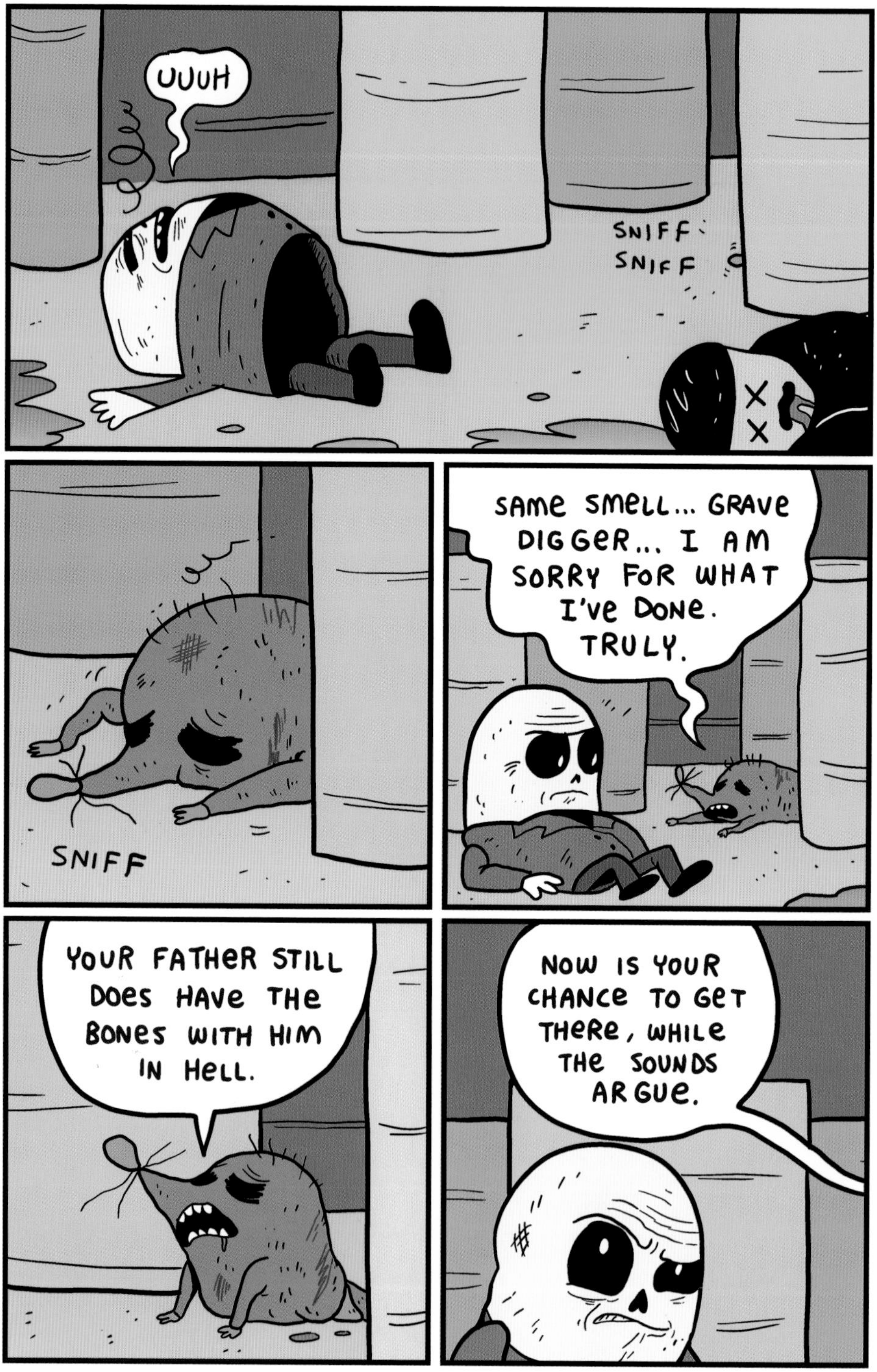
UUUH
SNIFF SNIFF
SNIFF
SAME SMELL... GRAVE DIGGER... I AM SORRY FOR WHAT I'VE DONE. TRULY.
YOUR FATHER STILL DOES HAVE THE BONES WITH HIM IN HELL.
NOW IS YOUR CHANCE TO GET THERE, WHILE THE SOUNDS ARGUE.

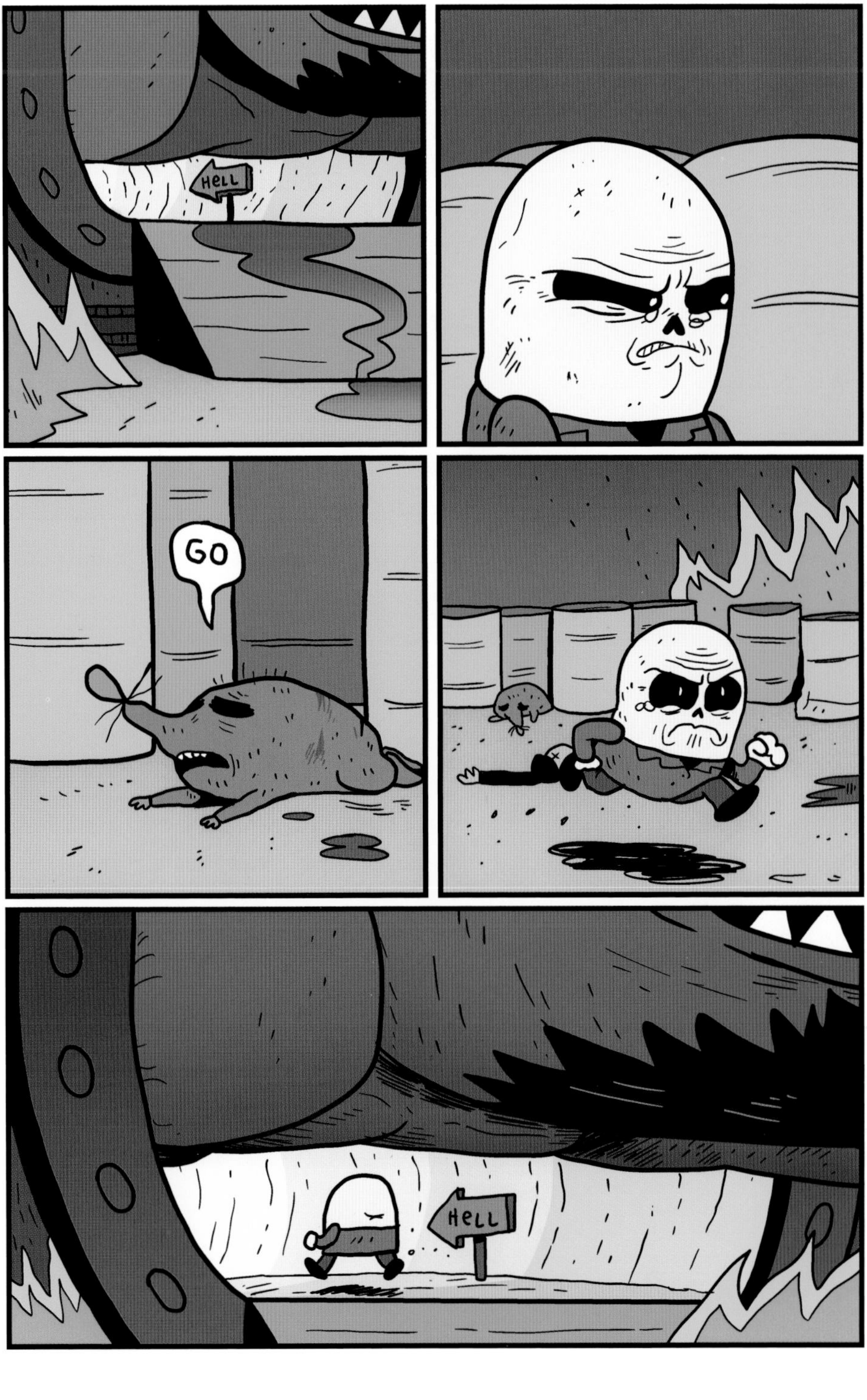
HELL
GO
HELL

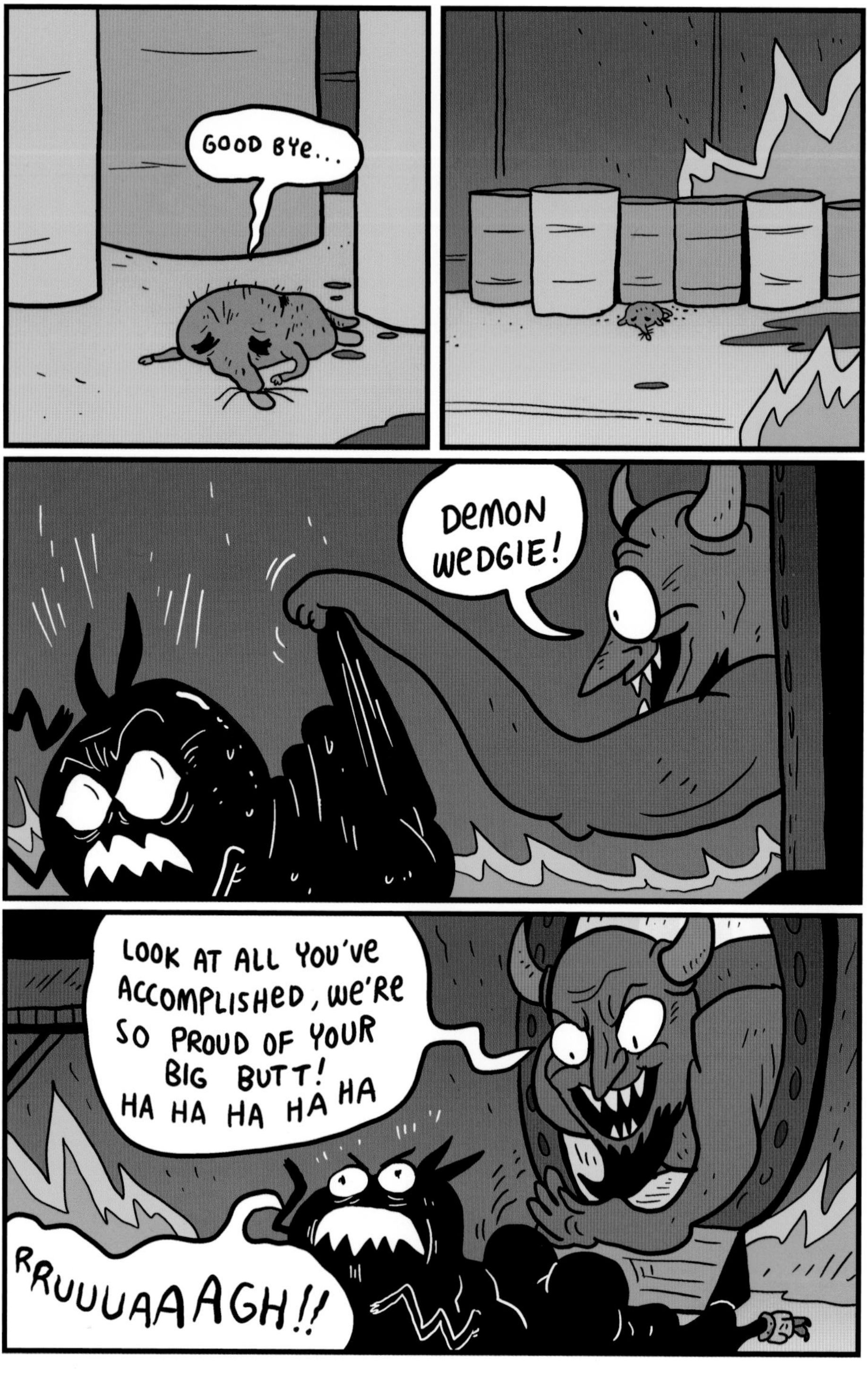
GOOD BYE...
DEMON WEDGIE!
LOOK AT ALL YOU'VE ACCOMPLISHED, WE'RE SO PROUD OF YOUR BIG BUTT! HA HA HA HA HA
RRUUUAAAGH!!

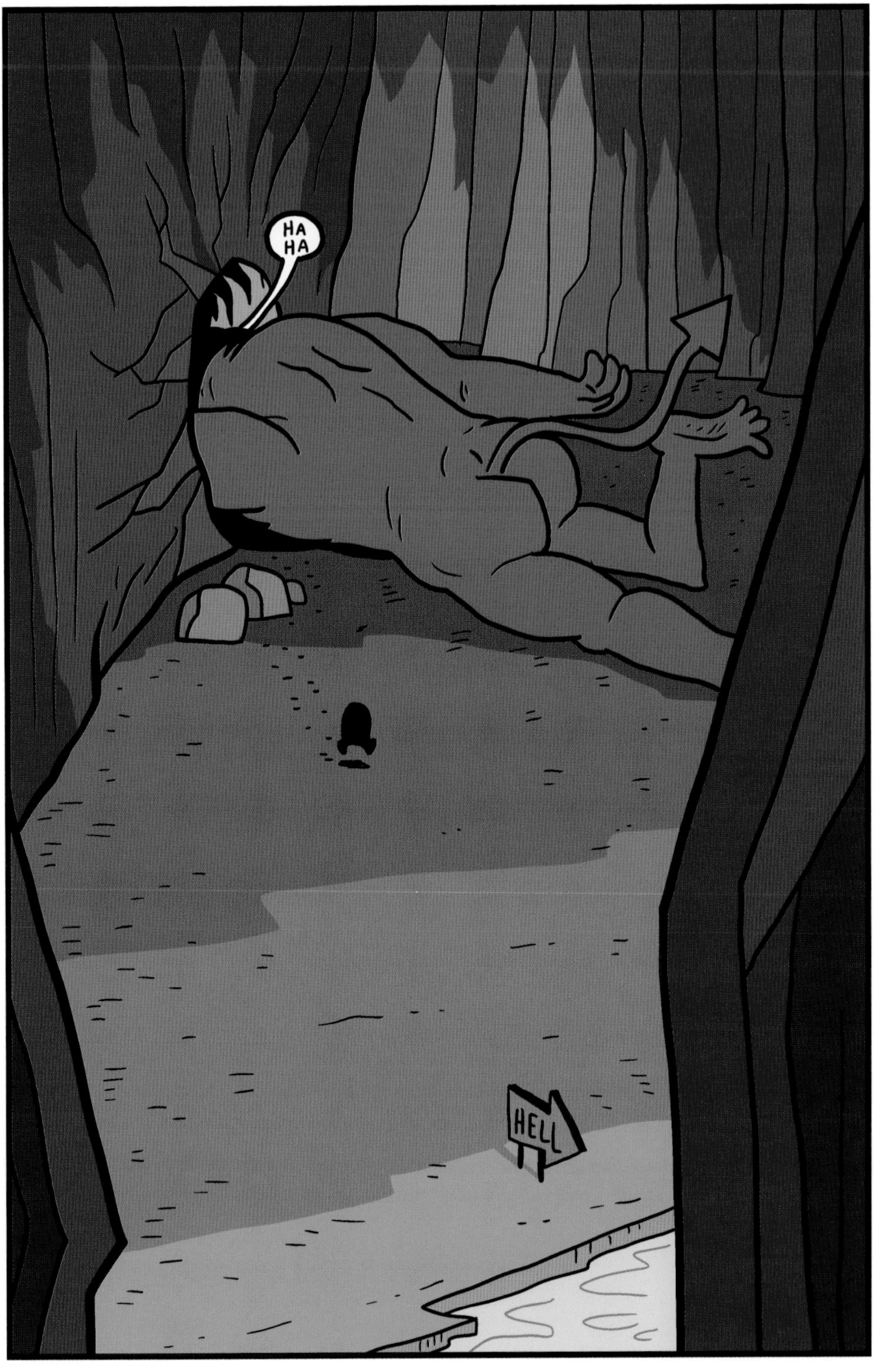
HA HA
HELL

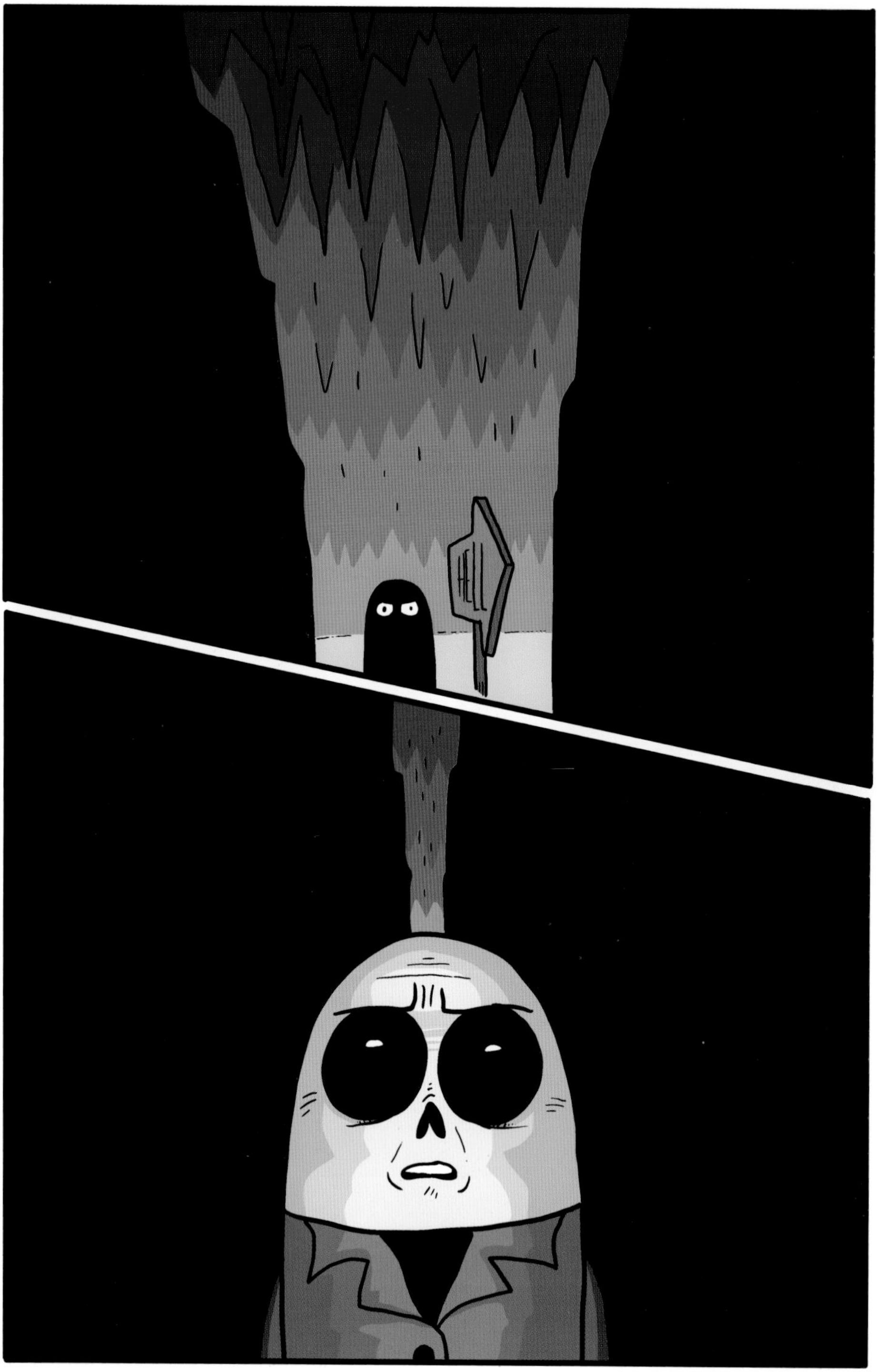
HELL

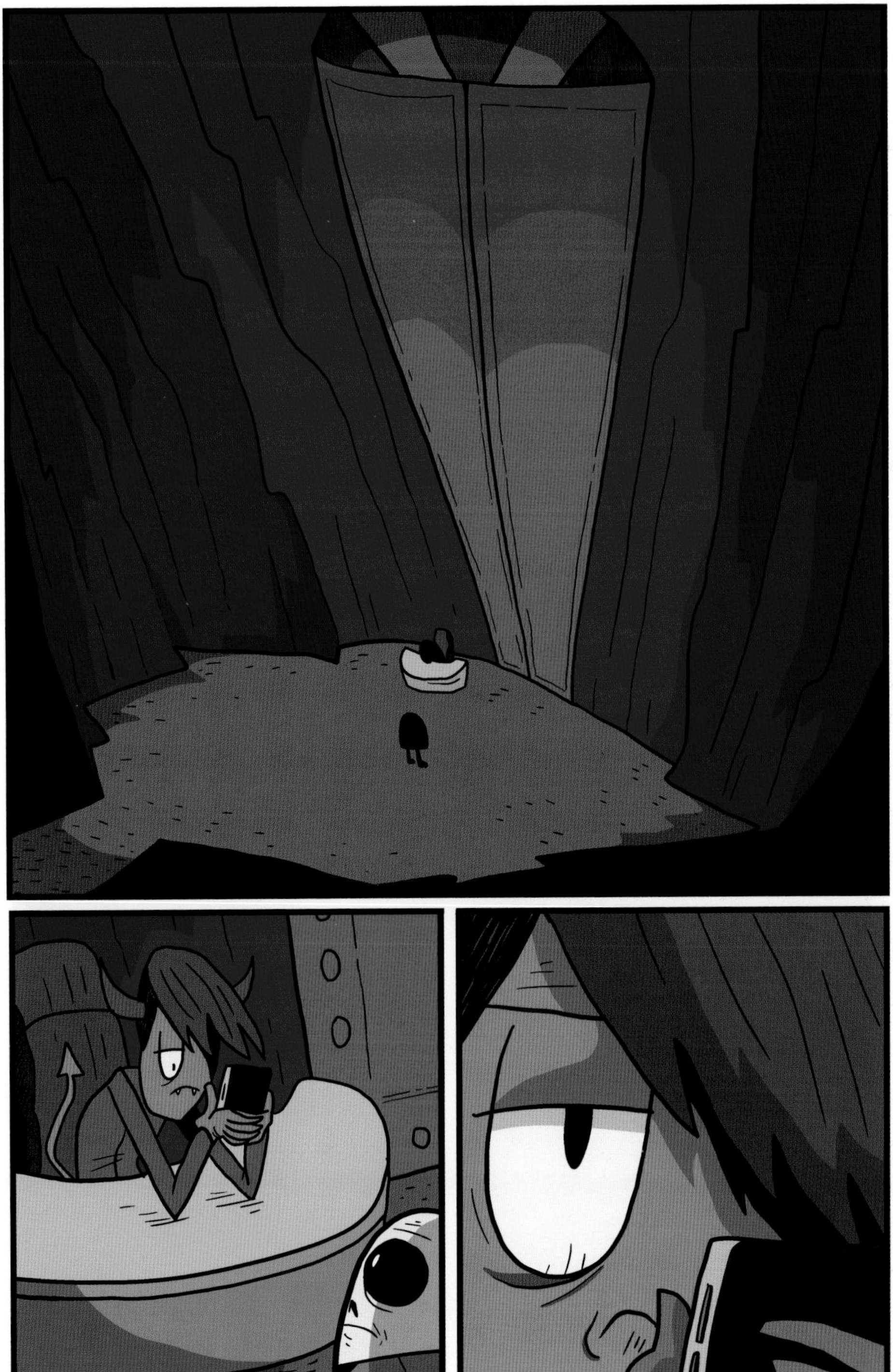

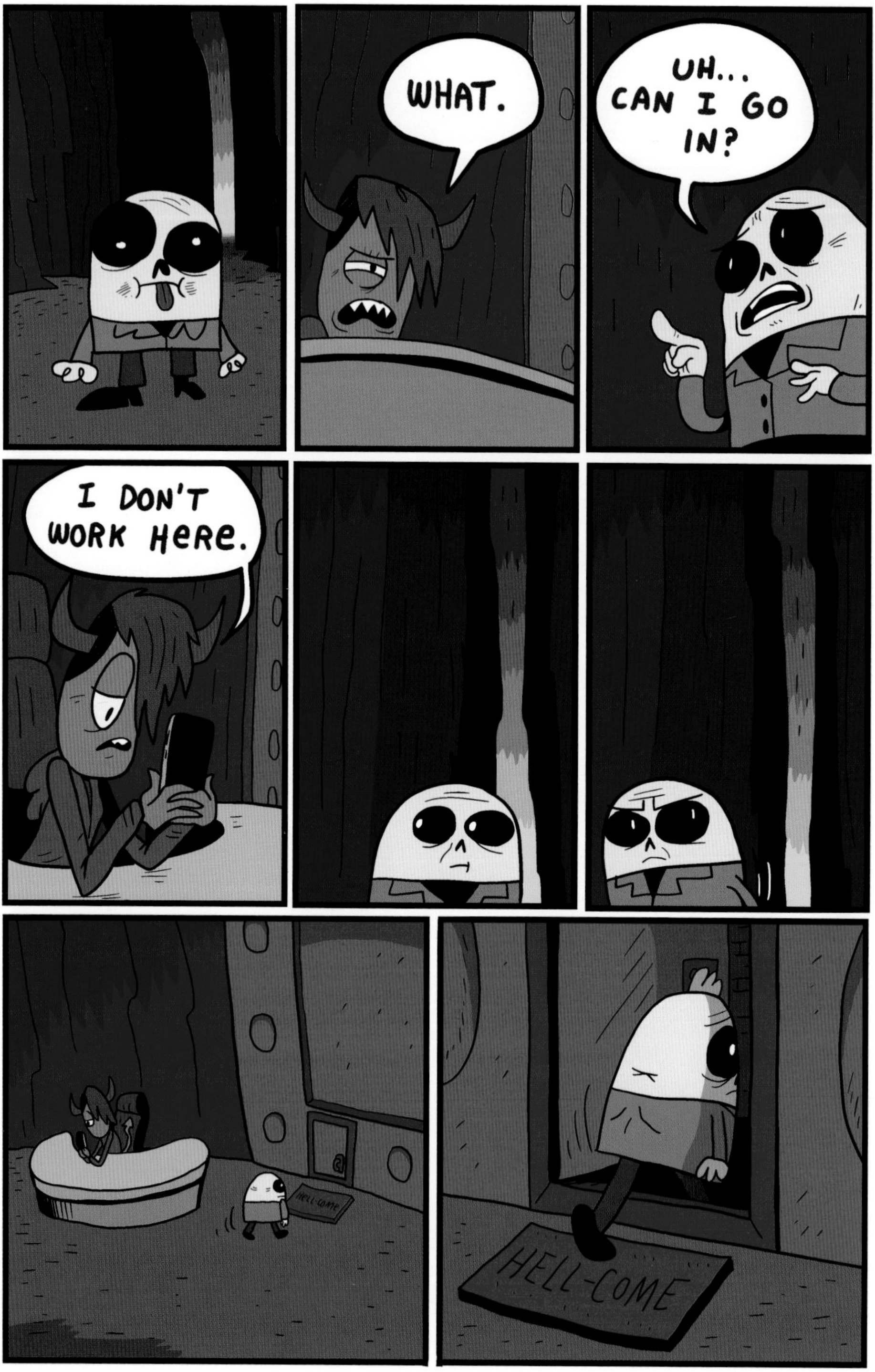
WHAT.
UH... CAN I GO IN?
I DON'T WORK HERE.
HELL-COME
HELL-COME

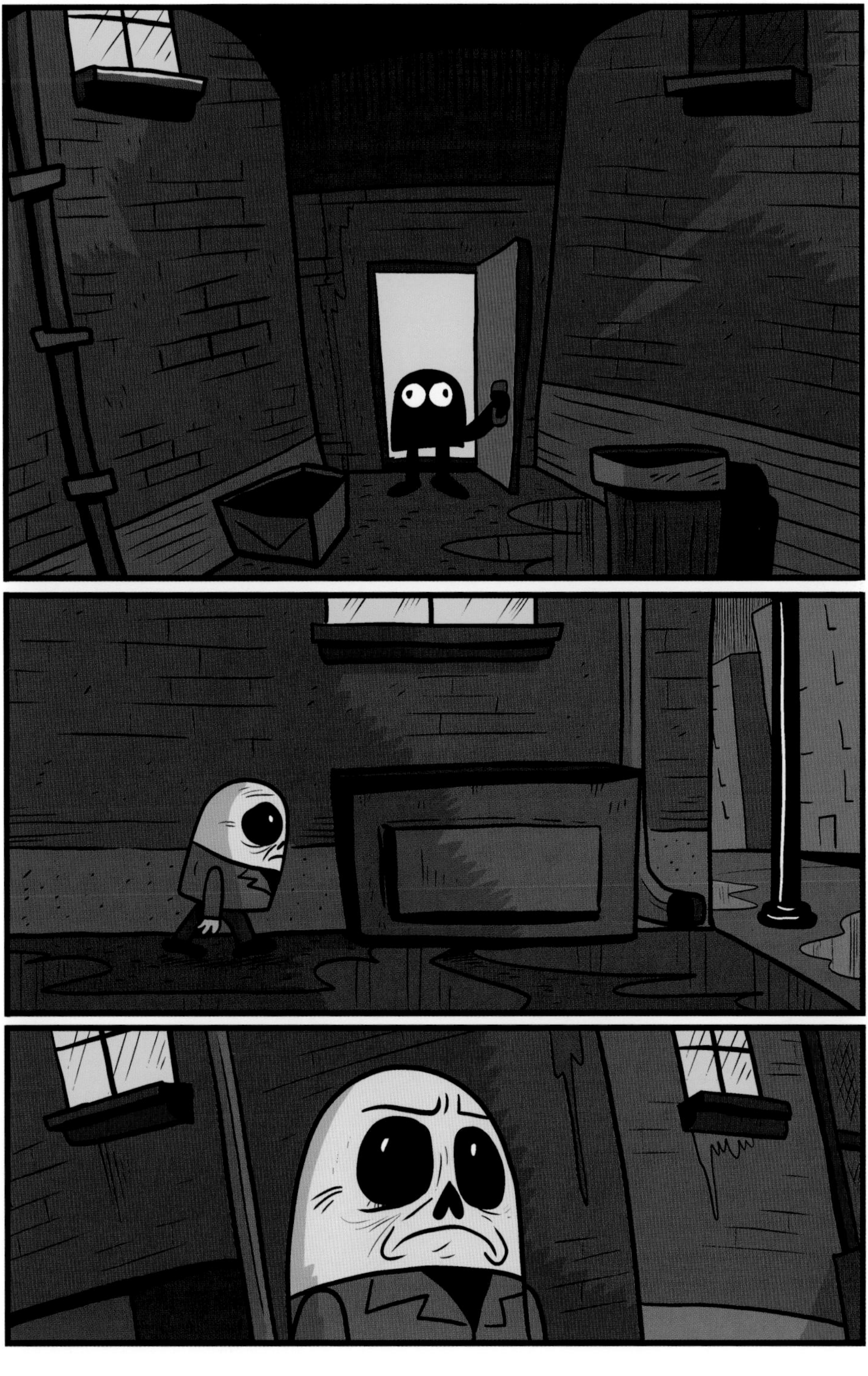

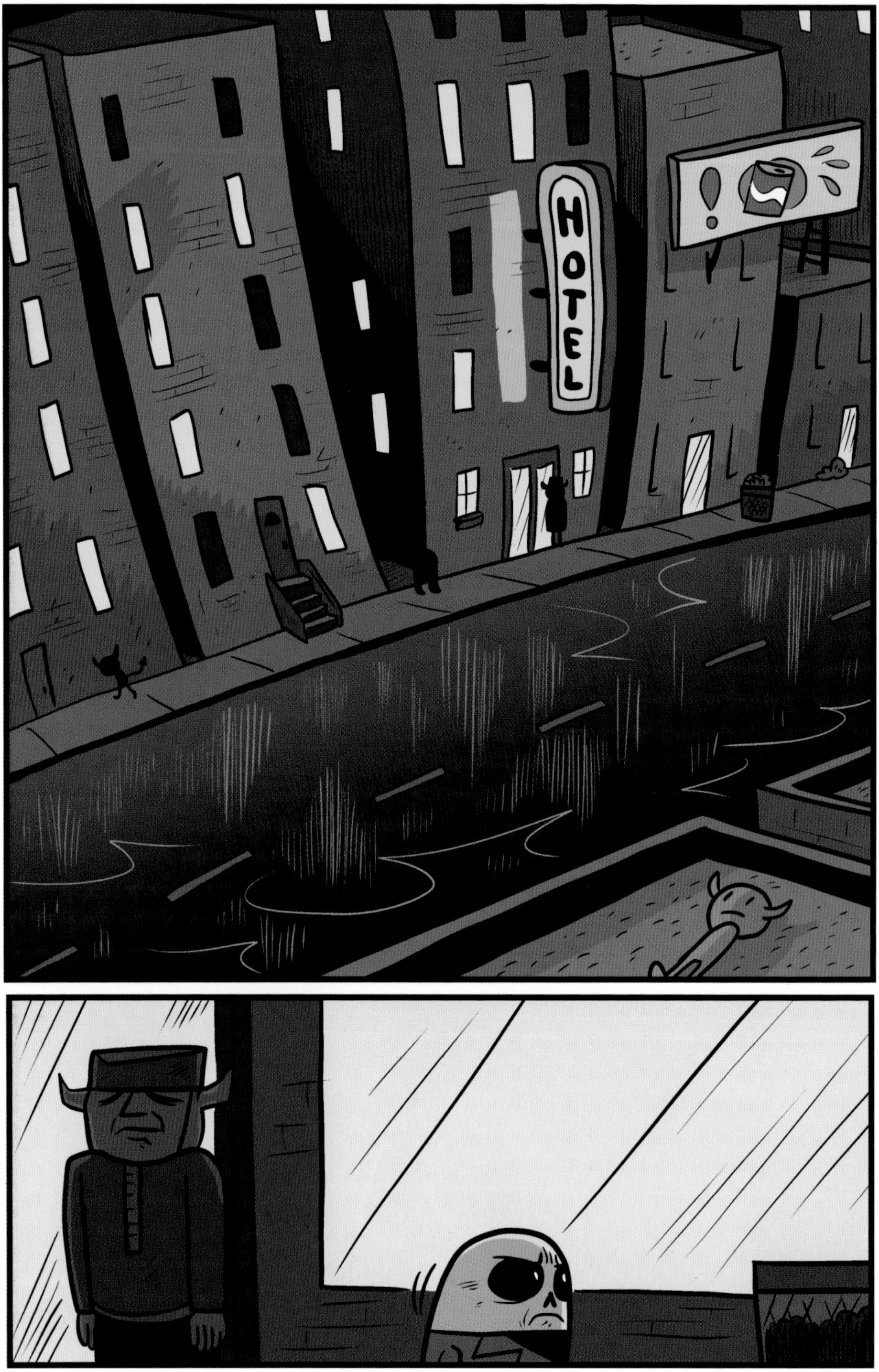
HOTEL

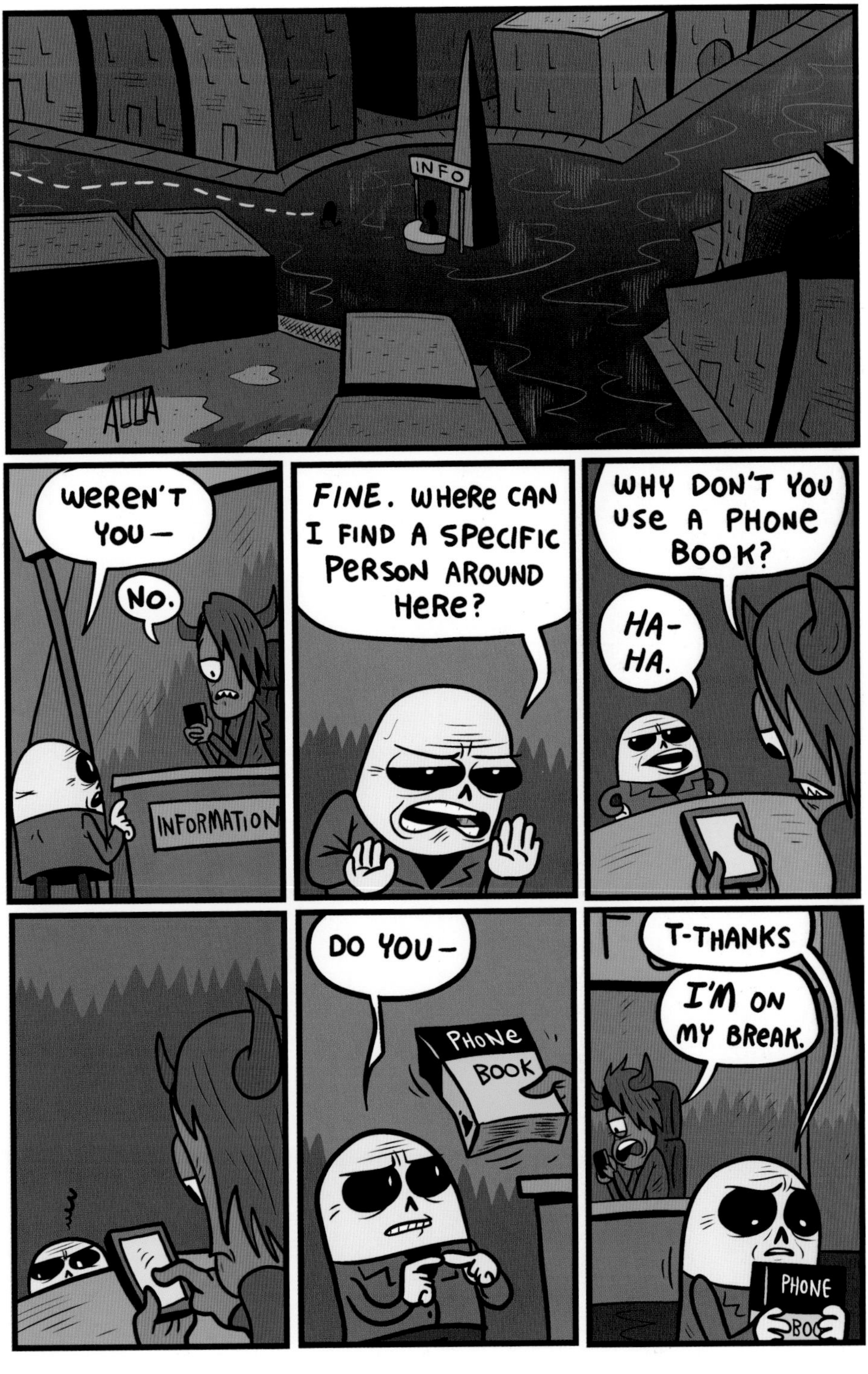
INFO
WEREN'T YOU—
NO.
INFORMATION
FINE. WHERE CAN I FIND A SPECIFIC PERSON AROUND HERE?
WHY DON'T YOU USE A PHONE BOOK?
HA-HA.
DO YOU—
PHONE BOOK
T-THANKS
I'M ON MY BREAK.
PHONE

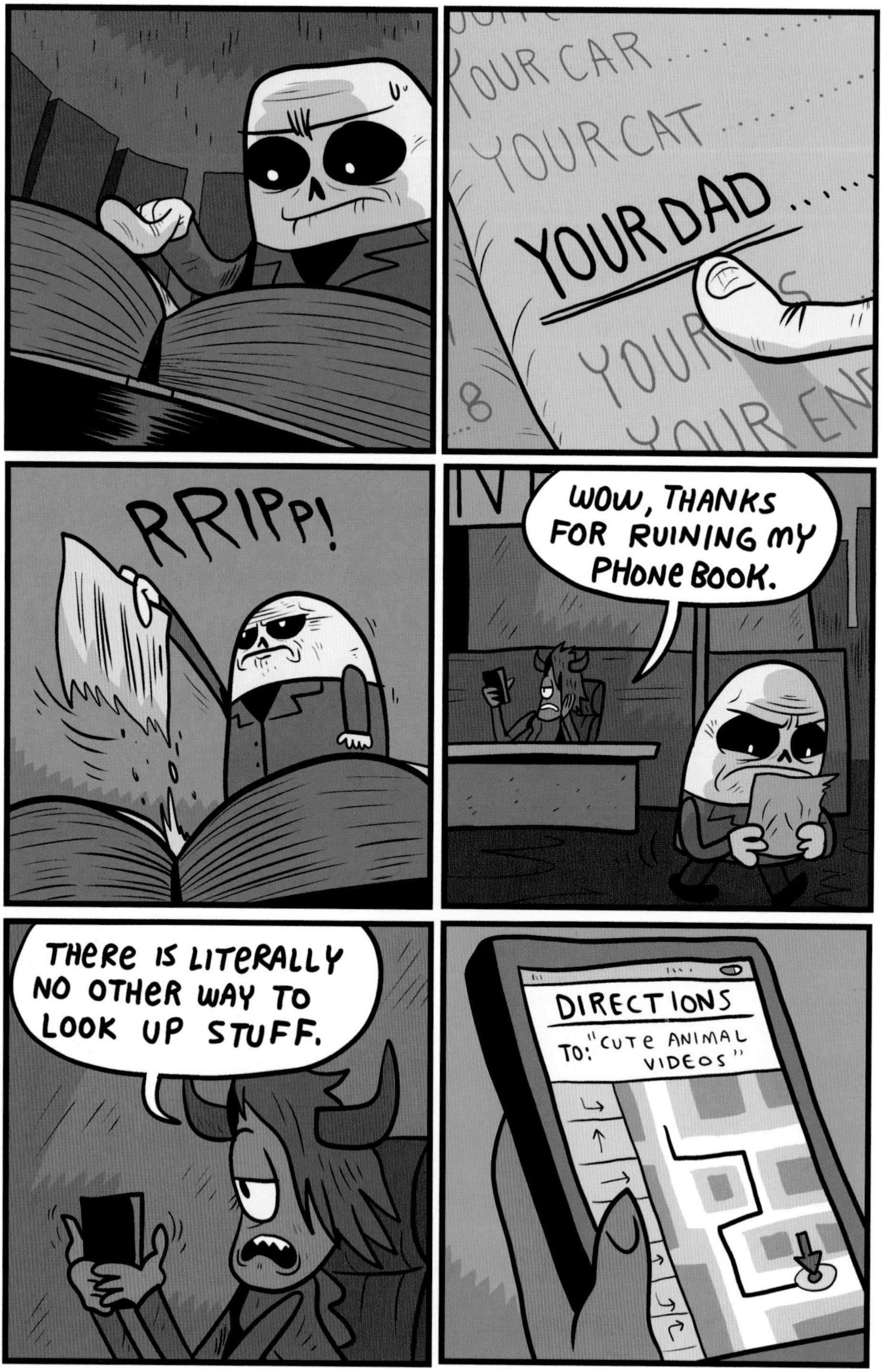
YOUR CAR
YOUR CAT
YOUR DAD
RRIPP!
WOW, THANKS FOR RUINING MY PHONE BOOK.
THERE IS LITERALLY NO OTHER WAY TO LOOK UP STUFF.
DIRECTIONS
TO: "CUTE ANIMAL VIDEOS"

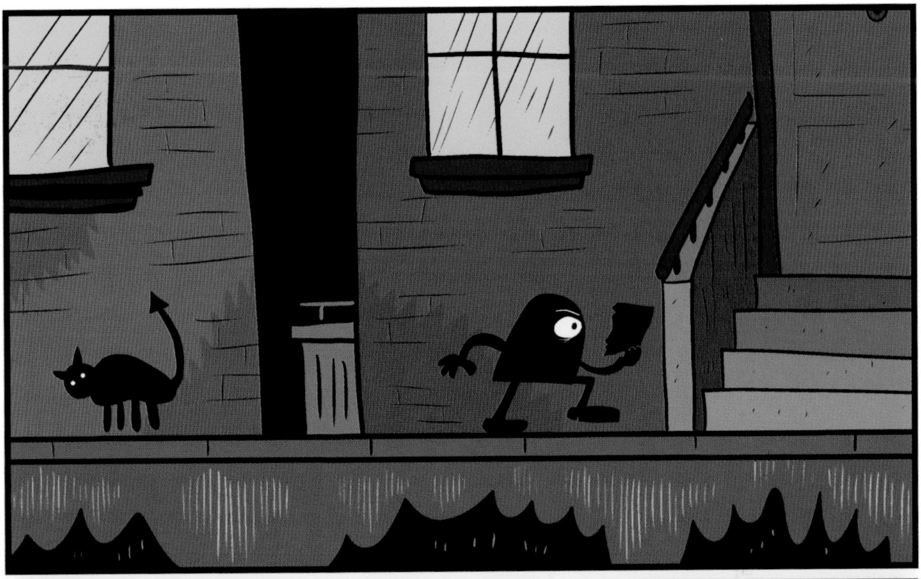

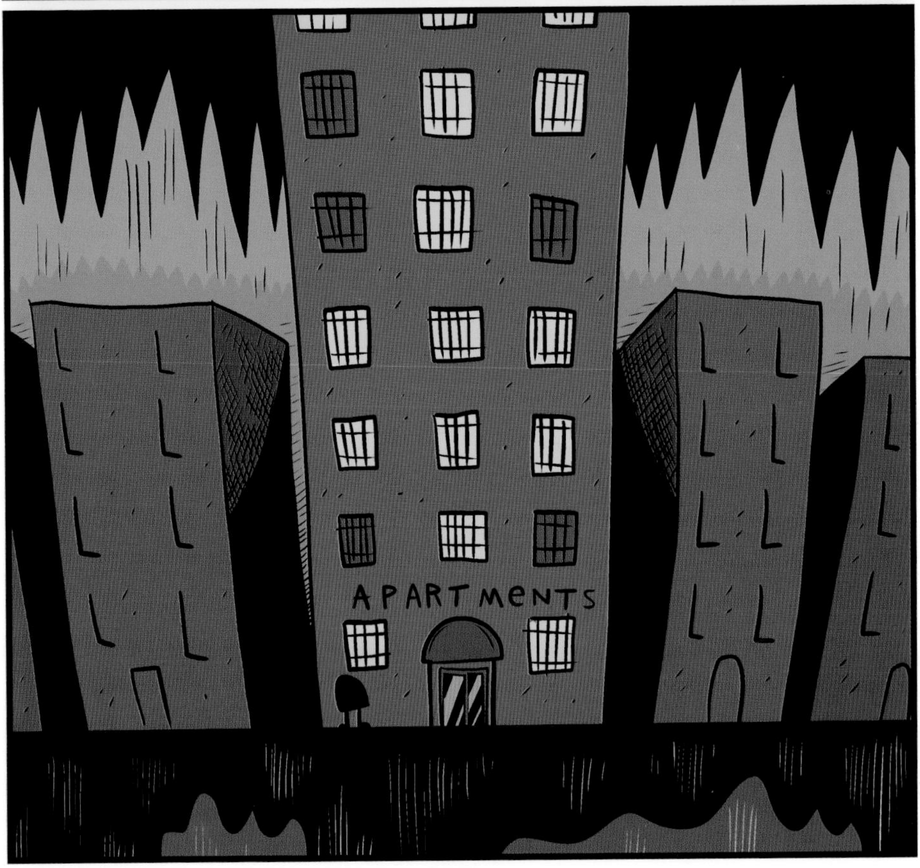
APARTMENTS

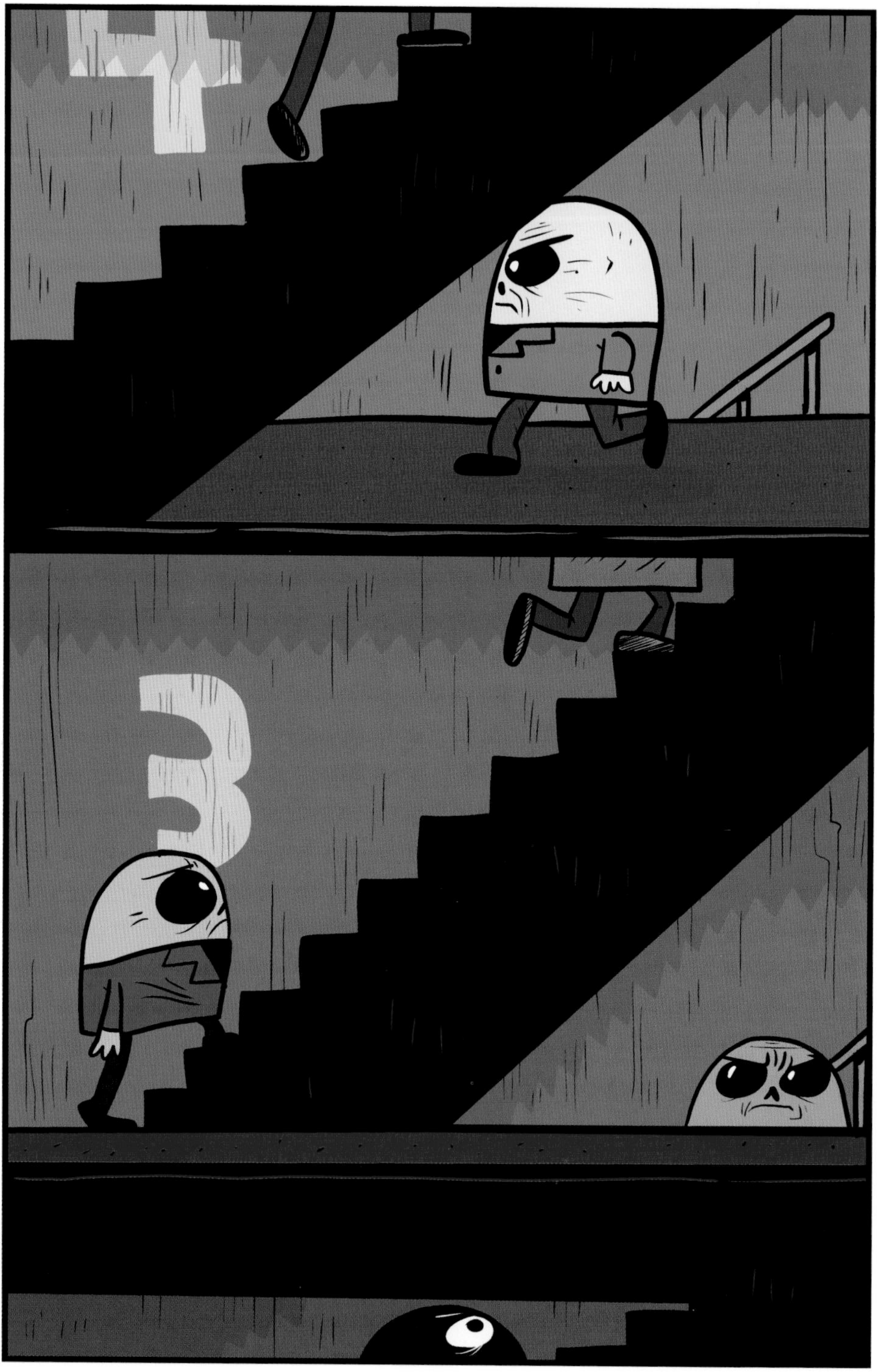
4
3

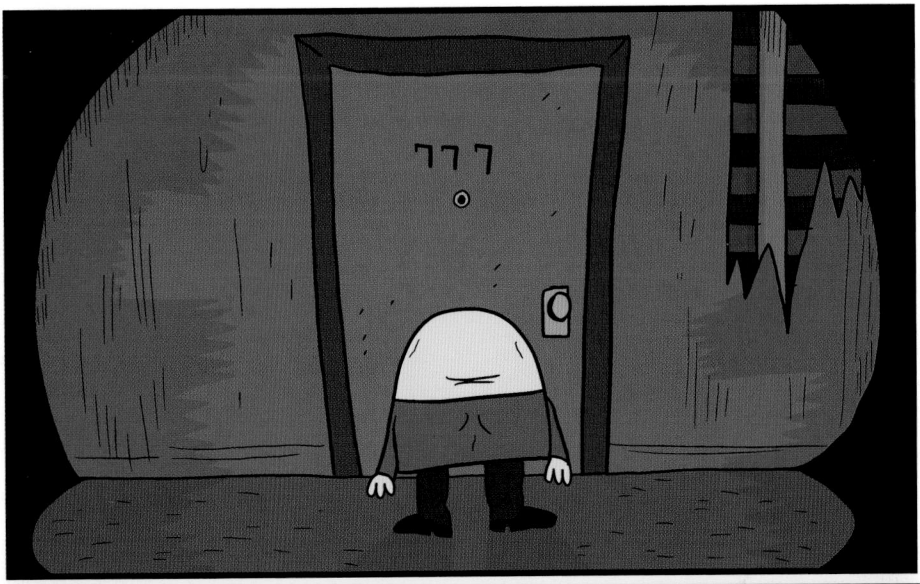
777

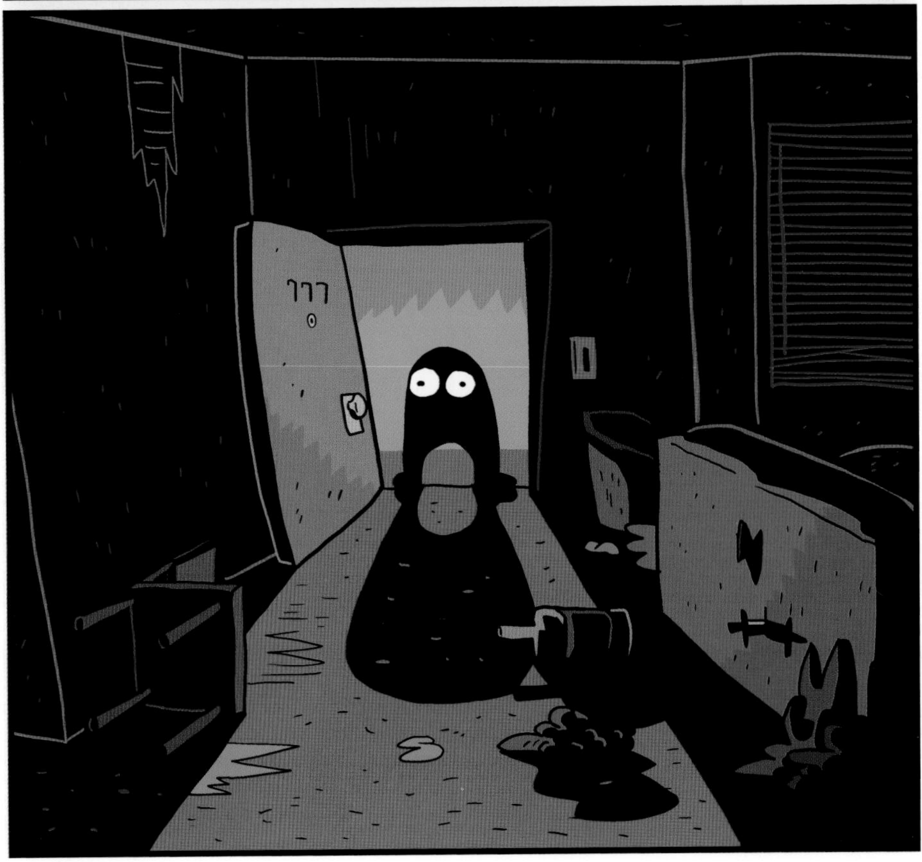
777

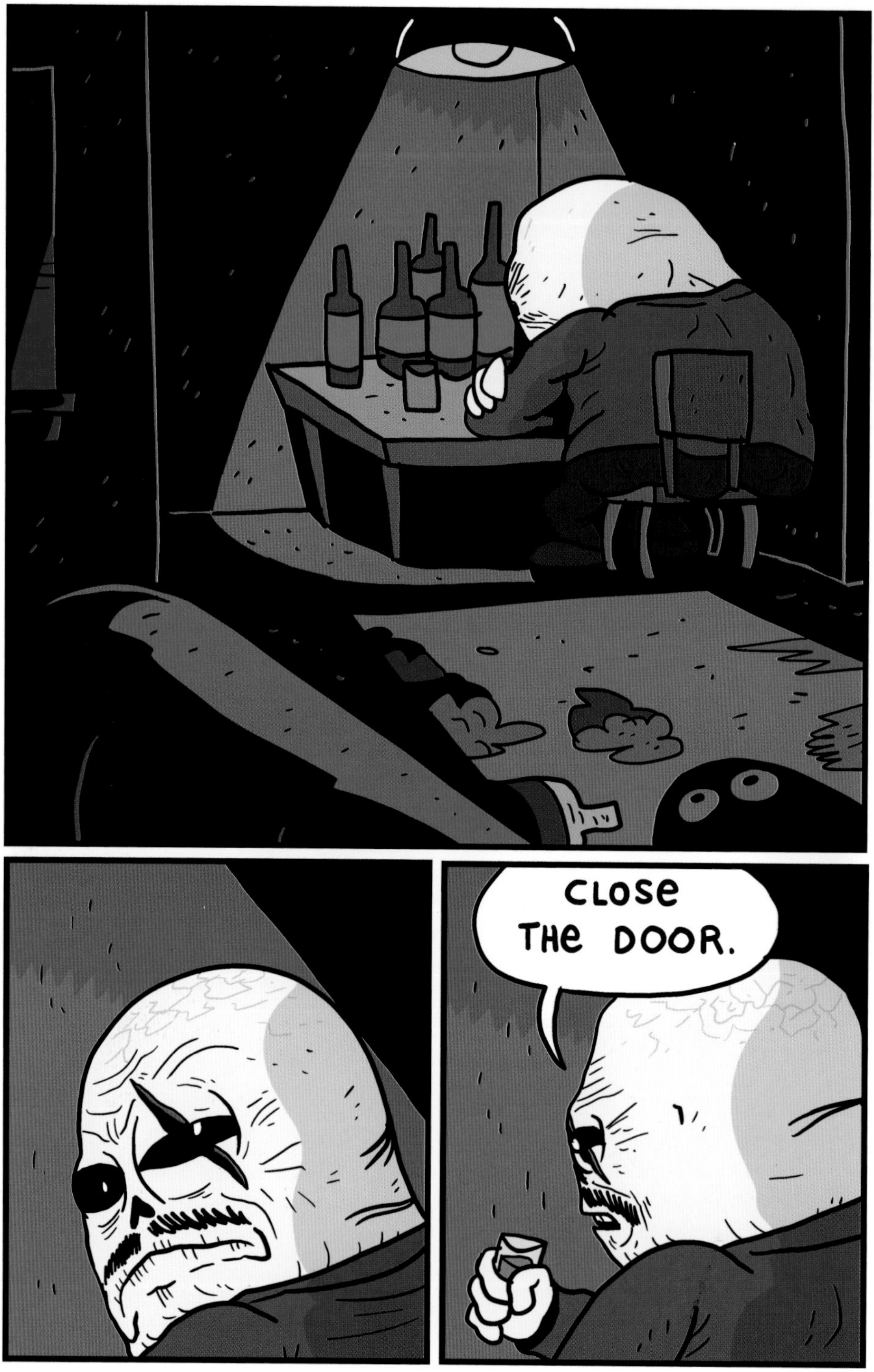
CLOSE THE DOOR.

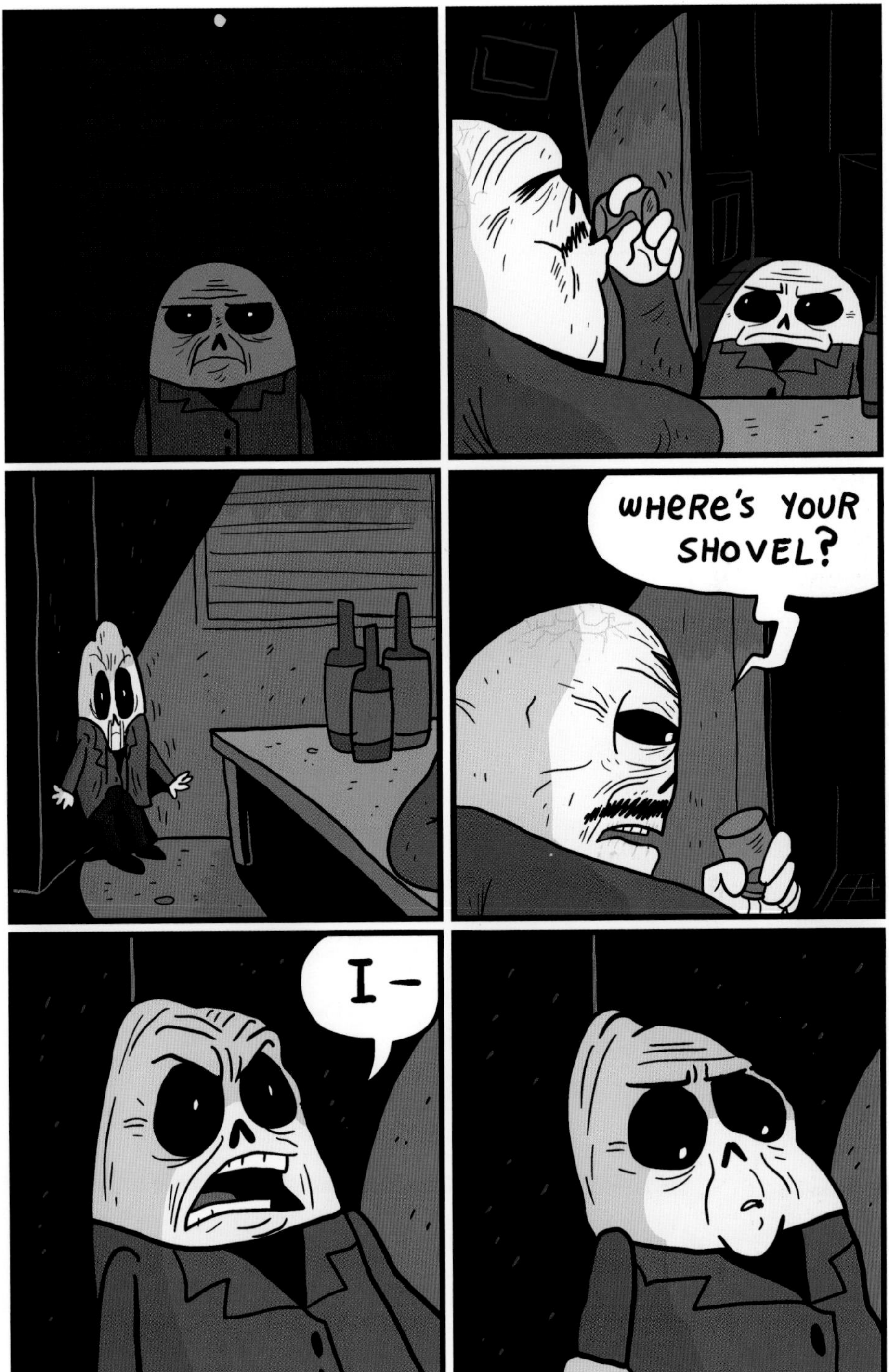
WHERE'S YOUR SHOVEL?
I-

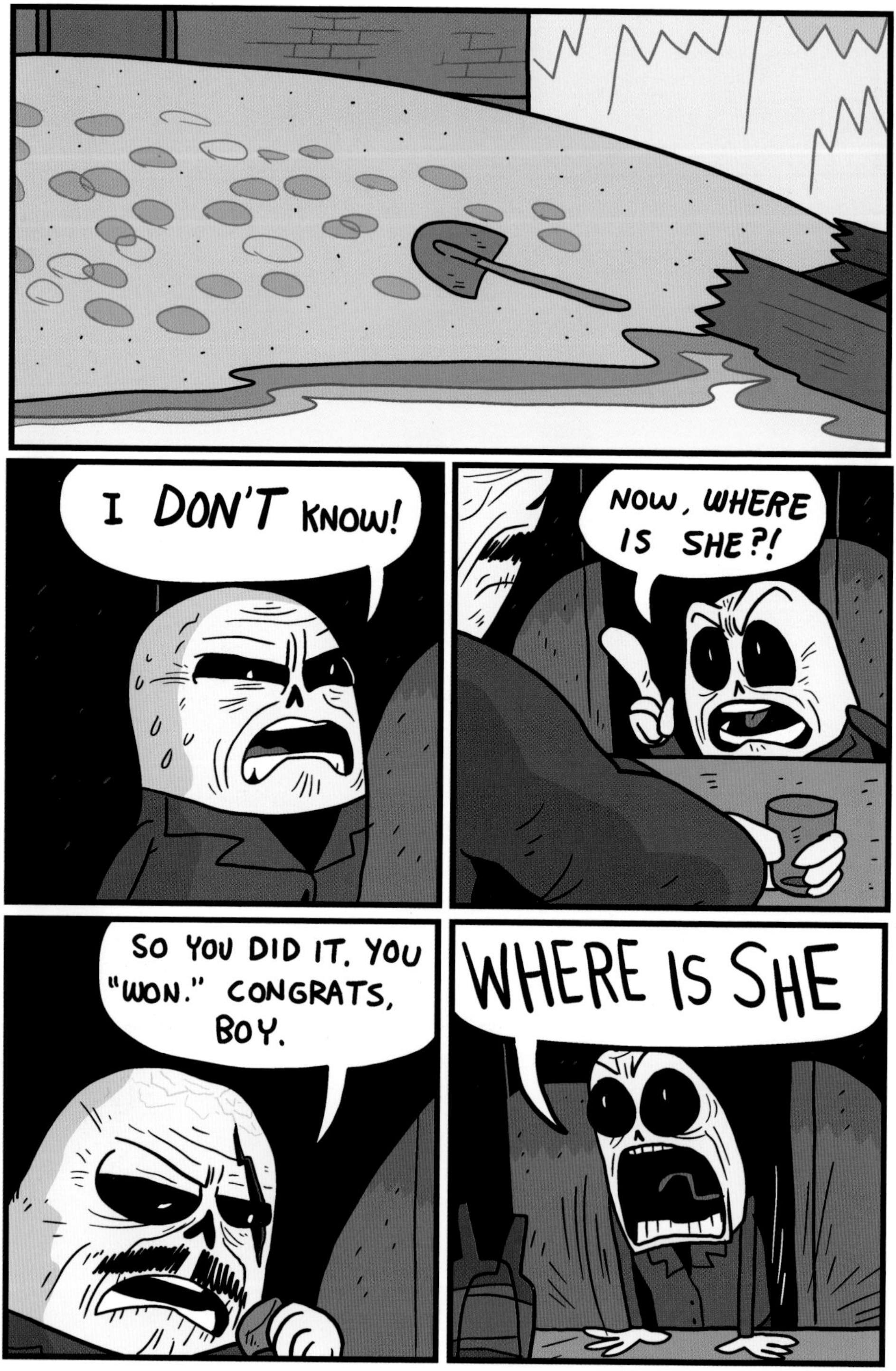
I DON'T KNOW!
NOW, WHERE IS SHE?!
SO YOU DID IT. YOU "WON." CONGRATS, BOY.
WHERE IS SHE

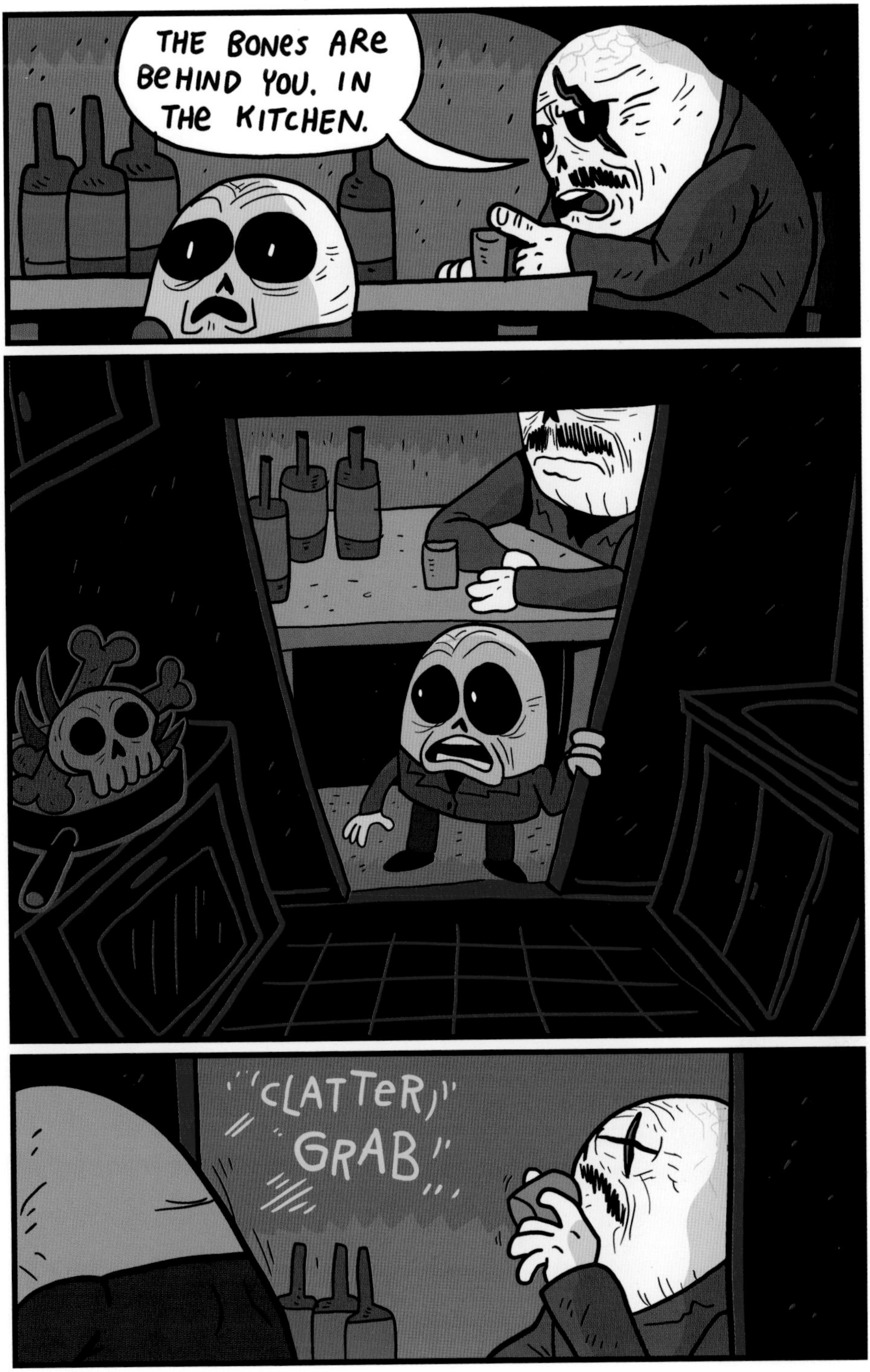
THE BONES ARE BEHIND YOU. IN THE KITCHEN.
CLATTER
GRAB

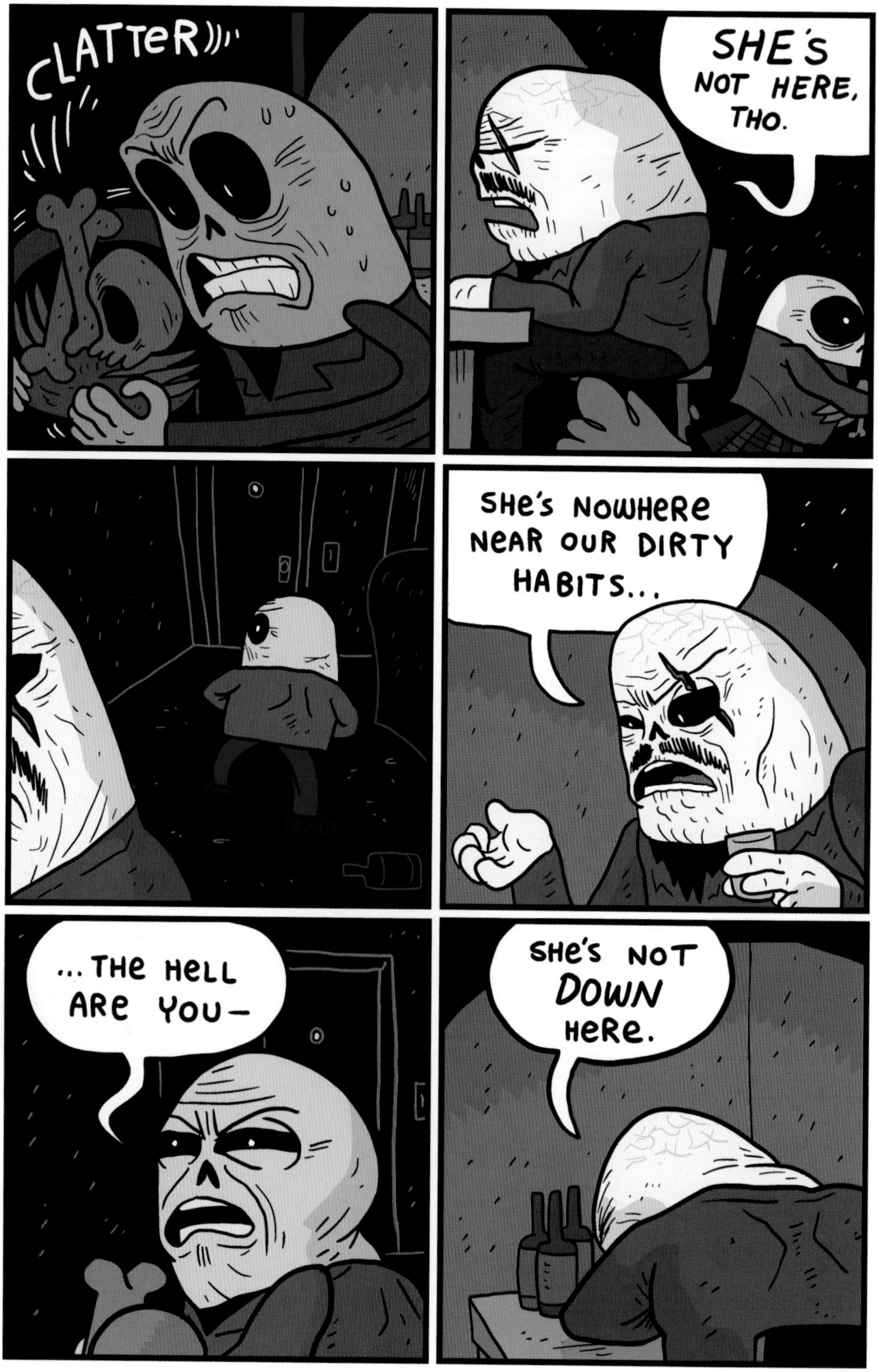
CLATTER
SHE'S NOT HERE, THO.
SHE'S NOWHERE NEAR OUR DIRTY HABITS...
...THE HELL ARE YOU—
SHE'S NOT DOWN HERE.

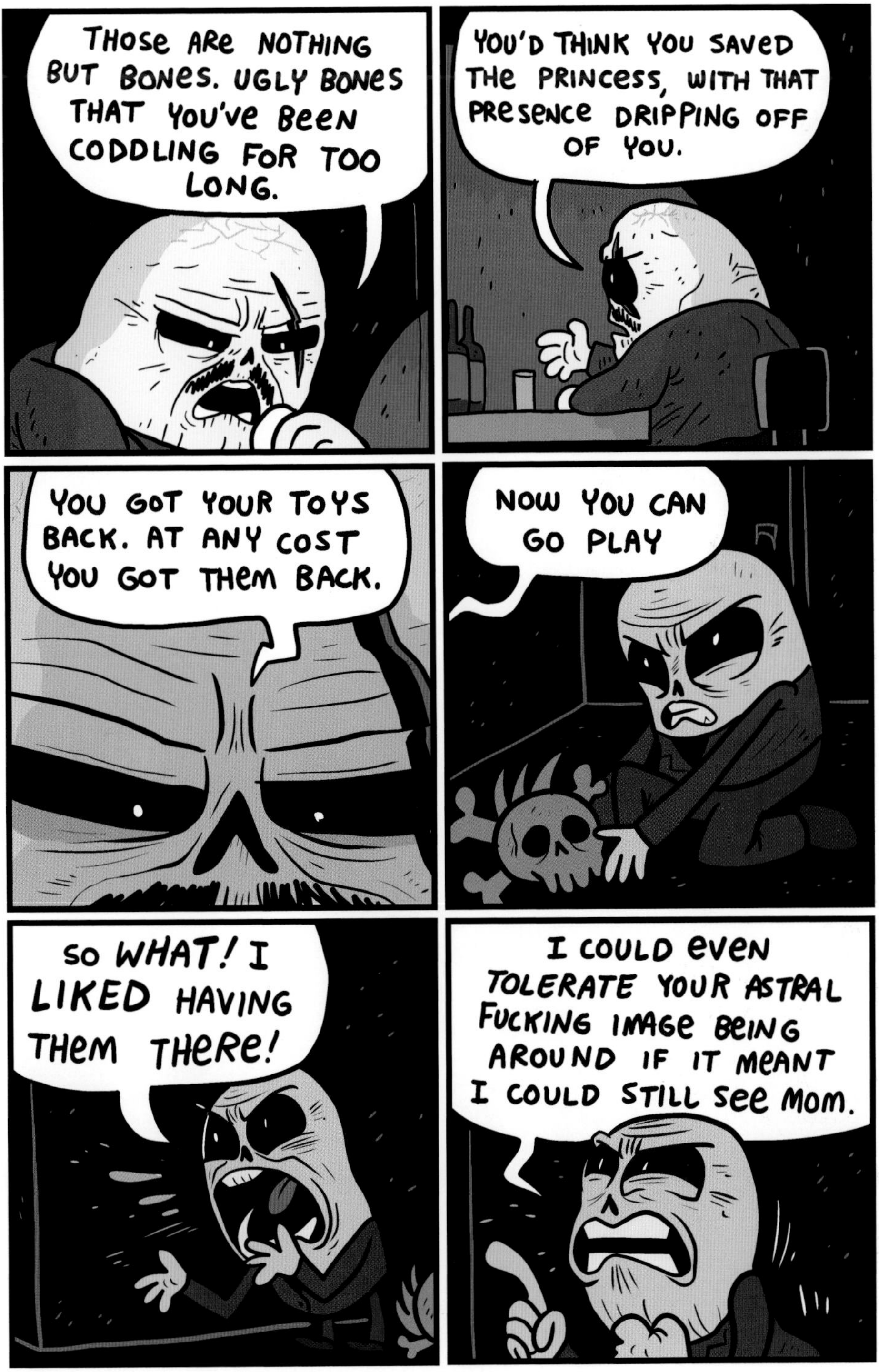
THOSE ARE NOTHING BUT BONES. UGLY BONES THAT YOU'VE BEEN CODDLING FOR TOO LONG.
YOU'D THINK YOU SAVED THE PRINCESS, WITH THAT PRESENCE DRIPPING OFF OF YOU.
YOU GOT YOUR TOYS BACK. AT ANY COST YOU GOT THEM BACK.
NOW YOU CAN GO PLAY
SO WHAT! I LIKED HAVING THEM THERE!
I COULD EVEN TOLERATE YOUR ASTRAL FUCKING IMAGE BEING AROUND IF IT MEANT I COULD STILL SEE MOM.

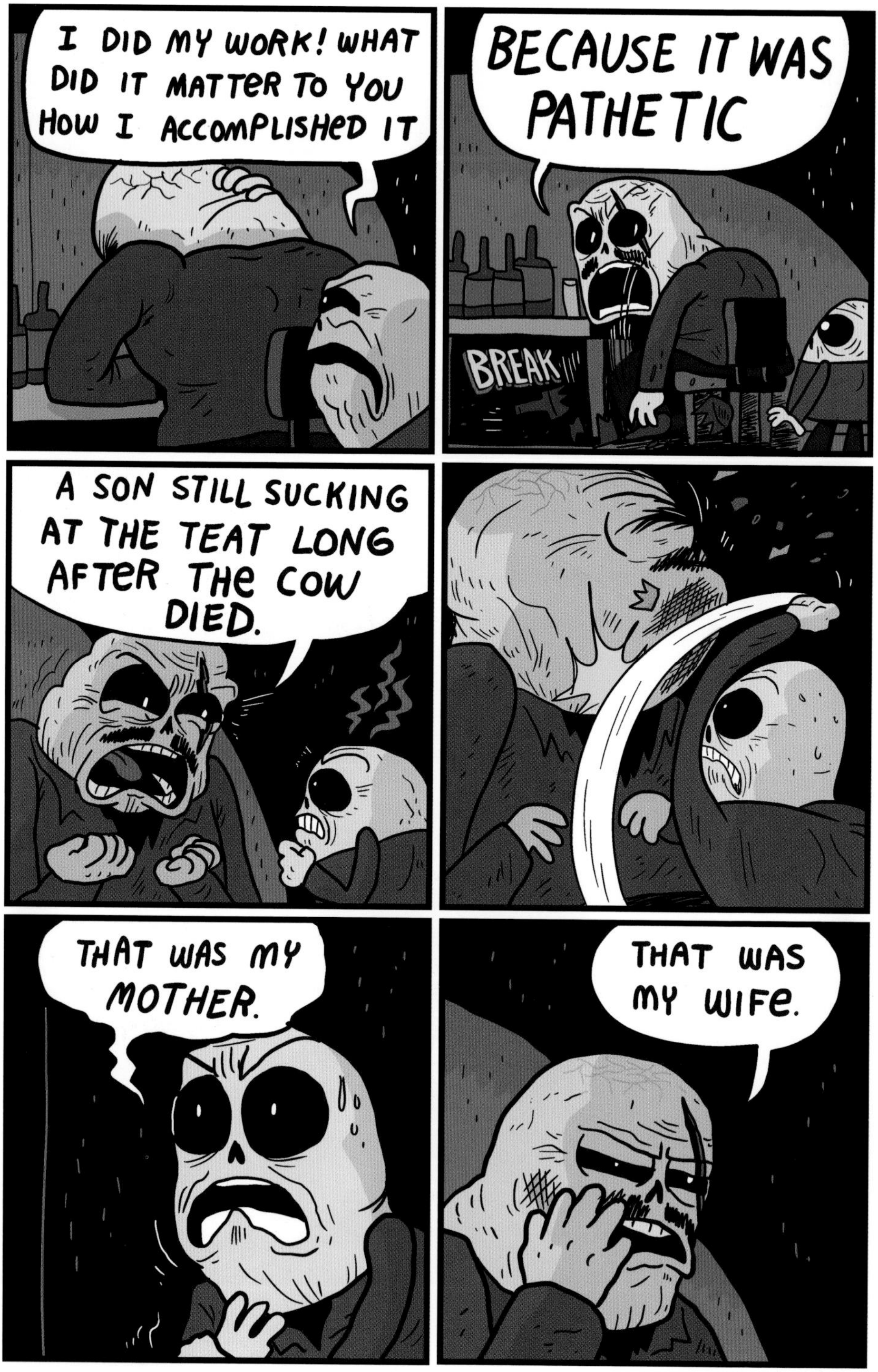
I DID MY WORK! WHAT DID IT MATTER TO YOU HOW I ACCOMPLISHED IT
BECAUSE IT WAS PATHETIC
BREAK
A SON STILL SUCKING AT THE TEAT LONG AFTER THE COW DIED.
THAT WAS MY MOTHER.
THAT WAS MY WIFE.

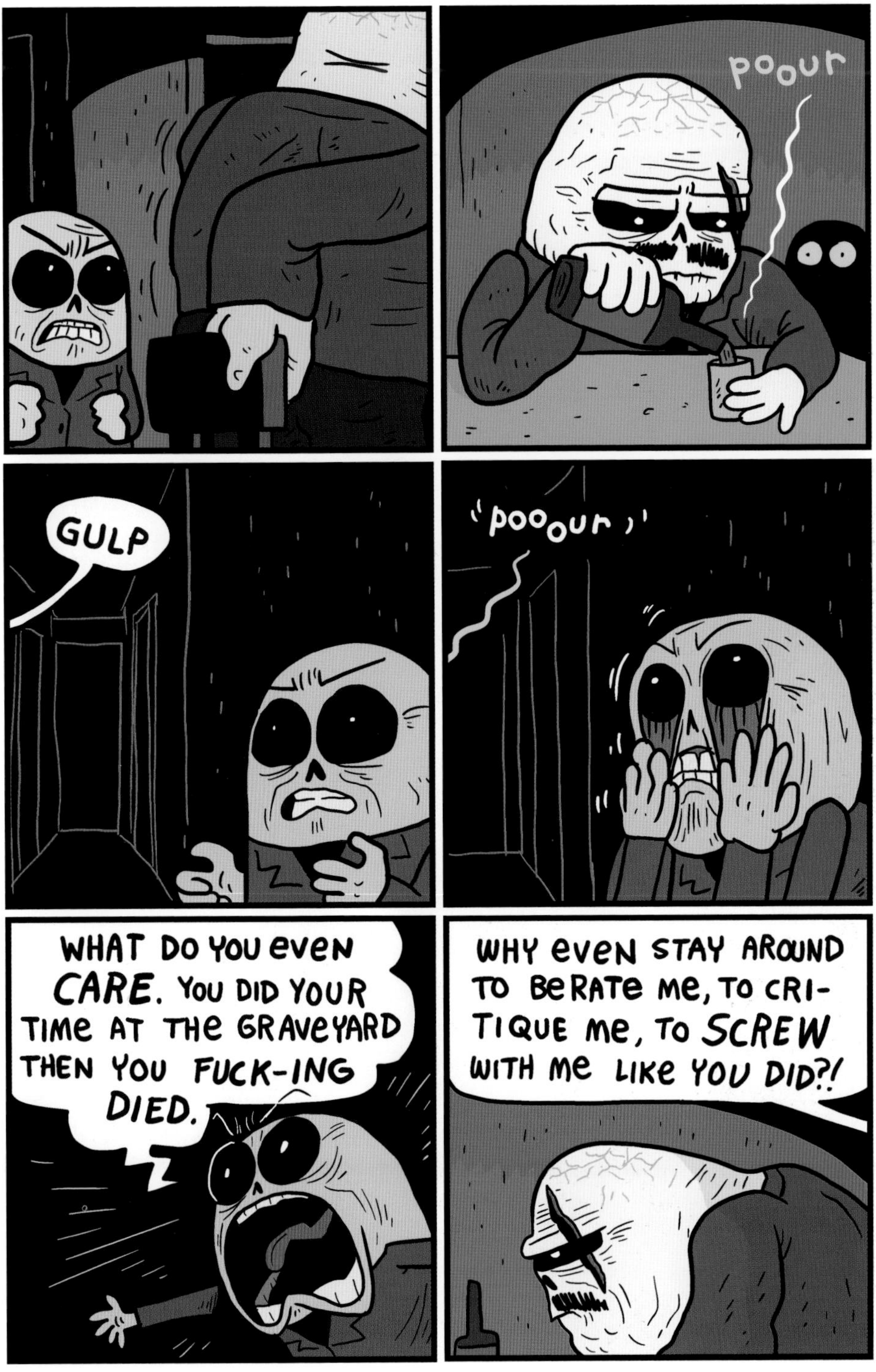
poour
GULP
poooour
WHAT DO YOU even CARE. YOU DID YOUR TIME AT THE GRAVEYARD THEN YOU FUCK-ING DIED.
WHY even STAY AROUND TO BERATE me, TO CRI-TIQUE me, TO SCREW WITH me LIKE YOU DID?!

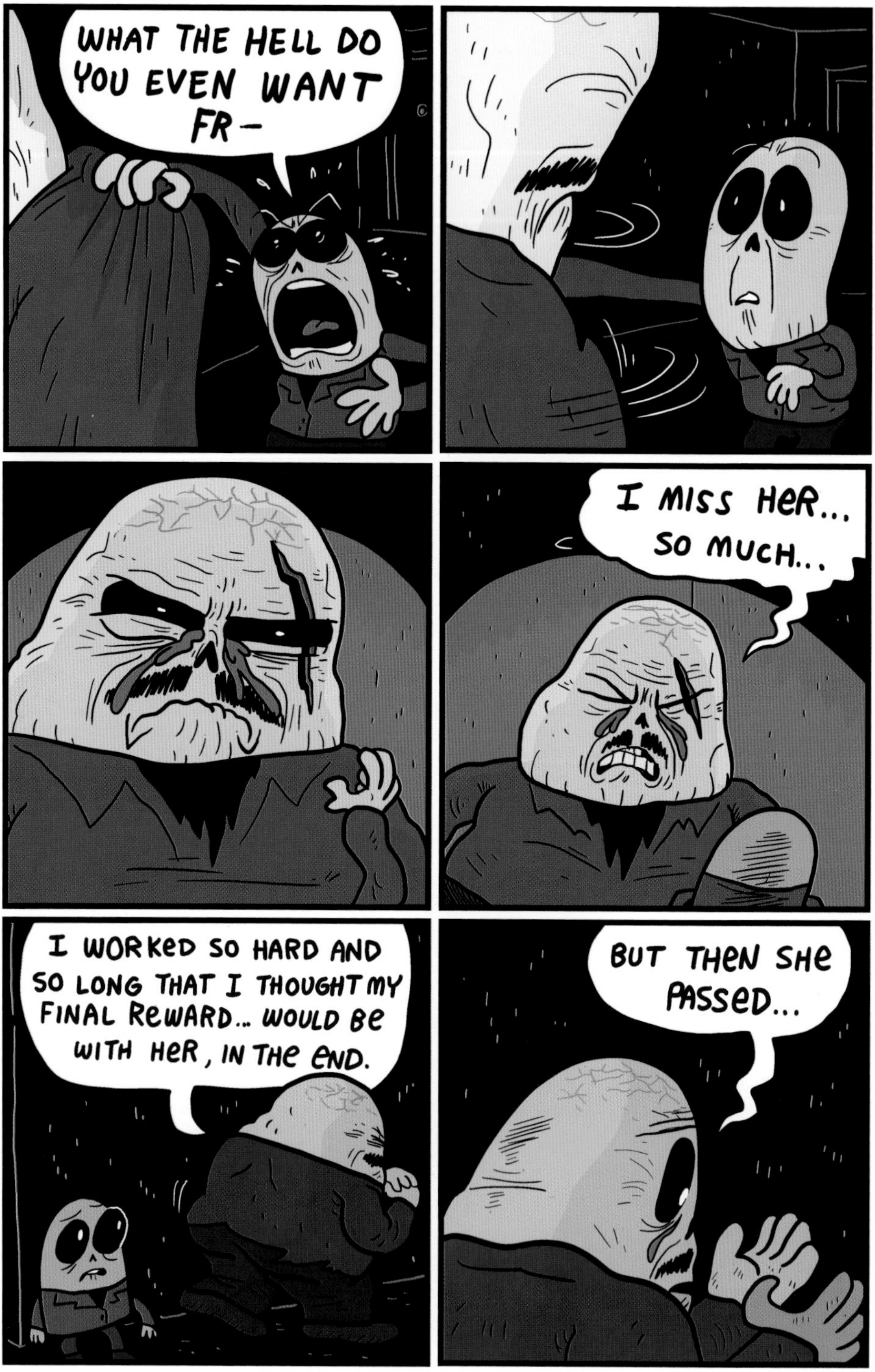
WHAT THE HELL DO YOU EVEN WANT FR–
I MISS HER... SO MUCH...
I WORKED SO HARD AND SO LONG THAT I THOUGHT MY FINAL REWARD... WOULD BE WITH HER, IN THE END.
BUT THEN SHE PASSED...

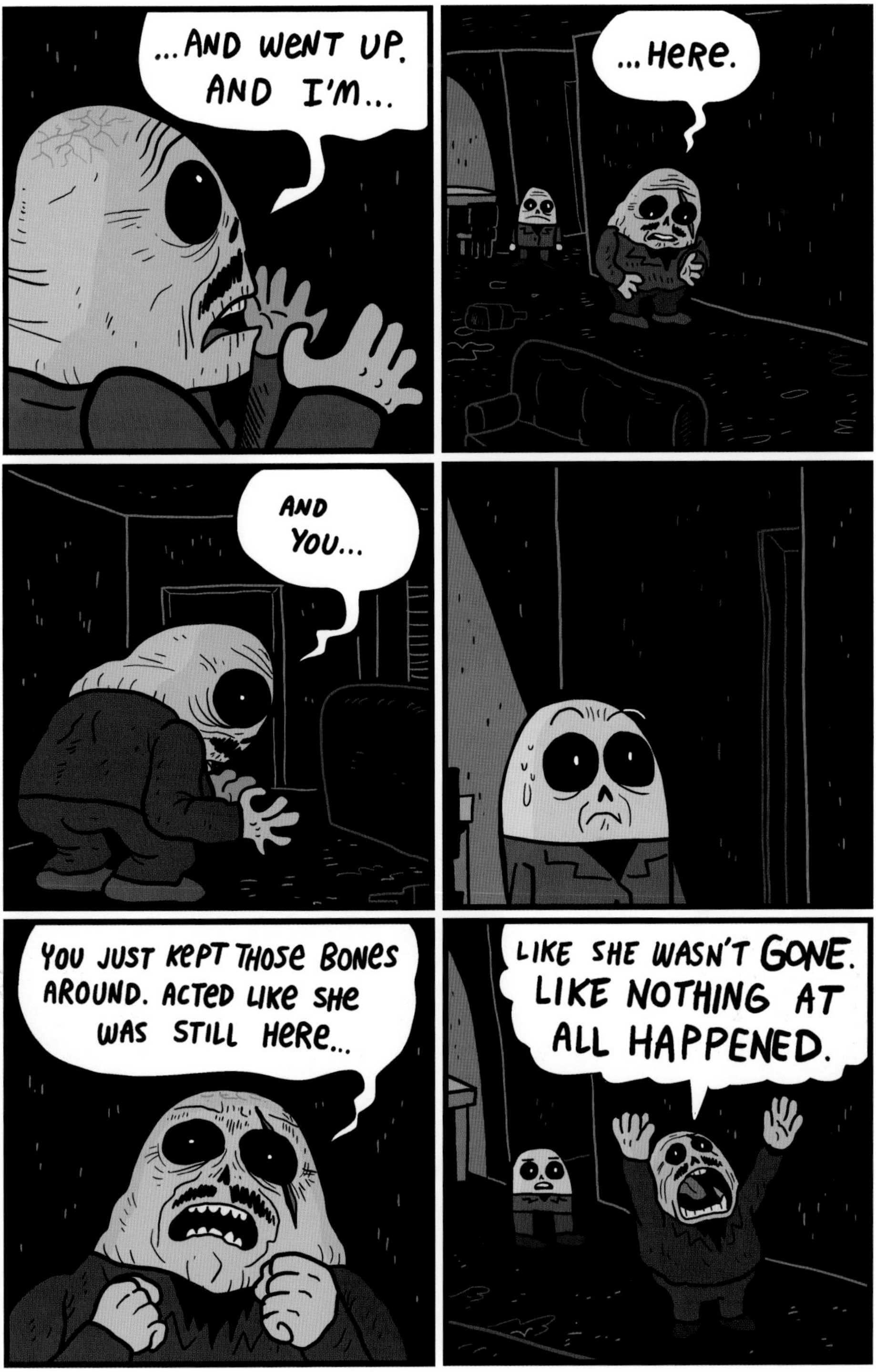
...AND WENT UP. AND I'M...
...HERE.
AND YOU...
YOU JUST KEPT THOSE BONES AROUND. ACTED LIKE SHE WAS STILL HERE...
LIKE SHE WASN'T GONE. LIKE NOTHING AT ALL HAPPENED.

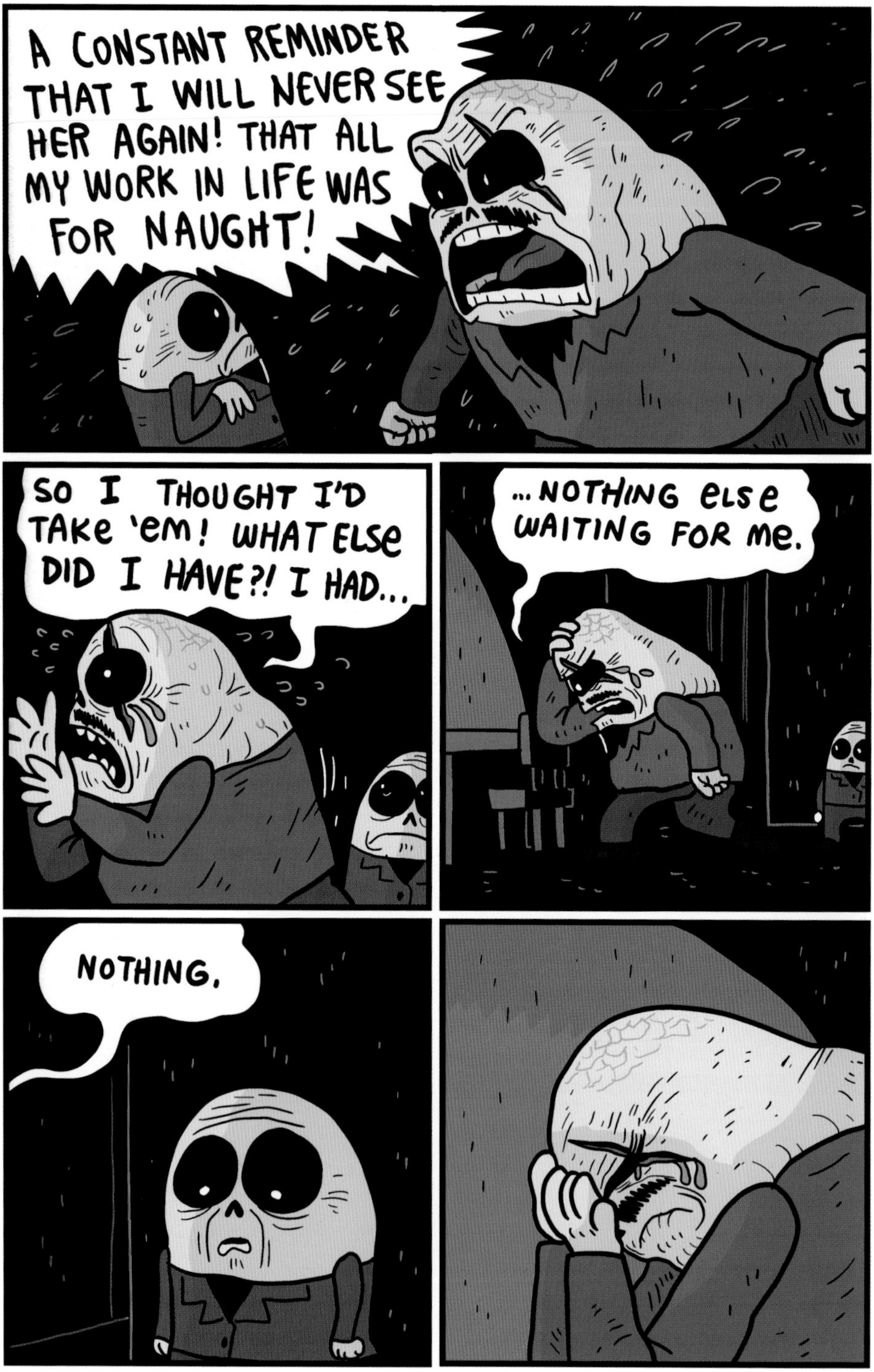
A CONSTANT REMINDER THAT I WILL NEVER SEE HER AGAIN! THAT ALL MY WORK IN LIFE WAS FOR NAUGHT!
SO I THOUGHT I'D TAKE 'EM! WHAT ELSE DID I HAVE?! I HAD...
...NOTHING ELSE WAITING FOR ME.
NOTHING.

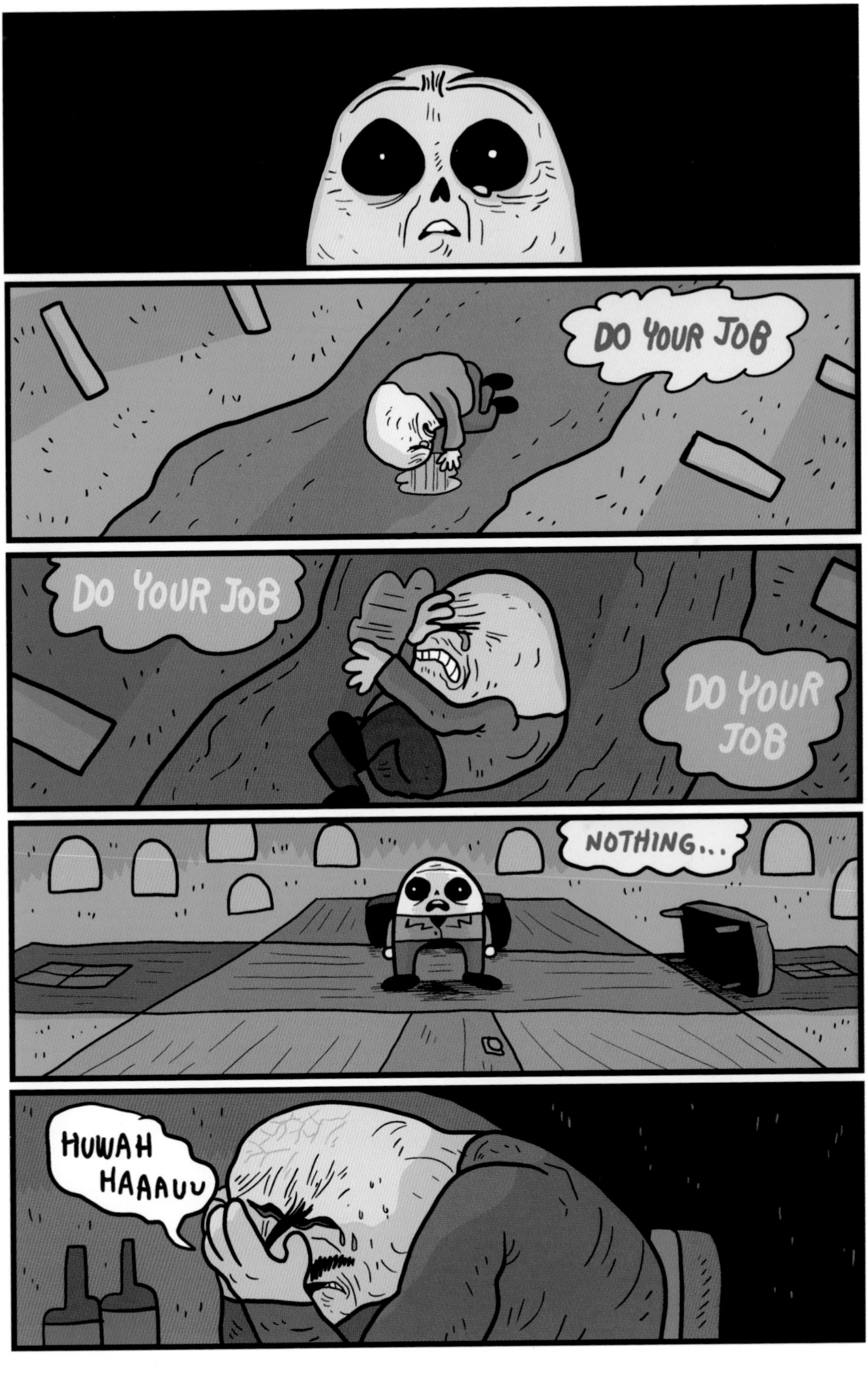
DO YOUR JOB
DO YOUR JOB
DO YOUR JOB
NOTHING...
HUWAH HAAAUU

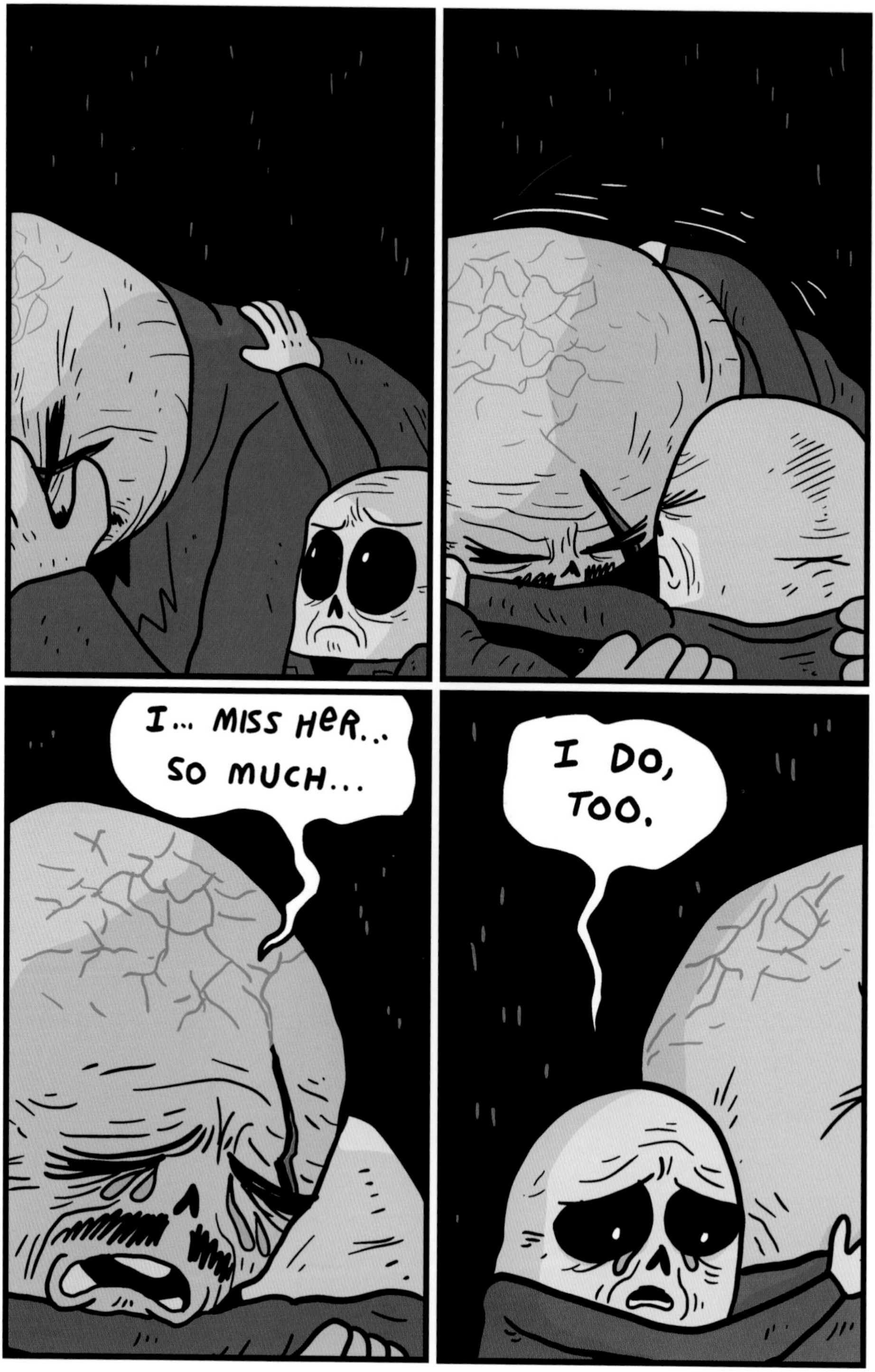
I... MISS HER... SO MUCH...
I DO, TOO.

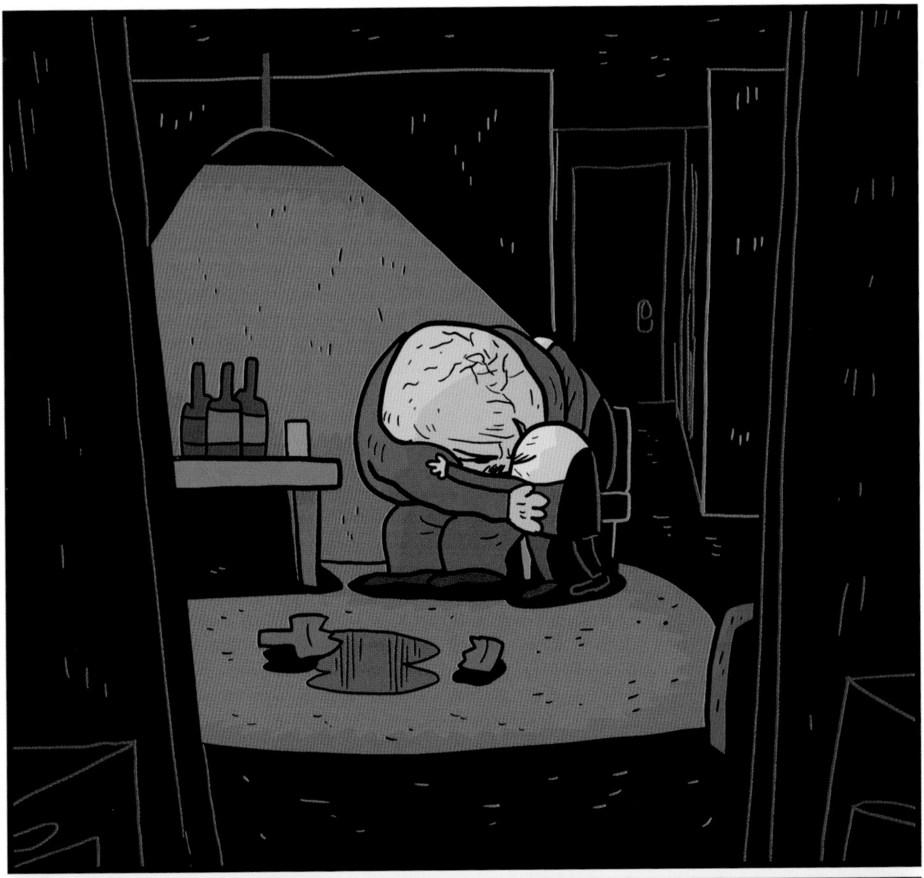

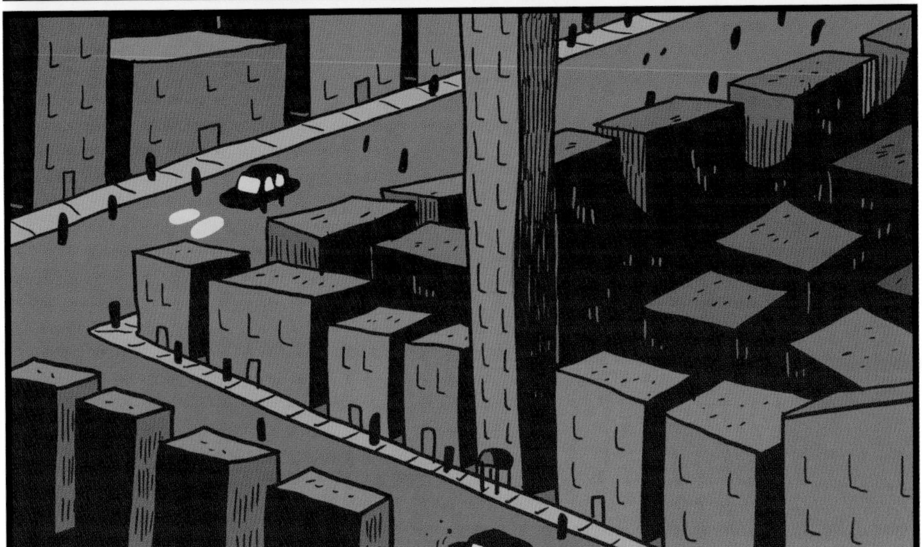

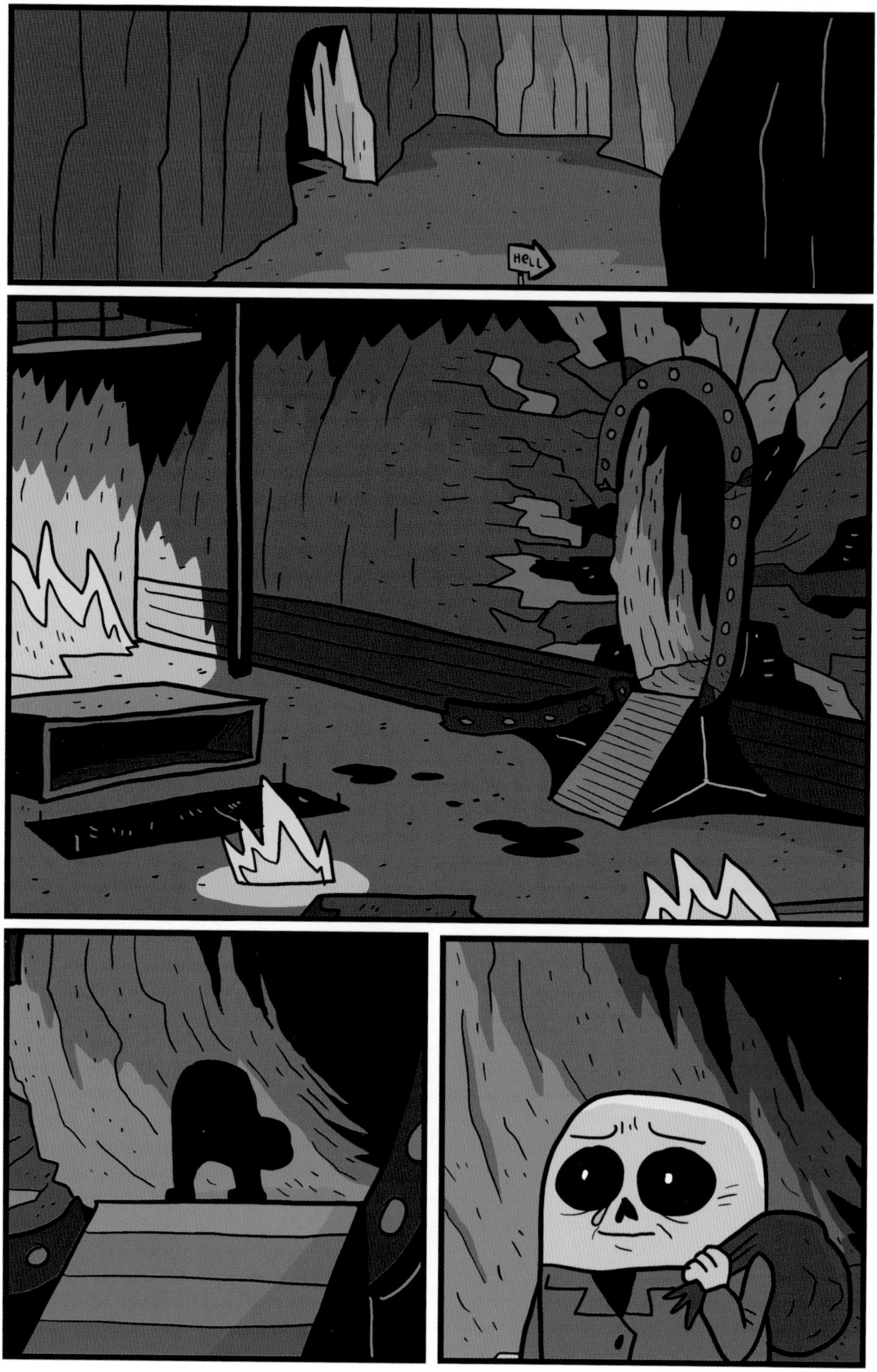
HELL

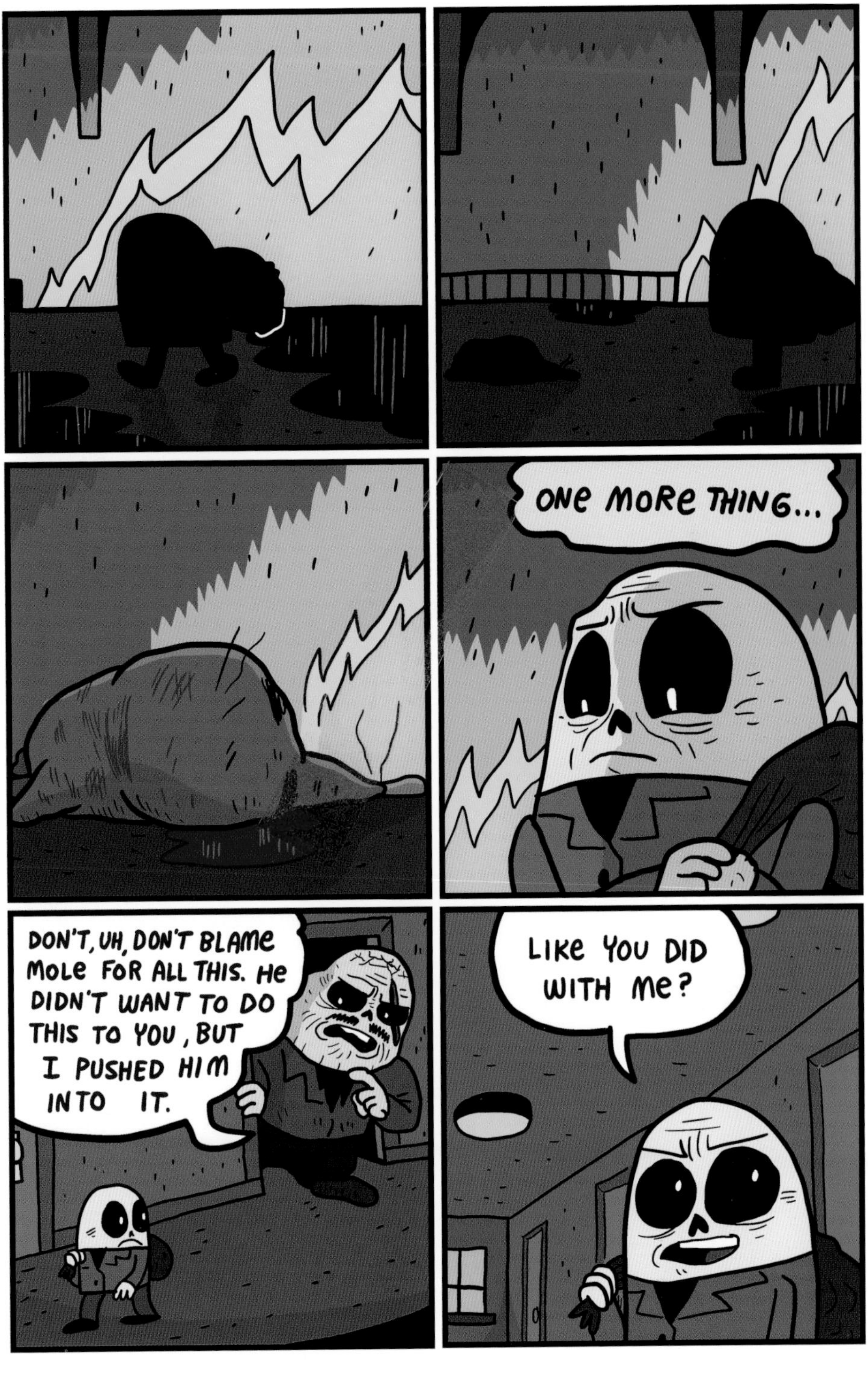
ONE MORE THING...
DON'T, UH, DON'T BLAME MOLE FOR ALL THIS. HE DIDN'T WANT TO DO THIS TO YOU, BUT I PUSHED HIM INTO IT.
LIKE YOU DID WITH ME?

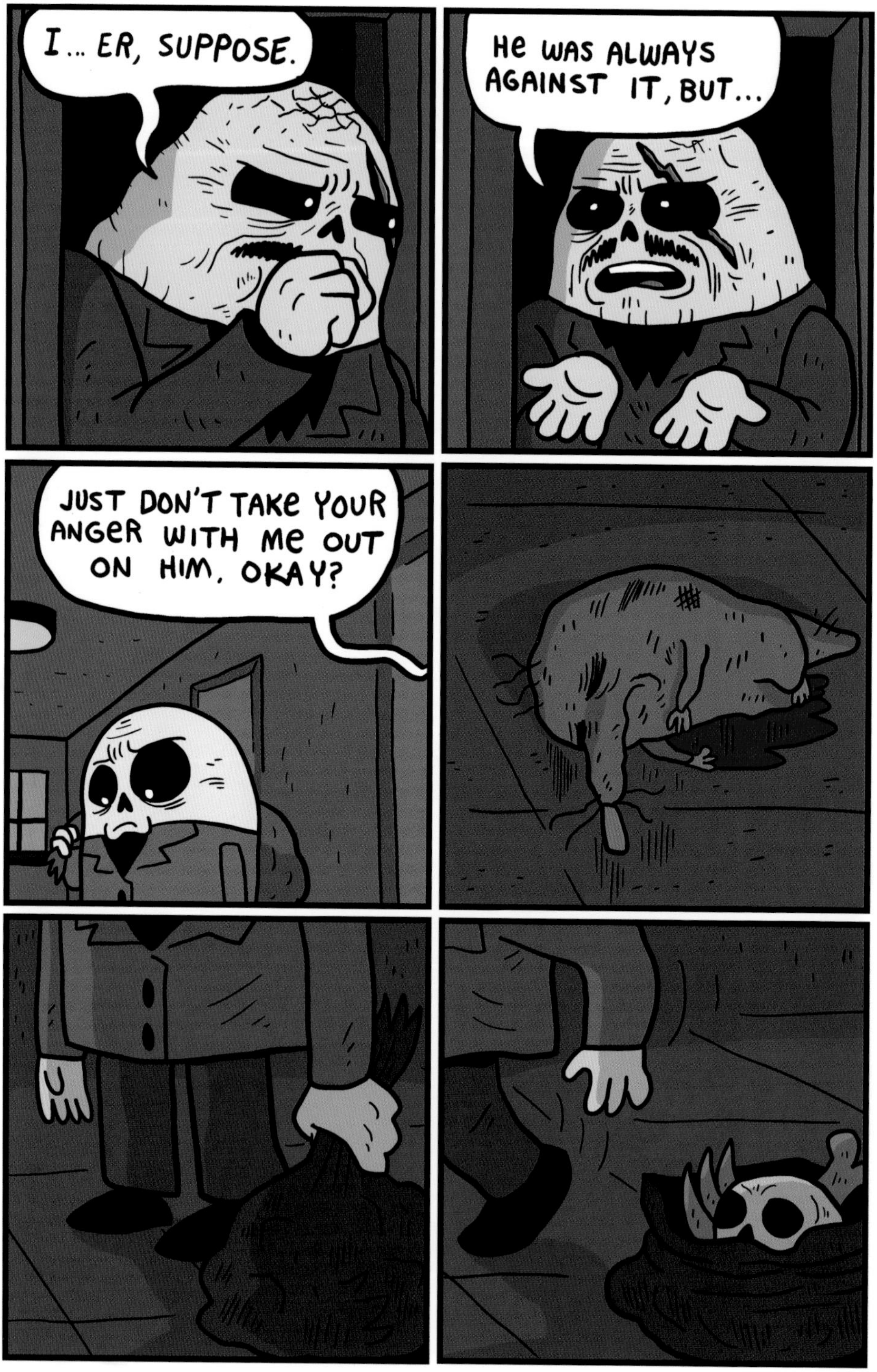
I... ER, SUPPOSE.
HE WAS ALWAYS AGAINST IT, BUT...
JUST DON'T TAKE YOUR ANGER WITH ME OUT ON HIM, OKAY?

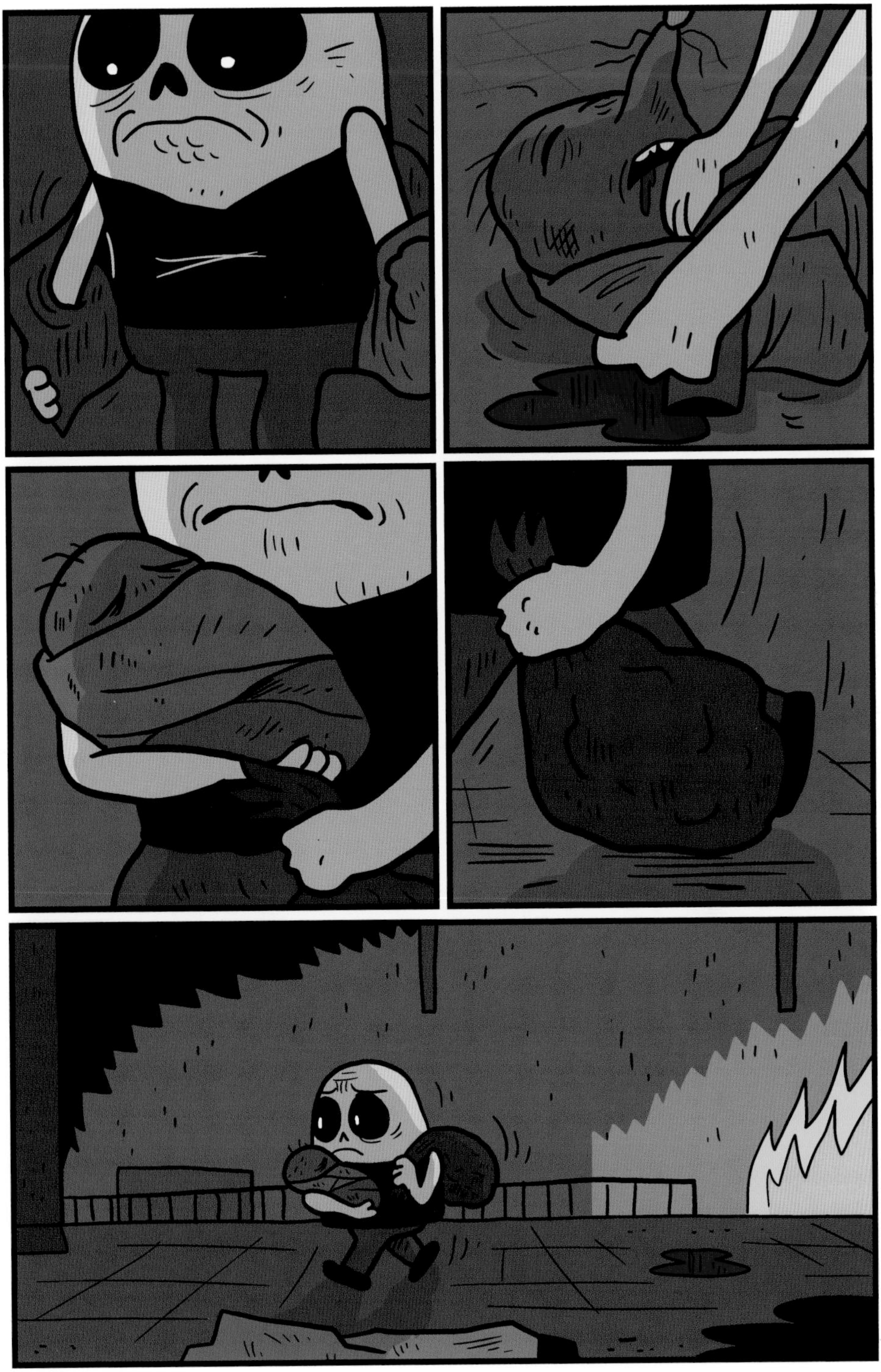

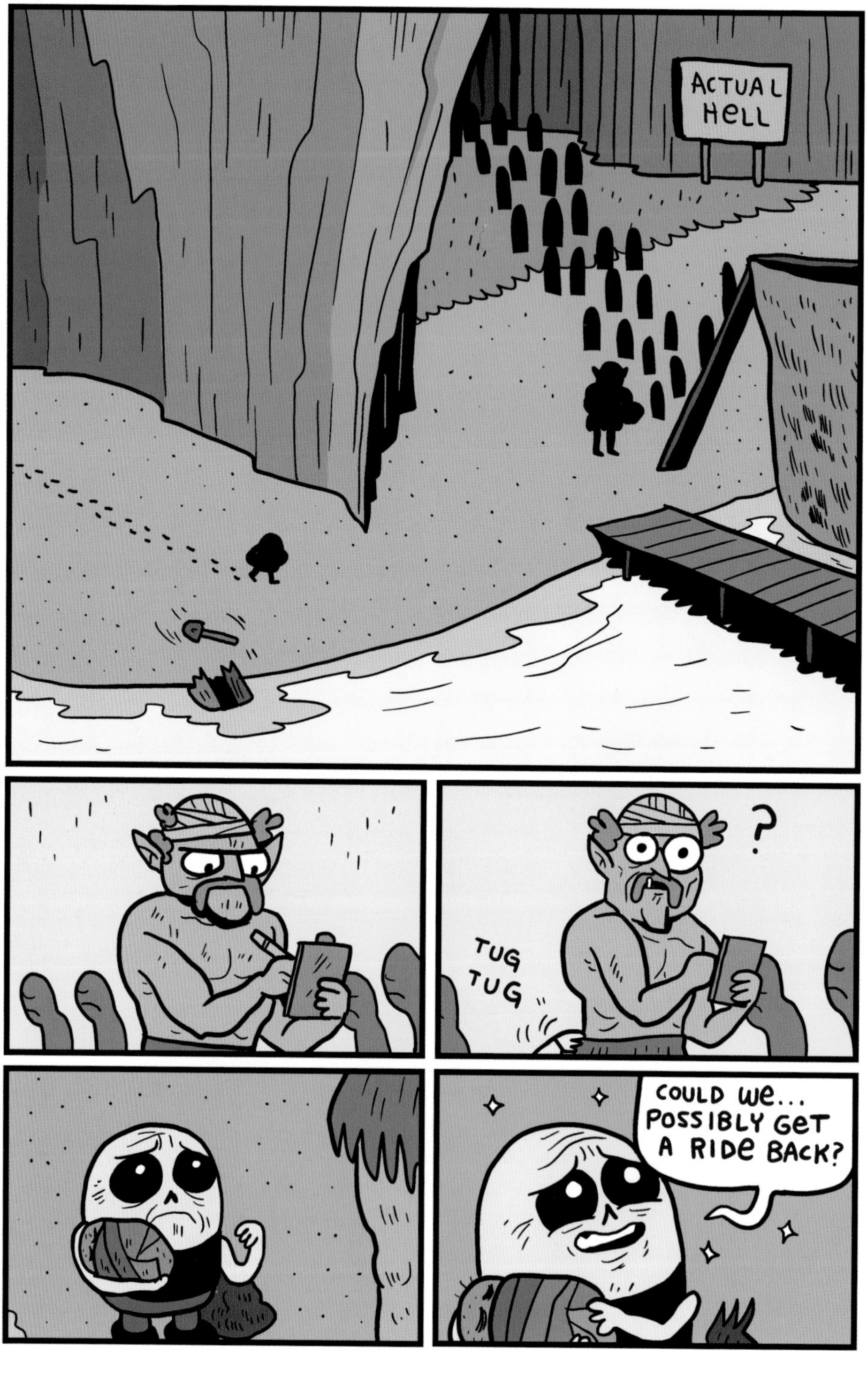
ACTUAL HELL
?
TUG TUG
COULD WE... POSSIBLY GET A RIDE BACK?

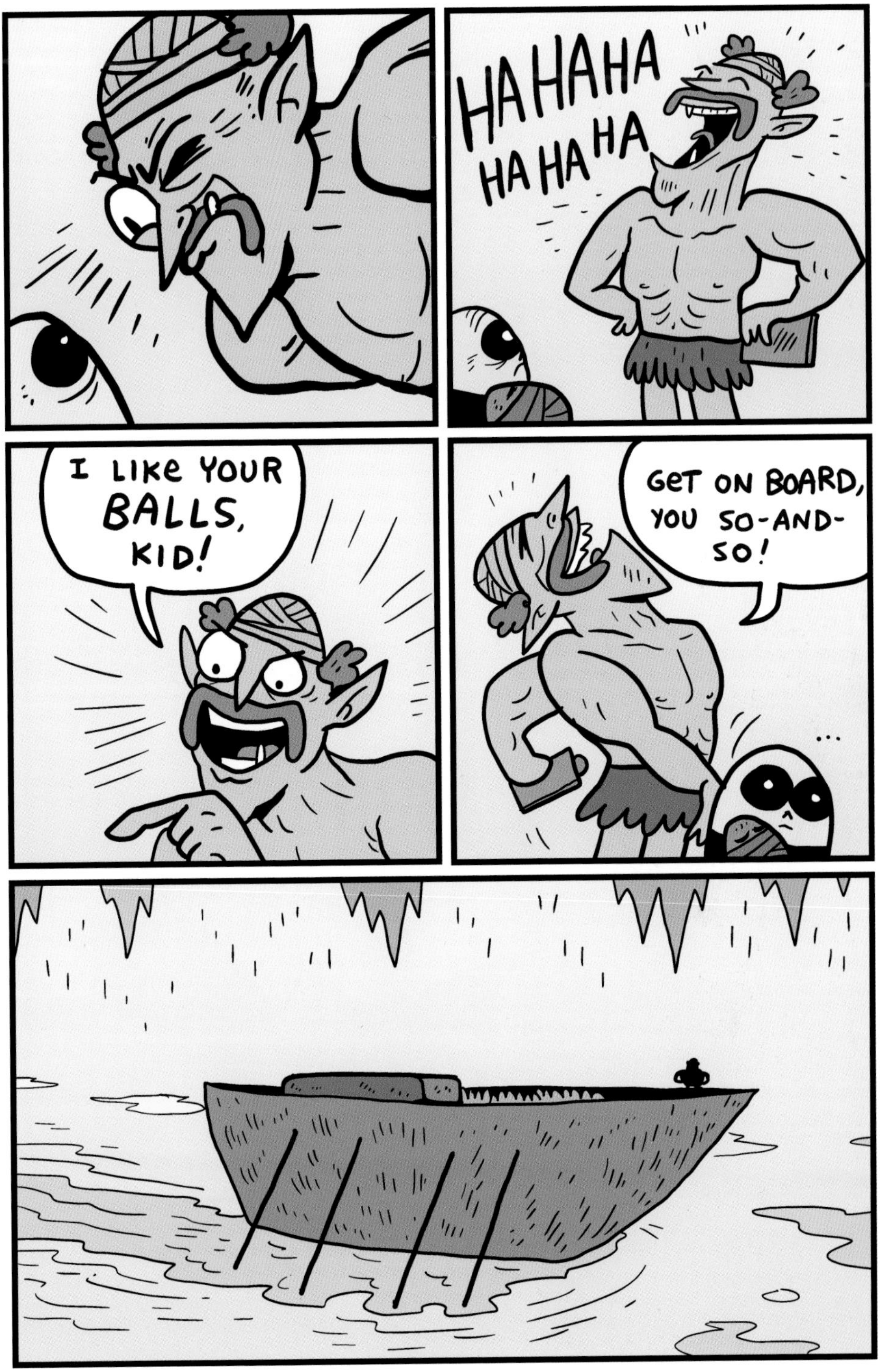
HAHAHA
HA HA HA
I LIKE YOUR BALLS, KID!
GET ON BOARD, YOU SO-AND-SO!
...

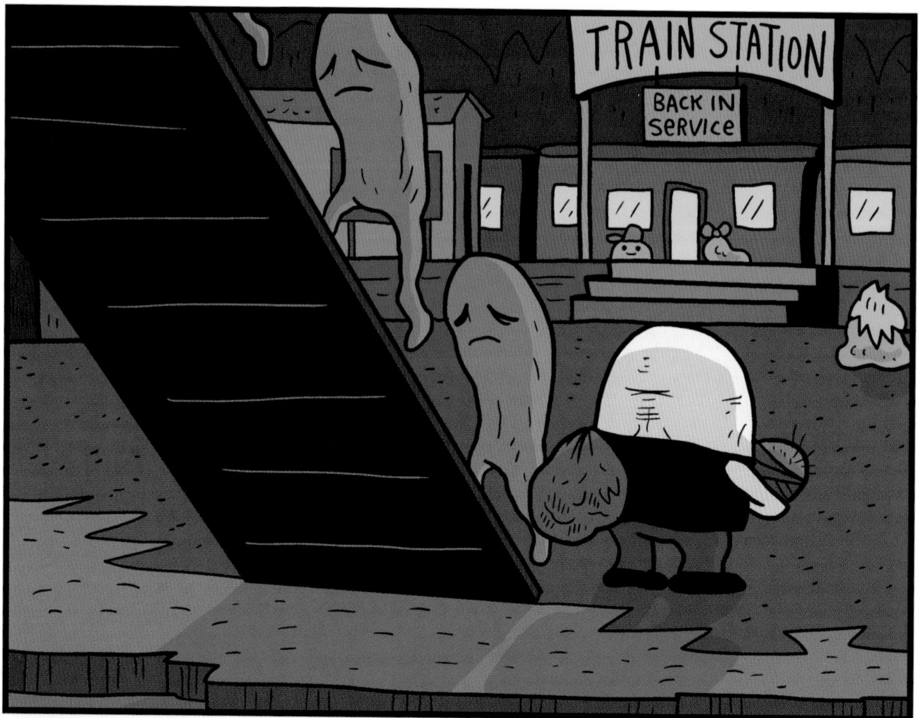
TRAIN STATION
BACK IN SERVICE

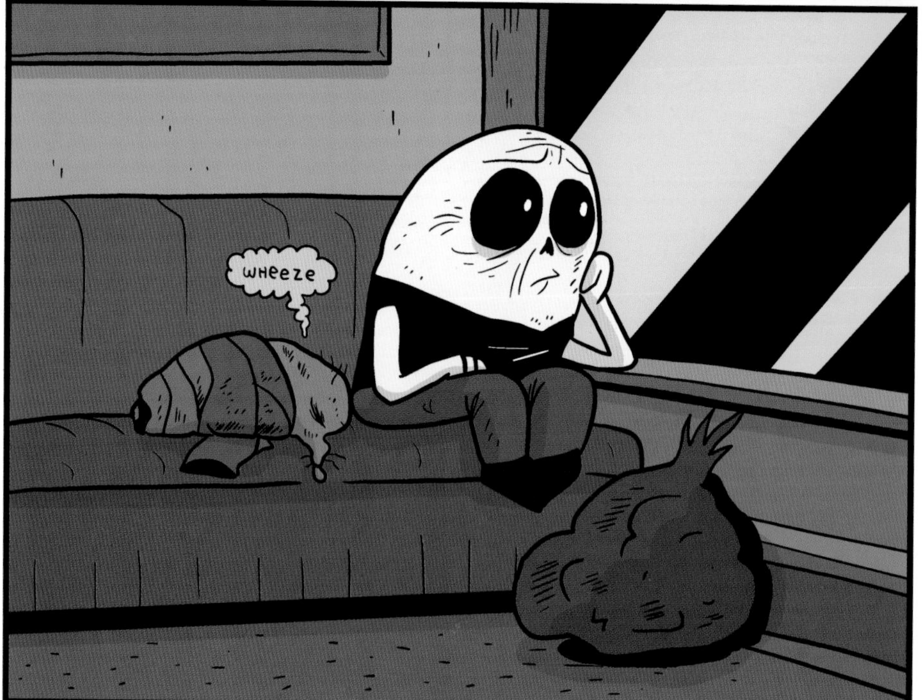
WHEEZE

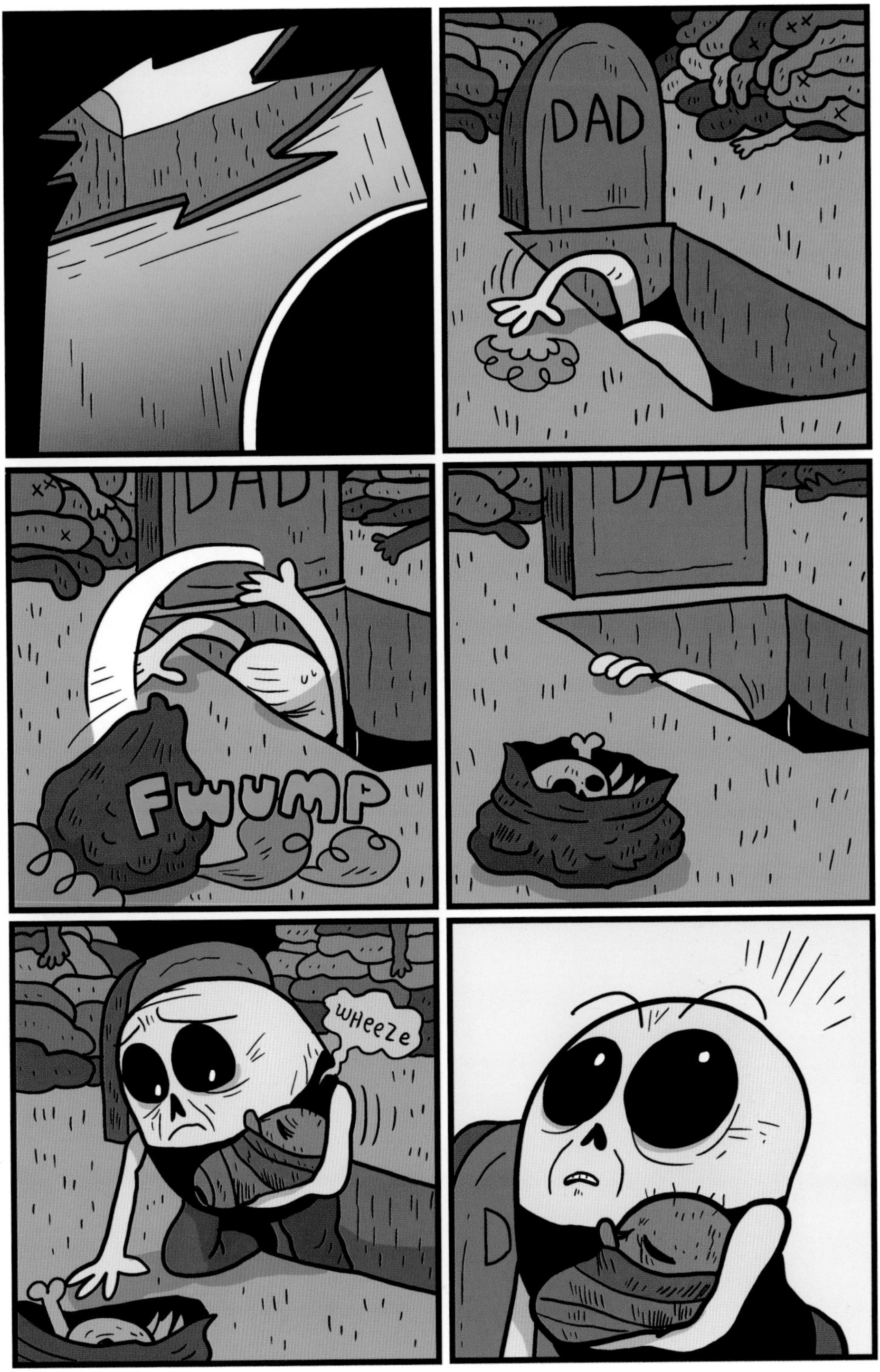
DAD
FWUMP
WHEEZE

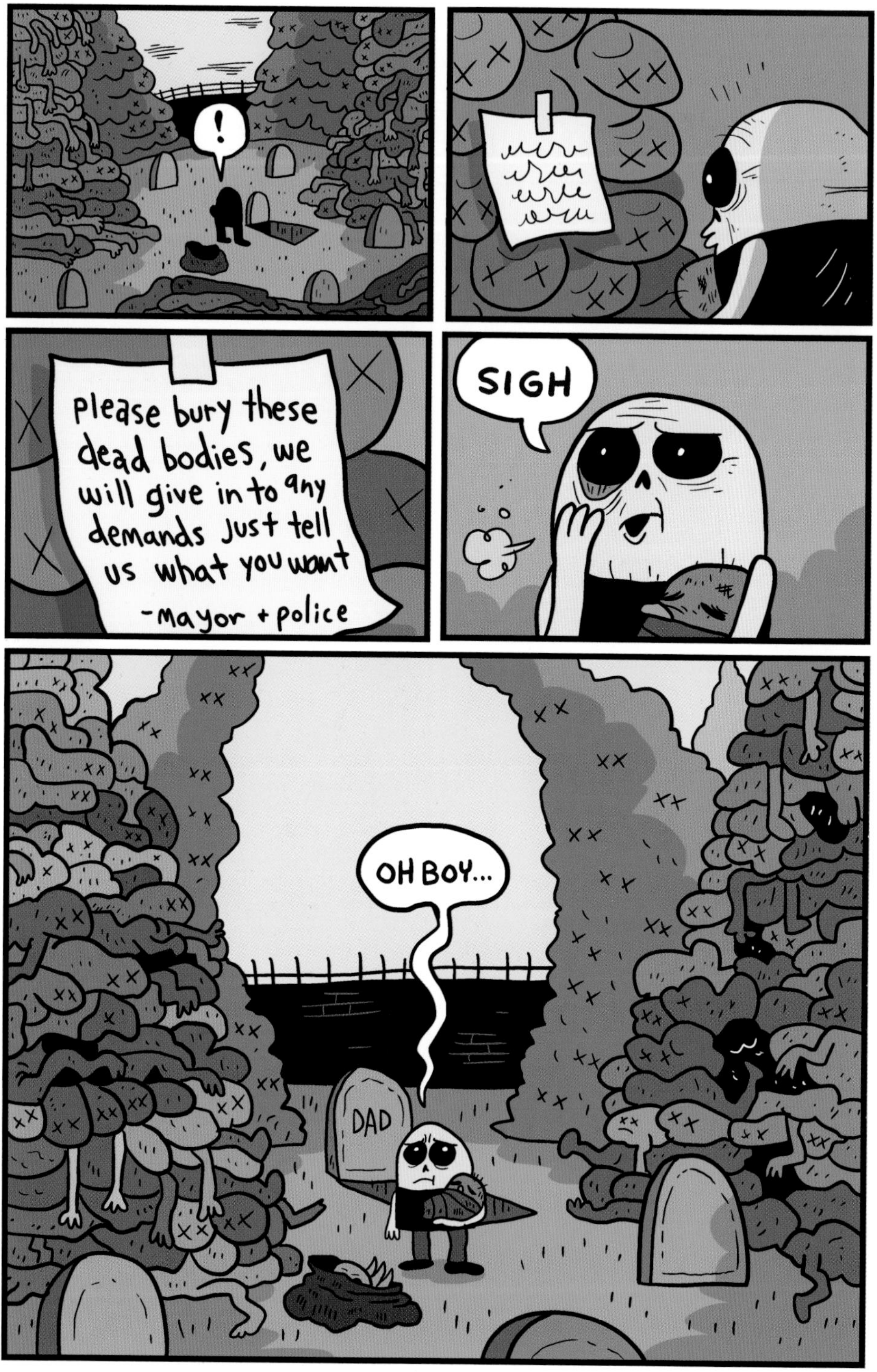
!
please bury these dead bodies, we will give in to any demands just tell us what you want
-mayor + police
SIGH
OH BOY...
DAD

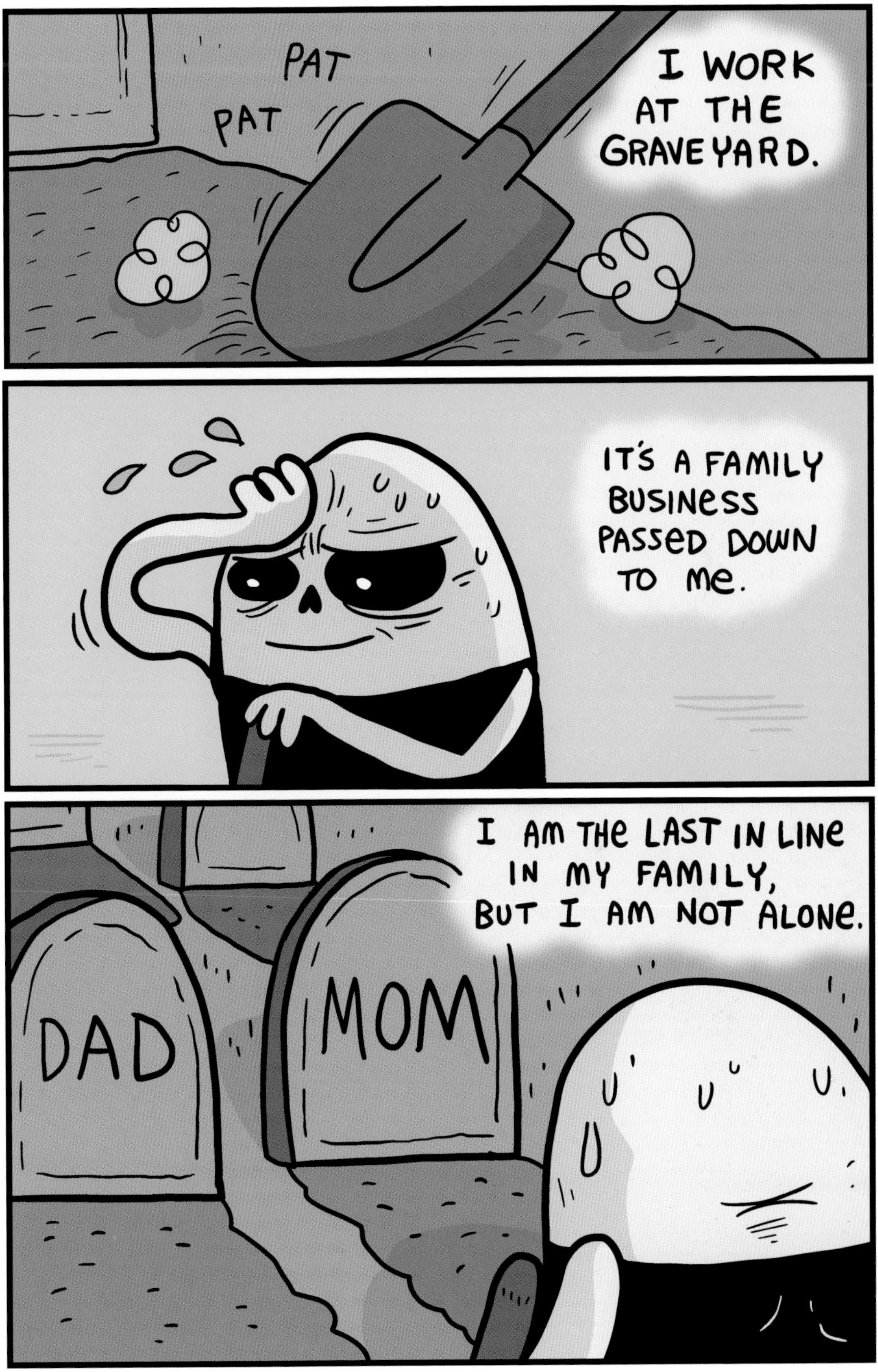
PAT
PAT
I WORK AT THE GRAVEYARD.
IT'S A FAMILY BUSINESS PASSED DOWN TO ME.
I AM THE LAST IN LINE IN MY FAMILY, BUT I AM NOT ALONE.
DAD
MOM

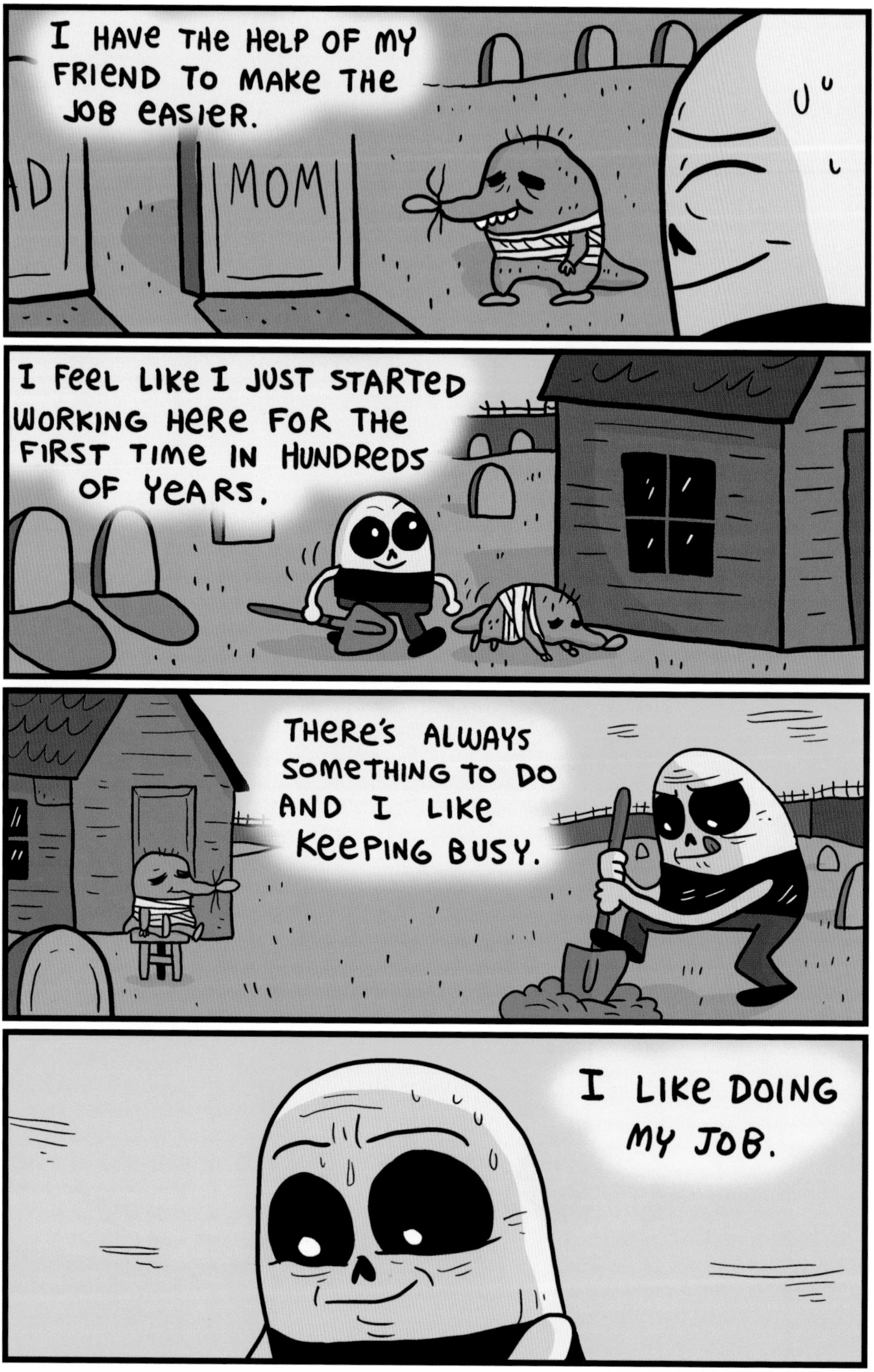
I HAVE THE HELP OF MY FRIEND TO MAKE THE JOB EASIER.
MOM
I FEEL LIKE I JUST STARTED WORKING HERE FOR THE FIRST TIME IN HUNDREDS OF YEARS.
THERE'S ALWAYS SOMETHING TO DO AND I LIKE KEEPING BUSY.
I LIKE DOING MY JOB.

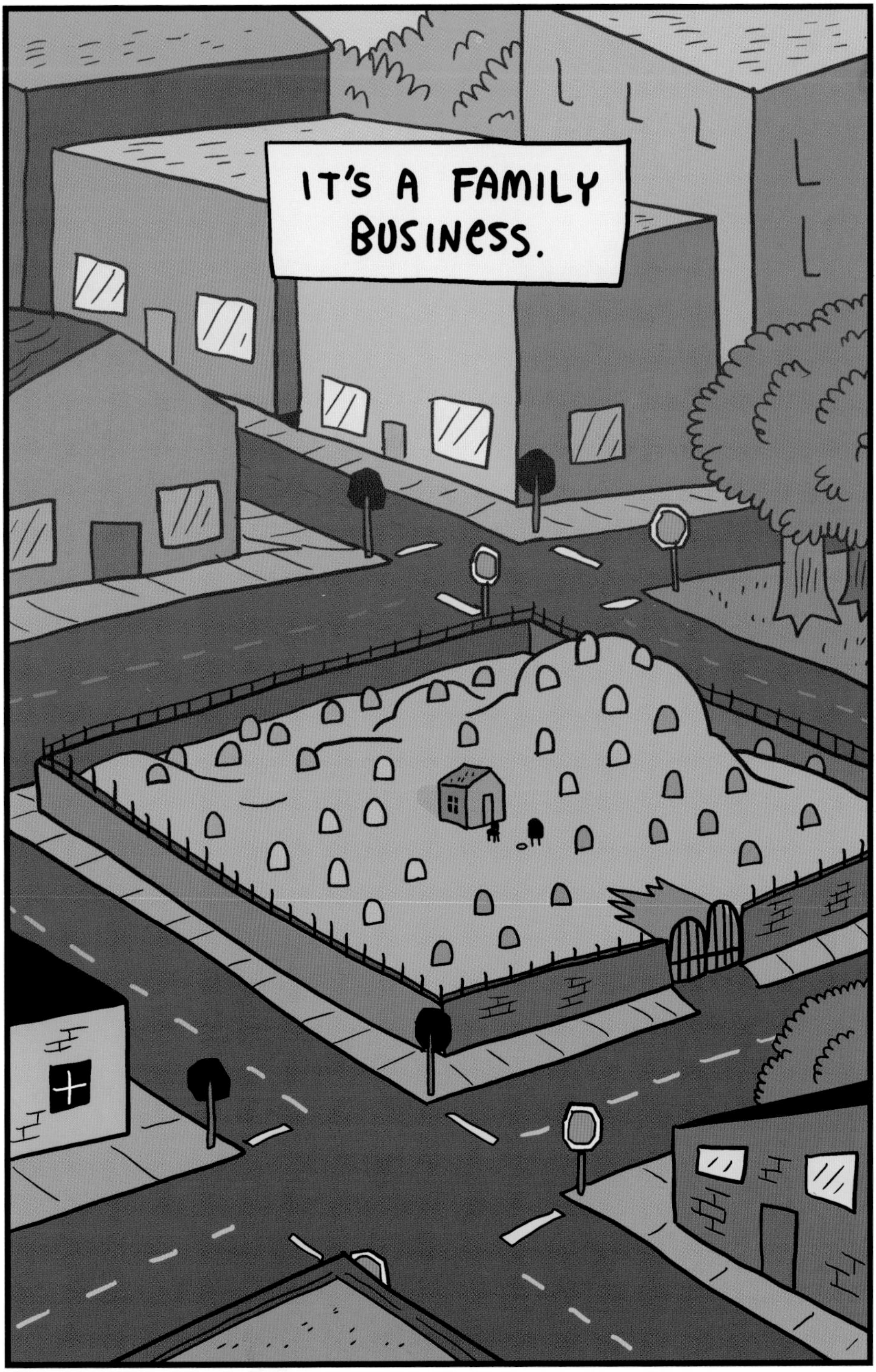
IT'S A FAMILY BUSINESS.

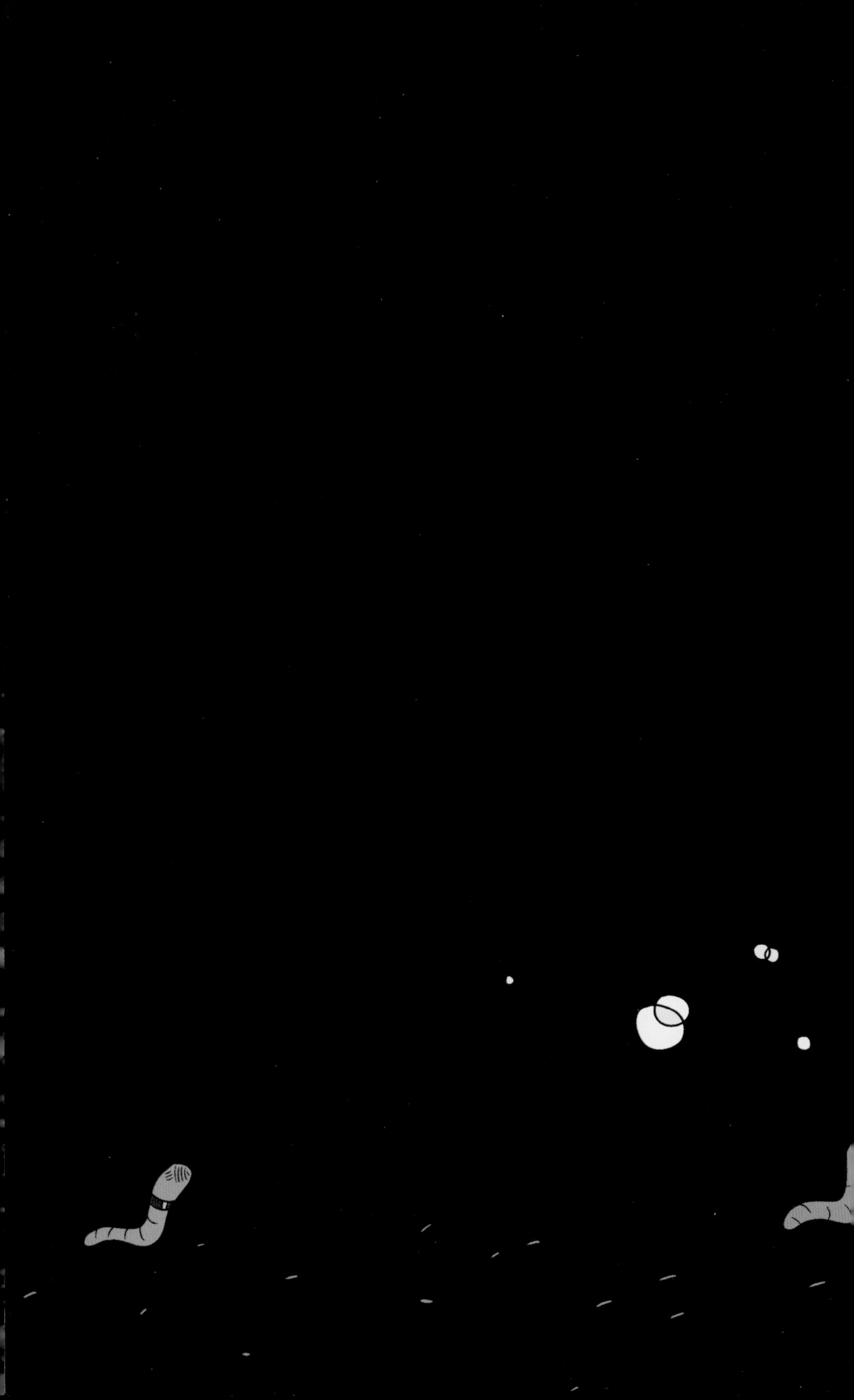

epilogue

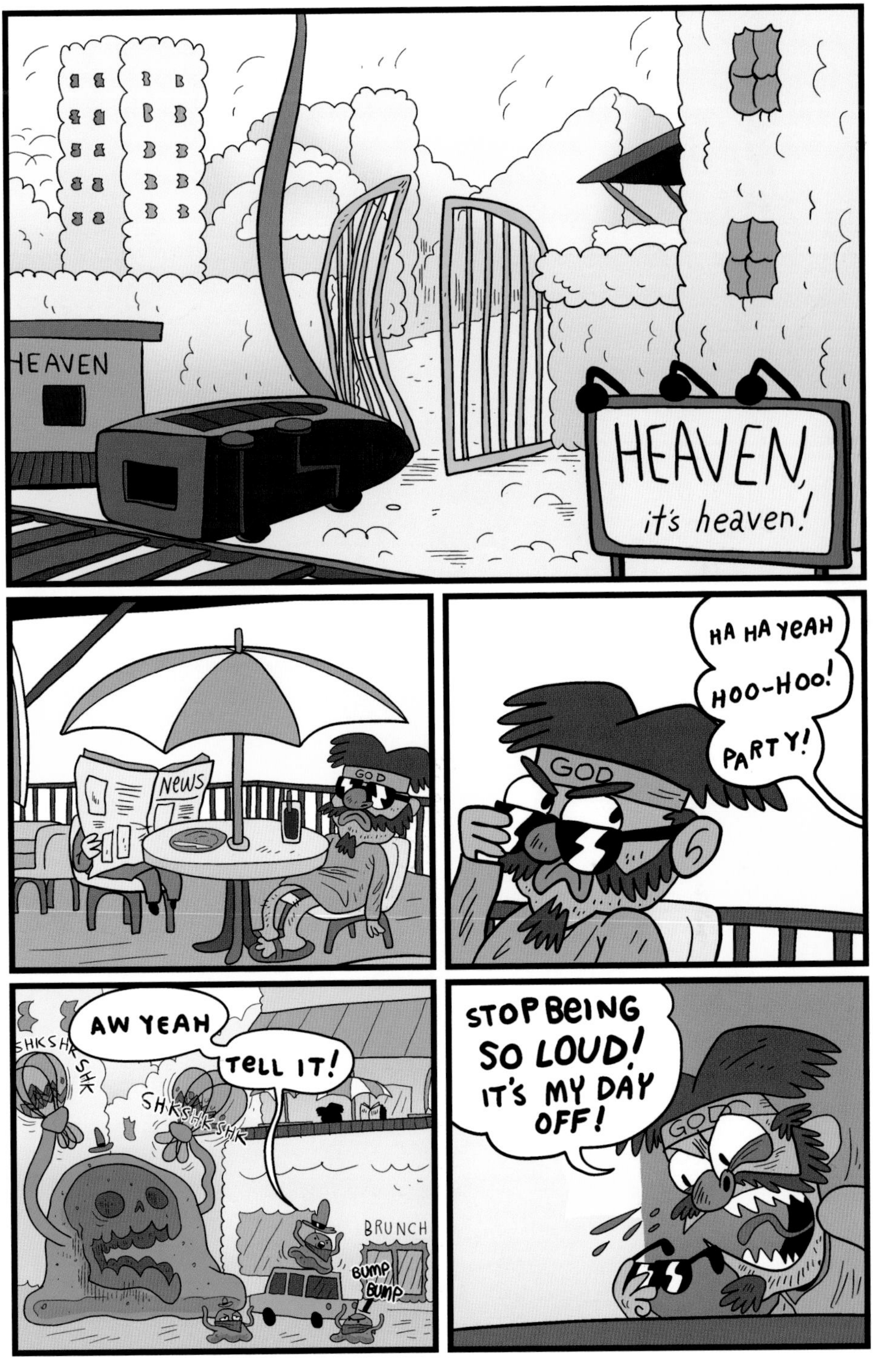
HEAVEN
HEAVEN,
it's heaven!
NEWS
GOD
HA HA YEAH
HOO-HOO!
PARTY!
GOD
SHKSHKSHK
AW YEAH
TELL IT!
SHKSHKSHK
BRUNCH
BUMP
BUMP
STOP BEING SO LOUD! IT'S MY DAY OFF!
GOD

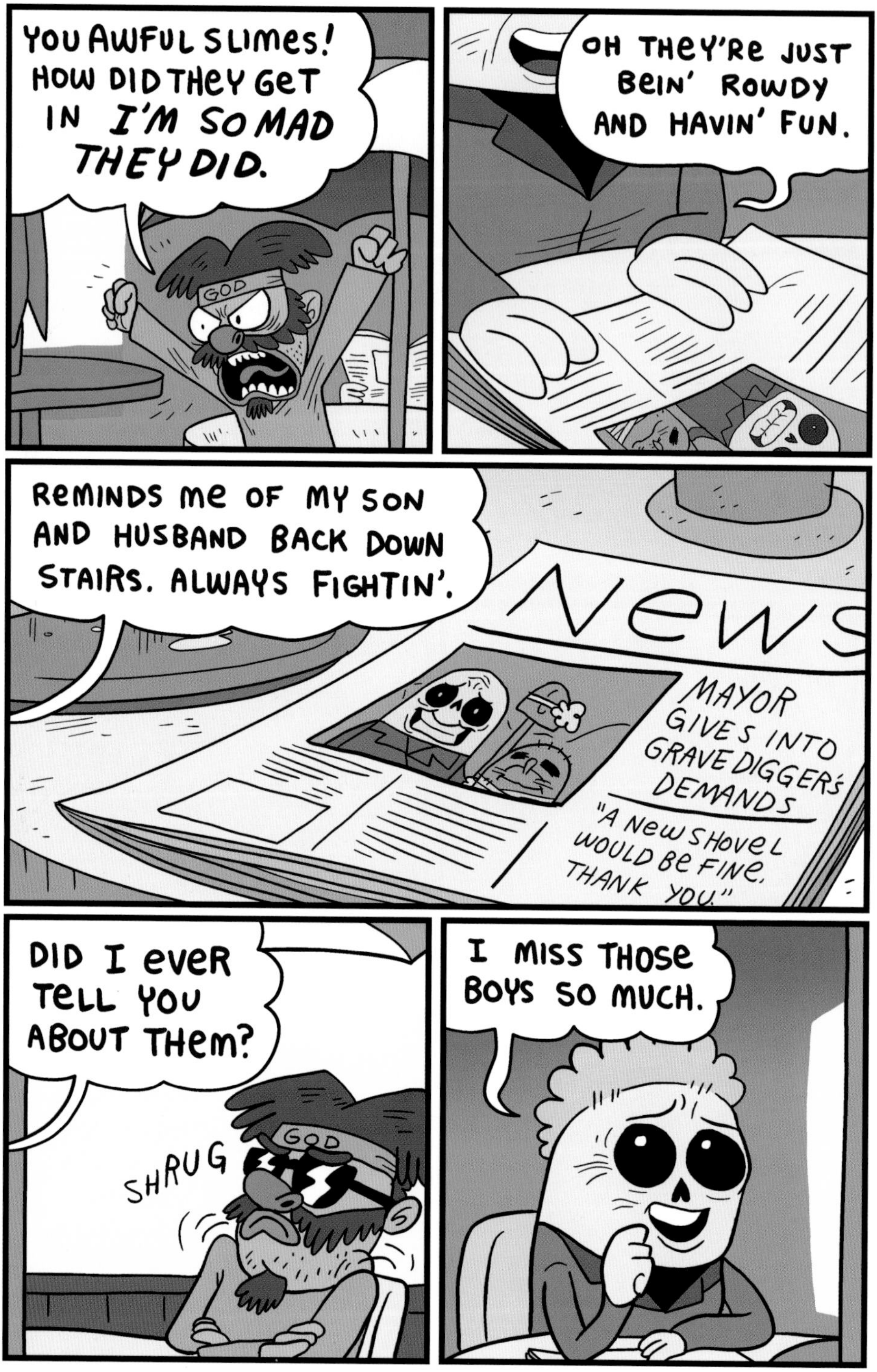
YOU AWFUL SLIMES! HOW DID THEY GET IN I'M SO MAD THEY DID.
GOD
OH THEY'RE JUST BEIN' ROWDY AND HAVIN' FUN.
REMINDS ME OF MY SON AND HUSBAND BACK DOWN STAIRS. ALWAYS FIGHTIN'.
News
MAYOR GIVES INTO GRAVE DIGGER'S DEMANDS
"A NEW SHOVEL WOULD BE FINE, THANK YOU."
DID I EVER TELL YOU ABOUT THEM?
GOD
SHRUG
I MISS THOSE BOYS SO MUCH.

GOD
NEWS
CRASH!
GOD
NEWS
GOD
HAHAHAHAHA HAHAHAHAHA
HOOOOOOOONNNNN
GOD DAMMIT CUT IT OUT
OOOOOONNK

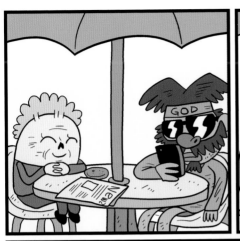

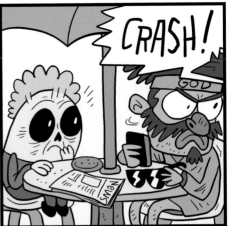

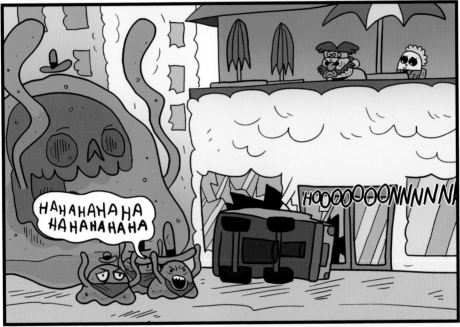

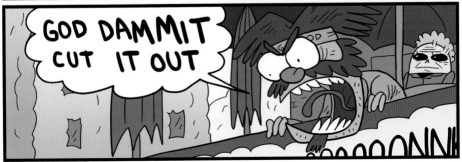

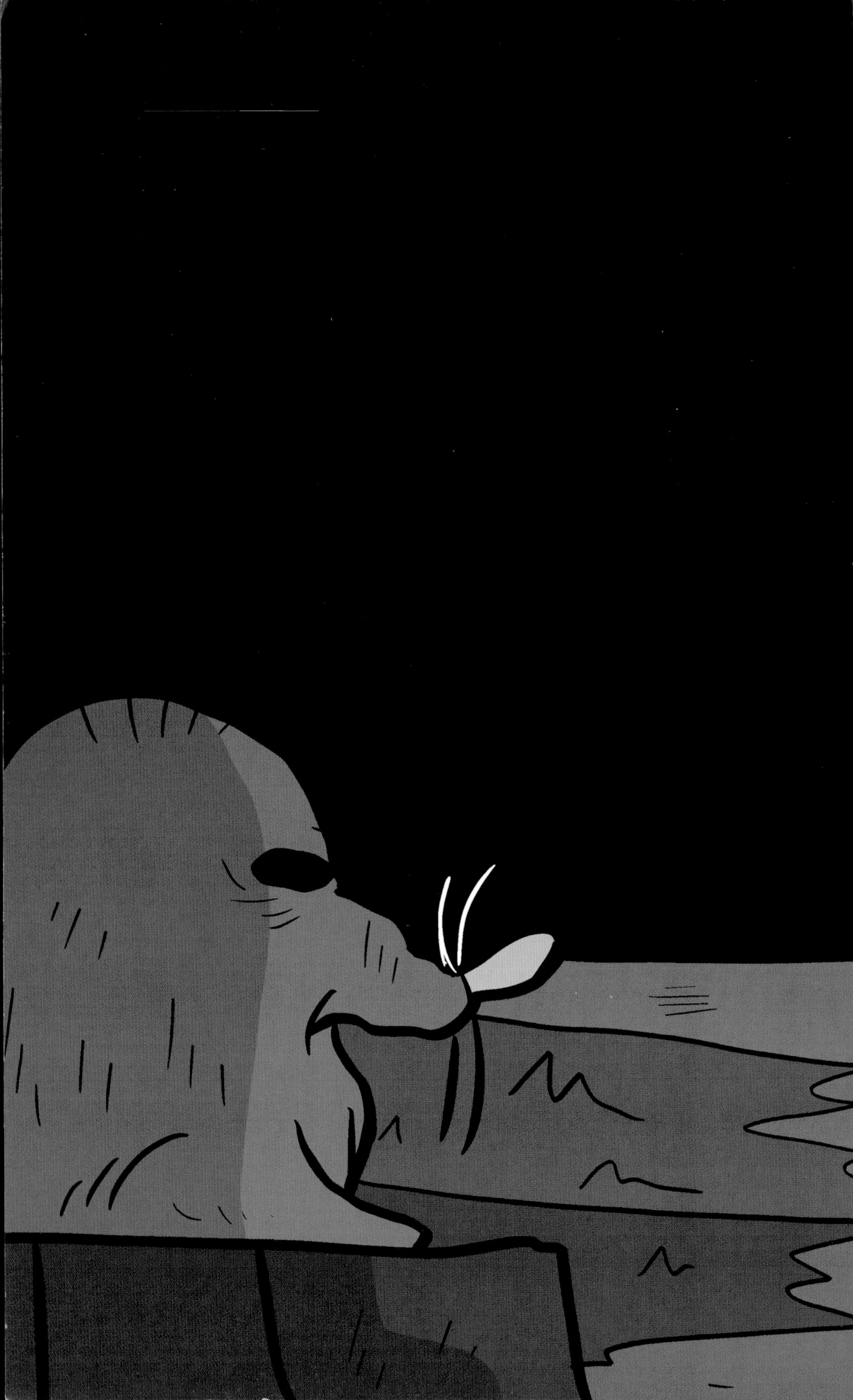

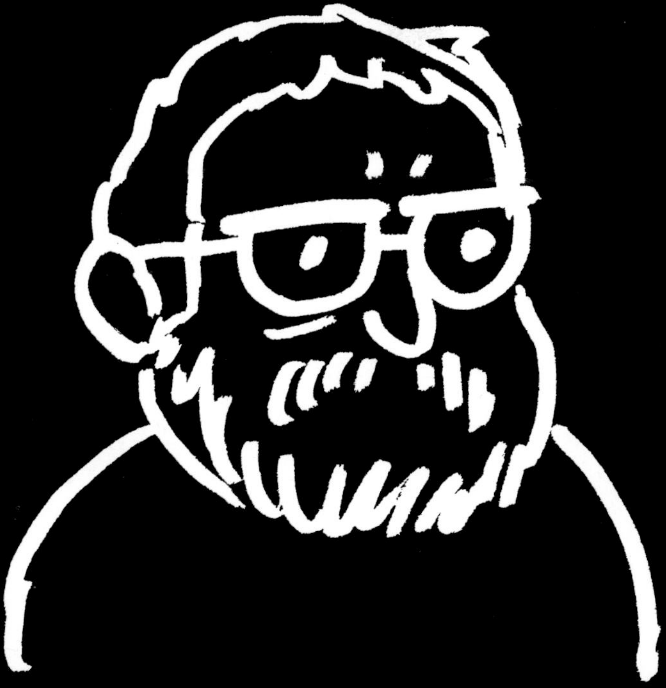

KC Green has been drawing comics since 3rd grade. He's older now and a little better at it. He did the webcomic *Gunshow*, which is where *Graveyard Quest* spawned from. *Gunshow* is over now tho, aw. You can read it online still if you want to. He lives in Massachusetts but is originally from Oklahoma, isn't that fun?

KCGREENDOTCOM.COM • @KCGREENN • PATREON.COM/KCGREEN

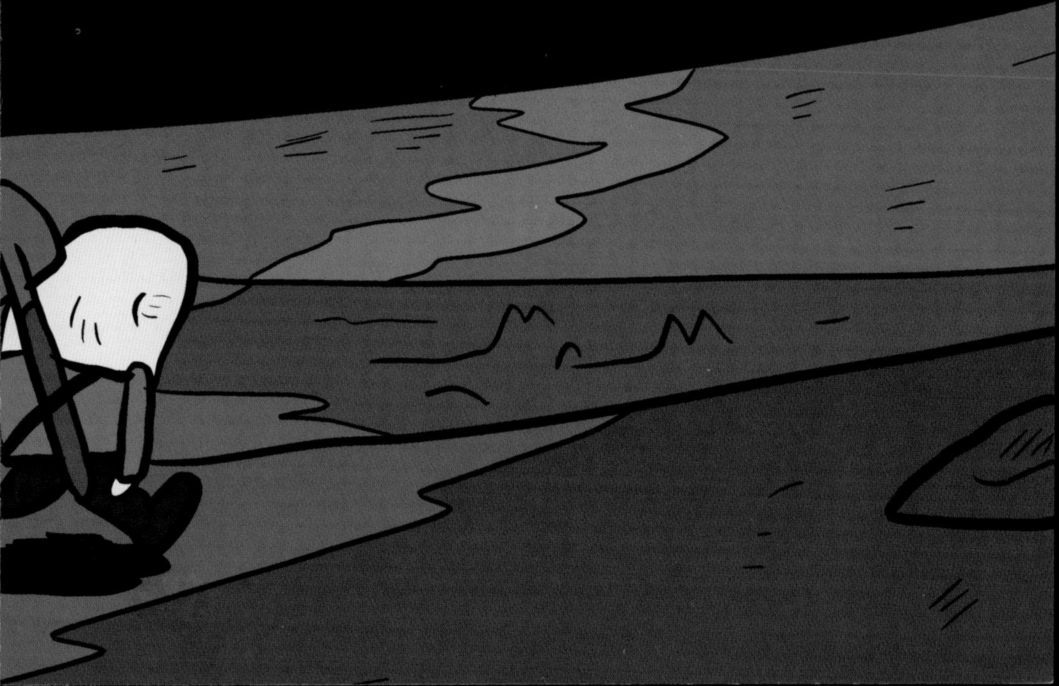

GUNSHOW

BY KC GREEN

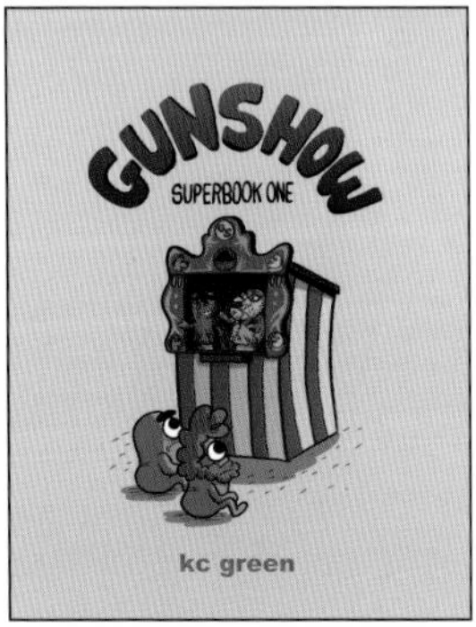

GUNSHOW
SUPERBOOK ONE
kc green

GUNSHOW SUPERBOOK ONE

Houses the original, out of print, volumes 1 & 2. PLUS Volume 0! Comics before *Gunshow* was *Gunshow* on the web!

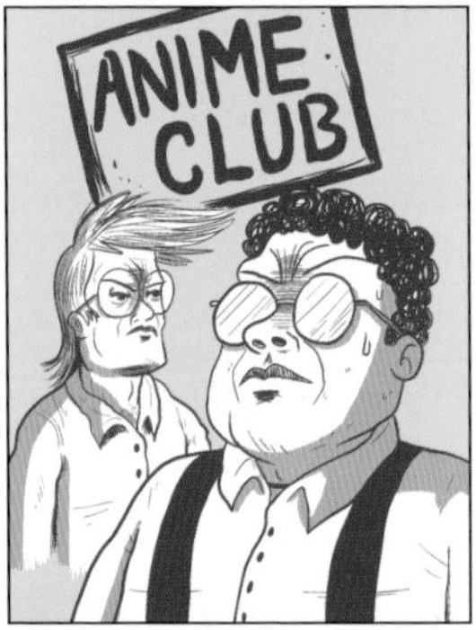

ANIME CLUB

ANIME CLUB

Contains the entirety of the *Anime Club* story, plus extra comics and art.

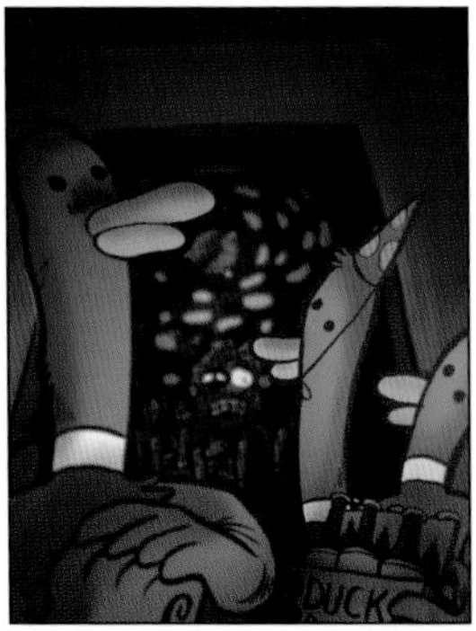

SECRET MIDNITE DUCK PARTY

Volume 3, collecting a good chunk of black and whites with a special 19 page opening story.

GUNSHOWCOMIC.COM

Gunshow woke up on the web and became a 6 year long running webcomic that housed such favorite stories as *Anime Club*, and *Graveyard Quest* (you're reading that now!) plus a bunch more. The archives are online as well as published in a wide 6 book variety (7 if you count *Graveyard Quest*, which I guess we should). 7 book variety!

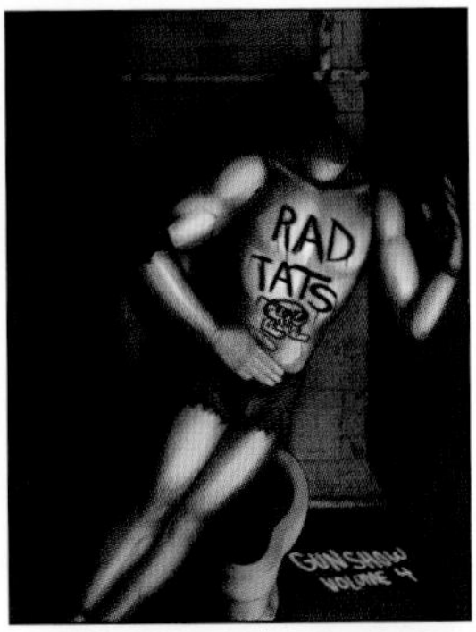
RAD TATS
GUNSHOW VOLUME 4

RAD TATS

Volume 4, containing the "skull w/ shoes" saga of comics that all sort of flowed into the next one by one way or another.

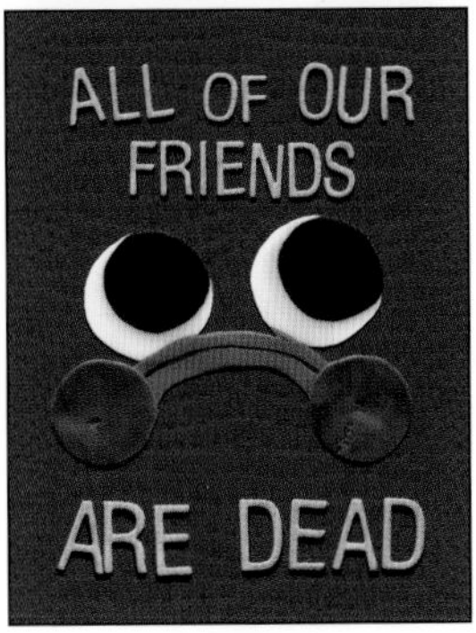
ALL OF OUR FRIENDS
ARE DEAD

ALL OF OUR FRIENDS ARE DEAD

Volume 5, containing a GOOD CHUNK of the start of the color strips and stories, including Jason's Road Trip and the start of the Dark Homer comics.

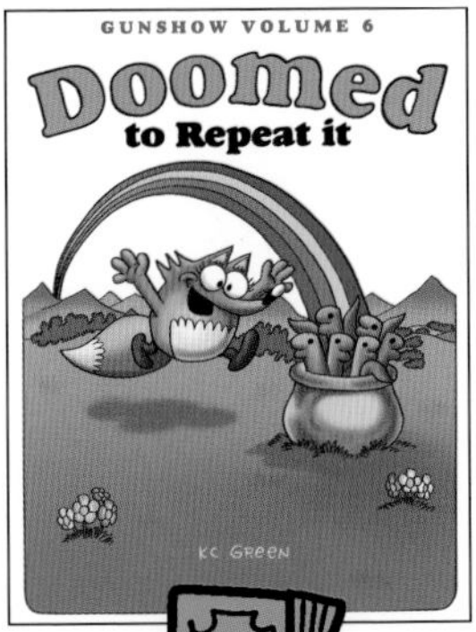
GUNSHOW VOLUME 6
Doomed to Repeat it
KC GREEN

DOOMED TO REPEAT IT

The final volume (6) containing THE REST of the ENTIRE COMIC (400 pages worth). Including stories like Ring, The Dog's Sins, and others.

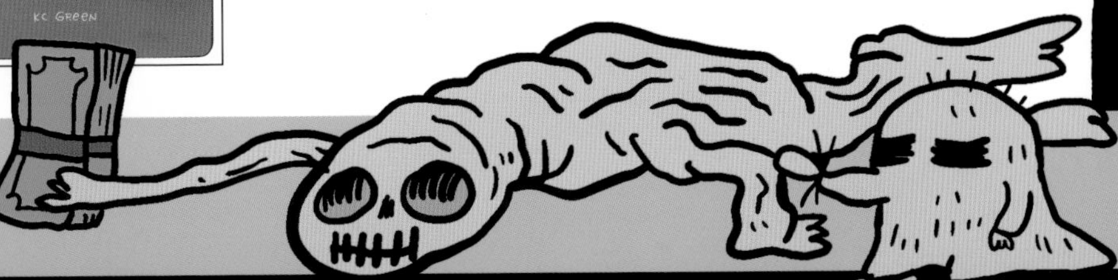

BACK

BY KC GREEN AND ANTHONY CLARK

Abigail woke up in a grave and the witches told her she's the key to the end of the world. Sounds good enough to her. Join Abigail and the druid Daniel as he tries to talk her out of it and fight obnoxious no-gooders along the way to see the King and end their world as they know it.

BACKcomic.com

HE IS A GOOD BOY.

BY KC GREEN

Crange (an acorn) woke up in his tree like normal, but has been unceremoniously kicked out from his tree and is charged with having to plant himself like his brothers and sisters before him. He's not really having that and instead just sort of wanders around drinking and coming across horrible weirdos and coming to terms with growing up. Did I mention the horrible weirdos? A lot of them die, so it's okay. Crange doesn't mind, for the most part, as long as he's left alone.

HIAGB.COM

"I LOVE IT! Penny is a human disaster after my own heart!"
- Noelle Stevenson, *Nimona*, *Lumberjanes*

LUCKY PENNY

ANANTH HIRSH **YUKO OTA**

A new graphic novel from the creators of *Johnny Wander*!